The Intimate Letters of
Piozzi and *Pennington*

Mrs Hester Lynch Piozzi
Engraved by H. Meyer from an original drawing by J. Jackson

The Intimate Letters of *Piozzi* and *Pennington*

Edited by Oswald G. Knapp

NONSUCH

First published 1914
Copyright © in this edition 2005
Nonsuch Publishing Ltd

Nonsuch Publishing Limited
The Mill, Brimscombe Port, Stroud, Gloucestershire, GL5 2QG
www.nonsuch-publishing.com

British Library Cataloguing in Publication Data.
A catalogue record for this book is available from the British Library.

ISBN 1-84588-025-0

Typesetting and origination by Nonsuch Publishing Limited
Printed in Great Britain by Oaklands Book Services Limited

CONTENTS

INTRODUCTION TO THE MODERN EDITION

> She was, in truth, a most wonderful character for talents
> and eccentricity, for wit, genius, generosity, spirit and
> powers of entertainment.
>
> *Madam d'Arblay*

Although probably best known for being 'Doctor Johnson's Mrs
Thrale', Hester Lynch Piozzi was an important historical figure in her
own right. Her literary tendencies expressed themselves at an early age
and before she reached the age of fifteen she had written papers in the
St. James' Chronicle. However, it was through her marriage in 1763 to
Henry Thrale, a match Hester herself violently opposed but was unable
to prevent, that she was introduced to the leading literary figures of her
age. Her friendship with Samuel Johnson started when Henry Thrale's
oldest friend, Arthur Murphy, introduced him to the Thrales in 1765.
Johnson became a frequent visitor to their London and Streatham
houses and through his influence Hester could soon count among her
friends such literary luminaries as Edmund Burke, Oliver Goldsmith,
and Samuel Pepys, who composed verses to commemorate the Thrale's
thirteenth wedding anniversary in 1777. Yet during this period Hester
herself produced no published work.

After the death of Henry Thrale in 1781, Hester started a relationship with an Italian singer, Gabriel Mario Piozzi, which was to lead
to her social ostracism and to the end of her friendship with Johnson.
For English society of that era, a relationship with a Roman Catholic
foreigner was unacceptable, to the extent that Hester's own children
refused to accept the match. Despite this the couple were eventually
married in 1784 and Hester records in her *Thraliana*:

> I am returned from church the happy wife of my lovely,
> my faithful Piozzi:—Subject of my Prayers, Object of my
> Wishes, my Sighs, my Reverence and my Esteem.

The couple remained happily married until Piozzi's death from gout in 1809.

It was in 1785 that Hester began to publish her own work, starting with contributions to the *Florence Miscellany* during the period spent living in Italy just after her marriage. Despite their estrangement in the latter part of his life, Hester's first major publication was *Anecdotes of the Late Samuel Johnson* (1786), which led to a very public falling out with Johnson's biographer James Boswell, satirised by Peter Pindar in *Bozzy and Piozzi, or the British Biographers. Anecdotes* and her *Letters to and from the Late Samuel Johnson L.L.D* (1788) remain her best known and most widely read works. Her last published work *Retrospection or a Review of the Most Striking and Important Events, Characters, Situations and their Consequences which the last Eighteen Hundred Years have presented to the view of mankind* was released in 1801 but was a critical disaster and may have adversely affected any further attempts at a literary career. Her next work *Lyford Redivivus or a Granddame's Garrulity* failed to find a publisher.

However, Mrs. Piozzi left behind another literary treasure in the form of her letters to her friend Penelope Pennington (*née* Weston). What prompted the start of such a long and friendly correspondence, of which we have letters surviving from 1789 to 1821, is unclear, as is the reason for the break in communication from 1804 to 1819. However these letters present the modern reader with an unparalleled and fascinating insight into the history and society of the late eighteenth and early nineteenth centuries and reveal in Hester Lynch Piozzi a writer of learning, vivacity and charm.

Retaining a zest for lift right up to her death, Hester, when nearing the age of eighty, took a fancy to a young actor called William Augustus Conway, who it has been suggested, though without hard evidence, that she proposed to marry. She continued to write her letters until a few weeks before her death at the age of eighty or eighty–one – there is some confusion as to her exact date of birth – and retained her sense of humour to the last, saying 'Ah! now I can die in state!' when hearing of her daughters' arrival during what was to be her last illness. She died on 2 May 1821.

PREFACE

THE letters included in this volume have been printed without alteration, except that some of Mrs. Piozzi's redundant initial capitals have been suppressed, and that her somewhat erratic punctuation has been, to a certain extent, systematised. Her spelling, save for the correction of obvious slips, which are very rare, has not been altered. The omitted passages, which have been indicated wherever they occur, mainly consist of formal "compliments" at the beginning or end of letters, to which she was much addicted, unsavoury medical details, or casual allusions to insignificant persons and trivial events of no interest in themselves, and having no direct bearing on the story of her life.

For the outline of her career before her second marriage I have to acknowledge my indebtedness to previous writers, particularly Hayward and Mangin, and the more recent works of Mr. Seeley and Messrs. Broadley and Seccombe; not forgetting the indispensable *Dictionary of National Biography*, for the identification of many persons incidentally mentioned. I have also to express my thanks to Miss Thrale of Croydon for interesting information respecting her family; and above all to Mr. A. M. Broadley, not only for his generous permission to make use of Mrs. Piozzi's unpublished Commonplace Book, now in his possession, but also for allowing me to draw freely upon his unrivalled collection of prints, &c., relating to this period, from which the greater part of the illustrations has been taken.

Oswald G. Knapp
Inwood, Parkstone,
July 1913

CHAPTER I

INTRODUCTION TO MRS. PIOZZI

IN the course of the last hundred years the horizon of woman's work and interests has been extended so widely, and in so many directions, religious, educational, political, economic, and social, that already the Blue-Stockings of the eighteenth century seem almost as far removed from us as the Précieuses Ridicules of Molière. The student of the period takes note of them as products of a social and intellectual movement characteristic of their day; and the general reader knows a few of them by name, though chiefly as satellites revolving round the greater luminaries of the age: but their works are, for the most part, unread and forgotten. This is not, perhaps, a matter for surprise, seeing that they were not profound or original thinkers, and even their works of fiction are too stilted and prolix for our impatient age. Indeed their contemporaries were probably less impressed by the learning, even of the leaders of the movement, than by their brilliant conversational powers, in which, perhaps, they have never been surpassed; though this is a matter on which, from the nature of the case, we have, for the most part, but imperfect materials with which to form a judgment.

If there be an exception, it is to be found in the case of the writer of the following letters. Of the literary society in which she moved she was an acknowledged queen, who hardly yielded precedence on her own ground to Mrs. Montagu herself. Indeed Wraxall was of opinion that she possessed "at least as much information, a mind as cultivated, and even more brilliancy of intellect"; while Madame D'Arblay thought that her conversation was "more bland and more gleeful" than that of either Mrs. Montagu or Mrs. Vesey. "To hear you," wrote Boswell (before their great quarrel), "is to hear Wisdom, to see you is to see Virtue." It may be said that this was merely the partiality of friendship, or an example of the mutual admiration which was rather characteristic of the coterie. But Anna Seward, who roundly condemned her literary style, declared that her conversation was "the bright wine of intellect, which has no lees"; and the great Lexicographer himself, who was not wont to be unduly lavish of his praises, vouchsafed on one occasion to tell her that she had "as much wit, and more talent," than any woman he knew. And what is still more remarkable, her power of pleasing continued, with but little diminution, to the end of her long life. Sir William Pepys, who had known her for many years, writing after her death, says he had "never met any human being who possessed the talent of conversation to such a degree."

And more easily than in the case of most of her contemporaries, the charm of her conversation can be gathered from her letters. To it Fanny Burney's criticism seems to apply as fitly as to the record of her Italian tour, of which it was originally written: "How like herself, how characteristic is every line! wild, entertaining, flighty, inconsistent, and clever!" The spontaneity and freshness of her style is the more remarkable when we remember the taste of the circle in which she moved, and compare her letters with the laboured and formal productions of her friend Anna Seward, the much-admired "Swan of Lichfield," and particularly when we recall her intimate relations with Johnson for a period of nearly twenty years. The fact is that he found her mind already formed, and though it was for a time "swallowed up and lost," as she says, in his vast intellect, it was not absorbed, but emerged later on, strengthened and clarified indeed, but with its original characteristics little changed.

A good many of her letters have already seen the light. Those written to Dr. Johnson she herself published after his death. Her friend, the Rev. Edward Mangin, included about thirty, written for the most part to himself, in his *Piozziana*; while Hayward, in the so-called *Autobiography*, gives about a hundred and forty, of which a few were written to the brothers Lysons, and nearly all the remainder to Sir James Fellowes. But these differ in some important respects from those in the present volume. They were nearly all written to men, and though they may possibly be somewhat more brilliant, and make rather a greater show of learning, they are hardly so frank and unaffected, and do not reveal the personality of the writer so clearly as those which she wrote to an intimate friend of her own sex; in whose case she had no temptation to pose, even unconsciously, nor any lurking thought of a reputation as a wit to be kept up.

Their recipient was fully alive to their importance, and in a letter in Mr. Broadley's collection, dated 1821, quotes her as saying that she had "a larger and perhaps better collection of dear Mrs. Piozzi's letters than any other correspondent." And she backs her opinion by that of Dr. Whalley, who had probably seen most of them, to the effect that "was any publication intended, they would be a most rich and valuable addition, and altogether form a collection of letters more eagerly sought after, and more agreeable to the general public than any that have been ever published."

The letters in question, some two hundred in number, begin in 1788, not long after Mrs. Piozzi's second marriage, and continue (though with a break of fifteen years) to within a few days of her death in 1821. The friend to whom they were written first appears on the scene as Penelope Sophia Weston, a friend of Mrs. Siddons, Helen Williams, and Anna Seward, whose published letters contain many addressed to "the graceful and elegant Miss Weston," who was then the leading spirit of "a knot of ingenious and charming females at Ludlow in Shropshire," where Anna paid her a visit in 1787. She was then living with her widowed mother, who had not much in common with the literary proclivities of her daughter. She writes in 1782: "My mother is a very good woman, but our minds are, unfortunately, cast in such different moulds—our pursuits and ideas on every occasion are likewise so—that it is of very little moment our speaking the same language. Indeed I see very little of her; for she is either busied in domestic matters, praying, gardening, or gossiping most part of the day; while I sit moping over the fire with a book or pen in my hand, without stirring (if the weather is unfavourable), for weeks together … Remember me to your charming Mrs. Siddons." This passage appears in the published correspondence of her "dear cousin Tom," the Rev. T. S. Whalley, D.D., who was not, strictly speaking, related to her at all, but had married her first cousin, Miss Jones of Longford. As he had a house at Bath he may have been the means of making her acquainted with Mrs. Piozzi.

It does not fall within the scope of this work to give a detailed account of Mrs. Piozzi's life: this has been done, though in a somewhat piecemeal manner, by A. Hayward,[1] and more recently by Mr. H. B. Seeley.[2] But for the better understanding of the letters it will be necessary to give a brief outline of her career up to the date at which they begin; and this may fitly be preceded by some account of her family, a matter in which she was keenly interested, and to which she frequently recurs in her correspondence.

Mrs. Piozzi was the last of an old knightly Welsh family, Welsh by long residence, if not by blood, called in the early records Salbri or Salsbri, and Englished as Salesbury or Salisbury, and in more recent times as Salusbury. It produced a goodly number of soldiers, scholars, and divines; the latter chiefly in a younger branch seated at Rûg in Merioneth in the sixteenth century. Among these were William Salesbury, "the best scholar among the Welshmen," who compiled a Welsh dictionary, and made the first translation of the New Testament into that language; Henry Salesbury, a noted doctor and grammarian, and John Salesbury, a Jesuit, Superior of the English Province. In the same century the elder or Llewenny line boasted of John Salesbury, a Benedictine monk who forsook his vows and married, but was made by Queen Elizabeth Bishop of Sodor and Man; Foulke Salesbury, first Dean of St. Asaph, and Thomas Salesbury, who was executed for his share in Babington's Plot.

In the course of centuries a goodly number of romantic legends had attached themselves to the earlier generations, particularly in connection with their armorial bearings, in which Mrs. Piozzi was an enthusiastic believer. As far back as the sixteenth century the Salesburys had claimed as their eponymous ancestor a certain Adam, believed to be a younger son of Alexander, Duke of Bavaria, hence known as Adam de Saltzburg, who made his way to England, and was appointed by Henry II Captain of the castle of Denbigh. Another and less probable version of the story, favoured by Mrs. Piozzi, makes him a follower of William the Conqueror, and gives him a fair estate in Lancashire, on which he built a seat called Saltsbury or Salisbury Court. Of her descent from this Adam she says: "I showed an abstract to the Heralds in Office at Saltzburg, when there, and they acknowledged me a true descendant of their house, offering me all possible honours, to the triumphant delight of dear Piozzi, for whose amusement alone I pulled out the Schedule." This may be satisfactory evidence for the existence of Adam, but of course the Heralds had to take the descent on trust. The fact appears to be that Adam of Llewenny was an Englishman who settled in Wales after its conquest at the end of the thirteenth century, and was a member of the family of Salesbury of Salesbury, co. Lancs. Adam's descendant, Sir Henry Salesbury "the Black," "having taken three noble Saracens with his own hand on the first Crusade, Cœur de Lion knighted him on the field of battle, and to the old Bavarian lion which adorned his shield added three crescents." This Henry is supposed to have built Llewenny Hall. The name of another Henry, who fought in the Wars of the Roses, "stood recorded on a little obelisk, or rather cippus, by the roadside at Barnet, ... so long that I remember my father taking me out of the carriage to read it, when I was quite a child. He had shown mercy to an enemy on that occasion, who, looking on his device ... flung himself at his feet with these words—'SAT EST PROSTRASSE LEONI.' Our family have used that Leggenda as motto to the coat armour ever since." The arms of the present Piozzi-Salusbury family are: Gules, a lion rampant argent, ducally crowned or, between three crescents of the last, a canton ermine, with motto as above.

We are on firmer ground when we arrive at Sir John Salesbury of Llewenny, Kt., M.P. for Denbigh in the sixteenth century, and his family of fourteen children, of whom the eldest and youngest sons were the ancestors of Mrs. Piozzi on the maternal and paternal side respectively. John, the eldest, married Catherine of Berain, a lady who deserves a paragraph to herself. Their grandson, Sir Henry Salusbury of Llewenny, was created a Baronet by James I, but this line came to an end with his granddaughter Hester, who married Sir Robert Cotton of Combermere Abbey, co. Chester, Bart., ancestor of Lord Combermere. Their granddaughter, Hester Maria Cotton, was Mrs. Piozzi's mother.

Catherine of Berain
By W. Bond after J. Allen 1798

Catherine of Berain above mentioned, called from her numerous descendants Mam y Cymry, or Mam Gwalia, "Mother of Wales," was a great-granddaughter of Fychan Tudor of Berain, a personage claimed by Mrs. Piozzi, though not acknowledged by the genealogists, as a younger son of Sir Owen Tudor, Kt., by Queen Catherine, widow of Henry V. That the Mother of Wales (who would, on this hypothesis, be a cousin of Queen Elizabeth) was a lady of great attractions, both in person and in purse, may be gathered from the story of her four matrimonial ventures, which cannot be better told than in the words of Pennant, the historian and naturalist, who was himself one of her descendants. "The tradition goes that at the funeral of her beloved spouse (Sir John Salesbury), she was led to Church by Sir Richard (Clough), and from Church by Morris Wynn of Gwydyr, who whispered to her his wish of being her second. She refused him with great civility, informing him that she had accepted the proposal of Sir Richard on her way to Church; but assured him—and was as good as her word—that in case she performed the same sad duty, which she was then about, to the Knight, he might depend on being her third. As soon as she had composed this gentleman, to show that she had no superstition about the number three, she concluded with Edward Thelwall of Plas y Ward, Esq., departed this life Aug. 27, and was interred at Llanivydd on the 1st of Sep. 1591."

For the paternal ancestry of Mrs. Piozzi we must return to Roger, the youngest son of Sir John Salesbury, M.P. He married Anne, one of the daughters of Catherine of Berain by her second husband, Sir Richard Clough, Kt., another picturesque figure who deserves a separate mention. He was the youngest son of a Denbigh glover, who became a prosperous merchant, and was a partner of Sir Thomas Gresham, whom he assisted to found the Royal Exchange, and whose continental business he superintended. This necessitated a residence at Antwerp, where he also acted as a kind of unofficial agent of the English Government. His mercantile pursuits were not, however, so absorbing but that he could make a pilgrimage to Jerusalem, where he was made a Knight of the Holy Sepulchre, and thereafter bore the five crosses of Jerusalem in his arms. During one of his brief visits to England, about 1567, he married, as we have seen, Catherine of Berain, then widow of Sir John Salesbury of Llewenny, and began building two mansion-houses, one called Plas Clough and the other Bachygraig, both in Flintshire, and both in the Dutch style, perhaps by means of imported workmen. The former was inherited by his son Richard, by a former wife, an Antwerp lady named Van Mildurt, whose descendants still possess it. The latter he bequeathed to Anne Salesbury, one of his daughters by Catherine of Berain. It thus became the seat of the younger line of the family down to the time of John Salusbury, Mrs. Piozzi's father, and came to her on the death of her parents.

Mrs. Piozzi herself was born 16th January 1740 (Old Style), or 27th January 1741 (New Style), at Bodvel, near Pwllheli, and was christened Hester Lynch, the names being derived from her mother, Maria Cotton (granddaughter of Hester Salusbury, the last of the elder line),

Sir Richard Clough
By Basire after M. Griffith

and from her maternal grandmother, Philadelphia, daughter of Sir Thomas Lynch. Her father, John Salusbury of Bachygraig, left an orphan at four years old, was high-spirited and attractive, but careless and extravagant, and even before his marriage had succeeded in heavily encumbering his property. His wife's fortune of £10,000 barely sufficed to pay his debts and to provide a modest cottage in which to start housekeeping. Before long she and her only child found a more comfortable abode at Llewenny Hall with her eldest brother, Sir Robert

Salusbury Cotton, who took a great liking for little Hester, and being himself childless, promised to provide for her; but his sudden death before he had carried out his intention left them in great straits. John Salusbury had been sent out by Lord Halifax to assist in re-settling the colony of Nova Scotia, but it was not a lucrative employment, and his wife sought a home for her child first at East Hyde, Beds., with her own mother, Philadelphia, then the widow of Captain King, and afterwards at Offley Hall, Herts., the seat of her brother-in-law, Sir Thomas Salusbury, Judge of the Admiralty Court.

So far Hester's education had been of a very desultory kind, though she had been well grounded in French by her parents from a very early age. At East Hyde she learnt to love and manage horses, startling, and somewhat shocking her grandmother, by driving two of the "ramping warhorses" who drew the family coach round the courtyard. But her first systematic instruction she received at Offley, where she learnt Italian and Spanish, apparently from her uncle's wife, Anna, daughter of Sir Henry Penrice, and "Latin, Logic, Rhetoric, &c." from a Doctor Collier, for whom she had a warm regard, and who did more, she considered, to form her mind than anyone with whom she afterwards came in contact, Johnson not excepted. Greek she did not learn from him, for she laments her ignorance of it some years later, when, in the course of her Italian tour, she was unable to read an inscription in that language which was shown to her. So Mangin was no doubt unconsciously exaggerating when he wrote that she had "for more than sixty years ... studied the Scriptures ... in the original languages." But it seems fairly certain that she acquired some knowledge of Greek, and possibly also of Hebrew, in later life, though she makes no parade of her acquirements. The stray words in these languages which are found in her letters are not conclusive evidence, as they may have been merely copied from some work which she had been reading. But in her Commonplace Book, now in the possession of Mr. A. M. Broadley, and written only for her own amusement, occur several Greek phrases, and an epigram of some length, with a translation, apparently her own. And it is noteworthy that the Greek is written with the breathings and accents, in the clear, firm hand of one well used to the script, very unlike the tentative efforts of a beginner.

By this time suitors for the hand of the prospective heiress began to arrive, among whom was Henry Thrale, proprietor of a lucrative brewery in Southwark, who commended himself to the uncle as being a "thorough sportsman," and to the mother by his assiduous attentions to herself. But he does not appear to have taken the trouble to be more than barely civil to the bride elect, who naturally resented his attitude, and heartily disliked the idea of a marriage with him. She appealed to her father, who had now returned from America, having no aptitude or liking for a colonial career, and who sympathised with her feelings, but his sudden death in 1762 put an end to any hope of intervention on his part. Her mother and uncle pressed on what they considered a desirable match, and she was married to Thrale, 11th October 1763.

At this period, at any rate, Henry Thrale was by no means the dull, heavy, self-indulgent being that some accounts of him in later life might seem to suggest. His father, Ralph Thrale, a shrewd, self-made man, used the fortune he had amassed at the Old Anchor Brewery to give his son the best education the period could afford. Much of his boyhood he spent at Stowe in Buckinghamshire where his associates belonged to a group of great county families; for Ralph Thrale's cousin, Ann Halsey, had married Sir Richard Temple of Stowe, created Viscount Cobham, whose sisters had married into the families of Grenville and Lyttelton. As some of them were indebted to the father, motives of policy may have had something to do with their friendship for the son. At the age of fifteen he was sent to Oxford, which he left without taking a degree, though he was afterwards created a D.C.L. Then he was sent on the grand tour, on an allowance of £1000 a year, with William Henry Lyttelton, afterwards Lord Westcote and Lyttelton, whose expenses were also paid by the elder Thrale, and at the time of his marriage he was a finished "man about town." His artistic and literary tastes are indicated by the gallery of portraits by Reynolds which he formed at Streatham Park, and by the literary society he loved to entertain there, from Johnson downwards. The latter spoke of him as "a real scholar," and said that "if he would talk more, his manner would be very completely that of a perfect gentleman"; and he had, what Johnson entirely lacked, a keen appreciation of natural scenery. His religious and moral principles might be expected to be those of his associates, who at the time of his marriage, with the exception of one Romanist, all seemed to his wife to be professed infidels. But his outward conduct was at least decorous, and she remarks that his conversation was wholly free from all oaths, ribaldry, and profaneness. In 1779 she wrote in *Thraliana* (her private diary): "Few people live in such a state of preparation for eternity, I think, as my dear Master has done since I have been connected with him: regular in his public and private devotions, constant at the Sacrament, temperate in his appetites, moderate in his passions,—he has less to apprehend from a sudden summons than any man I have known who was young and gay, and high in health and fortune."

Their usual residence was a pleasant country house known as Streatham Park, standing in grounds of about a hundred acres, but in winter she was expected to live at his business premises in Deadman's Lane, Southwark, a stipulation which had put an end to several of Thrale's previous matrimonial negotiations. Her acceptance of it she believed to have been the determining factor in his final choice of a wife. He possessed also a hunting-box near Croydon, where he kept a pack of hounds, and a house in West Street, Brighton. But with all the comfort, and even luxury of her surroundings, she enjoyed no confidence and little sympathy from her husband. He required a wife to do the honours of his table and to bear his children; other forms of activity were frowned upon or banned. Riding to hounds was too masculine to be tolerated; she was not permitted to have any voice in the management of her household, and she did not even know what there was for dinner till it appeared on the table. She was not allowed to know anything of his business affairs till a serious crisis occurred, when she saved the situation by her promptitude in raising some £20,000 from relatives and friends to meet pressing demands. This, and her energetic canvassing of Southwark when Thrale was standing for Parliament, seems to have convinced her husband of her capabilities, and to have generated in him a certain amount of respect, if not of affection.

The sphere of her activities being thus restricted, and having no taste for gay society, she was driven to occupy herself with her books and her children, of whom she had twelve, though only four survived their childhood. While still in her teens she had contributed verses anonymously to the *St. James' Chronicle*, but at this period she probably had little opportunity and no encouragement to practise composition. Thrale, however, was interested in men of letters, and the introduction of Johnson to Streatham Park in 1764 helped to make it a meeting-place for many literary and artistic celebrities, such as Murphy, Reynolds, the Burneys, the Sewards, and others. Johnson himself came to be looked upon as one of the family, having a room reserved for him at Streatham and Southwark, and accompanying them as a matter of course on their visits to Bath and Brighton, and on longer expeditions to Wales in 1774 and to Paris the following year.

Thrale retired from Parliament in 1780, and died 4 April 1781, of apoplexy, largely the result of over-indulgence at table, to which in his later years he had become addicted. Both his sons had predeceased him, Henry, the elder, in 1766, and Ralph in 1775; and his widow was left with five daughters, all under age. Harriet, the youngest of these, died at school in 1783, shortly before Mrs. Thrale's second marriage; the four survivors were as follows.

Hester Maria, born 1764, known in her childhood as Queeny, a name given her by Dr. Johnson, who supervised her education, and with whom she was a great favourite. She inherited much of her father's strong, but cold and reserved character, and was never on very affectionate or sympathetic terms with her mother. She married at Ramsgate, 10th January 1808, Admiral Lord Keith, G.C.B., then a widower, son of the tenth Lord Elphinstone, and who was created Viscount Keith in 1814. She died at 110 Piccadilly, 31st March 1857, leaving an only daughter, the Hon. Augusta Henrietta Elphinstone, who married twice, but left no issue.

Susannah Arabella, born 1770; who died unmarried at Ashgrove, Knockholt, 5th November 1858, and was buried at Streatham.

Sophia, born 23rd July 1771; who married, 13th August 1807, Henry Merrick Hoare, son of Sir Richard Hoare of Barn Elms, Bart. She died at Sandgate, 8th November 1824, leaving no issue, and was buried at Streatham.

Cecilia Margaretta, born 1777. She married, 1795, John Meredith Mostyn of Segrwyd, who died 19th May 1807. She survived him half a century, dying at Sillwood House, Brighton, 1st May 1857. They had three sons, of whom the eldest was christened John Salusbury, but all died unmarried.

Her widowhood, 1781–4, was the most stormy period of Mrs. Piozzi's life. Her first anxiety was to dispose of the brewery, which neither she nor the executors felt competent to carry on. After some negotiation it was purchased by the Barclays for £135,000, and so provided a respectable portion for each of the girls. Bachygraig, her ancestral abode, had come to her on the death of her mother, and Thrale had left her Streatham Park for life, but the one was ruinous and the other expensive, and on the score of economy she determined to let Streatham and live at Bath. This course also had the advantage—in her eyes at least—of removing her somewhat farther from Johnson's sphere of influence. His eccentric habits and domineering temper had for many years been somewhat of a trial to her, though delight in his conversation, admiration for his talents, and regard for his character had hitherto induced her to bear them with patience. She was anxious to avoid a rupture with him, but it was more than probable that, both as an old friend and as one of her husband's executors, he would strongly disapprove of the second marriage which she was now beginning to contemplate with Signor Gabriel Piozzi, an Italian musician and singer.

He had been recommended to her in 1780 as a man "likely to lighten the burden of life to her, and just a man to her natural taste," by Fanny Burney; but it is recorded that on the first occasion on which they met in company, when he played and sang at Dr. Burney's in 1777, Mrs. Thrale stood behind him as he sat at the piano, and mimicked his gestures and manner, to the mingled amusement and embarrassment of the company. From this unpromising beginning grew a friendship which gradually ripened into love, and in 1783 it was apparent that Piozzi was seriously courting the widow, and that she was not ill-disposed to his suit. Then the storm burst. Mrs. Thrale was in no sense a public character, but she was violently attacked in the public prints, which had previously amused themselves by announcing her engagement to Crutchley, to Seward, and even to Johnson himself. Her friends were horror-struck, and remonstrated each after their kind. Johnson went so far at last as to charge her with abandoning her children and her religion, and with forfeiting both her fame and her country. But, as might be expected, her worst foes were those of her own household, and the opposition of her children, and more particularly of Hester, was the hardest thing she had to bear. It is somewhat difficult for us who are so far removed from the controversy to grasp the reason of all this outcry. But it must be remembered that Piozzi was a Papist, a foreigner, and a singer, a combination which to the average Englishman of the eighteenth century meant an untrustworthy and contemptible mountebank. The irony of the situation was that Piozzi met with similar objections from his own family, who were scandalised at his proposed alliance with a heretic, and could not conceive that a brewer's widow could be a lady, or a fit mate for a member of an old and well-connected family. Years afterwards, when Cecilia was travelling on the Continent, she made the acquaintance of the Piozzis, and wrote that she "liked them above all people, if only they were not so proud of their family." "Would not that make one laugh two hours before one's death?" is her mother's comment in 1818.

For some time she held out, but at last the combined opposition was too much for her; Piozzi was dismissed, gave up her letters, and went abroad. But the strain was too great, her health gave way, and her physician, considering her condition serious, recommended that Piozzi should be recalled, as the only hope of saving her life. Miss Thrale reluctantly acquiesced, and they were shortly afterwards married in London, according to the Roman rite, on 23rd July, and in St. James' Church, Bath, on 25th July, 1784. From this date her worst troubles were over, and she entered on what she describes as twenty years of unalloyed happiness. Having made what she considered suitable arrangements for her daughters, by providing a trustworthy companion for Miss Thrale, and placing the younger ones in a school at Streatham, she started, with her husband, on a long-projected Italian tour. Hayward says that Cecilia accompanied them, but this is contradicted by Mrs. Piozzi's own statements in the *Autobiography*. They had not long left England when Miss Thrale removed her sisters to another school, dismissed her companion, and retired with an old nurse to the Brighton house, where she shut herself up and spent her

Dr. Johnson's Biographers (Mrs. Piozzi, Carey? and Boswell)
From a caricature, 1786

time in the study of Hebrew and mathematics. Shortly afterwards, on coming of age, she rented a house in town, and took her younger sisters to live with her.

Meantime the Piozzis travelled via Paris, Lyons, Turin, and Genoa to Milan, where they wintered, being everywhere well received both by Italian friends and by the English colony, including the Duke and Duchess of Cumberland; a fact which probably had a good deal to do with the attitude of society at home on their return to England. The following summer they spent at Florence in the company of Merry, Greatheed, and the other Della Cruscans, to whose *Florence Miscellany*, published in 1785, she contributed some verses. Her literary instincts, long repressed, were at last encouraged, and Johnson being now dead she compiled at Leghorn in 1786 her *Anecdotes of Dr. Johnson during the last twenty years of his Life*; much to the annoyance of Boswell, who regarded everything relating to his hero as his own peculiar preserve, and resented her refusal to add her reminiscences to Johnson's Pyramid, as he styled his own great work. The book, for which she got £300, was well received, the whole edition being sold out in three days, and four editions appeared the same year; but Boswell's strictures on her alleged inaccuracy led to a lively "Bozzy and Piozzi" controversy, with accompanying caricatures, which amused the town, and doubtless helped to keep the author in the public eye. The Piozzis returned to England through Germany in 1787, and lived for a time in Hanover Square with Cecilia, the elder daughters at first keeping aloof, though they often met in public. But society had forgiven her if her children had not, and sooner or later the old friends who had protested most loudly took the opportunity of making their peace.

About this time, as it would seem, she made the acquaintance of Miss Weston, now about thirty-six years of age, who had moved with her mother from Ludlow to London, and was living with a relative in Queen Square, Westminster, and therefore not far from the Piozzis. A letter she wrote to Dr. Whalley in 1789 shows that she was then in charge of a young pupil, with whom she had but little in common, as the girl was interested in nothing but dress. She adds that the kindness of dear Mrs. Piozzi towards her, on all occasions, exceeds all expression.

1. *Autobiography, Letters, and Literary Remains of Mrs. Piozzi*, 2 vols., 1861.
2. *Mrs. Piozzi: a Sketch of her Life, and Passages Irons her Diaries, Letters, &c.*, 1891.

CHAPTER II

EARLY CORRESPONDENCE

IN July 1788 the Piozzis took rooms at Exmouth, from which they had views "of sea and land, Lord Courtney's fine seat and Lord Lisburne's pretty grounds all facing us." But though there was "a very pretty little snug society" there, Mrs. Piozzi votes it "a dull place," where "if one is idle, one is lost." Idleness, however, was not one of her failings. Early in the year she had published her *Letters to and from the late Samuel Johnson, LL.D.,* which made £500, and had a large sale. Some allusions in the correspondence more truthful than complimentary to Joseph Baretti, who had at one time acted as tutor to Miss Thrale at Streatham, roused him to make a coarse and violent attack upon her in the *European Magazine*, which caused her much pain. He also satirised her in a farce entitled *The Sentimental Mother*, in which she figures as Lady Fantasma Tunskull, and her husband as Signor Squalici. Yet she forgave him, and when he died in the following year, sent a kindly notice of him to the *World*. This year too, as she records in her Commonplace Book, she wrote a dramatic masque called *The Fountains*, which was much admired by Miss Farren, and which Sheridan and Kemble "pretended to like exceedingly," but contrived to lose the copy. She adds: "It has often been in my head to publish it with other poems—but 'tis better let that alone." About this time she must have been engaged on a more ambitious task, the record of her continental tour, which appeared in 1789 under the title of *A Journey through France, Italy, and Germany*. This was well received by the general public, though some of the Blue-Stockings objected to its colloquial style. Anna Seward, for instance, gently reproved "the pupil of Dr. Johnson" for "polluting with the vulgarisms of unpolished conversation her animated pages," and wrote as follows to Miss Weston, who defended her: "You say Mrs. Piozzi's style, in conversation, is exactly that of her travels. Our interviews were only two; no vulgarness of idiom or phrase, no ungrammatic inelegance struck me then as escaping, amidst the fascination of her wit, and the gaiety of her spirit; but inaccuracies and ungraceful expressions often pass unnoticed in the quick commerce of verbal society, that are very disgusting after their deliberate passage through the pen." The critics found fault with her matter as well as her manner, as did Gifford in the often quoted lines:

> See Thrale's grey widow with a satchel roam,
> And bring in pomp laborious nothings home.

But she bore him no malice, and took her revenge by obtaining an invitation to a house where he was dining, to his obvious embarrassment, from which she relieved him by proposing "a glass of wine to their future good-fellowship."

As long as the Piozzis and Westons were living close together in town, there was naturally little occasion for letters, but they recommence in 1789 when Sophia had gone to Bath after an illness. On 13th April Mrs. Piozzi writes from Hanover Square, after a visit to Drury Lane: "I have scarcely slept since for the strong agitation into which Sothern and Siddons threw me last night in Isabella"; while her husband adds a P.S.: "I assure you I cried oll (*sic*) the Tragedy." This was no doubt Sothern's *Fatal Marriage*, in which Mrs. Siddons took the part of the heroine Isabella, a character in which she was painted by William Hamilton. Mrs. Piozzi was much interested in the thanksgiving for the King's recovery after his first illness, "the most joyful occasion ever known in England"; for which she wrote an Ode, which was printed (with emendations that greatly annoyed her) in the *Public Advertiser*. For the State procession to St. Paul's on 23rd April, Miss Weston had secured them places in a balcony, "which, if it tumbles down with our weight, why we fall in a good cause, but I wish the day were over."

This summer the Piozzis went northwards, intending, as it would seem, to emulate Johnson's Highland tour. On 11th July she writes from Scarborough: "We like our journey so far exceeding well, but 'tis as cold as October, and just that wintry feel upon the air; a Northern Summer is cold sport to be sure, but Castle Howard is a fine place, and the sea bathing at this town particularly good. What difference between Scarbro' and Exmouth! yet is this bay by no means without its beauties, but they are more of *Features* than *Complexion*." They made their way north as far as Edinburgh, but the projected Highland tour was given up; the biographers say on account of Cecilia's delicacy, but in a letter in Mr. Broadley's collection, written from Glasgow, 26th July, she says: "Our weather has been so very unfavourable here, and my own health so whimsical, I fear Mr. Piozzi will not venture far into the Highlands." The first letter of sufficient interest to be quoted at length is written from the Capital.

EDINBURGH, 10 *Jul.* 1789.

And so you will not write again—no, *that* you will not, Dear Miss Weston,—with all your mock Humility!—till Mrs. Piozzi answers the last letter, and begs another. Well! so she does then: I never was good at *pouting* when a Miss; and after fifteen years are gone, one should know the value of Life better than to *pout* any part of it away. Write me a pretty Letter then directly, like a good girl, and tell me all the News. The emptier London is, the more figure a little News will make, as a short Woman shows best at Ranelagh when there is not much company. Echoes are best heard too when there are few People to break the sound, you know, so let the Travelling Trunks, Hat Boxes, and Imperials that pass over Westminster Bridge every Day at this time of the Year, be no excuse for your not writing. We have had a good Journey, and the Weather cannot be finer; a Northern Latitude is charming in July, and the long Days here at Edinburgh delightful—but no Days are long enough to admire its Situation or new Buildings, the symmetrical beauties of which last quite exceed my expectations, while the Romantic Magnificence of the first is such as gives no notion at all of the other. So I like Scotland vastly; and as we have Engagements for every Day, one should be ungrateful not to like the Scotch too. But for that my heart was always equally disposed … I am much flattered with finding my Book read here, and everybody talks about *Zeluco*, but I hope no one more than myself, or with more true esteem of its Author …

The full title of the work just mentioned was *Zeluco, various views of Human Nature, taken from Life and Manners, Foreign and Domestic*, its object being "to trace the windings of vice, and delineate the disgusting features of villany." Its author, John Moore, M.D., an army physician, tutor to Douglas, eighth Duke of Hamilton, and father of General Sir John Moore, is frequently mentioned in the letters. He was in Paris during the massacres of the Revolution, and published the Journal kept during his residence there in 1793.

The Piozzis returned southward by Glasgow and the Lake District to Liverpool.

LIVERPOOL, *Sat. 22d Aug.*

So dear Miss Weston, and her Hanover Square friends, have shared all the delights that *Water* can give this hot weather, while

> A River or a Sea
> Was to us a Dish of Tea, &c.

Meantime I do not tell you 'twas judiciously managed to run from Lago Maggiore to Loch Lomond, and finish with the Cumberland Meres, any more than it would be wisely done to put Milton into the hands of a young beginner; and when good taste was obtained, lay Thomson's charming *Seasons* on the desk; then make your Pupil close his studies with Waller's poem on the Summer Islands.

Beg of Major Barry to make my peace with his countrymen; some one told me the other day they were offended at a passage in *yᵉ Journey through Italy*, and I should be very sorry on one side my head, and much flattered on the other, *that they should think it worth their while* …

We spent a sweet day at Drumphillin, near Glasgow, in consequence of Dr. Moore's attentive kindness, and even from that charming spot continued to see the majestic mountain which attracted all my admiration, and which still keeps possession of my heart. I took *my* last leave of it from the Duke of Hamilton's Summer House, but at a distance of seventy or eighty miles it may be discerned. If you ask me what single object has most impressed my mind in this journey of 800 miles round the Island, I shall reply BEN LOMOND ...

If I promised you an account of Glasgow, I did a foolish thing; what account can one give of a very fine, old-fashioned, regularly-built, continental-looking town?—full as Naples, yet solemn as Ferrara: after Glasgow too, everything looks so little.

I think Mr. Piozzi must write the account of *this* town, he is all day upon the Docks, and all night at the Theatre; both are crowded, yet both are *clean*: the streets embellished with showy shops all day, and lighted up like Oxford Road all night; a Harbour full of ships, a chearful, opulent, commodious city. Have you had enough for a dose? and will you give all our compliments to all our friends, and will you love my husband and Cecilia?

The Major Barry above mentioned, apparently a member of an Irish family, is frequently referred to in the letters. He became a Colonel in 1790, and acted as A.D.C. to Lord Rawdon (afterwards Marquess of Hastings) in the American War, in which capacity he sent home "the best despatches ever written." Retiring from the Army in 1794, he settled in Bath, where he was a prominent figure in literary and scientific circles till his death, which occurred shortly after that of Mrs. Piozzi.

From Liverpool they went to inspect Mrs. Piozzi's Welsh property, and the next letter gives the first hint of the idea of building a house on it, which was carried out later on. Perhaps the postscript was hardly meant seriously, as no steps were taken in the matter for some years, and Mrs. Piozzi herself states that the suggestion was made by the Marquis Trotti, who does not appear upon the scene till 1791.

DENBIGH, *Tuesday* 1 *Sep.*

DEAR MISS WESTON,—I thank you for your invitation to pretty Ludlow, and shall let you know when we are likely to arrive there, that all possible advantage may be taken of your friendly hints. Mr. Knight is an old acquaintance of my Husband by the description you give of his taste and elegant conversation; at least it would be strange should there be *two* such men of any *English* name. Scotch and Welsh families are disposed in a different manner: *we* have but so many names, and all who bear those names are related to each other. I find a great resemblance between the two nations, in a hundred little peculiarities, and the Erse sounded so like my own native tongue that I wished for erudition to prove the original affinity between them.

The French nation was never a favourite of mine, and I see little done to encrease one's esteem of them *as* a nation. Their low people are very ignorant, their high ones very self-sufficient: you now read in every Paper the effects of that self-sufficiency acting upon that ignorance. Fermentation however will, after much turbulence, at length produce a *clear* spirit, though probably 'twill be a *coarse* one. They will know in a dozen years what they would have, and I fancy *that* will be once more an Absolute Monarchy …

Mr. Piozzi adds a P.S. "In a few days I intend go to see our little estate, and choose the place to building a little Cottage, and a little room for our dear friend Miss Weston … G.P."

In her remarks on surnames Mrs. Piozzi does not display her usual acumen. There is hardly any English name of which it can safely be predicated that all the individuals who bear it are related to each other, and assuredly this is not the case with a name like Knight. She shows more penetration in her estimate of the trend of events in France, where the mutterings of the coming storm were already making themselves heard. The States-General had assembled in May, in June the Commons had constituted themselves the National Assembly, the Bastille had fallen on 14th July, and on 4th August the nobles had relinquished their hereditary privileges. Well within the twelve years which she postulates, the Revolution of Brumaire (1799) had practically put the supreme power in the hands of Bonaparte as First Consul, though he was not proclaimed Emperor till 1804.

From North Wales they went, by way of Ludlow, to Bath, probably for the benefit of Piozzi, who was already beginning to suffer from the attacks of gout which finally proved fatal.

BATH, 2 *Nov.* 1789.

DEAR MISS WESTON,—Not *one* letter do I owe you, nor *three* nor *four*, but forty if they would make compensation for your kind ones to Ludlow, where Miss Powell's politeness made the time pass very agreeably indeed, spight of rain, which, however provoking, could not conceal the beauty of its elegant environs, even from an eye made fastidious by the recent sight of richer and more splendid scenery.

Mrs. Byron read me the kind words for which Mr. Piozzi and I owe you so many thanks: she gains strength daily, and will be quite restored if kept clear from vexation, and indulged in her favourite exercises of riding and the Cold Bath. My husband and she have many an amicable spar about *Bell's Oracle*, on account of his savage treatment of dear Siddons, whose present state of health demands tenderness, while her general merit must enforce respect. I wonder, for my own part, what rage possesses the people who wish to see, or delight in seeing, virtue insulted. Let us not learn to tear characters in England, as persons are torne in France, and drink the *intellectual life* of our neighbours warm in our Lemonade.

Major Barry has written me a charming letter, Do tell him that he shall find my acknowledgements at Lichfield; I mean to write a reference to Miss Seward, about a critical dispute we had here at Bath some evenings ago, concerning the two new novels, which I find are set up in opposition to each other, and people take sides. You will easily imagine that *Zeluco* and Hayley's *Young Widow* are the competitors.

Give my kind love to Miss Williams when you see her, and tell her that she is one of the persons I please myself with hoping to see a great deal of this winter.

We are all going to the Milkwoman's Tragedy to-morrow; I fear with much ill will towards its success. Her ingratitude to Miss More deserves rough censure, but hissing the play will not mend her morals.

Miss Wallis is to play Belvidera next Saturday. She is scarcely more of a woman than Cecilia Thrale, and quite as young looking; very ladylike though, and a pretty behaved girl in a room. I advised Dimond in sport to act Douglas to her Lady Randolph, as a still more suitable part than Belvidera. Here's nonsense enough for one pacquet. 'Tis time to say how much I am dear Miss Weston's affect^e servant.   H.L.P.

Mrs. Byron, whose name frequently recurs in the letters, was a daughter of John Trevannion, who married, "pour ses péchés," as Mrs. Piozzi elsewhere remarks, Admiral the Hon. John Byron, known in the Service as Foulweather Jack, the grandfather of the poet.

The attack on Mrs. Siddons in *Bell's Oracle* was one of the rare exceptions to the general chorus of praise she commonly evoked from the Press; it seems to have been quite undeserved, and her reputation was far too firmly established to be shaken by it.

Zeluco has already been referred to. Its competitor, *The Young Widow, or a History of Cornelia Sudley*, was the work of William Hayley, the poet, of whom Southey said: "Everything about that man is good, except his poetry." Yet it hit the popular taste, and he was even offered the Laureateship in succession to Warton.

The Milkwoman, Anna Maria Yearsley, otherwise "Lactilla," was a rustic genius discovered by Hannah More, who brought out a volume of her poems, for which she wrote a preface. But her action in investing the proceeds for the benefit of the authoress, without giving the latter any control of the money, produced a rupture between them, and the quarrel was carried on in the Press "to a disgusting excess," as their contemporaries thought. Besides her play of *Earl Godwin*, she wrote a novel called *The Royal Captives,* which met with some success, so that she was enabled to set up a Circulating Library at the Hot Wells, Clifton.

Miss Wallis, whose career began in the Smock Alley Theatre, Dublin, had just made her first appearance in England at Covent Garden, where she played Belvidera (in Otway's *Venice Preserved*) and other leading parts, with some success. But she seems to have found provincial audiences more appreciative, and played regularly at Bath and Bristol for five years.

In 1814, several years after his death, Mrs. Piozzi writes in her Commonplace Book: "Dimond the Bath Actor was, of all *common mortals* I have known, completely the best. So honourable that he left no debts unpaid, so prudent that he never overran his Income, Pious in his family, pleasant among his friends. Temperate in his appetites, and courageous to conquer the passion which no man could have felt more strongly."

With the return of the Piozzis to Town the letters cease until the summer of 1790, when the tenant vacated Streatham Park, and Mrs. Piozzi found herself again established there, but under happier auspices. In May and June she scribbles hasty notes of invitation to Miss Weston, explaining that "the Hay is carrying, the Weather changing, and even the Master of the House going to Town on horseback, because Jacob must not be disturbed." The special attraction held out was the presence of Mrs. Siddons, but illness prevented Miss Weston from coming till it was too late to meet her. Mrs. Siddons was herself suffering from some trouble, apparently rather mental than physical, for she adds at the end of one of Mrs. Piozzi's notes: "I fear my heart will fail *me* when *I* fail to receive the comfort and consolation of our dear Mrs. P. There are many disposed to comfort one, but no one knows so rationally or effectually how to do it as that unwearied spirit of kindness."

STREATHAM, 12 *Oct.* 1790.

I am watching the Moon's increase with more attentive and more interested care than ever I recollect to have watched it since your project of coming hither with the Colonel has depended on her getting fat. I am glad he is much at Lord Sydney's, and hope it bodes well for us all, and that he will soon have his orders to fight these hateful French, whose pretended love of England and English Liberty—in good time!—ends at last in real attachment to Spain, and to the gratification of old Family Compacts. I never expected better for my own part, and long for you to come and tell me all the harm of them you know. My Master looks better, and gains strength every day …

The Colonel here referred to was Colonel Barry, who had recently obtained promotion, and was hoping for active service. His patron was

Streatham Park
By J. Landseer after S. Prout

Thomas Townshend, second Viscount Sydney, who was Paymaster-General 1767, and Secretary for War 1782.

STREATHAM, 10 *Nov.* 1790.

Dear Miss Weston is always partial to *me*, but I think she now extends her kind thoughts, very charitably indeed, to the whole race of Authors, when a finely written book so convinces her of his virtue who wrote it. I do believe however that Mr. Burke has, in the glorious Pamphlet you so justly admire, given us *his own true and genuine* sentiments; and 'tis on such occasions that a writer shines, like the Sun, with his own native and unborrowed fire. This book will be a most extensively useful production at such a moment! and from such a man! Tell me what charming Miss Seward thinks of it …

The Pamphlet was, of course, Edmund Burke's *Reflections on the Revolution in France,* published this year, which ran through many editions, and was translated into several foreign languages.

Anna Seward, though a constant correspondent of Miss Weston's, was never very intimate with Mrs. Piozzi, whose literary style, as previously mentioned, she detested, though she admired her wit. This year she lost her father, the Canon of Lichfield, who had long been an invalid, but she continued to live at the Palace, which he had for many years occupied.

For the first half of 1791 only two letters are preserved, the first being written just as the Piozzis had decided to set out on a visit to Bath.

Tuesday, 11 *Jan.* 1791.

My dear Miss Weston did not use to be so silent, I hope it is not illness or ill-humour keeps her from writing. Here have been more storms, and very rough ones, since you left us; Lady Deerhurst apprehends the end of the World, but I think her own dissolution, poor dear, is likeliest to happen, for she is neither old nor tough like that, but very slight and feeble ...

Peggy, Lady Deerhurst, was the daughter of a neighbour of the Piozzis at Streatham, Sir Abraham Pitches, Kt., and became the second wife of George William, then Lord Deerhurst, and afterwards seventh Earl Coventry. In spite of her feeble health she outlived her husband, and the dissolution which Mrs. Piozzi anticipates did not happen for near half a century.

Early in February the Piozzis went to Bath, from which place the next letter is written.

11 *Feb.* 1791, *Fryday.*

My dear Miss Weston must be among the very first to whom I give an Acct. of our safe arrival at a comfortable House, corner of Saville Row, Alfred Street. We ... ran hither in one day from Reading, but I found a strange Giddiness in my Head that was not allay'd by the noisy concourse of young Gamesters, Rakes, &c., at York House, where we staid till this Lodging was empty: and here I have good Air and good Water, and good Company—and at last—*good Nights*; so that I mean to be among the merriest immediately. The Place is full, and the pretty girls kind, as my Master says, so you must write pretty eloquent letters to hold his heart fast ...

Miss Hotham's accounts of our sweet Siddons are better than common, so when things are at worst they mend, you see. Mr. Kemble's illness, gain'd only by shining too brightly, and wasting the Oyl in the Lamp, while here at Bath, is recovered by now I hope, and his spirits properly recruited ...

Cecilia was fourteen years old three days ago, and all the ffolks say how she is grown, &c. ...

The letters cease after their return to Streatham, until Miss Weston in her turn went to stay with friends at Bath. Those which follow are full of an incipient romance which appealed strongly to Mrs. Piozzi, inasmuch as it bore a strong resemblance to her own. An acquaintance of her husband's, a certain Lorenzini, Marquis Trotti, their guest at Streatham, had been struck by the charms of Harriet Lee (afterwards joint authoress of the *Canterbury Tales*), who was now helping her sister Sophia in the school at Belvidere House. But considerations of worldly prudence, which had so far held him back from an actual declaration, seem finally to have prevailed, in spite of Mrs. Piozzi's well-meant encouragement. The final act of the drama is somewhat obscure, but from hints let fall in subsequent letters Harriet Lee would appear to have had rather a fortunate escape.

STREATHAM PARK, *Thursday*, 28 *Jul.*

MY DEAR MISS WESTON,—I was happy to find the Prescription, which, after all, I did not find, but made little Kitchen copy. Do not forget Streatham, nor remit of your kindness towards me, or towards those I love, dear Harriet in particular: I hope you will contrive to see her very often.

Marquis Trotti is sensible of your partiality, and deserves all your esteem. His behaviour is such that were he my son I should kiss him, were he my brother I should be proud of him, and as he is only my good friend, I pity and respect him. There is much tenderness, joined with due manliness, in his character; he is a very fine young fellow ... But as Hermione says in the *Midsummer Night's Dream*:

> I never read in Tale or History
> That course of true Love ever did run smooth,
> But either it was crossed in *Degree*, &c.[1]

Well! if 'tis of the right sort, opposition will but encrease it, and as Marquis Trotti said to Buchetti in my company yesterday, "The time is approaching when aristocratic notions about marriage will fall to ground, and then those who have sacrificed their happiness to such folly will look but like Fools themselves."

Show this letter to our lovely and much beloved Harriet; she is, I think, the object of a very honourable and a very tender passion, and to a mind like hers that ought to be a very great comfort …

Write to me only in general, not particular terms. Write very soon tho', or I shall be gone to Mrs. Siddons's.

The great actress was seeking retirement and country air at Nuneham Courtney, on the banks of the Thames below Oxford, and thither all the Streatham household shortly betook themselves.

Buchetti, whom Mrs. Piozzi had known for some years, was evidently a friend of Trotti, but seems, in spite of his Italian name, to have been a Frenchman. There is a letter from him in Mr. Broadley's collection, dated Paris, 11th June 1789, written in English, and signed Abbé de Buchetti, telling Mrs. Piozzi that he had written to her from Cadiz in October 1788, giving an account of his travels in Andalusia, &c. He goes on to mention the forthcoming meeting of the French Estates to debate on the new Constitution, which he expects will be very interesting, and at which he hopes to be present. He adds compliments from Trotti.

The following lines by Mrs. Piozzi, dated Streatham, 6th July 1791, occur on a loose sheet among the letters:

> By Friend Howard instructed our Virtue t'advance,
> The difference is found 'twixt Great Britain and France;
> Old England her Pris'ners to Palaces brings,
> While the Palace in France makes a Prison for Kings.

Rectory House, Nuneham,
6 Aug. Saturday.

I promised my dear Miss Weston a long Letter from sweet Siddons's fairy Habitation, but had not an Idea of finding as elegant a Thing as it is. England can boast no happier Situation; a Hill scattered over with fragrance makes the Stand for our lovely little Cottage, while Isis rolls at his foot, and Oxford terminates our view. Ld. Harcourt's rich Wood covers a rising Ground that conceals the flat Country on the Left, and leaves no Spot unoccupied by cultivated, and I may say peculiar Beauty. How I should love to range these Walks with my own dear Streatham Coterie!—but now it is all broken up. The Marquis and my Master with M. Buchetti left us this Morning in search of Sublimer Scenes: I have given them a Tour into Wales— Cecilia and myself sit and look here for their Return—*that is for my Husband's*—unless Miss Owen's summons or Signal of distress lures me to Shrewsbury, where I could wait for *him* and be nearer. They will reach Worcester tonight, and visit Hagley tomorrow I trow. Never did mortal Nymph speed her *polish'd* Arrow more *surely* than has our Harriet done: never did stricken Deer struggle more ineffectually against the Shaft which has fix'd itself firm in his Heart than does her noble Lover. He has however no Mind, I fancy, to give up without an Effort—but no one better knows than I do the difficulty, up to impossibility, of such an Operation. *She* too feels, and feels sincerely, I'm sure; these are the true lasting Passions; when a serpentine Walk leads they *know not whither*: for in Love, as in Taste, I see

> He best succeeds who pleasingly *confounds*;
> Surprizes, varies, and *conceals* the *Bounds*.

Console and sooth her, *do*, my charming Friend, she will find these five or six Weeks as many Years—but by then she will have her Admirer at the Hot Wells, where he may drink the Water to advantage. He is already much altered in countenance, but *so* interesting! …

There is nothing like living near a Nobleman's house for making a *Democrate* of one: here has been such a deal of Ceremony and Diddle Daddle to get these Letters frank'd as would make a plain Body mad—and I see not that you or Harriet will get them either quicker or cheaper for all the Ado we have made at last, but now I am out of Parliament myself I will beg no more Free Cost directions. Oh! would you believe the Gypsies have told Truth to Marquis Trotti? They said he would have a great Influx of Money soon—*Yellow Boys* you know they called them: and he said what stuff that was, because his Fortune could not easily admit of Increase, as it was already an entail'd Estate—and all his expectations well known to himself. But a few days ago a Letter from Italy informed him of unclaimed Dividends found in the Bank of Genoa, which might be his for asking. *He will not go over* to ask for them however; but sent his Father word he was indifferent about the Matter—he had enough &c.—he is of Aspasia's mind entirely—

Love be our Wealth, and our Distinction Virtue.

His Income can be in no Danger though, do what he will: at least a very considerable one, of which I am glad: he is a deserving Character indeed, and will, I hope, lose very little by his Sentiments of Dignity and Sensibility of Heart. Let our Harriet read all this, I had no room for another Word in that I sent *her*. How beautiful a bit of writing did she send me upon leaving Streatham! I wish, when her Hand's *in*, some clever verses would but drop from it: tell her I say so: this is Inspiration's favourite Hour. How pleased it would make me if I were but addressed in them! Her Talents have really made a glorious Conquest, and, she ought to cherish them. I long for the sight of her dear pale Ink, that I do …

It appears so strange and so shocking to put up my Letter without speaking of Miss Seward, that I can't bear it; nobody has such a notion of her Talents as I have, though all the world has talked so loudly about them. Her Mental and indeed her Personal Charms, when I last saw them, united the three grand Characteristics of Female Excellence to very great Perfection: I mean Majesty, Vivacity, and Sweetness.

Well! you may speak as ill of Bath as you please, but I wish I was there, and never look at old White Horse Hill, which one sees from the

Anna Seward
By W. Ridley after Romney 1797

Terrace, without sighing to pass it on the Road—but Fate calls to Shrewsbury—and thither I shall hie me on the 20 of this Month. And now remember Missey, that to kindle and keep up a Man's Love so as to make him ardent enough for the *overleaping* Objections, is the true duty of prudent Friendship; not to make him *talk* of those *very Objections* which we know already, and which will only strengthen by talking of. So God bless you all, and love your   H.L.P.

The Aspasia here quoted appears to be the heroine of Beaumont and Fletcher's *Maid's Tragedy*.

Harriet Lee, as desired by Mrs. Piozzi, wrote the verses on Streatham Park which are given below.

VERSES TO MRS. PIOZZI,
10 Aug. 1791.
(By Harriet Lee)

From the bright West the orb of Day
　　Far hence his dazzling fires removes;
While Twilight brings, in sober grey,
　　The pensive hour that Sorrow loves.

Tho' the dim Landscape mock my Eye,
　　Mine Eye its fading charm pursues:
Ah! tell me, busy Fancy, why
　　Thro' the lone Eve thou still would'st muse?

More rich perfume does Flora yield?
　　Blows the light breeze a softer Gale?
Do fresher dews revive the Field?
　　Does sweeter music fill the Vale?

No, idle Wand'rer, no!—in vain
　　For thee they blend their sweetest Powers;
Thine ear persues a *distant* Strain,
　　Thy gaze still courts far distant Bowers.

To that loved Roof where Friendship's fires
　　With pure and generous ardor burn,
Lost to whate'er this Scene inspires,
　　Thy fond affections still return.

E'en now I tread the velvet plain
　　That spreads its graceful curve around;
Where Pleasure bade her fairy train
　　With magic influence bless the ground.

Now, on that more than Syren song,
　　Where Nature lends her grace to Art,

My Sense delighted hovers long,
 And hails the language of my Heart.

And thou, much loved, whose cultured mind
 Each Muse and every Virtue crown,
If aught to charm in mine thou find,
 Ah, justly deem that charm thine own!

From thee I learnt that grace to seize
 Whose varying tints can gild each hour;
From thee that warm *desire* to please,
 Which only could bestow the *power*.

Then let me court pale Fancy still,
 Still bid her bright delusions last,
The present hour she best can fill
 That kindly can recall the past.

And oh! that past!—fond heart forbear!
Nor dim the Vision with a Tear!

Having successfully invoked her friend's muse, Mrs. Piozzi herself felt inspired to pay a poetical tribute to the absent Piozzi and Trotti; both poems, as it happened, being composed on the same day. It will be noticed that her fourth stanza contains a pretty pointed allusion to the marriage she hoped to bring about between the Marquis and Harriet Lee.

STANZAS TO THE TRAVELLERS
(Marquis Trotti and Mr. Piozzi)
Written at the Rectory, Nuneham, 10 *Aug.* 1791

I

While you your wandering footsteps bear
To harsher climes and colder air,
 Nor once our absence feel;

Here still beneath the shady tree
We sip our solitary Tea,
   Or turn the pensive Wheel.

2

Yet oft our thoughts recur to you
As the rich landscape lies in view,
   And spreads its beauties wide;
Such beauties once were found, we cry,
In our loved Friends' society,
   By us 'ere while enjoyed.

3

In the pure current as we gaze,
Where Isis through the valley strays,
   Far from her silvery source;
From Pride and Prejudice as clear,
We read our *noble Traveller,*
   Refining in his course.

4

Like him she haunts the rural shade,
Nor loves the clam'rous, proud Cascade,
   Loudest in stormy weather:
Nor scorns to mix her *ancient Name*
With honest, artless*, British Thame,*
   And seek the Seas together.

5

But if around we turn our eyes
Where Learning's lofty turrets rise,
   Dropping their classick Manna;
How swift does fancy back reflect
The hours devoted to collect
   Our fav'rite Buchettiana!

6

When Cynthia swells with silver light,
Lending new lustre to the night,
   If Philomel we hear,
Pouring her wood-notes o'er the plain,
How does our Piozzi's sweeter strain
   Still vibrate in our ear.

7

Too empty then your projects prove,
To run from Friendship and from Love,
   And call it Separation;
Reason admits of many a cheat,
But never yet was found deceit
   Cou'd trick the Imagination.

With regard to her own compositions she writes in her Commonplace Book: "Grave verses have seldom, I think, dropt from my pen. Poor dear Jane Hamilton, afterwards Holman, used to say she was at a loss to decide whether the ground work of my character was seriousness embellished with gaiety; or a blythe, pleasant temper, shaded with very serious, and not seldom melancholy, reflexions."

The next letter, though undated, was evidently written before that dated 18th August, and within a few days of receiving Harriet Lee's verses.

I know not, my dear Girl, whether the great Dictionary is a good incentive to Love or no, but if agreable letters produce it the Gypsie prophecy towards *you* will not surely be long in completing. I never read any Book so interesting or entertaining, therefore recommend no Novels, but write again, and that directly ...

Dear, lovely, sweet Siddons is better; and at last tolerably reconciled to parting with me for the relief of those whose anguish is of the soul, while hers, I thank God, is confined wholly to the beautiful clay that fits it so neatly with its truly well suited inclosure ...

And now my beloved friends do not think me wanting, in my duty about our Lorenzini; I never was remiss in bringing the subject forward, never lost sight on't but from thinking it prudent so to do; as Adriana says,

> It was a Copy of our Conference,
> Alone it was the subject of our Theme,
> In company I often glanc'd at it,
> Still did I place it in his constant view.[2]

The *verses* I dispatched after them to Denbigh, which they cannot yet have reached, a proof I never shrunk one instant from the cause, and as this moment has brought me a *cold, stiff* letter from him, dated Shrewsbury,—this moment shall carry one back from me to tell him *I think it such*. Meantime you know I never said that it was likely he should marry in this manner unless from irresistible impulse; the obstacles I *know* to be *all but*, if not *wholly* insurmountable. Only my notion of his *Love* is stronger than yours can be, who have seen so little of him; and proportionable power will vanquish proportionable, or rather disproportionable resistance. If Gunpowder *enough* is put under Mont Blanc—*it must give way*. Such was my reasoning always, and I still think it just. The last evening he spent here, crying over Piozzi's Song, and applying every word on't, as I could see, mentally to his own situation; looking all the while like *very Death*, and never sleeping in the night, but employing himself in penning his Journal forsooth, which consisted only of tender sallies at the sight of the Bath Road; at thoughts of leaving Streatham; &c., till his very heart was breaking with passion, apparently increased instead of diminished by absence. Vindicate my hopes and even *belief* that he will relieve his anguish, when become totally insupportable, by a union which every *natural* friend he has in the world will certainly disapprove. As to the letters which he brought down to the Library in his hand the morning we left Streatham, they were letters he had himself *written*, not *received*: I suppose to say that he was resolved on remaining another year in England. They had, as he confes't, cost him even tortures to write them. O my sweet Sophy! I know most fatally from experience every pang that poor young man is feeling; yet I was an *Englishwoman*! of a country where no such aristocratic notions are acknowledged as taint his hotter soil; and yet three years did I languish in agony, absence, and lingering expectation. "If fortune," said he to me one day, (dancing to the tune in his own head, for I had not mentioned fortune,) "If fortune were the only obstacle, I hate it, I despise it; I have been offered fortunes enough, the first in Lombardy I may say; but I abhor them all." "One may see," was the reply, "you have no such mean notions." "My Father pleased himself," said he, "I made no objections. *If people were generous!* but——" "But what, my Lord?" quoth I. He put his handkerchief to his eyes, and changed the conversation. Who would have pressed him further to tell that which I know already, and which no power on earth can cure; the difference of Birth, Religion, and Country? If however he has but *love enough*, all those three things which would drown him if he tried to swim across, may be *leaped* over; and I, who have taken the jump before him, never cease to show him how well I feel myself after it. For the rest, he is now in bad company for our cause to be sure; but I shall have another sight of him at Shrewsbury, before he gets to Bath, and will send thither all the particulars …

NUNEHAM, *Thurs.* 18 *Aug.* 1791.

One more long letter, dearest Miss Weston, and then away to Shrewsbury, whither direct your next. This last has been just as long reaching Oxford, whence I almost see myself within five hours of you, as a letter yesterday received from Marquis Trotti at Wrexham, a place not less, surely, than 140 miles off. They make a mighty slow progress, which tires my spirits to follow; and seem exceedingly well amused, a thing I was not absolutely dying to hear. Meantime, what he has written, tho' cold, has pensive passages in it which keep my hopes alive; and 'tis not cold neither, but *guarded*. Now I tho't it my duty to keep Harriet ignorant of nothing I knew, and as I have told her every good and desirable symptom, so have I left in no doubt his present disposition, for the first letter I *copied* for her, and this last I *enclosed*.

Was there ever such a storm seen in England as this last dreadful one of the 15th? Our December lightning that frighted you so was nothing to it. Where was my poor Husband *then*, I wonder? Perhaps on Snowdon, incumber'd with a horse no less confounded than himself. We were all here much alarm'd indeed, though Mrs. Siddons has mended ever since, I think …

Now for more public concerns, of which your last letter but one gives me the best information. It does really appear, contrary to my predictions, that all Europe will joyn to re-instate a descendant of that House of Bourbon, which, when represented by his ancestor *Louis Quatorze*, all Europe united to humble: but this should be considered as justice, not caprice. That last mentioned Prince sought openly to seize the rights of others, while his wretched successor has been cruelly deprived of his own; and the world will not look on, it seems, while the Crown of France is trampled on, though none stir'd a step even when the Sacred head of an *English* monarch was sever'd from his body by the *Democrats* of that day.

Helena Williams is a courageous damsel, and will, I hope, never be a distressed one in consequence of that conduct, which, if anything happens but good to her, will be condemned as rashness; and if she returns safe will be applauded as curiosity after the great objects in life, while we are listening only to hear how go the small ones. I find that fierce doings are expected, and I am much delighted with your *nine thousand* men: 'tis an admirable anecdote of old Marshal Saxe, and to me a new one. It will, may be, divert you to hear that he married a Lady he did not much like, merely because her name was *Victoria*, and that when he died, one of the female French wits said, what a pity it was that no *De Profundis* should be said for him who had so often made France sing *Te Deum*. He was a Lutheran, you know.

You never sent me word you liked my Verses, and they were really ingenious ones too; did Harriet ever shew them to you? If much applause ensues, I shall be tempted to copy over some stanzas made for pretty Siddons's little red book, where she keeps everything y^t has been ever said or sung in her praise, *unprinted* …

I expect a letter from my Travellers before I send this: meantime Heaven forefend that I should meet the Marquis at Shrewsbury. He will quit my Master at Denbigh, *sure*, and go thro' S. Wales to Bristol. Say everything that expresses esteem, love, and gratitude, to Mr. and Mrs. Whalley, and tell Miss Seward how valuable her health is even to *me*, who see so little of her: if she neglects it, she is doing public injury, and is worse than a Democrate ...

French affairs, as reported in England at this juncture, were no doubt very confusing. The King's attempt to leave Paris in July had been frustrated, but he had been making overtures to most of the crowned heads in Europe, and intervention on the part of some of them must have appeared imminent.

It seems likely that Mrs. Piozzi made the acquaintance of Helen Maria Williams through their common friend, Dr. Moore. She was a girl of great natural ability, but of scanty education; for though born in London, she was brought up at Berwick-on-Tweed. She returned to town with her mother in 1781, being then about twenty years of age, bringing with her a romantic poem, "Edwin and Eltruda," which, like several subsequent works, met with considerable success. In 1788 she went with her mother to France, on a visit to a sister who had married a Swiss Protestant minister; and having enthusiastically adopted the principles of the Revolution, she made that country her home, and wrote a good deal on French politics, as will be noticed later. These proceedings, and her intimacy with J.H. Stone, who had been separated from his wife, provoked a good deal of hostile comment, both among her acquaintances, and in the papers like the *Anti-Jacobin*, of which she was not aware till much later. It was currently reported that she was living under Stone's protection, a view accepted in the *Dictionary of National Biography*. But it is not quite fair to judge her conduct solely on such *ex-parte* evidence, though perhaps it was all her biographer had to go upon. Her own letters, written to Mrs. Pennington, put a somewhat different complexion on the case. In the first of these, dated 2nd July 1803, she mentions that she is taking charge of the orphan children of her sister, who had died suddenly. She lives with her mother and another relative, Mrs. Persis Williams, whom she has never quitted for three days together since she left England, except for her journey to Switzerland, which was undertaken to save her neck. Stone procured her passport, but she travelled, not with him alone, as had been represented, but with three other gentlemen, one of whom was an English M.P., and on her arrival was placed under the charge of her brother-in-law's relatives. In 1811 she writes that her mother is dead, but that she is still living with Mrs. Persis Williams and her nephew. In another letter, dated 26th January 1819, after Stone's death, she mentions that his matrimonial troubles had begun before she knew him, and that it was his wife, "an odious woman," who provided herself with gallants in Paris, and then, seizing on the new Law of Divorce, "in spite of all our counsels," separated herself from her husband, who had by this time lost his fortune. After this they took Stone in, and he lived for twenty-five years as a member of the household.

Mrs. Piozzi, who abhorred her books, though she never quite lost her affection for their author, writes in her Commonplace Book: "I think Helen Williams turned wholly foreigner, and considered England only a place to get money from." Though her poems, novels, and politics may alike be forgotten, she has a certain claim on the gratitude of generations of play-goers, for it was her tale of *Perourou the Bellows Mender* that the first Lord Lytton adapted for the Stage as the *Lady of Lyons*.

SHREWSBURY, 29 *Aug. Monday.*

You are a noble girl yourself, dearest Miss Weston, and a true friend; if to be an elegant letter writer was praise fit to mix with this, I think you the best in England. *Both* the sweet Epistles came safe; the *first* pleases me best tho', because most natural. But if the thing is *credible*, believe it, they have been come a little bit, and no enquiries has he made; but he treats me with a haughty reserve, in consequence perhaps of my verses, or I dream so: for when Buchetti praised 'em, he said nothing. We are *none* of us going through S. Wales to Bath and Bristol. He has *business in London*, he says, and God knows we have little pleasure here; so we all set out on Thursday morning together. You will be sadly hurt at all this, but 'tis true. No more does he follow me fondly about, as at Streatham or the Rectory, but I think apparently avoids me. Bad symptoms these; while poor

Helen Maria Williams
From an engraving by J. Singleton

Miss Owen, polite by habit, and desirous of keeping her own anguish down by hospitable attentions in which *the mind* has no share, though the kind heart wishes it had, leaves me not an instant to myself or to him.

Oh! but I have caught my Spark at last. He began talking to me of the Assizes, "Where," said I, "Marquis Trotti shall be indicted on a new Statute, for Heart-stealing without intentions of payment." He coloured, laughed, and stared,—well he might,—but asked my proofs, and I produced *your letter*. We should have made a good picture enough. "And what," says I, "is to be the end of all this?" "A ride to

Bath," replied he. "I have begged Jacob to buy me a horse, and I will go, and go alone; and I will see S. Wales and all. As to the letter, Miss Weston is charming, but, I hope, has embellished a good deal. And who is going to sea-bathe?" "Only her sister-in-law," answered I. "Oh! that sea-bathing frighted me!"—We were interrupted, but I find by Mr. Piozzi that this matter has been discussed among them, and my husband *thinks now* that there is *somewhat in it*. But he is always right friendly and charming, and says just what he ought, but wishes our Harriet well too, and is reading your letter *now*.

No description can tell what I have suffered in another friend's cause since I came here; but my death is not catched, and my leg is not broken, so I'll say as little as possible on a subject of more horror than one can express in words, though dear Miss Weston chose them …

From the next letter it appears that all the party had returned to Streatham Park.

Monday 5 Sep.

Kind! charming Miss Weston! your letter was a sweet cordial after the journey, for I did get home very tired and fatigued and latish on Saturday evening, after suffering something, sure enough, in the cause of friendship …

The Marquis is making Jacob buy him a horse, to ride over *South Wales*, and Mr. Davies tells him that Bath and Bristol is the nearest way thither; sure he will never *ride* that way, however earnest to rid himself of his companion's good advice, which his head probably applauded while his heart resists it. There is a cold reserve about the man, mixed with fine qualities too, but he has only a half confidence in me certainly; and seems, odd enough! to like teizing my curiosity with conjecture about his intentions towards Harriet, which I have not yet penetrated. He waits in this neighbourhood for his servant from Paris, whither he has sent him to fetch all his goods away. So far looks well, and runs as he told me long ago, when he said "I can at least give you *that* satisfaction, that I do not leave England this year." For my own part he puzzles me completely, and *so* confounds my conjectures, that were I to hear within a month that Harriet was

Marchioness Trotti, or were I to hear he had informed her that such an event was impossible, I should in neither case be surprised. He is gone to London this morning, under promise to return o' Thursday, and says his servant will not be here before the end of the week. So much for Lorenzo.

My own health has been shaken, but will tie up again with use of the tub, or perhaps we may try the Sea too. But I feel so glad to get home that scarcely will pleasure or profit tempt me out again in a hurry. Harriet talks of going to Weymouth or Southampton: if he should go to find Belvidere House without his favourite Bird, how would he feel? Yet will I not tell him the project, lest he should make that an excuse for not going: let him go, and hear, perhaps see that she is ill, from those whom he will believe. Better so; she may change her mind too, and I hope she will; but I only give her information always, not advice. I have this day acquainted her with all he says and does, 'tis she must act accordingly. My dear Master is pleased to find me at Streatham Park once more in a whole skin; the danger will be better to talk than write about, and we shall meet again some time, I trust, and exchange minds …

Dear, charming Siddons is better; we stopt at her *village*, not at her *house*, returning, and heard y^t Sheridan and Kemble were with her; on *business* no doubt, so we would not go in, but sent com^{ts}. They may see I do not want any favours they have to bestow.

Adieu! my charming friend! Poor Harriet laments your loss most pathetically, and I am very, very sorry for her: yet let us remember 'tis not now above six or seven weeks suspense. I should, from the first, have thought it very fortunate if she had not to count by *months* at least, if not *years.* Adieu and love your   H.L.P.

John Kemble, Mrs. Siddons's brother, became manager for Sheridan at Drury Lane in 1788. His sister's retirement during the season of 1788-9, though mainly due to ill-health, was not altogether unconnected with the difficulty of extracting her salary from the brilliant but unbusinesslike Sheridan.

At this date Miss Weston was staying at Corston, near Bath, with the Rev. F. Randolph, D.D., Canon of Bristol, who afterwards acted as Domestic Chaplain and English Instructor to the Duchess of Kent in the little Court at Amorbach, shortly before the birth of the Princess Victoria.

The Rev. Reynold Davies, M.A., of Streatham, who is frequently referred to in the later letters, was much esteemed by Mrs. Piozzi, who entrusted him with the education of John Salusbury Piozzi for some years after he was brought to England. In the Oxford Matriculation Registers he is described in the usual way as Reynold Davies, son of David, &c.; but on the monument he erected to his parents it is stated that he was the son of David Powell of Bodwiggied in Penderyn, co. Brecknock, an unusually late instance of the old Welsh system of nomenclature, by which the father's Christian name was taken as a surname by the son.

Tues. 28 *Sep.* '91.

Your letters, my lovely friend, are like the places they describe, cultivated, rich, and various: the prominent feature elegance, but always some sublimity in hope and prospect …

Our Italian Friends are still with us; the Marquis talks seldomer than ever of his intended tour through S. Wales to Bath, yet may mean it ne'er the less; and I dare say he will go and refresh his passion. Make Harriet Lee tell you Cecilia's saucy trick; it will divert her to tell it, and I won't take the tale out of her hands: her spirits mend, I see, as to her heart, it scarce *can* receive improvement; and the strong sense she posesses, with such variety of resources too, will guard those passes where tenderness prevails over prudent apathy …

My Master went last night to Town with good old Mr. Jones, to see what sport the transmigration of Old Drury can afford. We hear that all goes well, and that the Town accepts Kemble's new terms willingly and generously …

During 1791-2 Drury Lane Theatre was rebuilding, and Kemble and his company were acting at the Haymarket until the new house was ready for occupation.

"Good old Mr. Jones" was a connection by marriage of Mrs. Piozzi's, having married a daughter of Sir William Fowler, her mother's cousin. He was instrumental in bringing about the public reconciliation between Mrs. Piozzi and her daughters, as narrated later on.

STREATHAM PARK, Sat. 15 Oct.

My dear Miss Weston's letter contain'd more agreeable descriptions of the places I love, than of the people. I must hear better accounts of our sweet Harriet before my heart is easy, yet I doubt not her command over a passion which no longer appears to disturb the tranquility of her once half-frantic Admirer; who told my Master, in confidence *no,*—was his expression to me,—but in common discourse, that if he married a woman of inferior birth, such were his *peculiar* circumstances, that exactly one half of his estates would be forfeited. He remains constantly with us, but the world seems a blank to him: he takes no pleasure, as I can observe, and either feels no pain, or pretends to feel none. If he ever does marry an Italian lady he will be a very miserable man however, from being haunted by our Harriet's form, adorned with talents, and radiant with excellence. Should he renew his attachment to her, and sacrifice half his fortune to his love, every child she brings will seemingly reproach him for lessening an ancient patrimony.—*Such is life.*

Mrs. Siddons is at Harrogate, and, we hope, mending. Poor Sir Charles Hotham is going to change the *Scene,* I hear: his state of existence, so far as relates to this world, draws to an end. Yet though the Physicians send him to Bath, he and Lady Dorothy resolve, it seems, to see the *new* Drury Lane Hay Market before their curtain falls. Who says there is no ruling passion? It appears to me that *any* passion, or even inclination, nursed up carefully, will rule the rest, tho' naturally larger and stronger; as our little Flo lords it over the out-door dogs, merely on the strength of being his Mistress' *favourite.*

Chevalier Pindemonte has written me a long letter. He sends particular compliments to all our Friends and Coterie almost, and says a vast deal about dear Siddons. "What," cries Mr. Buchetti, "does he say of Helena Williams?" "Oh! not a word," replied I, "men never speak at all of the woman whom they really like." A painter would have enjoyed Marquis Trotti's countenance at this conversation. Meantime our little democratic friend is not doing a foolish thing at last by leaving England, I do believe. Such is the advantage, of exchange between London and Orleans, that they say the very difference may make it worth her while; nor is that position a weak one, if it be true that a British Guinea is worth thirty-two French Shillings; and it was a man just arrived who told it me for a fact …

Della Crusca has married a Woman of elegant person and address, and who will bring him perhaps £500 o' year, with an unblemished character, as people tell me: the husband meantime will congratulate himself charmingly on his own *superiority*, no small pleasure to some minds; and the world will always be on his side in every dispute, tho' he had neither character *nor* fortune when they met. His family, I hear, are very angry.

The Kembles get money apace. Mr. Chappelow says he is sure that the Pit *alone* pays every night's expence, and people in general seem highly satisfied. *Here's* a long letter from your ever affectionate

H.L.P.

Sir Charles Hotham lived long enough to see the new theatre after all: his curtain did not actually fall till 1794.

It was during her Italian tour that Mrs. Piozzi had met Mr. Chappelow, who remained her firm friend till his death. Her connection with Robert Merry (" Della Crusca") at Florence has been mentioned in the Introduction. He returned to England in 1787, and published some rather turgid poems of a sentimental character, which were satirised by Gifford in the *Baviad.* At some time in the course of this year he was in Paris, being, like Helena Williams, an ardent sympathiser with the Revolution.

STREATHAM PARK, *Tues.* 8 *Nov.*

My dearest Miss Weston would readily forgive my long silence, if she knew how heavily my hours are passing, and how happy a moment I think even this that I have stolen to write at last. Poor Mr. Piozzi has been, and is as ill with the Gout as I do believe a man can possibly be. Knees, hands, feet,—crippled in all, and unable even at this hour to turn in the bed …

Marquis Trotti and Mr. Buchetti have both been excessively kind indeed, and I shall feel eternally obliged by their attentive friendship. The Marquis has delayed his journey till he sees our Master on his legs again, and Mr. Buchetti keeps his courage up, as nobody but a countryman *can* do in a strange land …

I rejoice in our dear Harriet's recovery, which *you* say proceeds from her fate's being decided, a position I never believed, yet cannot contradict, for to me he never names her; notwithstanding I am confident he thinks of her still, nor would I bet a large wager he does not yet marry her; but it was not an event ever likely to happen in three months, and in three years she may, for aught I see, still be his, tho' I never more will tell her so.

Agitation of spirits is the worst illness, of which my present situation is a proof, and too much love is good for nothing, as I see, except to make one wretched. Mr. Piozzi has had Gout upon his throat, his voice, all that could agitate and terrifie me, but now *Safe's* the word, and I care little for his *pain*, poor soul, if we can but keep away danger …

STREATHAM PARK, *Sat.* 20 *Nov.*

My dear Miss Weston deserves twenty letters, yet can I scarce write her *one* somehow. That all have their vexations is very true, and perhaps my share has been hitherto not quite equal to my neighbours'. Notwithstanding they would make no inconsiderable figure if prettily dressed up,—I mean *my own*. Poor Piozzi gets on as the Crabs do, he says, backward. Yesterday no creature could bear to see his agony, and tho' we all dined in the Library, we wished ourselves back a'bed …

I have had a letter from sweet Helena [Williams] this very post, telling how she is got safe to Orleans; 'tis however written in a strain less triumphant than tender, I think; and if as she purposes, we may hope to see her next Summer, I shall have few fears of her return to France.

As to our dear Harriet, you know how much I love her, but old Barba Jove and I have a vile trick of laughing at Lovers' resolutions.

No matter, my heart wishes her sincerely well, and I have too many obligations to Marquis Trotti's politeness and attention while Mr. Piozzi was ill, not to wish and desire all good for him which he can desire for himself ...

Owing, no doubt, to Miss Weston's return from Bath to Westminster, there are no letters for the next three months; the next, though as usual, undated, is shown by the postmark to have been written from Bath in 1792.

> *Monday 5 Mar. No. 15 Milsom Street.*
>
> My dearest Miss Weston will not wonder I write so little while my hands are full of engagements, my heart with anxiety, and my head,—as old Cymbeline says,—amazed with too much matter.[3] Harriet will have let you into a great deal of my story, and you will be surprised less at the behaviour of a man who, it seems, had no birth nor education to found good manners upon. The only difficulty is whether we shall tell the lady what we know, or suppress it. I am for the latter, because like Zara she may care little whether he is Osmyn or Alphonzo, for aught I know. But my Master, ever steady to the care of *his own honour*, says she shall be told *that which we have heard*, because 'tis our duty to speak as much as hers to listen. Send me some good counsel, and continue to love your
>
> H.L.P.

So ends Harriet Lee's romance. No clue is given as to what had been heard to Trotti's prejudice, but it must have been something serious, and as Harriet had met him, as a friend of the family, at Mr. Piozzi's house, the latter felt bound to clear himself of any suspicion of collusion. The Marquis, if not altogether an impostor, was clearly not what he seemed; the curious thing is that the Piozzis had not had their suspicions aroused sooner.

The characters alluded to by Mrs. Piozzi occur in Congreve's *Mourning Bride*, in which Osmyn, otherwise Alphonzo, son of the King of Valentia, is wrecked on the coast of Africa, where Queen Zara falls in love with him.

The next letter, undated, but bearing the postmark of July '92, alludes to a pecuniary loss Mrs. Weston had sustained, apparently through the fault of her son. Perhaps as the result of this they left the house in Queen Square, and till September the Westons took up their abode at Lewisham.

I would not, dearest Miss Weston, for the World, add to your torments. Comfort your poor Mother, and present her my cordial good wishes and compliments. Tell her that I say one good child out of only two is a good proportion, and I am sure God Almighty will not forsake her if the World does. While I have a house you command an apartment; consider it as your own, and come when it suits you. Cecilia will get her arm again, but 'twas a dreadful accident; that Girl is always saved from the brink of a precipice somehow: nothing could be more painful or more dangerous, she must wear it in a sling for a week at least ... Could not Mr. Vandercorn be useful? he would make a point of serving you, I'm sure; but I fear, I fear the poor £1000 is irretrievably gone. Despair not of Fortune however, she is never long in a mind, and will not be always so cross, I am *sure* she will not ...

Marquis Trotti was here yesterday, to my amazement, who concluded him gone abroad; he brought Zenobio, Merlini, and Buchetti with him, and we had no manner of talk: he looks very well, says he leaves London for Paris next Wednesday,—I will not tell Harriet for fear of keeping her away. Would he had never come! We wanted him not, Heaven knows ...

No sooner is one romance ended than another begins, destined, like the last, to give Mrs. Piozzi a good deal of anxiety to equally little purpose. Cecilia's first admirer appears upon the scene, in the person of a Mr. Drummond, and prosecutes his suit with an ardour which for a time carries all before him.

Whatever faults the Marquis may have committed, he did not consider himself in any way cut off from intercourse with the Piozzis, or feel any difficulty about keeping up a correspondence after he left England, which he did just in time to be present at Paris during the September massacres.

STREATHAM PARK, *Tues.* 17 *Jul.*

Mr. Piozzi has so many things to call and to hurry him—he can only come on *Monday* next to fetch his dear Miss Weston and mine. Be ready then kind creature and come away …

I am wholly of your Mother's opinion, that 'tis best be *near the spot*: and if *she* is contented with her situation, what need you care to change it? … My vote is for doing nothing, it commonly is you know, if one stirs, 'tis always to hurt oneself, I think, literally and figuratively and all …

No news has been heard of the Federation, but all is supposed to be quiet in France, as an effect of the late coalition between the King and Jacobins. We shall see how matters end; I wonder one has no letter from Marquis Trotti.

Mr. James Drummond has pranced over the Common now with comical effect enough; for he half frighted a quiet old Gentleman of our Village here by stopping him on his ride, and telling his tender tale to most unwilling ears, as no man could like a love story less: and he had no claim to his confidence, for he could not guess who he might be. Mr. Thomas—a man you have heard Mr. Davies call his Oracle—was the person so unwillingly trusted, and while they were together, Drummond called to Miss Lees, who were walking on the lawn, and renewed his acquaintance with them: he likewise halloo to Jacob in a gay tone. Such Geniuses are entertaining and comical as Larks, but I like them not about my house, and shall feel uneasy on the 25th lest some frisk may be performed.

The elder daughter of Mrs. Siddons, Sarah Martha, known among her friends as Sally, was just now staying with the Piozzis, as a companion for Cecilia, who was her junior by about two years.

STREATHAM PARK, *Sun.* 9 *Sep.* 1792.

My dearest Miss Weston, this is my last letter from home; we go tomorrow, and I am now so glad we are going, because Kitchen looks and talks as if Cecilia's cold had fastened seriously upon her breast and lungs. She certainly does breathe with less freedom, and the cough, though the slightest possible, is not removed. Lord! Lord!

what an agony does it give me to think on possibilities! But change of air is the first thing in the world for such disorders, and *she* must have Asses' milk now, instead of Sally Siddons, who grows fat and merry. Be happy if you can, sweet friend, 'tis a hard task, even with all *I* have to make me so: but let us never provoke God's judgements by repining even at his *mercies.* Accept the present offer as such, if you *do* accept it; and carry this kind hearted man a chearful countenance, for that he has deserved. What does Mrs. Weston say? Write me all, and write me soon, remembering how truly I am yours   H.L.P.

This letter gives the first hint of Miss Weston's approaching change of condition. That it had not occurred before was not due to any lack of admirers. In 1779 she was indulging in a semi-Platonic friendship for the half-genius, half-charlatan, and wholly egotist, long patronised by the Whalleys, who signed himself Courtney Melmoth; who wrote to her from Longford Court letters of seven foolscap sheets, filled with rhapsodies about his charmer, or rather about his own feelings for her, in which he seems to have been much more interested. This extraordinary being, who in real life was named Samuel Jackson Pratt, was a man of good family and education, being a graduate of Cambridge, and son of a High Sheriff of Huntingdon, had in his life already played many parts, having been by turns priest, actor, fortune-teller, bookseller, playwright, poet, and essayist. He was a thoroughly untrustworthy person, as Sophia seems to have discovered in time, though he was the only one of her admirers whose letters she was at pains to preserve. William Siddons had reason to believe that he was the original author of the anonymous attacks on his wife, previously alluded to, and the Swan of Lichfield was convinced of similar duplicity on his part towards herself. It is from her letters to Sophia that we get some information as to the latter's more serious admirers.

Of these the first was Major Cathcart Taylor, who evidently made some impression on her heart, but proved himself "unworthy," and was dismissed before 1784. Later on a strong mutual attachment grew up between her and Mr. W. Davenport; but the engagement was broken off by what Anna Seward terms "the rascality of a parent." The last of the series, who made the Swan his confidante, and whom she calls "the gentle Wickens," had a "little temple of the Arts" at Lichfield. But "prudence laid a cold hand upon his hopes"; the lady was far above him, and he gave her up for her own sake. "He admires the brightness of the Star, but will not draw it from its habitual sphere."

The match she was now contemplating was not brilliant, or even romantic, and probably her head was much more concerned in the decision than her heart. But the suitor, in spite of a somewhat scandalous story retailed to Sophia by her cousin Mrs. Whalley, was evidently an honourable man, and certainly his suit was not prompted by mercenary motives. William Pennington probably belonged to a Bristol family, for a merchant of these names was living there earlier in the century; but he himself, according to the editor of Whalley's correspondence was a loyal colonist ruined by the American War of Independence. This account goes on to relate how, on the way home, he made the acquaintance of another colonist returning to find relations in the Old Country with whom he had long lost touch. The latter fell ill on the voyage, and, in spite of all Pennington's care, died before they reached England; but not before he had made a will leaving everything to his new friend. Pennington's first care on landing was to seek out the dead man's relations, and then, having torn up the will, to put them in the way of obtaining the property.

This must have been before 1783, as in January of that year Sophia, writing to Whalley, incidentally mentions that Mr. Pennington is sharing a house with "cousin Somers." In 1785 we find him acting as Master of the Ceremonies at the Clifton Hot Wells. A contemporary Guide Book informs us that he was "inducted" to this important office "under the patronage of the Archbishop of Tuam, and the Bishop of Cloyne, and with the unanimous voice of a numerous circle of nobility and gentry." Here, "distinguished by a medallion and ribbon," he presided over the Assemblies, and legislated for the better preservation of their dignity, ordaining, *inter alia*: "That no Gentleman appear with a sword or with spurs in these rooms, or, on a ball night, in boots. That the Subscription Balls will begin as soon as possible after seven o'clock, and conclude at eleven, on account of the health of the Company." He continued to officiate as M.C. for twenty-eight years.

Portrait of Mrs Thrale at the age of 40
From the original picture by Sir Joshua Reynolds about 1781
This was just about the time of her first meeting with Piozzi

CROWN INN, DENBIGH, 15 *Sep. Sat.*
I make haste to assure my kind friend that all apprehensions for Cecilia are at an end. The change of air relieved her oppression the first day, and carried off what remained of cold, or cough, or whatever it was, the *second*. But soon as arrived here, after the rainyest journey ever seen, I suppose, poor Sally Siddons was taken ill of an excessive sickness and pain, and our whole night has been spent as yours was, when I was just as ill at Streatham Park … She is now risen and better, and eating Chicken Broth. I am very sorry to think you have

been suffering the same torture, but do make haste and get well, and take Bark; it is the best thing after all for *you* who have, I think, few complaints except what proceed from irritated nerves and perpetual anxiety of heart. A decided situation will tranquilize every sensation, and calm the tossing of the waves, which keep on their turbulent motion very often long after the storm is over. Yours is surely past, and so Dear Coz, (as Cecilia says to Rosalind,) Sweet Coz, be merry.[4] Your Mother is right, I daresay, about going to London; Lewisham is a dull place, it were better live here at Denbigh. We have Coals at 10*d*. per C.—and they say how *dear* it all is! and Chickens 1*s*. a couple,—and *such* a prospect! Well! I do think my own poor Country a very pretty one, that I do: and cheap, for though we are called the Squire and his Lady, who live upon *the best*, and pay *for the best*, they cannot for shame ask more than seven Guineas o' week for our lodging and boarding and linnen and china and all included;—four people and three servants, and we have one very long *staring* room and clean beds.

So much for Wales, meantime our letters from France will come slowly, for though they boast their brisk intelligence, I believe the Duke of Brunswick may be in quiet possession of Paris, or beaten back to Coblentz, before we shall hear a bit about the matter, as this town lies in the high road to no town, and smaller events than the deposition or restoration of Sovereigns make much ado here. We shall be quiet tomorrow, and go to Funnen Vaino on Monday, if Sally recovers quite well, and I doubt not her doing so; our Medical Man here is very kind and comfortable.

Helena Williams should mind who she keeps company with; so indeed should Hester Piozzi: that fine man she brought to our house lives in *no* Emigrants' Hotel at Paris, but a common Lodging, in a place where numbers lodge. He carried *no* wife over with him, nor *no* children; they are left at Hackney I am told. Her mother and sister are at Montreuil …

P.S.—(by Mr. Piozzi.)

Dear friend, we are arrived at Denbigh very safe; the Crown Inn is prety comfortable, and I've got a very fine room for Company; next Monday morning we'll go all togheter to see our place for the new

House, and I hope in two years she should be finisd to receive our selves, and our dear friend; be merry and comfortable if you can, and believe me for alway your G.P.

If letters from France came slowly, yet they did arrive. Mr. Broadley's collection contains two written from Paris by the Marquis Trotti, who found himself in the thick of the September massacres, of which he speaks in guarded terms. In the first, dated 3rd September, he says: "I did not run any risk in the terrible bloodshed of yesterday. It was an horrid havock: but I forbear to come into any detail, as it would very likely prevent your receiving this letter. The King and Queen are still living … I am a Traveller, and never meddled in anything, and as such I trust to come out safe." He writes again on 13th September: "So it is, Madam, I long to be in some peaceful, retired place, where people are happy and free without such violent exertions to be so. What I saw lately in Paris is quite enough for me, and I would hate myself if I was to grow familiar to such horrid scenes. Slaughter in cold blood, and murder without provocation, bring us straight back to the state of a brute, which would be ten thousand times worse, living as we do now in populous cities, than as we did formerly in forests … O how often shall I remember the sweet tranquillity of Streatham Park, and the circumstances which will always endear it to me."

He goes on to allude to the project of building a house in Wales, and assuming the role of Prophet, foretells the founding and growth of a "New Salisbury" around Brynbella, greater and more imposing than the old one, with a monument to the "Illustrious Lady" erected in its great square.

The constituent Assembly, having framed the new Constitution, had dissolved itself, and left Louis to work it with the aid of the Girondins, who declared war on Austria in April, but were soon dismissed by the King. A threatening manifesto by the Duke of Brunswick helped to bring the Jacobins into power, who deprived the King of what little authority he possessed, while the new Assembly was succeeded by the Convention. These changes were speedily followed by the imprisonment of the Royal family, and the massacres by the Paris Commune in August and September; but of these Mrs. Piozzi had evidently not yet heard.

Helena Williams' friend was evidently John Hurford Stone, whose name occurs several times in the succeeding letters. He was a Unitarian, and originally a coal-merchant in London, and a prominent member of the Society of Friends of the Revolution. He had thus brought himself to the notice of Fox and Sheridan in England, and had made the acquaintance of Talleyrand and Madame de Genlis in France. He was now paying a visit to Paris from which he returned early in 1793, but soon took up his permanent abode in France, where, on the outbreak of the war, he was imprisoned as an Englishman. In 1794 he was divorced from his wife, and thereafter lived with Helena Williams. His tombstone in Père Lachaise styles him an "enlightened champion of Religion and Liberty."

The idea of building a residence on Mrs. Piozzi's Welsh property, first mooted in 1789, was now taking shape. The old mansion of Bachygraig, besides being inconvenient and ruinous, occupied a low and rather damp situation on the banks of the Clwyd, so a higher and drier site was chosen for the new house.

Sally Siddons soon recovered, but in a few days Cecilia had a serious relapse.

Sat. 29 Sep. [1792]

My head full of opium, my heart of anguish, I will write to my valuable friend about *her* affairs, my own I cannot trust the pen with; dear Sally must write *them* for me. Mr. Whalley is angelick, you should be happy to call him cousin, sure; and the sweet, artless, *hoping* man's letter enclosed, that quotes my verses—in good Time!—and gives the lye to all old maxims which say that we lose our Lovers when we lose our fortune. How can you be so cold to him? But 'tis illness makes you so; be well, sweet friend, and reject not Heaven's offer of temporal happiness in its *natural form*: that of a good husband. Every hour shows me there is no other comfort in this world but what we receive from indissoluble union with a soul somewhat like one's own. Even in my case I feel consolation in my Husband's disinterested goodness. Your Husband, I am sure, has a heart in which meanness will not make its abode. Then why should you scruple to honour or obey him? *I* honour him from my heart. Have him! Have him! and try not to disappoint his romantic expectations of felicity never to be found. Cecilia mends hourly, or I could not write thus much; yes, hourly!—and yet,—Sally takes the pen. Show Sir Lucas Pepys this letter; if mortal pow'rs can save her, *his* will; he saved her once, why was he out of Town?

Ah! dear Miss Weston, what affliction have we all been in! what anxious days and sleepless nights has poor Mrs. Piozzi pass'd! Cecilia has been ill, *very* ill, a Physician from Chester has been call'd; we now hope to God she will recover, sure, almost, that there is no immediate danger. *Not immediate*, but dearest Miss Weston, how afflicted will you be to hear that Dr. Hagarth indicated but too plainly that Cecilia, whom we thought so strong, so free from every complaint, will fall into a consumption. Dear Mrs. Piozzi has fear'd this since the first day Cecilia ail'd any thing, which was last Sunday, when she directly sent for Mr Moore the Apothecary of Denbigh. He said nothing was the matter but cold; she cough'd and complain'd of a pain in her shoulder and side, Monday she was worse, Tuesday and Wednesday she still got worse, Thursday she kept her bed, and Dr. H. was sent for. That day she spit a good deal of blood and was bled. Dr. Hagarth and Mr. Moore differ'd in opinion concerning what part the blood came from. Dr. Hagarth feared it was from the lungs, and that was a bad symptom,—they let her blood again at night. Yesterday Dr. Hagarth left us, and Cecy, after a good night was surprisingly better; she was in better spirits, sat up some time, and was very well disposed to talk and laugh, but she is ordered not to do either. To-day she is still much better, and we hope soon to see her well. In the meantime dear Mrs. Piozzi through anxiety and grief has caught a violent cold, to-day she seems better. Oh, my kind friend, how would your tender heart have bled for her! Mine was ready to burst, in the midst of her affliction on Cecilia's account, to see her compose herself, and assure Mr. Piozzi that for his sake she would bear all patiently, and take care of her own health: indeed, indeed, it was a heart breaking sight. Cecilia does not in the least suspect her complaint, she was only frighten'd when she spit the blood. Tho' to be a spectator of such affliction is a sad thing, yet am I happy in being here. Cecilia is pleas'd to have me near her; she turned everyone but me out of the room when she was bled, and me she held fast and close to her. I think I am a small comfort to poor Mrs. Piozzi too,—at least she told me so. What melancholy reflections does Cecy's illness bring into one's mind; that one who yesterday was young, healthy, strong, prosperous in her fortunes, belov'd by her Parent and friends, in short, with every thing conspiring to render her happy, should to-day be within an inch of death, and quitting for ever all these blessings, is a sad and striking lesson. To make things still more vexatious, poor Jacob has had a terrible fever and sore throat; he is to-day mending. Mr. Piozzi is all tenderness; he is, you may easily conceive, low spirited enough. Let us pray to God that Dr. Hagarth has been deceiv'd, or at least, if he has not, that the complaint may be got the better of. I am sorry indeed to hear how ill you have been, do, dear Creature, get well, and accept of the comfortable independence which is offer'd you by so amiable a person. Will it not in some measure soften the affliction the former part of my letter must have given you, to tell you that my belov'd Mother is at length cur'd of her complaint, and quite an alter'd woman? What a happy being was I when I received this charming news from herself, in her own handwriting! The intended journey to Guy's Cliff must, I fear, be given up, I will hope that when dear Cecy is recover'd, we shall yet pass some happy days there together. The weather has prevented our enjoying this lovely country sufficiently; I have seen enough to make me never forget the beautiful Vale of Clwydd. The new house is to be call'd the Belvedere. Yours sincerely,

S. SIDDONS.

This letter is addressed to 14 James Street, Westminster, where Mrs. Weston had taken rooms, and where she remained at any rate till her daughter's marriage. Sir Lucas Pepys, in whom Mrs. Piozzi reposed so much confidence, was the leading physician of the day. He had been created a Baronet in 1784, was President of the Royal College of Physicians, and attended the King in several of his illnesses.

The suggested name of Belvedere for the new house was not adhered to. The one finally chosen was a hybrid Cambro-Italian form, Bryn-bella, meaning the Beautiful Bank, or Brink.

CROWN INN, DENBIGH, 1st *Oct. Monday.*

I write myself now, kindest Miss Weston, and I write with steadier fingers. The cough has yielded to repeated bleedings, and she mends as rapidly as she grew ill. Dr. Haygarth it was who threw me in that agony, by pronouncing Cecilia in serious danger from the blood spit up, which *he* said came from the lungs; and never did twenty Guineas purchase as much affliction at one dose, I do believe, as those we gave to him. Dear Mr. Moore, an agreeable Practitioner settled here as Accoucheur, Surgeon, &c., who cured Sally Siddons, had repeatedly assured me that it was *not* from the lungs … Her quick recovery gives great reason to think *him* right; and he *so* smiles, and *so* rejoyces, yet insists on my telling nobody that he differs from Dr. Haygarth, who is a man of very high reputation, and in earnest a very pleasing Physician—skilful too I dare say—and fully perswaded of his own opinion, which is supported by Science, as the other's by Experience.

Dear Cecy's recovery will, if complete, prove the old adage that an Ounce of Mother is worth a Pound of Clergy; meaning that good Common Sense, or *Mother Wit* as we call it, beats learning out of doors.

So may it prove! I will now pluck up courage and write to Sir Lucas myself. Doctor Haygarth recommended us to take Cecilia to a warmer climate, and that *instantly*: at the same time he said she must not be *hurried*, or even suffered to *talk* much, or move. *Naples* was the first place that occurred: but how should we get to *Naples*? Thro' France? They would refuse Passports, perhaps *hurry* her into *worse apartments* than these we are in: a prison, and present her with the sight of heads streaming with blood. Thro' Germany? Through marching armies into miserable towns, where want of horses to get forward would detain us in a climate worse than that of Great Britain; a German inn to escape catching cold at is a good joke to be sure. 'Tis a residence for Pigs only, not delicate Damsels, sure.

Let it be *Lisbon* then! Very well, Lisbon be it; but now do not you open your lips, or black one bit of paper with this intelligence, for if she really ails nothing—which Mr. Moore says will very soon appear to be the case—all these phantoms vanish, and poor Mr. Piozzi and I are *not* to be driven forcibly, expensively, dangerously, and suddenly from all our comforts, all our friends, present enjoyments, and future projects. The little *Belvedere* may yet go forward at Funnen Vaino, and we may yet be merry with *you* in many a beautiful spot, but none like the *Vale of Llwydd*. My health, tho' horribly shaken, *may* tye up again, and I may kiss my pretty black Cock and Hen (that I forgot to thank you for,) at poor old Streatham Park. They are of the Polish breed; we will call them the King and Queen of Poland, there will never be any other, I fancy …

Jacob's dangerous sore throat and fever has been a great addition to my agony, but he will live, poor fellow, I thank God; and so the favourite horses got lamed with neglect while he was sick, and Phillis came to evil, and all went *consistently.* I expect my poor Husband to get a fit of the gout every day, and that would *do* for me. I should remind myself of the Welch Parson's letter saying

"Dear Sir, as I was passing the heights of Snowdon last week, with Mrs. Jones behind me, I got in much distress, for night came on, my horse tired, and my Wife fell in labour …"

Of Sally Siddons I say, like as Imogen says of Pisanio, "thou art all the comfort the gods will diet me with."[5] Her mother's recovery is however one solid and certain felicity to us all. I do thank God for that: she is an invaluable Creature.

Thursday 4 *Oct.* DENBIGH.
Well! My dearest Miss Weston, you are a *true* friend if ever any one had a *true* friend, and you will think of nobody but me, and of nothing but my miseries; from some part of which however charming Sir Lucas's letter and yours together have relieved me. I write to him to-day, and I beg'd Dr. Haygarth to write. *His* will doubtless be a *despairing* letter, he despair'd even of Jacob, who, Mr. Moore protested, was never in actual danger. No matter now tho', for he certainly is recovering; and I earnestly *hope* I did not neglect

my duty to him, while my heart was full of everything else in the world.

Indeed, indeed, Cecilia has, between her lovers and her illness, worked my poor heart very hard this year. I marvel Drummond is not come down yet, for he knows all that happened, but the same avarice which prompted his original pursuit of her restrains him from spending seven Guineas to follow *her,* and fret *me.* Some certain comfort every state affords, you know. Cecilia does mend to be sure as fast as ever anybody did mend: ay, and as fast as she grew worse, which was with a rapidity I never before was witness to …

Dear Piozzi does *not* get the gout, so we shall surely move hence o' Monday, but Haygarth is very good, that he is, and comes at a call very quickly too. He has made two visits, and kind Mr. Moore nurses, and sends his wife to nurse, and help sit up, and everything,—that is, he *did* do so when wanted,—as if he were one's oldest and sincerest friend. He *never* thought her in danger, and is now the happiest person, except myself, in the Town of Denbigh. The neighbouring Gentlemen send in baskets of fruit and sallads, and all they think she can want: so if she *does* hate Wales, which I do believe she does most heartily, the People could do no more to make her love it.

Remember, that tho' the Dr. came twice, she spit blood but once; remember too that I did not wait till she spit blood before I sent for him,—*that* agony was while he was coming hither,—this day sennight, and Mr. Moore had just bled her as he walked in. The state of her blood however, and of her case, made Haygarth order the operation to be repeated; and 'tis to bleeding alone that I impute her cure.

She was as well, as lively, and as handsome as ever you saw her just before this attack: she lost the cold *you* had observed by the time she reached Meriden. I remember her running up and down the garden slopes like a school-girl; so she ran up and down the Castle Hill here, to fright me and Sally Siddons at the heights she shew'd herself from,—for mere sport and frolick. The disease was sudden and violent. She had caught the cold when Jacob caught *his,* riding in the rain to the Belvedere, and then coming home in the chaise with us, her habit wet thro'. She *would* ride that day tho' it was showry when she set out, but the roads are so bad for a carriage that every body will ride that *can;* and she is not used to mind a cold, poor soul …

This is, I think, my most rational letter yet … Sally Siddons is my darling daughter, and *so* affectionate. Farewell; beg dear Mr. Whalley's prayers for me, and write to Chester to yours *gratefully,*

H.L.P.

Sat. 6 *Oct.* 1792.

My dearest, truest, kindest Miss Weston's sympathizing letter makes a nice contrast to cruel Doctor Haygarth's, this moment received,—wherein he bids me not relax my caution, for that diseases of these kinds are peculiarly insidious;—says Miss Thrale ought to be watched with the most sedulous attention, &c., and brought to him, if able to move, next Monday, to Chester,—where however he *despairs* again of finding us any comfortable accommodations.

How can dear Sir Lucas Pepys love a man so unlike himself?—and how can a creature who witness'd my anguish suspect, or pretend to suspect, my care of a child whose welfare precludes every other thought and consideration?

Well! Cecilia has no sweats, no febrile heat, no chills, no pain in the breast *at all.* She sleeps uninteruptedly seven hours at a time, and coughs only *now and then,* as we say, but it certainly is not cured. This morning we try her with an airing, but I'm forced to send my letter away, because our Posts come and go very slowly, as you see. Sally Siddons scolds me for crying over Haygarth's letter, because she says *she* sees Cecy mend every moment.

The remaining page and a half is filled up by Sally, who enlarges on this text in great detail, and with much common sense. She seems to have converted Mrs. Piozzi to her opinion, for the next letter, instead of being written at Chester, is dated from Guy's Cliffe, near Warwick, then the seat of the Greatheeds. Mrs. Piozzi had become intimate with Bertie Greatheed at Florence, and wrote the Epilogue for his blank-verse tragedy, *The Regent,* which was performed at Drury Lane in 1788. It was not a great success, in spite of the acting of John Kemble and Mrs. Siddons. Here the object, though not the nature, of Mrs. Piozzi's anxiety suffered a change; for Sally had a bad attack of the spasmodic asthma from which she suffered all her life, and of which she eventually died.

GUY's CLIFFE, *Sunday* 14 *Oct.* 1792.

Never, my dearest Miss Weston, never *try* to oppose the immediate dictates of Heaven. I was miserable, yes *miserable* at coming to this sweet hospitable house, because I wanted to be at home with Cecilia, to see and embrace my kind, my true friend—and to endeavour at sleep in *my own* bed—for from every other it has long been flown. On the road hither however, for we came softly, not to hurry poor Cecy, only 44 miles o' day, Sally Siddons was taken *illish*. I hop'd it was the Influenza, for cold she could not have catch'd, and I have kept her at all possible distance from my own girl ever since she threw up blood at Denbigh. Here however was she seized yesterday with *such* a paroxysm of Asthma, cough, spasm, *every* thing, as you nor I ever saw her attack'd by … But as God never leaves one deserted, *here* most providentially was found Mr. Rich'd Greatheed, who you know practised physick many years in the West Indies; and under his care we are now *existing*, not living. He is very charming, and so is his dear sister, who desires her love to you, and all possible happiness. I told her *my* infinite obligations to your generous friendship, and she says how good, and clever, and how much admired you always were. Sally in her bed begs to be remembered to you, who have so often watched her bedside. She has reason to adore Mrs. Greatheed though, who ransacks the country for relief to the dear creature, and we expect her mother every instant to add to our agony.

Meantime Cecilia remains *just the same* as when Haygarth pronounced her *well*; but she is *not* well, no nor *ill* neither … Well, her sisters had the best of my flesh and of my purse; poor Cecilia can but pick the skeleton of either, and she is welcome to *that*.

I knew from the Lloyds that Drummond was acquainted with all; he doubtless attributes her illness to disappointed love of *him*. I *knew* it from them, but they did not *tell* me so, mind: oh, had I never known anything of Drummond but what I had been *told,* my information had been very shallow, sure.

Adieu! if no new affliction arises we shall be at Streatham Park on Thursday night, 18, and you shall see what yet remains of your poor

H.L. Piozzi.

Mrs. Siddons was no stranger at Guy's Cliffe. More than twenty years before, when her parents were trying to break off her engagement to William Siddons, she had lived there for two years, nominally as lady's-maid, though it is said that her chief employment was to read poetry to the then master of the house, Mr. Samuel Greatheed. After her marriage in 1773 she often stayed there as a friend of the family.

STREATHAM PARK, Wensday, 7 Nov. 1792.

I am truly delighted, dearest friend, with your charming pacquet ...

We are all in the right to love Mr. Pennington, 'tis for all our credit to love him, and will be ever so to yours. Never were so many knowing ones taken in at once as would be if he proved worthless. You will follow him *soon,* and the moment we have half a crown *in hand* we will follow you. Let mine be the first letter sign'd P. S. P. Siddons says you must say nothing from her, but you may tell Mr. Whalley from me, that I think her as yet neither well nor happy, soon to be so however, as we all hope; that's enough, she will always do right, we are sure of her principles, *unbending* as her best admirer said they were.

So you are a widow when this reaches you, and your true love is gone away, What mistakes he will be guilty of till you come, I am thinking; for he, poor soul! dreams only of his Sophia. May your Mother end her days peaceably under his protection and your care, and quite forget she ever had any other son! *'Tis best.*

My Master will call some day, if he *can,* that is. Mr. Ray has given him tickets for Lord Mayor's Feast, so he is to see London's Glory,— *in good time*; he has seen the Apparitions, which he greatly approves.

Helena Williams should not be sick now all goes her own way; Is this a time, brave Caius, to wear a Kerchief? &c.,[6] as Brutus says. I will write to her some of these days ...

Mrs Siddons
By R. J. Lane after Sir Thos. Lawrence

In France the Prussians had been driven back, the National Convention had abolished Royalty, proclaimed the Republic, and were now preparing to try the King, though it is not likely that the last item of news had yet reached Mrs. Piozzi. The Republic at once took up the offensive, and its troops occupied Savoy and Nice, which no doubt gave rise to the expectation of an attack on Rome, as mentioned in the next letter.

Streatham Park, *Wensday* 21.

My dear Miss Weston's kind letter came safe to my hand, 'tis the last I shall read with that signature. Do pray tell me whether your Brother knows how matters go, and when he found it out. Does good Mamma set out at the same time you do? Yes, I dare say. Give my truest regards to charming Mr. Whalley, and your *real* cousin, his amiable Lady, and tell my Harriet Lee how I expect her, and long to see her, and tell all my tales of sorrow and of joy about poor Cecilia, whose kind and wise Physician came here out of pure good will two days ago, and signed *a good Bill of Health* for all the family,—honest Jacob included; and said moreover that sweet Siddons would recover in due time, and that time not distant. He is one of *us* her adorers ...

How happy Mr. Pennington must be in Mrs. Tryon's admiration of his Sophia's fine qualities. These are the bright moments, the lucid spots of life, which those who never marry never see. Mr. Whalley's is really a lucky house, I seldom have seen it without a courting scene upon the fore-ground. Tell him, (if you can remember,) that his democratic friend, Count Andriani, asked for him the other day, tho' I perfectly recollect his turning quite pale with passion while they disputed about politics. Meantime the French are expected hourly at Rome, and at Loretto, to pay their troops with the rich spoils of Palaces and Churches. Some Italian noblemen dined here last week, and actually wept with reflexions upon past terror and apprehended injuries. Excellenza Pisani in particular, at whose throat, and at those of his little girls, ten and eleven years old, they held knives and pikes for the space of *four* hours, surrounding his coach as he came away, and loading him with the bitterest curses; adding Rogue and Rascal, etc., till his daughters' Gouvernante, in perpetual fits, seem'd wholly dead from fright, and his Steward came out in a spotted fever with the agony. I never heard anything so dreadful. Little Lady Caterina says she thought they would kill Papa every minute. Remember that Pisani is one of the first families in Europe, and that his person ought to have been sacred as Ambassador from one of the first Republics in it.

Poor Marquis Spinola has the same tale to tell; but he had lived twenty years in France, and acquired kindness enough for the Nation to be sorry for *them*. Well! we will now think of nothing but private happiness, and rejoice that 'tis still within our reach. May you, my kind friend, long remain a proof and pattern of it, prays your truly affectionate and obliged   H.L. Piozzi.

1. *Midsummer Night's Dream*, I. i,134.

2. *Comedy of Errors*, V. i, 62.

3. *Cymbeline*, IV. iii. 28.

4. "Sweet my Coz, be merry."—*As You Like It*, I. ii. 1.

5. *Cymbeline*, III. iv. 183.

6. "Oh what a time have you chose out, brave Caius," &c.—*Julius Cæsar*, II. i. 315.

CHAPTER III

REVOLUTION AND CHANGE

BY the time the next letter was written Miss Weston had become Mrs. Pennington, and had taken up her abode at the Hot Wells, in a house in Dowry Square. It points to a serious estrangement between Mrs. Siddons and her husband, though nothing is said as to the cause. Mr. Siddons, like Mr. Thrale, seems to have been reserved, and somewhat lacking in sympathy for, if not actually jealous of, his brilliant wife; but so far as one can judge, his conduct as a husband was outwardly quite correct, and even exemplary.

Mrs. Piozzi's Commonplace Book, now in the possession of Mr. Broadley, contains a note on Count Andriani, whom she describes as "a Milanese nobleman, a bold dashing fellow, who went up in an air-balloon about 1781–2, when such exploits were rare." She goes on to relate how his outspoken preference for Killarney as compared with Loch Lomond offended Helen Williams, who, though born in London, chose to consider Scotland her native country, on the strength of having been brought up at Berwick-on-Tweed.

My dear sweet friend, rates my little tokens of goodwill too high … But let us talk of nothing but *your* happiness, and *my* comfort in the thought of it. Dear Mr. Pennington is already sensible of your worth, and will be more so, when he knows you as I do! He has won all our hearts here, and his charming wife will do the same with his friends wherever they are …

Poor Siddons pities my very soul to see her: an indignant melancholy sits on her fine face, and care corrodes her very vitals, I do think. God only can comfort her, and His grace alone support her, for she is all resentment; and that beauty, fame, and fortune she has now so long posess'd, add to her misery, not take from it. I am sincerely afflicted for her suffering virtue, never did I see a purer mind, but it is now sullied by the thoughts that she has washed her hands in innocence in vain! How shall I do to endure the sight of her odious husband? I suppose he comes tomorrow.

STREATHAM PARK, *Thursday*, 10 *Jan.* 1793.

Who is silent and sullen *now* of these two scribbling Mrs. P.P.'s? not Mrs. Piozzi, sure. No, nor her poor Husband, who, tho' now laid up with the gout worse than ever I knew him, thinks of you often, and added a Postscript to my last letter with the Ballad in it. Oh, but the Church and King Ballad is a great deal better than mine; 'tis really a sweet copy of verses, and *you* will cry over it. Enquire and get it to read. I doubt not of its being the production of some very capital hand.

Our Master is too bad to be diverted by anything: 50 hours has that unhappy Mortal lain on an actual rack of torment, nor ever dozed once except for 7 or 8 minutes, not ten. 'Tis truly a dismal life, and Mrs. Siddons has called home Sally, and Mr. Davies is making holyday at Brighthelmston, and there is nobody to make out Whist with good old Mr. Jones. I just had a peep of the Lees and Greatheeds, it was however *but* a peep. We went to Town one night and saw Euphrasia, and caught a cold which Piozzi attributes to the Kanquroo, etc., that we carried the children to look at next morning. "Ah! those Ferocious Beasts are been my Ruin" quoth he ...

Marquis Trotti writes from Vienna, where he is retired, like Isabinda in The Wonder, to avoid matrimony, as the Italians here tell me; and they fancy him attached to Miss Hamilton, who, they say, is highly accomplished, tho' plain, and a prodigiously well known and admired authour. When we talk of people's affairs, I hope and suppose we always make just such wise assertions, for who at last *really* knows the affairs and thoughts of another? You are however ignorant of nothing belonging to *my* family concerns, you'll say; 'tis true; but one reason may be there is nothing I wish to conceal. We have no money for Bath this year, Brynbella drains all away; and Cecy prefers a week's flash in London to a month at Bath, she says. And she perhaps knows why better than she will tell to you, or to yours ever,   H.L.P.

Say you are alive, and well, and happy, and tell Mr. Pennington how much we all wish him so. Adieu! Master's bell rings, I run. Farewell.

By "Euphrasia" she probably meant to designate Murphy's play, usually known as *The Grecian Daughter*, in which the heroine Euphrasia, daughter of Evander, saves her father's life in prison by suckling him. In her reference to Isabinda she seems to have suffered from a momentary (and unusual) lapse of memory. The name of the heroine in *The Wonder*, otherwise *A Woman keeps a Secret*, by Mrs. Centlivre, is Isabella; Isabinda is a character in *The Busybody*, by the same writer.

The Miss Hamilton here referred to seems to have been Eliza, sister of Captain Charles Hamilton, a member of the Woodhall family, who was living in London shortly before this date; but her most successful work, the *Letters of a Hindoo Rajah*, was not published till 1796.

Mr. Broadley's collection contains a letter written this year to Mrs. Piozzi by Harriet Lee, which shows that the latter had not quite banished Trotti from her thoughts, though she does profess her determination to live and die an old maid. "Should you have any letter from Vienna,—and I know not why, but am disposed to believe you have had the last,—pray be so good as to ask in your answer whether he knows anything of the fate of Gen. de Paoli, and if he is really dead. You may, if you please, add that I begg'd you to make the enquiry."

Just at this time Mrs. Pennington fell ill, and Mrs. Piozzi writes an anxious letter of enquiry, but of no particular interest, to her husband on 14th January; but by the time it reached him, the invalid was sufficiently recovered to answer for herself.

STREATHAM PARK, 17 *Jan.* 1793.

Oh what pleasure did the sight of your handwriting give us all, my ever kind, my ever partial friend! Poor Mr. Piozzi really suffered for you in the midst of his own pains, and they have been great and serious. He is now just trying to crawl, and that very miserably indeed, and his hands, etc., so entirely useless for a whole week he could not even use the pocket handkerchief for himself. Are not you very sorry? 'Tis my fear that it will be long before he can ever play the Pastorale, etc.

Here is bitter weather too, and that retards both his and your recovery, and sweet Siddons has relapsed, and Sally is with her, as bad as bad can be, and Pepys attending them both. I'm told London has a violent Influenza in it, and will keep my Miss out while I can, but one's arms do so ache with pulling at an unbroken Filly that longs to hurt herself by skipping into some mischief or other, that, like the old Vicar in Goldsmith's Novel, I get weary of being wise, and resolve to see people once happy in almost any way.

Meantime Harriet Lee quits London, after making me only one pityful visit or two. I gave her the elegant verses called a Ballad for Church and King, she may copy them for you; I fancy them written by Bishop Porteous, without knowing very well why. Poor Louis' fate was decided on last Monday, but we know not yet what that fate is. Your anecdote is very interesting, I shall read it to all the Democrates. Meantime 'tis supposed that a plague is begun in Austria. Long live the Turnep Cart, say you. If things go on so rapidly I shall become a list'ner. The King of Naples has really behaved very paltrily, and poor Pius Sextus is forced to solicit help from his excluded and excommunicated brother Martin at last. I suppose we shall send a fleet into the Mediterranean for protection of Italy; they will all be contented to see us pay the expence of a war they have not spirit to fight for themselves. Fye on 'em all! *Tutti Compagni*, says yours,   H.L.P.

Dr. Beilby Porteous was now Bishop of London, to which see he had been translated from Chester in 1787. He had a greater reputation as a preacher than as an author, but was said to have had some share in Hannah More's *Cœlebs in Search of a Wife.*

Hugues Basseville, an envoy of the French Republic, having been murdered at the foot of Trajan's Column in Rome on 13th January, Pius VI was charged with complicity, and so was driven in self-defence to join the League of the Germanic States against France. Martin, as typifying the Lutherans, is as old as Dryden's *Hind and Panther*, and stands for Luther himself in Swift's *Tale of a Tub*, but Mrs. Piozzi probably had in her mind its use by Dr. Arbuthnot in his *History of John Bull.*

Ferdinand I, King of Naples, was at first disposed to sympathise with the Revolution, but the execution of Louis drove him to join the league of Austria and England against the Republic.

STREATHAM PARK, 24 *Jan.* 1793.

MY DEAR FRIEND—It *is* very vexatious that we cannot come to Bath this year, and I am excessively grieved at it for a thousand reasons ...

I *hope* we shall make a point of showing our attachment to Royalty and Loyalty by wearing black for the poor King of France, whose murder is meant only as prelude to still more extensive ruin and destruction of all things most dear and sacred in the eyes of Christian and civilised nations: destruction to the Arts, the Altar, and the Throne. Have you seen the large spot upon the Sun's disk, discernible to a naked eye, and large as a button on a man's coat? None was ever seen without a telescope till now; and last Sunday, when London's caliginous atmosphere had stript old Titan of his rays, and render'd his face as you have often seen it, red and round, like a piece of iron heated in the fire, a considerable crowd gathered about St. Paul's, and viewed the phenomenon distinctly. So at least Mr. Greatheed informed us, who was himself among the starers ...

Piozzi continues immovable; he says "I advance towards recovery indeed like the Lobsters—I go backward. Tell so to Mrs. Pennington." You see I have not changed his mode of expression. Sweet Siddons has been here to careen and refit after her terrible cold. She returns to duty this moment, and carries this letter to the Post Office, only waiting while I assure you of the continued affection of your ever faithful and affect[e]   H.L.P.

Mr. Pennington's turn came next; for it appears that an attack of gout had prevented his directing some special entertainment, perhaps in the nature of a benefit, at the Hot Wells.

STREATHAM PARK, 30 *Jan.* 1793.

Poor, dear, kind Mrs. Pennington!

I am glad and sorry and all in a breath from what your letter tells me: had we been at Bath, matters would have gone just the same …

Why does not that hapless Queen of France dye of grief at once, and spare Frenchmen the crime of murdering an Emperor of Austria's daughter, whom they have already reduced to the disgrace of begging a black gown of his murderers, to wear for her Consort's death? I never heard anything so horrible as the account of the King's execution, and I fear there is no war to be made upon the wretches neither. Mrs. Mackay gives us to understand that Rome is ripe for rebellion, and Ireland is half under arms. All private concerns seem lost in public amazement somehow. But dear Miss Owen's brother has got a large windfall, it seems, by his crazy cousin of Porkington's burning himself to death, airing his shirt: and that nasty Mr. Stone, that we all hate so, is come away from France; I'm glad of that too …

Marquis Trotti is safe at Vienna. I want a letter from him concerning the plot there. Mrs. Siddons is in her business, and Sally with her; Maria coming home. Major Semple was one of the active men, I find, at Louis XVI's execution. His wife returns to England with her little flock, on pretence of broils in France, but I suppose in order to avoid her husband. I have read the 5th edition of Village Politics, but I had seen another thing written before that, called Liberty and Equality, prettier still in the same way, and fancy it the production of Mr. Graves of Claverton. 'Tis in his style, and very interesting and very clever indeed …

James George Semple wrote his autobiography in Tothill Fields Prison in 1790, from which it appears that his wife was a daughter of Elizabeth, the "amazing" Duchess of Kingston, that he had served in America and on the Continent, and being then on General Berruyer's staff, had witnessed the execution of Louis XVI. But this was the more respectable side of his career, against which must be set the fact that he had found it convenient on certain occasions to pass under four or five different aliases, and that he had been twice sentenced for fraud, and once to transportation, which he narrowly escaped. So his wife may have had good reasons for putting the Channel between them.

"Village Politics, by Will Chip," was the work of Hannah More, published in 1792, which was thought so highly of that it was distributed gratis, not only by patriotic societies, but even by the Government. The proceeds of its sale enabled her to begin her series of Cheap Repository Tracts. The Rev. Richard Graves, who held the living of Claverton, near Bath, till he was nearly ninety, had been a prolific writer of poetry, but was best known as the author of a novel, *The Spiritual Quixote*.

Maria, the second daughter of Mrs. Siddons, now about fourteen years old, had been educated at a boarding-school in Calais. She, like her sister Sally, was beautiful but delicate, and was carried off by consumption a few years later.

Thursday, 7 Feb. 1793.

And so your kind heart beats still for those helpless ladies in the prison at Paris: so does Mr. Piozzi's; he cannot rest for thinking on the accounts (I hope greatly exaggerated,) of insults offered to their persons,—the *young* Princess Royal's in particular. Can such things be, and no lightning fall yet? The Sun may well hide his head ...

Dear, charming Siddons goes on as usual, and another fair daughter is come home to give her something more to do; and an old Tragedy, written ages ago by Mr. Murphy, is coming out at last, a mythological play of the dark days, Theseus and Adriadne, and *that* old ware. I guess not how it will be liked. Meantime we hear no more news than you do. You know that the King and Nation cry War! War! glorious War! while Opposition longs for Peace and dull Delay, and an Ambassador to the Fish-women of Paris. *You* know that Mr. Grey would not wear black for the King of France; and *you* know the story of the Dauphin running out and crying "I'll go, and beg, and kneel to

Maria Siddons
By G. Clent after Sir Thos. Lawrence

them to send home my Papa alive"; and the brutal centinel catching up the child, and thrusting him in with "Get back, you troublesome Bastard, he's no Papa of yours." The insulted Sovreign only said "*Too much! too much!*" and stept into the coach. This anecdote from *Mr. Ray*, who had it in a private letter from a friend at Paris: I call that good authority. *Everyone* knows he rode *backward* in the coach: two impudent Officers of the National Guard sitting in the front seat; and how oddly they must feel the while, methinks! Well! if we live we shall see some signal vengeance overtake these gallants, that I do believe; and in the meantime war is hourly expected by all, desired by the Court no doubt, and wished for by the bulk of mankind in general. It will be good sport for Naples, Spain, etc., to see France humbled, and England impoverished, and their dastardly selves sitting snug; but I believe Holland will be lost if we don't stir, *and those things must not be.* Dumourier has promised to plant his tree in Amsterdam on the 17th, and none but ourselves can hinder it. Venice has been overflowed with a high tide, so has Rotterdam; "the sea and the waves roaring, men's hearts failing them for fear, and for looking on those things that shall come upon the earth." What says dear Mr. Whalley? Miss More has written very sweetly, and is applauded by all the world for her nice Village Politics. 'Tis more read than that little Pamphlet *I* like so, called Liberty and Equality; but the more of those things go about the better; if one misses, another may hit. *My* stuff will please perhaps: I sent a sheet to the Crown and Anchor for distribution this morning,—a threepenny touch, but you shall not be told till you find out which is mine. Mr. Greatheed being asked which side Mrs. Piozzi was of quickened my zeal. I hope it cannot be ever asked again.

Farewell, dear Friend; wish my rheumatism well,—if it is rheumatism, I take James' Analeptic Pills for it, they cannot hurt me, and while I remain above ground, most gratefully and affectionately shall I ever be yours,   H.L.P.

The "old Tragedy" was that of the *Rival Sisters*, written in 1786, but not acted till 18th March when it was staged for the benefit of Mrs. Siddons, who took the part of Ariadne. Its author had in his own life played many parts, having at one time or other been a bank clerk, an actor, an author, a barrister, and a commissioner in bankruptcy. He was an old friend of Thrale, who was indebted to him for the introduction of Johnson to his circle; and about this time he was the means of making the Piozzis acquainted with Samuel Rogers the poet.

Though Mrs. Piozzi does not seem aware of it, the French had declared war on England on 1st February; but just then the Republic was more engaged on the regeneration of Holland by means of the army of Dumouriez, which, after the defeat of the Austrians, had occupied Belgium.

LONDON, 12 *Mar.* 1793.

Do not despond so, dear Friend, all will be well. I saw Mr. Parsons lately, who was full of your praise, and said how that conduct which always did please the World, now pleased it more.

Public matters have at length taken the wished for turn, and France must soon be humbled. No longer will our worthless Democrates boast the friendship of a *powerful* and *victorious* Republic, as they called her: she will be tatter'd and torne in pieces now very soon, I doubt not.

Meantime here are we, *amusing* ourselves, and the weeks *do* fly so heavily, compared with what I find them in the Country, while Flo barks, and the Parrot takes him off. Well! but I really have neither been sullen nor sick. I have covered Cecy with finery, and sate up till morning at every place without repining, while she was diverted, I hope. Drummond took no notice of her at the only Public Place we saw him at, so I trust that foolery is finished, and nine days more shall see me counting my Poultry, and kissing my *Canes* at home, where Spring pours out all her sweets to tempt us back, and there will I finish this letter.

STREATHAM PARK, 20 *Mar.* 1793.

Here we are again, and in new characters somehow, or else old ones revived. Last Saturday, at Mr. Jones's, Piozzi received a Billet from Miss Thrale, requesting to see him next morning. He attended her summons while I went to Church, and heard, at my return, her intention of coming to see me the day following, *at my own hour*, with her Sisters. I appointed 12, and she promised for the other Ladies and herself. My Master saw only the *eldest*, but our good hospitable Landlord, rejoicing in this new and strange event, (which gives every one's curiosity an air of *tender interest* that it would be ill manners in me to repress,) spread his finest tablecloths, and invited them to *breakfast at ten*, an hour they appear'd eagerly to catch at,

and coming to their appointment, sate down with us and Mr. Rich'd
Greatheed, and Baron Dillon, who came in by chance; while each,
thinking I trust on everything else in the world, agreed to *converse*
only on popular topics. Susanna felt nervous, however, and left the
room with Cecy for a moment, but Miss Thrale and I stood our
ground admirably, and I beg'd Mr. Richd Greatheed to tell dear
Siddons how well (like Rosalind,) I had *counterfeited.* Night carried
me to *her* Benefit, and Company crowded round all day, so that my
spirits were so oddly kept afloat that, upon my honest word, I have
never been *sleepy* since Saturday that Piozzi received the letter, and
this is Wednesday morning.

Well! we returned the visit, and invited the Ladies here on Easter
Monday to *Dinner.* All the Town would buy *tickets* I'm sure, with
pleasure, could they procure 'em, and pass through danger itself
willingly, *to see the sight.* I told my Master it would have been best
to take the little Theatre, and give them the whole show at once.
Nothing does revolt me so as that true British spirit of tearing out
every private transaction for public discussion and amusement: it
makes one's feelings appear affected if indulged, and annihilated if
they are repressed. But this luxurious Nation longs to learn what
cannot be known, and see what its own very light renders incapable
of being clearly discerned. For when they *have* stared in our *faces* on
such an occasion, how much do they find out of our *hearts*?

Farewell! and do write to me: I can talk of nothing but *this*, and
will talk no more about that, so Adieu, and love your true friend

H.L. Piozzi.

Easter Tuesday.

My dear Mrs. Pennington has often seen people talked into
misery, 'tis the way now to talk me into happiness; but I am content
to be happy the way other people please, and I am sure *they are
right.* I returned the visit I told you of next day, and they all din'd
and supped here last *Monday,*—oh! yesterday—after an interval of
fourteen days, in which I saw nothing of them. However all is vastly
well, they are contented to take me up, as they set me down, without
alledging a reason; and I am contented to be taken and left by *them*

without reasoning on the matter at all. We had a brilliant day, with feast, and dance, and song, and broke not up till four o'clock in the morning. Our elastic house pulled out to embrace *them*, and the Hamiltons, kind and sweet, the Greatheeds, Miss Owen, dear old Mr. Jones, and all the Siddons family. One of my delights was to see Cecilia dancing with Mr. Richard Greatheed, who, when be felt her pulse at Guy's Cliffe, I feared would never have made Allemande with her. Everybody seemed pleased, however, and we all *were* pleased. Our acquaintance will henceforth be theirs, and things will shake naturally into their proper places. Nothing could exceed the kindness of our common friends, except my sensibility of it. The Girls seemed less shy of Mr. Piozzi than of me, comical enough! But he is *so* good, and *so* attentive to them! How you would love him! And public concerns were prohibited the conversation, so Mr. Greatheed was quite charming. The dear Broadheads could not come, their uncle is dead, and has disinherited them, leaving £50,000 to a little Currier's boy, who as I say will jump out of his *skin* for joy I suppose, while they fret as I once did on a like occasion …

The reconciliation thus unexpectedly brought about was perhaps a little too formal to be permanent, being the result of policy rather than affection. The daughters seem to have inherited a large share of their father's cold and reserved nature, and never to have been sufficiently in sympathy with their mother to understand her impulsive disposition. There was never any open rupture, but as causes of friction arose, chiefly in connection with business matters, they drifted gradually apart; more rapidly after Piozzi's death, when his widow found another and more absorbing interest in the career of their adopted son. She, on her side, does not appear to have made any sustained effort to keep in touch with them, and at the close of her life she was almost a stranger to her own children, who seldom wrote—she mentions Lady Keith's "annual letter" on 1st January 1818—and never visited her at Bath.

STREATHAM PARK, 21 *Apr.* 1793.

I am truly sorry, dear Friend, that things go no better, but 'tis a sad world, and so we always knew it was: kind Piozzi is quite grieved for Mr. Pennington's long continued illness.

Joe George, the sick labourer, was turning the earth over this morning among the clumps, and saw me feeding your black cock;— "And pray, Madam" (said he,) "what is become of Miss Weston? I never see her now,—and so good she was!" "Didn't you know, George, that Miss Weston was married, and lived at Bristol?" "No, Madam, because they never tell poor folks anything,—and I am as glad as the best of them, and I'll drink her health." You may guess how the dialogue ended.

We are to dine in Town and meet charming Siddons at Mr. Greatheed's on Fryday next; our own Ladies too—alias Titmice—will be there. Nothing serves them but fagging me out, that we may show ourselves together *in public*, Susanna says; so out I march, and do not laugh nor cry, though under perpetual temptations to both, for why did we not always do so? or what has happened to make us do so *now*? My comprehension reaches not these wonders. Cecilia thinks 'tis a merry life, and when she is in a calm, as mine Hostess Quickly says by Doll Tearsheet, she is *sick*.[1]

Drummond follows us about with his baffled countenance, making my words good, who told him the Girl would never be nearer marrying him than she was that day, when I had the honour of predicting how I should see them pass each other in public, saying to their separate parties, "That's the man who was troublesome to me,"—and "That's the girl who jilted me." Just so was it at Yaniwitz's Benefit …

Your favourites in the Temple tower are yet alive, but help is further off than we thought for. Dumourier's army were not of his mind, you see; France will not yet be quiet under kingly government, her convulsions must be yet stronger before the crisis comes on, and this frenzy fever abates. Madame Elizabeth's character rises upon one every day; had you heard Mr. Stretton, who saw it all, tell the tale of the 22nd of June, I think you would have cry'd till now; so sweet yet so steady a creature! Sure, she will not *yet* be sent after the brother she alone can ever resemble.

Adieu dear soul! My arms ach with putting the Library to rights. The old work, say you, and I would I had my old assistant, says your faithful   H.L.P.

The allusion to Dumouriez recalls a curious episode in the history of the Revolution. That general had for some time been distrusted by the Jacobins, and after a defeat at Neerwinden he made terms with the Austrians, by which he agreed to abandon Belgium. This of course meant ruin, if not death, and as a last desperate resource he started to lead his army on Paris, hoping, with the aid of the Gironde, to overthrow the Jacobins, as a preliminary to setting up a constitutional monarch in the person of the Duc de Chartres. But the Girondists were not prepared to adopt such a scheme, which only served to throw more power into the hands of the Jacobins, who proposed the creation of the Committee of Public Safety to deal with the situation, and summoned Dumouriez to give an account of himself before the Convention. At this critical moment his army failed him; his old troops might have followed him, but the new Jacobin Volunteers mutinied, and he was driven to take refuge, with the Orleans princes, in the Austrian camp.

STREATHAM PARK, *Fryday* 26 *Apr.* 1793.
I hasten to thank dear Mrs. Pennington for her kind letters. We have got a man, and his name is *Goodluck*, and I hope it will be ominous … You know the state of my heart pretty exactly, how then can you say that you are ignorant of my political opinions. God forbid that, among Christian people, there should be *two* opinions concerning the impiety of these French rebels, who trample under feet every sentiment of honour and virtue, everything sacred and everything respectable.

Lady Inchiquin, who met us at Mr. Macnamara's yesterday, has seen a letter from Miss Edgeworth, sister to the late King of France's Confessor. Her brother told *her* that the poor injured Sovreign said, when they drowned his voice on his attempt to harangue his subjects from the scaffold, "They will not listen, well! I shall be heard in Heaven," and so to prayers; where Mr. Edgeworth, kneeling down and endeavouring to collect his thoughts, felt himself suddenly covered with the royal blood, so speedy was the execution of their guilty sentence. We see however divine vengeance overtaking them daily; and 'tis *my* belief that no *men* are to have the punishing of these crimes, but that the perpetrators of them will fall by their own, or their companions' hands, or perish by famine, storm, or other dreadful judgements. You see we take no ships, yet all their fleets are ruined. The combined armies gain few signal victories, yet their forces moulder away.

Lady Inchiquin told a tale of the poor victims in the Tower, not exactly, but much like yours; and if 'tis sure that they are to be seen for sixpence thus, everybody will have a tale to tell, and we shall hear as many false as true. Mr. Stretton said *he was shown them;* but I had not, when he said so, a notion of the sight being a thing paid for ...

Harriet [Lee] says in her last letter that the fellow who stole an heiress, Miss Clarke, from a Boarding School in Bristol, is afraid the girl will hang him after all; a pretty youth he must be to have obtained no more tender interest than *hanging* in a lady's heart of thirteen or fourteen years old all this while, for no one but *she can* hang him, that's sure. Do send me some particulars, I forgot to bid Harriet write concerning it. Bristol has always some wonder to exhibit, an impostor, or a poet, or a devil, or some *strange creature* ...

The Lady Inchiquin here referred to must have been the wife of Murrough, fifth Earl of Inchiquin, afterwards created Marquess of Thomond, who married in 1792, Mary, daughter of John Palmer of Torrington, and niece of Sir Joshua Reynolds. Abbé (Henry Essex) Edgeworth de Firmont, who belonged to a junior branch of the Edgeworthstown family, was confessor to the Princess Elizabeth, and to Louis XVI on the scaffold, and after the restoration became chaplain to Louis XVIII. He was granted a pension by Pitt, and died in 1807 of a fever contracted while ministering to the French prisoners.

Sarah Martha Siddons
By R.J. Lane after Sir Thos. Lawrence

Wensday, 22 May.

I am always ready to converse with my dear Mrs. Pennington, and always ready—so is Mr. Piozzi—to love your excellent Husband ... I rejoyce Mrs. Weston is so happy, and hope her good son will lure away all her affection and even remembrance from the bad son.

We were all together at Ranelagh two nights ago, and staid till morning, Mrs. Greatheed and the young Siddonses with us; Sally quite outlooked her sister by the bye, and was very finely drest. Of *our* Misses, Susanna is ever most admired, but I think the eldest and youngest very pretty dears too.

Meantime the young King of France is dying, poysoned I suppose; but to quiet the peoples' minds about him, he and his mother are removed to a better place than the Temple, the Palace de Luxembourg. Well! and we none of us hear a word from Helena Williams since I wrote last. Dr. Moore got £800 for his book, so we cannot doubt its excellence. I wish I could give you just such a proof of the merits of our poor Synonymes. Streatham Park does look beautiful, my Master has new gravelled the walks, and *your* Lilac is in *such* beauty.

Sweet Siddons will be quite well. Farquhar, like a wise fellow, goes to Sir Lucas to ask how he shall manage her; let a Scotchman alone for doing nothing, and yet keeping every one pleased. That man knows the mind's anatomy nicely, whether he is skilled in the body's or no.

Brynbella goes on; the water surrounds the house in a full stream ten feet deep, and the maids may catch the Trout in the frying pan, Mead says, without more ado; while the men may cart home the coals from a pit two miles off.

If Cecilia would marry and take Streatham from us, I should like to hie *home*, and dye, like a Hare, upon the old *form*, near the place I was *kindled* at. We should be as near you there as here. Cecy is very naughty; runs bills of £40 at Bague the Milliner's, and hides the dresses she sends home, hashing them about, and spoiling the look and appearance of them that *we may not know*. Silly little Titmouse! Always in a secret, and always in a scrape, and no Miss Weston to preach her over. Oh dear! ...

Adieu! I shall be very happy to receive Harriet Lee. You will be all of one mind, and ask that fellow to supper at last, as I said you would. If the girl is contented no one alive has a right to call his conduct in question, after she comes of age and acknowledges him, which I never doubted her doing ...

Dr. Moore's successful book must have been his "Journal during a residence in France, from the beginning of August to the middle of December, 1792," containing an account of the massacres, a work which is often quoted by Carlyle.

Mrs. Piozzi was just now bringing out a somewhat ambitious work in two volumes, under the title of "British Synonymy, or an attempt to regulate the Choice of Words in familiar Conversation." It was a chatty, discursive book, "entertaining rather than scientific," as the *British Critic* said, its chief interest lying in the store of anecdotes introduced as illustrations; but it contained some rather acute distinctions and clever analysis. Her old adversary Gifford and others again fell foul of her style, charging her with bringing to her task "a jargon long since proverbial for its vulgarity, an incapability of defining a single term in the language, and just so much Latin, from a child's Syntax, as suffices to expose the ignorance she so anxiously labours to conceal."

Tuesday, 10 *June.*

My dear Mrs. Pennington's accidents and afflictions have really given us very serious concern … Mrs. Siddons is handsomer and more charming than ever. Lady Randolph took leave of the stage last Fryday, and I saw the exertions she made with some little anxiety; but here she is, as well and as chearful as can be. Mr. Murphy too is now almost perpetually in our society, and my own Lasses beat up our quarters whenever London affords little of that tumultuous amusement which delights the first 30 years of life. Mrs. Greatheed has not *yet* done delighting in them however; Susan Thrale says *they two* are the last in every publick place, the last in every great Assembly. Well! I tried a little raking myself this year, but it does not suit me somehow, I can make too little sport out on't, and the people tell me nothing which I did not know before, and *that* is what I want from company always.

Mr. Stone at Paris, the man who went over with dear Helena Williams, is guillotined. 'Tis now said he ruined a good wife, who brought him £20,000, and did a hundred shocking things, I know not how truly; but his worthy brother here is a horrible fellow, and will soon make a most dishonourable exit, I am told. You must read a Pamphlet, translated from the French, a very short one, called *Dangers which threaten Europe*. I have seen nothing as wise a long time,—always excepting my own stupendous performances, of course. Apropos, the European Magazine speaks very kindly of my little Synonymes, very kindly indeed, and selects the Adieu and

Farewell as a specimen. Harriet Lee never writes to me hardly, and her Marquis, who used to be punctual at *Whitsuntide* and *Christmas*, supposing her *here*, has failed these holydays. How all the Foreigners must wonder at the fate of their heroe, Horne Tooke! That fellow was a great seducer, I am happy he is out of the way. Farewell *and* Adieu, dear Friend …

The report of Stone's execution was unfounded; he lived, as stated above, till 1818. His brother William justified Mrs. Piozzi's prognostications, being tried for high treason along with Jackson in 1796. Horne Tooke is best known, apart from the stormy politics in which he was immersed, as the opponent of Junius, and author of *The Diversions of Purley.* The son of a poulterer named Horne, he took the name of Tooke in compliance with the terms of a will, in 1782. He was educated at Cambridge, and entered as a student at the Inner Temple, but relinquished law to take holy orders, though he soon abandoned both the dress and duties of his office. A friend of Wilkes, he was drawn into politics, became a member of the Corresponding Society, and founded another known as the Society for Constitutional Reform. His republican and revolutionary views brought him under the notice of the Government, who decided to make an example of him. He was accordingly arrested on a charge of high treason by a warrant from the Secretary of State, and brought to trial, but was acquitted in 1794.

STREATHAM PARK, 16 *Jun.* 1793.

Every letter I receive from you, my dear Friend, not only convinces me most unnecessarily of the loss I sustain in wanting your conversation, but shows me that we do not understand each other half as well at a distance. What could I ever have hinted to make you suppose I consider'd the diminution of your just dislike of Mr. Drummond as possible? He looked like a baffled Blockhead at Yaniewitz's concert; and if he had any memory might recollect what I said to him early in the business, when my tongue pronounced his fate precisely as it happened that night. "Sir," said I, "the child is but a child, and knows not what love is: she may be amused with having a *Lover* for aught I can tell, but in two years I shall see you pass each other in a Public Place,—she saying to her friends 'that's the man that was troublesome to me,'—you saying to yours 'that's the girl that jilted me?'" And so the matter ended …

The dear Siddons left me yesterday. She has charming daughters now, and so have I, so we can see little of each other. The currents of life draw those who delight in mutual and friendly chat apart from one another, without fault or blame of anyone's,

> But busy, busy still art thou
> To join the joyless, luckless vow;
> The heart from pleasure to delude,
> And join the gentle to the rude.

Sally is exceedingly well, and just as pretty as every pretty girl of the same age, and prettier than Maria, because her face looks cleaner.

You are lucky in Lady Asgill's friendship, the Miss I count little upon. A conversible companion of six and thirty years old is a good thing, and an infant under seven a delightful thing; but a Miss of 17 can charm nothing, as I should think, but a Master of 27. I grow too old for either, but the last is far most agreeable …

Do not you enjoy the thoughts of our late discovery that this famous Anacharsis Cloots, so well known in the National Convention for forwarding the cause of apostacy and rebellion, is no greater nor no less a man at last than *Dignum,* our thief, who worked on the Justitia Hulk about 15 years ago, and people used to go and see how daintily he fingered the wheelbarrow, I remember. Well! this is the hero of modern Democracy, the legislator of France, the renouncer of his baptismal vow, the champion of Atheism, and *orator of the human race*. Mr. Lysons came over from Putney late one evening o' purpose to tell it me, and is it not a capital anecdote? …

Not a word of poor Helena in all this long letter; that's a shame, yet I think *her* much more sincere than Dr. Moore, who, while he condemns every fact, justifies (you may observe,) every principle on which the facts were committed …

The identification of the English thief with the French orator, though doubtless a "capital anecdote," seems to be of the *ben trovato* rather than of the *vero* order. The individual in question was the Baron Jean Baptiste Clootz, who assumed the prenomen of Anacharsis to suggest his resemblance to the character of Anacharsis the Scythian in the Abbé Barthélemy's Romance.

The Lady Asgill here referred to would seem to be the wife of Sir Charles Asgill, who succeeded to the Baronetcy in 1788, and in the same year married Sophia, daughter of Admiral Sir Charles Ogle.

Fryday 19 *Jul.*

My dear Mrs. Pennington is a good Girl to write as often as she does while so many avocations call her: may the Ball turn out everything she wishes, and far away fly the Gout! Dear Siddons has had an alarm for her husband and Maria, who were overturned somewhere, and a little hurt; she keeps well herself however, and Mr. Gray, (who has been there to see,) says that she and Sally are as charming as ever …

The French are in a sad plight, but you may observe that God Almighty resolves to punish them without our meddling. The offences were certainly greater towards Him than towards us, and I perceive as yet that the combined armies have done France nothing but good. All the union they have shown among themselves has been occasioned by the Princes who invade them. Meantime it was meet, right, and our bounden duty, to oppose their principles and practice; I only mean that they will at length (as it appears,) fall by their own swords, not ours.

Mr. Este, more democrate than ever, is going to Italy, and asked me for letters. You may be sure I refused them, tho' so much obliged to him, and so full of personal good wishes for his welfare as an individual. It hurt me at the moment, but

> Beyond or love, or *friendship's sacred band*,
> Beyond myself, I prize my native land.

And so I refused letters of recommendation to a man whose only business and pleasure is the dissemination of principles I abhor, and

Mrs. Piozzi
From an engraving by Dance, 1793

who goes out of England only to return with those principles more firmly adhering to him. He was a delightful creature before ever he went to France, and Abate Fontana will not mend his notions in Italy. Mr. Dance the profilist is making a collection of celebrated heads; I have sate, but nobody knows me, they say, so I am to sit again. Lysons runs about with great zeal on the occasion, and I fancy they will go down to Nuneham ...

Poor Barron Dillon has had his Daughter in law killed, and his house in Ireland torne down by the rabble who call themselves Defenders—I am exceeding sorry. Piozzi talks about going down with Mr. Ray, or Mr. Chappelow, or both, to see Brinbella, and come back without delay; how dull we shall be the while! Cecilia without her sisters,—they are gone to Southampton,—and I shall have lost Harriet Lee ...

Here is rain at last,—we were all burn'd up till it came, and I really found London, when we dined there and took leave of our fair Daughters three nights ago, as cool, and almost as *green* as poor Streatham Park. No fruit, no after-pasture, no milk have we had this long time, and shall actually kill and eat the fatted calf on our wedding day next Thursday, because nobody would buy it to feed ...

"Baron Dillon" was Sir John Dillon, M.P., who had a free Barony of the Holy Roman Empire conferred upon him in 1782 by the Emperor Joseph II, which title he was authorised to bear in this country. He was created a Baronet in 1801. His murdered daughter-in-law was Charlotte, daughter of John Hamilton, who had married his eldest son, Charles Drake Dillon. The "Defenders" were the Roman associations corresponding to the Protestant "Peep o' Day Boys": both were now beginning to be merged in the "United Irishmen."

The Rev. Charles Este, Reader at Whitehall Chapel, published in 1785, *A Journey through Flanders, Brabant, and Germany, to Switzerland*, which the *British Critic* describes as "chatty, and brightly written." He was subsequently proprietor of the *Morning Post, the World*, and the *Telegraph*.

STREATHAM PARK, *Sat.* 10 *Aug.* 1793.

MY DEAREST MRS. PENNINGTON,—Nothing was ever so well or so truly said as your observation concerning public notions in France, except what you said likewise about private notions in England, and *my* Husband and *your* Husband's true taste for an elegant Knick-Knack.

I have had a letter from an old acquaintance, Helen Williams, my eyes could scarce believe it; but she says it was with difficulty she found means to get it over, and certain is the case, it came hither by

Penny Post. No tenderness was ever so seducing as her tenderness, no lamentation ever so pathetic; begging and intreating to know how we all do, and whether we still recollect her with kindness, etc. Many sweet words to Harriet, many to Mrs. Siddons, with enquiry if she remains still upon the Stage, "for not even *her* fame can reach me now at this sad distance," is the expression. Poor soul! she adverts to our felicity at Streatham Park, and says how happy we all are here, (I think so truly,) while she listens only to the sound of the Tocsin, in which "*more is meant than meets the ear*." Such is her quotation, and it impresses me strongly, for on this very day, the 10th of August, my heart tells me dreadful deeds will be performed in that theatre of massacre and madness—Paris. God keep her in personal safety! Meantime I will not write to her: she has given me directions, but as I told dear Mr. Este the other day, who put me to similar pain by begging letters for Italy, I will not help those forward who are doing, or trying to do, mischief,—

> Beyond or love, or friendship's sacred band,
> Beyond myself, I prize my Native Land.

And our sweet Master, whom the King has lately been graciously pleased to make an Englishman, in act and effect, as well as in true heart and firm loyalty, says I am in the right …

I shall scold Mr. Pennington if he suffers moody and still pensiveness to petrify your active qualifications and I understand even the situation of your affairs requires a chearful carriage, and gay manners. Assume them, and they will cling to you. Miss Farren tries that trick, and it succeeds too, notwithstanding her *real* health and looks are much impaired, but I hope bathing in the sea may in some measure restore them. We hear that Miss Burney has a Tragedy acted,—accepted I mean,—and *to be* acted by Sheridan's Company, who are all delighted with it. We hear too that she is married to a foreigner of fashion; and we *did* hear her brother was dead at Bath, but he contradicts the report himself in the Newspapers; so, perhaps will his sister tomorrow. Adieu …

Elizabeth Farren was the daughter of George Farren, a surgeon of Cork, who joined a strolling company of players. After acting at Bath and elsewhere in the provinces, she appeared at the Haymarket and Drury Lane, where she played leading parts till her marriage with Lord Derby.

Fanny Burney had married M. D'Arblay, a French refugee officer, 31st July and 1st August 1793. Her tragedy of *Edwy and Elgiva* was not acted till 1795, when Mrs. Siddons and her brother assisted at its production. The breach between her and Mrs. Piozzi, which dated from the latter's second marriage, was not healed for many years. The reconciliation is thus recorded in the Commonplace Book. "Madame D'Arblay, always smooth, always alluring, passed two or three hours with me to-day. My perfect forgiveness of l'aimable Traitresse was not the act of Duty, but the impulsion of Pleasure, rationally sought for, where it was at all times sure of being found—in her conversation."

STREATHAM PARK, 19 *Sep.* 1793.

My dear Friend, and your letter says I must call you my *old* Friend too. "*Ma'am I'm sorry.*" …

Helena Williams's situation is a strange one, but though my affection and esteem is all for her, my compassion leans towards the poor Mother and Sister whom she has dragged into this Hornets' nest. Mr. Chappelow is of your mind, that they will never come out on't …

Your namesake was always scrupulously steady never to wear rouge, so that may account for *her* ill looks,

> Though Rouge can never find the way
> To stop the progress of decay,
>   Or mend a ruined face.

Miss Farren alters terribly too, and dear Siddons, after all her lamentations about ill health, looks incomparably handsome, I am told …

Those [events] which occur in this part of the world are not exceedingly important; the best thing I know is dear Siddons's return to it, though for so short a time; the worst is her setting off for Ireland in this stormy season, but it will answer to her husband and family, *she* has fame and fortune enough without running further hazards. All will go well however, I doubt not, and if they ask why she tears herself to pieces so, she must say with Abigail in the Drummer,

> I'll clap my hand upon my purse, and tell 'em
> 'Twas for a thousand Pounds and Mr. Vellum.

More news from the Continent. Now if the Royal Family can 'scape their murderous pursuers but a few months more, one may pronounce them safe, I think, and they may be permitted to dye in their beds by the effect of past terrors and ill-usage, instead of expiring by the hand of sudden and immediate massacre …

The "namesake" who abjured rouge (which Mrs. Piozzi always used) was very likely Sophia Lee. *The Drummer* was a play by Addison, otherwise known as *The Haunted House.*

STREATHAM PARK, 4 of Nov. Monday, 1793.

My dear Mrs. Pennington's handwriting always gives me pleasure … We shall surely come to you, at least I doubt it not, the end of next Autumn, and shall visit the Cottage, and see how like Streatham Park is to Longford Court, etc. … We shall by then, I fear, have to talk of poor Helen Williams in a way that shocks me. She said *here* she could dye with pleasure for French Liberty, but she will fall by French Tyranny at last. I verily think when those wretches have spilt all the Blood Royal, they will call out our Country Folks to feed the popular fury and turn the current of it from themselves … The Queen's murder has some circumstances of horror belonging to it which I fancy you have not heard, and which I will not be the first to tell. I gained them by conversing with the foreigners. My imagination often leads me to think that matters are tending forward towards some great event, interesting to all the Christian world, which is almost in serious danger *now* by the Turk's preparation for assisting these Atheists to destroy us …

You will have my Book soon, Mr. Robinson and I are bargaining for it now, but they shall pay me a just price; I have enlarged it considerably. Dear Marquis Trotti will come *home* to his English friends again; I am glad on't. He is at Warsaw this moment by what appears, and after a Polar winter will find Bath a nice warm place, and old Belvedere House will look *so* pretty after Petersburg, and he and Harriet may read my Synonymes of *Love* and *Friendship* together. I told you he had the arrow fast in his heart. I *told* you *so* ...

All the neighbourhood borrow Helen's last publication from me, so that I scarce have read it, but 'tis as you say. Come what will, dear Friend, let you and I hold fast by our Christian principles, assuring ourselves that this is not the world for remuneration, but for tryal; and satisfied that happiness will, in the next state of things, be consequent upon Virtue. Let every misfortune it meets with *here*, strengthen our assurance that *there* it will be finally and lastingly rewarded. I verily and from my soul believe that admirable girl will lose her life by violence among those cruel creatures. They have abolished Sunday now, and every sign and form of worship in France is at an end. In that frantic Nation *chaos is come again* ...

It is not quite clear what work by Helen Williams is here referred to. She does not seem to have written anything of importance since her *Letters written in France* in the summer of 1790 which were published the same year, and would probably have reached Mrs. Piozzi long before this date.

STREATHAM PARK, 2 *Dec.* 1793.

MY DEAR FRIEND,—Having got a Frank by chance, I sit by Mr. Piozzi's bedside, and tell you, for my own amusement, how ill he is. Lame, hand and foot, with Gout, and torne with spasms beside, which we know not exactly on what account to place ... You can probably give me as good and chearful a history of *your* Husband's case, possibly too, from the same cause—a Ball. Our Royal Surrey Bowmen gave a grand one at Richmond, where Cecilia danced till five o'clock in the morning, and whence, of course, we came not home till seven. A member of *that* Club being also a member of some other Club, we had another invitation for Fryday in the same week, and were at home by six, which I believe we thought too late, and Cecy too early. So differs the appearance of things between Spring and Autumn.

Well! we have had a crazy man in our neighbourhood lately, who imitates Goldfinch in the Road to Ruin: talks precisely his dialect, and drives four thoroughbred horses of *different* colours in hand, with six lamps to the Phaeton. He is a Welch Baronet of good family; we dined with him at my Lord Deerhurst's, and whilst all the world was interesting themselves about the present state of Europe, he raved about his Phaeton, and talked of the *Tipee*, the *Stare*, the *Go*, and a heap of jargon such as one never heard.

How like you Madame D'Arblay's Book? Pray tell what is said of it. Mine is in good forwardness, I am only afraid the title may prove a millstone round its neck: no one will think of looking for Politics in a volume entitled *British Synonymy*.

Can you figure to yourself a more execrable triumph than that of the Convention in this *forced* disgrace put upon the old House of Bourbon by *connecting* the last Princess of it with a brutal soldier, and proclaiming her pregnancy—poor child!—amidst the hootings of the Jacobins. Has not her aunt, the virtuous and hapless Elizabeth, *now* lived too long, and do you not wish her dismission to the brother she so justly loved? We are all gasping with hope of charming Lord Moyra's Expedition. I think he will bring the rogues to terms by cutting off internal communication with their Provinces through means of the Seine, and when they are starving, submit they must ...

Lord and Lady William Russell make us pretty neighbours enough, but Mr. Chappelow is always in Norfolk, and we have no Whist Players ...

The Road to Ruin, by Thomas Holcroft, who shared Horne Tooke's prosecution, appeared in 1792. Its hero, Goldfinch, thus describes himself: "Father was a Sugar Baker, Grandfather a Slop Seller, and I'm a Gentleman."

Madame D'Arblay's "Book," which would be more correctly described as a Pamphlet, was on the subject of the French emigrant clergy.

Francis Rawdon Hastings, who had recently succeeded to the title as second Earl of Moira, was sent in December to Brittany, in charge of a force designed to co-operate with the Royalists, but had to return without effecting anything.

Lord William Russell was the posthumous son of Francis, Marquess of Tavistock, and grandson of John, fourth Duke of Bedford, his wife being Charlotte, daughter of the Earl of Jersey.

STREATHAM PARK, *Sunday Morning* 15.

Dear Mrs. Pennington is exactly in the case I concluded she was. Mr. Piozzi *tried* to be well three or four days ago, and came downstairs, but has relapsed, and the Gout has laid fast hold of him again in both feet. He is in bed now again, incapable of motion, and pierced through with pain. We had begun to call the croud about us too; so here is Miss Hamilton, and here is a new man from Italy that sings divinely, and here is Cecilia's new Flirt, who draws caricaturas, and here is poor Dr. Perney for the benefit of them all; and here am I in one perpetual fever with fretfulness, and Mr. Murphy coming to talk upon business, about Cator, and his Answer to our Bill—in good time!—with Mr. Piozzi, who is scarce in his wits for very agony. But these are always my months of misery. Don't you remember what a winter I pass'd with that Drummond? It was just the same season of the year.

Well! public affairs do yet claim some attention, tho' private ones be never so pressing. You are an odd Girl to talk of Fleming's famous Sermon *now* for a newish thing. Were we not all raving about it last winter? And have not I mentioned it in my Synonymes? And did not I read you the passage? Or did all that I allude to pass between me and dear Mrs. Siddons? I thought it was with you. Michael Fleming was a Calvinistical preacher, and in the year 1701, when Louis XIV was in the plenitude of his power, did most ingeniously from his skill in calculating, predict the downfall of the French Monarchy, and ruin of that nation, *before the end of the year 1794.* The Sermon in which this odd menace was made some of his hearers preserved, for its rare confidence and uncommon predictions little thinking they would ever come to pass; and a few copies being printed, the discourse was kept in Sion College Library, and Sir George Young likewise had it in *his*. They have now reprinted it with remarks, induced, no doubt, by the striking situation of affairs upon the Continent. Fleming however did not *pretend to prophecy* what has followed, as claiming any peculiar insight into the schemes of Providence. He explained a passage in the Revelations of St. John, and by dint of mere calculation *predicted* what is now very nearly fulfilled.

Enquire, do, what went with that extraordinary story of a poor fellow of Bristol, one George Lukins, who made the people believe, (perhaps himself too,) that he had Devils inside him. I remember some pamphlets upon the subject, and how Mr. Easterbrook, a Clergyman but not of the Anglican Church, exorcised and cured him. What was all that stuff? Was the man cured at last, or did he ever ail anything, or was it all an imposture? You live near the spot, and might glean me out the truth by diligent search, and it would divert you besides. The affair was some time in the year 1788, as I recollect. We were in Devonshire.

Nothing was ever heard of equal to the atrocities committed, and blasphemies pronounced, by our horrible neighbours the French. There is to be one more grand effort made for subduing them this New Year, which brings down 100,000 Austrians, 50,000 Russians, 50,000 Prussians, and 30,000 English, all new-raised troops, beside what are already in the field. And if, upon this proof, with all that Spain can do beside, we find them invulnerable, the project will be given up, and they will be considered as having gained their invulnerability by dipping in Hell's best river, as Achilles did. They are a dreadful race. Mr. Rogers tells me Helena Williams *would* not come away. She is translating Marmontel. Mr. Stone is expected to make use of the times, I find, and be a *free man*. If his wife gets guillotined he *will* be so; but we will hope sweet Helen would not *have* him, were he so freed to-morrow. She is not in prison, only under arrest, with a Grenadier at the door of her apartment, relieved every six hours …

Mrs. Siddons is doing delightfully in Ireland, and when she returns is to shine out in Sophia Lee's new Tragedy.

Robert Fleming, who died in 1716, was a minister of the Presbyterian congregations at Leyden and Rotterdam, and afterwards in Lothbury, where he published in 1701 the sermon entitled "The Apocalyptical Key, an extraordinary discourse on the Rise and Fall of the Papacy." In this he fixes the close of the period of the fourth Vial of the Revelation about the year 1794, and supposes that "the French monarchy may begin to be considerably humbled about this time." The fifth Vial he expected to end about 1848, and this date coinciding with the widespread revolutionary movements on the Continent, caused another extensive reprinting of his work at this period. His other predictions, relating to the "drying up of the Euphrates," which he interpreted to mean the destruction of the Turkish Empire between 1848 and 1900, have not had quite so remarkably accurate a fulfilment; though the war now in progress in the Balkans certainly suggests that the process has begun.

Mrs. Piozzi was not so fortunate in her forecast of coming events. The great combination which she anticipates, against the French, never came off. Prussia abandoned the cause of the Allies, Spain and the German States followed her example, and England and Austria alone remained in the field against the Republic.

Sophia Lee's new tragedy was *Almeyda*, but it was not actually produced on the stage till 1796.

The Bill here alluded to was in connection with the Chancery suit between Lady Cotton and herself, respecting her interest in the Welsh estates.

There is a brief allusion in the Commonplace Book to "that poor innocent" whom Cecy Thrale and Sally Siddons taught the Streatham parrot to call "Sweet Dr. Perney," which was called forth by the news of his having been seized by an apoplectic fit in 1814.

STREATHAM PARK, *Tuesday* 14 *Jan.*

Dear Mrs. Pennington asks what is become of Mrs. Mackay? … You ask too who is Cecy's new Flirt? I answer, every man who comes

Arthur Murphy

to the house; he who franks this letter is the Gentleman I alluded to, but he makes no proposal of marriage, because he has no pretensions in point of fortune. Mr. Rogers, whose father's death has left him, in the City phrase, a warm man, does make proposals, and Cecy makes of him Caricaturas.

So we go on, and I am almost weary of keeping an expensive house and table to entertain Lovers who glide by like Figures in a Magic Lanthorn. Mr. Murphy, having found his way to the old house, likes it, and comes often, and stays long. Dear Siddons is yet in Ireland. Miss Farren was here last week, sadly altered ... Davies has taken a trip to Bath, and expected some attention from my fair Daughters there, who, I fancy, shut the door in his face. Doctor Perney supplied his place here, read, and preached, and played on his long neck. Young Bartolozzi, and Cimad'oro too, made us some sweet musick for two or three days, but Mr. Piozzi said no young man of *his* Country should have the entrée here, for obvious reasons; so there's an end of *them*.

So much for domestic felicity, and the happiness of individuals in this workyday world,[2] as Rosalind calls it. Public affairs go on much worse than they, and the fog thickens round us both literally and figuratively. Beating the French is kicking at a woolsack; 'tis elastic, and rises against every pressure, but perhaps emptying the bag may cure it of this elasticity: the captures of St. Domingo and Pondicherry are the only real advantages the Allies have had yet.

Lord Moyra and Col. Barry get no opportunity of shewing *their* prowess, on which I should however make no small reliance, could they once get footing in the Country; but seeing how hard it is to effect an invasion *with* ships, should cure us of fearing one from the French who have *no* ships: altho' I am perswaded that the hand of God is in all, and that these people come forth to scourge all Europe with his permission. Why does nobody quote a more immediate prophecy and less equivocal than any which have been mentioned, at least which *you* have mentioned? "And the second Angel sounded, and as it were a great MOUNTAIN burning with fire was cast into the *Sea,* and the third part of the Sea became *Blood*": etc. etc. etc. This prophecy is to be found in three passages of the Holy Scripture, but I can recollect only that in the 8th chapter of S. John's Apocalypse. Mr. Greg showed it me in the old Testament,[3] I have forgot where: but every one seems to think strange times are coming. There is a report of the Jews in Holland having sent circular letters to the learned of their Nation in every Country, to collate the evidences of our Saviour's mission, and to examine them against the prophecies contained in the Bible, spoken by his acknowledged precursors. Such a measure would prepare them for conversion, the moment God shall be pleased to remove the film which has been so long before their eyes …

The subject of Cecilia's caricatures was evidently no other than Samuel Rogers, the poet, best known as the author of *Italy*. He was now about thirty years of age, and had published in 1792 his *Pleasures of Memory*, which was probably his passport into the Streatham circle. But as a possible husband for Cecilia, Mrs. Piozzi evidently attached more importance to the fact that he was a partner in a flourishing London bank.

She notes in her Commonplace Book that Murphy was "the *only* man among the Wits I foster'd who did not fly from his colours, unless prevented by death." And so his portrait was the only portrait she saved when Streatham was broken up, and the Reynolds Gallery sold.

[Post Mark, Feb. '94.]

I hope Mr. Piozzi *is* recovering, dear Friend, that he is already recover'd, cannot yet be said. With regard to Cecilia, she does lead a life much like that of *Sweet Anne Page* in the Merry Wives of Windsor, but I suppose she likes it. Did I tell you Mr. Rogers had made formal proposals, or that Count Zenobio offered himself to *her*, before he was seized by Bailiffs, or dismissed by Ministry. I expect a man (as handsome as neither, nor as rich,) to ask her every day.

We go to Town however once o' week, to our once clean house in Hanover Square, now the dirtiest lodging in London, and dine with friends who will ask us; but make no return, as 'tis too odious to do anything but sleep in, and 'tis the present plan to go up on Tuesdays, and come *home*, as I call dear Streatham Park, on Saturdays. Those who I leave in care of it the while, do not give us any reason they can help to make it pleasant. For in my last four days absence they lost me two Asses, one in foal, *twenty* beautiful Ducks, one Guinea Fowl, one favourite Cock and Hen; so you see domestick cares and vexations prey upon everybody. They serve meantime to keep one from thinking on calamities which threaten us all, nor shall the Infidels have it to say that they had no warning of approaching confusion, while, in Dr. Johnson's phrase, used by Demetrius,

A thousand horrid prodigies foretold it.

Among the agreeable and consolatory events however, let Christians congratulate each other on the resolution taken by the Jews to examine into our evidences of Messiah's birth and passion. They have called a solemn Assembly at Amsterdam, and sent circular letters among all their brethren. Conversion will soon follow, and the other Tribes will hear it, and be found.

My Book is at the Press, and I correct the sheets very diligently, it will probably be devour'd, among other *Lambs*, about Easter. I may then run to Brinbella myself, for if *Sansculottism* prevails here, my neck will be one of the first to exercise the new Guillotine upon. Before that time comes, do you read the Articles Symbol, Device, etc., likewise Name, Nominal, Distinction, etc., with care, and you will see my sentiments completely. There are two or three more on which your favourite subjects are touched, but I forget 'em. I shall send you the first set that comes out.

Mrs. Siddons looks healthier and handsomer than ever. Her purse is heavy and her heart relieved … Her daughters spent this last Saturday and Sunday with Cecy …

(*P.S.* by Mr. Piozzi.)

I am alive still now, but, dear Friend, I cannot recover myself, the Gout never will go away, and so I am rather low spirits. God bless you, and remember me. Adieu.

"My Book" was the work on British Synonyms, previously referred to, which made its appearance before the next letter was written.

STREATHAM PARK, *Sat.* 26 *Apr.* 1794.

My dear Mrs. Pennington's two kind letters came together. I am delighted that you like my Book, if Mr. Whalley should not praise it, spare me the mortification of hearing so.

One would think the honest Lazzaroni at Naples, when they rescued their Monarch from that nest of noble traytors he was falling into, had resolved upon realizing my notions giv'n just in the Article so much your favourite, *Seditions, Troubles, Disturbances.* Briareus came in there, sure enough, with his hundred hands, and unloosed the knot. Mrs. Montagu is an enemy to my Synonymes after all, a declared one, and I wonder at it somehow, but they have many gallant friends.

Has not the young Emperor won your heart? He is really a fine fellow, and I sincerely hope will set his little nephew on the throne of France yet,—his first cousin I mean. Strange and dreadful events flow in upon us, (at least the *current* reports of them,) now every hour: and the rapidity with which this tide of Democracy rolls forward, shows the down-hill of regal and aristocratic days to perfection. I think all Europe is at length in arms, and my heart tells me that some great battle, siege, or massacre will distinguish this Summer beyond all the rest, and take up the attention of mankind from observing that first of wonders, the Jews' Restoration; which otherwise would so alarm our whole Christian world, that much mute expectation of Messiah's coming would pervade their minds, and in some degree militate against the suddenness of his appearance and the end of the world being, as he himself expressly tells us, totally unprepared for and instantaneous, like a thief in the night.

Meanwhile I had like to have been made a speedy end of, Thursday last week, by a bone in my throat, which called Surgeons and Doctors round me, and all in vain, for three long hours. Poor Miss Farren, who was with me, seemed half killed by the fright, but all is safe and well again.

Since then we have had Easter friends as usual; the dear Hamiltons,— who are going to Clifton this Summer full of friendly dispositions towards you,—the three Thrales, kind Kitty Beavor, with occasional Beaux and Belles, and as the Parrot now says, *Sweet* Doctor Perney. All of them left us today, contented with their entertainment I hope, and with the weather certainly. Never was so celestial a Spring …

The Emperor Leopold, brother of Queen Marie Antoinette, had been succeeded in 1792 by his son Francis II, who was therefore first cousin to the Dauphin. When Mrs. Piozzi wrote, a combined force of Austrians, Dutch, English, and Hanoverians was operating against the French in the Netherlands, at first with some measure of success.

It is remarkable that while Ferdinand himself had been cured of his incipient republicanism by the execution of Louis, revolutionary principles continued to spread among the Neapolitan nobility. The Lazzaroni, however, who were devoted to the King on account of his easy and familiar manners, were ready to give active support to the Dynasty against the plots of the aristocratic party.

STREATHAM PARK, *Fryday* 16 *May*, 1794.

Dear Mrs. Pennington will believe me sincerely afflicted for her accident and terror, the circumstances of which, so far as I am yet acquainted with them, we had from Harriet Lee. Will your Mother be well again soon? I hope and trust she may. My Grandmother broke her arm at 73 years old, and recovered so as to go out and enjoy herself again in three weeks time; tho' it was set by a common Farrier in the country, when surgery was less studied there than now.

The good news from our Armies on the Continent, and hopes of success by sea, will contribute to keep up your loyal spirits to enjoy them: and I verily hope our mad Democrates will be so crush'd by these late detections of their folly, as to attempt the sale of themselves to either the Devil or the French no more, when they find hanging their best payment, and contempt from the very People they profess to serve, their just and sole reward.

Were not my Synonymes right, when they said that our enlightened populace wanted no such friends or friendship? And have not the Neapolitan Lazaroni, (dear creatures,) come in like Briareus to unloose the knot in which some rebellious nobles would willingly have held their honest, single-hearted, well-intention'd King; who was always as much an object of my esteem as he appears to be of Dr. Moore's contempt. But *he* loves a more *subtle* character than *I* do.

Farewell, the guns are firing for some new successes; God continue them to this yet favour'd nation, and grant us gratitude, 'tis all we have to pray for ...

Mrs. Piozzi's somewhat misplaced admiration for Ferdinand of Naples dates from her Italian tour, when she was much struck by the easy bonhomie he showed in his intercourse with the poorest of his subjects.

Streatham Park, *Fryday* 11 *Jul.*

My dear Mrs. Pennington,—I was glad to see your handwriting, tho' it tells me little good. Be chearful, and a hoper, like myself. Things are never so bad but one may bear them; your Mother will get well, I fancy, had anything power to kill her, would she, nay *could* she have recovered that overturn? I hear of *your* pleasing everybody, and I hear it even from people whom I should scarce expect to have taste of your accomplishments. Be pleased yourself then; whilst one is liked there is always somewhat worth living for. What would your dear Husband wish me to say in your praise that I am not most cordially willing to join in? How few people are there in this world of whom I think more highly? …

Miss Mores told you no more than all our Town have told one another for these many months. Stone escaped, they say, from fear of jealous rage, more than from consciousness of any injury done to the *charming* Constitution of France, which he was very fond of. Much good may it do both himself and fair *Helena*, whose love to *Paris* will, I trow, prove fatal to her *at last*. But she has proved her partiality in a variety of ways, and it repays her *at present* with a splendid situation, I am told, for her family as well as for herself …

Direct your next to Denbigh, N. Wales; my Master says we go about this day sennight. He sends his love, etc. with Cecilia's.

The "splendid situation" of Helen Williams seems to be explained in a letter written by her to Mrs. Pennington in 1819. From this it appears that a friend in power put in the way of Stone and herself "an easy and honourable means of obtaining a fortune, and an ample fortune was soon obtained. We had a fine Hotel in Paris, and a delicious Country House in the English Taste." But they had not reckoned on two occupations of Paris by the Allies, which, with the knavery of some one they trusted, dissipated the fortune as rapidly as it had been acquired. Litigation was then pending, but she expected to lose everything, and become dependent on her nephews.

DENBIGH, 4 *Aug.* 1794.

How glad was I to see your handwriting here, my good Friend! It was like saying "Dear Mrs. Pennington, welcome to Wales!" Not to Brinbella tho'; we are not got *there* yet, but in a temporary residence here at Denbigh, in sight of the House, and perhaps little further from it than Dowry Square is from Rodney Place.

I am glad Mrs. Hamilton keeps so well, very glad indeed; this hot Summer has been good for *her*, however it has been bad for many things. No water in Thames to float away the ships at the great fire; no sluices with which to inundate the frontiers of Holland, I understand, and poor Sabrina's green hair all burn'd and dryed away. Shrewsbury Quarry looked over an empty ditch when I was there, to the amazement of all its inhabitants. But rain is coming forward in plenty, much more than Cecy likes, for riding is her only chance for amusement here, and if wet weather hinders *that*, what will become of her? Mr. Piozzi's Fortepiano is now as near us as Chester, I think we shall all be out of our wits for joy when it arrives. Would I could hear Miss Hamilton sing *La Dolce Campagna* to it, as I often have done with rapture.

Here is very little society indeed, half a dozen people, I believe, that like reading, not more, and *they* suffer sad intellectual famine. I reproach myself daily that I forgot to bring them down The Mysteries of Udolpho: it would have had such an effect read by owl-light among the old arcades of our ruined Castle here. Truth is Mrs. Radclyffe might find scenes to describe in this part of the world without rambling thro' the Pyrenees. Many detached parts of the valley of Llangollen are exceedingly fine indeed, very like Savoy; and from the rock above Brinbella, heavy with the gather'd winters of a hundred years, is seen Snowdon frowning in sullen majesty, like the *Gros St. Bernard*, but not over as rich a foreground. Ours is however admirably diversified; we have Cathedral, and Castle, and Country Seats, and Sea, which last is inestimable, and one *can* contemplate that yet, and say 'tis a Subject of England.

I feel sincerely grieved for the state of Europe, and must needs say that altho' it is the fashion to reproach our Allies without any mercy, they seem much greater sufferers on the whole than ourselves, who have gained both East and West Indies, and six ships of war in the scuffle; while the poor Emperor sees his coffers exhausting, his dominions diminishing, and his whole family upon the very verge of utter extinction. Our brave cousin Stadtholder too will soon, as it appears, have no *states* to *hold*, and has, for aught I see, a fair chance to outlive the celebrated name of Nassau. An event so improbable twenty years ago, that whoever had predicted it must have been accounted deranged in his understanding. I am sorry the Bristol people are so sullenly resolved to wish for peace with these spoilers, they are mistaken in thinking it *better than war*; it is *worse than war,* because peace will bring over full tides of Jacobinical principles, to the *ruin* of their *interest,* and *destruction* of their property. War at least keeps that infection at a distance. So much for politics.

Our dear Master did well to build a house in Flintshire; *he* never looked so well since I knew him as since we came here, I think, never had so good an appetite certainly, and provisions are excellent in their kinds, particularly fish …

Can you tell aught of Harriet Lee? *Our* correspondence is cool somehow, and unfrequent. What wonder? The *old* topick is lost, nor can I guess what is become of it, no *new* one can be interesting to her, and I feel as if ashamed, without any cause, God knows.

Mrs. Siddons' little Cecilia will, I hope, inherit her mother's beauty; virtue will, I fancy, be quite out of fashion before she can possess any. Sweet Helena's defection from the right path hurts all her friends exceedingly; but parents never appear to love children the worse for any ill behaviour. I suppose Mrs. W[illiams] sees nothing in her daughter's conduct that does not deserve admiration.

You are very good indeed in feeling for me about the little Spaniel. Immortal Phyllis, to the astonishment of physicians, friends, and nurses, now promises to be once more *her own dog again*. I never did see so surprising a recovery. The fall was above four yards perpendicular height.

Mrs. Radcliffe, née Ward, was an old acquaintance of Mrs. Piozzi's. For the *Mysteries,* which was just published, and made a great sensation, she received £500.

The state of Europe was indeed sufficiently gloomy as viewed by English eyes. We had, it is true, scored some successes. Howe's victory on "the glorious first of June" was to be the prelude to many others, and we took Ceylon and the Cape from the Dutch. But in France the "Great Terror" was at its height, and the news of its collapse after the death of Robespierre, at the end of July, had not yet reached Denbigh. The French generals acting against the Continental Powers were almost uniformly successful. In Holland, at the beginning of the year, under the eyes of the Emperor Francis himself, there had been a concentration of English, Hanoverian, and Austrian troops, with a view to check the French advance, but they were hampered by disaffection in the country itself. The Stadtholder William, with his English leanings, had never been popular with his own subjects, and indeed had only retained his authority in 1787 by the help of Prussian troops. Though the first Republican expedition under Dumouriez had failed, the new one under Pichegru was a brilliant success. Amsterdam was occupied by the French, and the Batavian Republic proclaimed. The Stadtholder fled to England, not to be recalled till 1813, and he was soon followed by the remnant of the now useless English force under the Duke of York.

DENBIGH, *Thursday*, 11 *Sept.* 1794.

I had not a notion that *our* correspondence was grown languid, dear Friend, and am now rather disposed to think a letter has been lost …

Marquis Trotti has written, he forgets no one old Streatham acquaintance but enquires very particularly for *you*. His own affairs at home go no better for these disturbances upon the Continent, yet will be not be drawn thither to see how they stand. The direction we are now using towards him is Hamburgh.

Kitty Beavor marries Dr. Gillies, and sets out for Scotland next week. I said to her once that all my single lady friends found husbands, and so I lost them. "*Oh*," says she, "*you will keep Kitty Beavor tho'*, for I shall never change *my* condition." But so the world wags, and the *old way* is the *best road* too.

Meanwhile, as you say, love seems banished from the novels, where *terror* (as in the Convention,) becomes the *order of the day*.

Miss (*sic*) Radcliffe however plays that game best which all are striving to play well. I am often weary of her descriptions, but she possesses great power over the fancy. Her tricks used to fright Mrs. Siddons and me very much; but when somebody said her book was like Macbeth, "Ay," replied H.L.P., "about as like as Peppermint Water is to good French Brandy."

I have written a Ballad for the Blackguards to bawl about the streets, imitated from Newberry's well known Chapter of Kings; written at first to teach Babies the English History, but lately set and sung at Catch Clubs, Bow Meetings, etc.

Here is the Chapter of King Killers.

The nine stanzas which follow, though doubtless good enough for the purpose which the writer suggests, are hardly worth preserving. One verse will probably satisfy the reader's curiosity.

> When France, mad for Freedom, her King controll'd,
> At first she was awed by Fayette the bold,
> Then came the Assemblée Nationale,
> And then she was governed by nothing at all.
>   But after all pother of this, and t'other,
>   They all lose their heads in their turn.

DENBIGH, 19 *Sep.* 1794.

Be not alarmed for me, kind Friend, I shall do as well as my neighbours, perhaps better, but nothing shall make me tell fibs,—I am not well …

Doubt not meantime that my old iron constitution will get thro' this business very stoutly. Think of your own affairs, and get thro' *them*, and we will be *old* friends twenty years hence. For look you, my dear, whether we think so or not, I, when my health shall be gone, and you, when your money shall be spent, are happier than half the human race collectively; and I know not how we have deserved the preference. We might have been born savages in America, condemned to hunt, and fish, and dress our game when caught, sick or well. Or we might have been some of those Begums, that Burke says were insulted and plundered by English Harpies in the East. Or we might have been African Blacks, stow'd in a slave ship. Or we might have been Mrs. Brown, or Lady Ann Fitzroy. I think we are very well off, with each of us a good husband, and safe in the only country where rational liberty prevails, true religion resides unmolested, and talents are valued according to *desert.*

What becomes of poor Helen Williams, I wonder! There is a strong rumour of Barrere's having followed his old colleague ...

Marquis Trotti began travelling so early that he will now, perhaps, never leave it off. You may find some *sage and grave* reflexions upon that subject at the close of a *famous fine* book, called Piozzi's Observations made in Italy and Germany. I'm glad you like my Ballad. The worthy French are making the words of it good as fast as ever they can ...

My maid fell from a horse two nights ago, scampering to see Brinbella, that at least was the excuse, and has disabled herself in a terrible manner; bruised and strained her wrist, etc. ...

DENBIGH, 20 *Nov.*

MY DEAR FRIEND,—So completely was I engaged, it seems, nursing my sick Husband, that even writing to you was forgotten. Mr. Piozzi's annual fit of Gout has caught him here, and will prevent all further journeys of business or of pleasure, save that which leads home the nearest way, when he shall be able to travel ...

The times wear a very threatening aspect, indeed they do; and here are storms ready to blow my Lord Howe's ships to pieces, when they shall have been damaged by engagement with an enemy hourly increasing in ferocity and force.

Horne Tooke's tryal is a most curious and interesting business; when Piozzi can listen, I translate him the passages which must, I think, arrest attention, even from pain and anguish.

Cecilia is *toujours gaie*, and helps to keep up all our spirits; she is young; so is no longer dear Mrs. Pennington's sincere friend and Faithful servant   H.L. Piozzi

Lord Howe's fleet was cruising between Ushant and the Scilly Isles from August till the end of October, when he was driven into Torbay by stress of weather. He put out to sea on 9th November, but was again driven back for shelter on 19th November.

Horne Tooke, Thelwall, and Hardy were arrested in November on a charge of high treason, for having issued invitations to a "National Convention," designed to bring about serious constitutional changes in the government of England. Though it was clear that they had been coquetting with treasonable practices, the jury did not consider their action justified a conviction which must have resulted in the penalty of death, and returned a verdict of "not guilty."

DENBIGH, 17 *Feb.* 1795.

What puts it in dear Mrs. Pennington's head that I wish to forget her? My only reason for writing nothing was that I had nothing to write. Mr. Piozzi had a long fit of gout certainly, and a sharp fit, but without one bad symptom, thank God; and his recovery was better than ever. Among other comforts, Denbigh possesses that of an excellent Physician.

All you say of public matters is more than true, but we are still further removed here from the talking world than you are, and what little we have heard of London and its environs in these late months, only contributed to keep us away, while many people suspect a tendency to sickness in the Metropolis, not of any one contagious distemper, but a disposition towards mortality in general. This *may* be exaggerated evil, but Beef and Mutton at 8*d.* o' pound is a real one, so is Bread at 9*d.* the quartern loaf, with coals at *six,* or at best, *four* Guineas the Chaldron. Strange allurements these to housekeeping with 18 or 20 servants at Streatham Park. At Easter however we *must* begin. You and I have often said that such times would come, and worse; *our* predictions are only verifying, others foretell fearful things indeed, but we are sure that neither they nor we know anything about the matter …

The rival Wits say that Helen Williams is turn'd *to Stone*, and tho' she was once second to nobody, she is now second to his wife; who it seems was not guillotined, as once was reported, but remains a living spectatress of these political and *im*-politic revolutions.

Kemble's advertisement, so like that of a penitent Hackney Coachman under the threatened *Lash* of a sharp prosecution, excites much notice, I understand; but am shocked to find his offence, though actionable, considered by the fashionists more as a jest than as an enormity. Harriet Lee seems to fancy her Sister has a play coming out, which Madame D'Arblaye's, late Fanny Burney's, Tragedy retards … Dear Siddons is sick again, but of a complaint common to many, as her family tell me: she must have been hurt by her brother's frolick I should suppose. *She* loved the girl, and thought her, as she proved, most excellent …

Cecilia is young, and gay, and frisky, and flighty, and so is her horse: I wish they were come safe home from a long ride to their and your   H.L.P.

P.S.—Dear Mrs. Pennington, don't forget your best friend, and come to see us at Streatham Park in the Spring.   G.P.

John Kemble's trouble arose from his having made advances to Miss Maria Theresa de Camp, afterwards wife of his brother Charles, who was acting with him at this date. For this he had to make a public apology in the newspapers.

1. "An they be once in a calm, they are sick."—2 *Henry IV*, II. iv. 40.
2. *As You Like It*, I. iii. 12.
3. Jer. li. 25; Ezek. xxxviii. 20.

CHAPTER IV

A MARRIAGE AND A DEATH

WHILE the Piozzis were staying at Denbigh, and superintending the building of Brynbella, Cecilia, still in her teens, met her future husband, John Meredith Mostyn.

DENBIGH, *March* 24, 1795.

My dear Mrs. Pennington will excuse her old Friend if, having long forborne to write because she had nothing to say, she continued that forbearance lately because she had too much. My heart has been very full: Cecilia seems to have seen the man she likes at last, and thinking about them occupies very, very much of my mind. As my Countryman is no Lord, nor no Wit, nor no Beau, nor no man of *monstrous Fortune*, I know not how the connection will be relished by London Friends, or by Cecy's Sisters, Guardians, the Chancellor, etc. But that she should pitch upon a youth of ancient and respectable family in my own neigbbourhood, grandson to an old intimate of my own Father, with a clear estate of £2000 pr. Ann.; independent in mind, manners, and fortune, with a *beautiful* person, and character highly esteem'd, cannot chuse but be agreeable to me. Meantime the World is *so* wicked, and one is so terrified at the thoughts of what *may* happen in it to two creatures, neither of them quite 20 years old, that I live in a fever ...

Write soon—directly if you can; we don't go to Streatham till the 14th of April. Adieu! I cannot make my pen obey me, it will neither stop nor run. Cecilia is out on horseback with her Sweetheart, but she bid me tell you all. And now I have forgot to add his name—'tis John Meredith Mostyn—of Segroid. We call the people by the names of their country seats, as in Scotland, 'tis necessary where there are so many old aristocrate families branch'd out into many separate houses and establishments.

Once more Adieu! Give my best regards to *your* Husband, and pray for a good one to Cecy, or what will become of your H.L.P.?

Mr. Piozzi is out at Brinbella. Building and planting, marrying and giving in marriage, you see we *do* go on till the very end of the world, undeterred by false Prophets which precede it.

This rascal Brothers will be *seriously* listen'd to, if the Prince of Wales's match goes off. He rested the truth of his mission upon that event, but we are expressly told that some of them *will* do signs and wonders; yet are we commanded strictly *not to go forth after them*,— as I find many do.

The Mostyns of Segroid (now of Llewesog, co. Denbigh) were a branch of the Mostyns of Mostyn, Barts., who claimed descent from Tudor Trevor. In previous generations they had intermarried with the Salusburys and Pennants, and J. M. Mostyn's sister Maria married Colonel Salusbury of Galtfynan. His grandfather, John Mostyn, was of Capel Gwyddelwern, co. Monmouth, and died 1731.

Richard Brothers was originally a Lieutenant R.N., but retired from the service, and set up as a prophet in London about 1787. His vegetarian diet, and conscientious objection to oaths, helped to bring him into notoriety, while his scruples about drawing his pay brought him into the work house. But he soon found admirers and supporters, and was enabled to publish his "Revealed Knowledge of Prophecies and Times, wrote under the direction of the Lord God," in 1794. Some of his predictions had a remarkable fulfilment: *e.g.* in 1792 he foretold violent deaths for the King of Sweden and Louis XVI, but others, such as the destruction of London by fire, were less successful. He now developed megalomania of a religious type, styling himself "Nephew of God" (explained as in virtue of descent from one of the "Brethren of the Lord") and the "Prince of the Hebrews" who was to lead the Jews back to Palestine. Some wild political utterances led to an examination before the Privy Council on suspicion of treason, but the fitting result was his confinement, not in a gaol, but in a lunatic asylum.

STREATHAM PARK, *Tuesday*, 5 *May.*

My dear Friend will, I am sure, be pleased to hear that we are safe arrived here, and our children about us: Mr. Mostyn grows every day dearer to me, and the connection with him more desired as we make closer acquaintance. Cecilia seems to resist, for his sake, all temptations from her Sisters to a London Spring; and Mr. Piozzi, in return, treats us all with frequent excursions for amusement, so as to render a *week's stay in Town* less necessary to her happiness. What a Town 'tis! And what strange events occur in it every hour! Prophets, Traitors, Lunatic Ladies who elope from their husbands, even without Gallants to seduce, or even feigned ill-usage to impell them. They run to *Bristol* however, you know I say that all the Wonder-doers, Conjurors, Poets, Impostors,—every one have something to do with Bristol … Mr. Jackson, tho' guilty, is recommended to mercy I perceive, but his condemnation will, in a certain manner, implicate Mr. Stone. Apropos, Helen Williams finds a defender in Col. Barry, who is as amiable, as clever, and as eccentrick as possible. Lovely Siddons is set out for Scotland in this moment, she will have cheated herself of Summer completely …

Whilst I am writing come my three Daughters, two of them at least, from Town, and bring the news of Jackson's suicide. What astonishing times are these! and the World, tho' wicked, is so enraged against my Lady Jersey, that people expect her to be hissed in her carriage, or at the theatres. Our new Princess's popularity daily encreases, I think, and if she *should* bring us a little boy the World would really be quite charmed with her. Is it not astonishing that she never learned English, when that study is grown even fashionable upon the Continent?

This is one of those days which Brothers pitched on for the Earthquake. Do you take any interest in his abettors and their pamphlets, Wright, Bryan, Halhead? …

William Jackson was an Irish clergyman, who had held a curacy in London, and acted as chaplain to the "amazing" Duchess of Kingston: afterwards, taking up journalism, he was editor of the *Public Ledger* and the *Morning Post*. Espousing the cause of the United Irishmen, he went over to France as their envoy, with a view to procure assistance for the projected Irish rising. Being brought to trial and convicted, he took poison, and died in the dock while sentence was being pronounced. His suicide was perhaps designed to save his property, which would have been forfeited to the Crown on conviction for high treason.

Frances, daughter of Dr. Philip Twysden, Bishop of Raphoe, and wife of George Bussy, fourth Earl of Jersey, had created considerable scandal, even in that lax age, by her relations with the Prince of Wales, afterwards George IV. The shameless way in which he forced her into the household of the Princess, was no doubt largely responsible for the sympathy so widely felt for the erring but injured wife. The Prince's marriage took place in April 1795, but the only child, born in 1796, was the Princess Charlotte, who married Prince Leopold of Saxe-Coburg, afterwards King of the Belgians.

Nathaniel Brassey Halhead, M.P. for Lymington, was a man of considerable attainments, as shown by his Bengali Grammar and "Gentoo Code of Laws"; but his learning did not save him from becoming the disciple, not to say dupe, of the mad prophet, under whose influence he wrote a treatise on the millenium, and a "Testimony to the Authenticity of the Prophecies of R. Brothers."

STREATHAM PARK, *Monday*, 11 *May* 1795.

......

Mrs. Siddons is gone to work her brother out of a gaol at Edinburgh, and was forced to leave her husband,—who, being security for him, is most deeply interested in his success,—*a cripple upon crutches*. Such stuff is this world made of, and 'tis time to look sharp about money matters *now*, when a common fowl is paid seven shillings for in Carnaby Market, and a leg o' mutton at the same place *eight* pence o' pound. For these uncommon misfortunes I refused to take common report; so left the carriage in Marlborough Street, and walked in my black bonnet and cloke all over that eminently cheap and plentiful market myself, in order to ascertain the real truth, and I now write down what I saw and heard in letters, not figures, to prevent the possibility even of *supposed* mistake. What however most amazes me is, that our Batchelor Friends say the prices are not raised yet in eating-house or tavern, nor are the dinners worse; and Virgo the poulterer told me he never sold more articles than since they have been at this unexampled price. Make these facts agree as you can.

With regard to Spring, all *order and gradation* seem as completely abolished as if the *Elements* had experienced a *Revolution*. The Walnut is now contemporary with the Primrose, a thing I never saw before, and all our Oaks are in broad leaf, before the Pear trees have shed their blossoms, a circumstance wholly new to me. Not a Blackbird is seen or heard in our desolated shrubbery, which, as you know, used to resound with them: and nobody but myself (who am ever on the watch,) has seen any Swallows. I observed six yesterday. But what strange times are these, with our false Christs too, and false Prophets! Mercy on me! But I do think Cecilia is beginning the World just in the *last Act* of it. May she at least play *her part* well! Mostyn and she are trying to get married, if possible, before he comes of age, and so they will amuse the time till he is of age, I suppose ...

Apparently the Chancellor proved obdurate in the matter of the marriage of the legal "infants," so the impatient Cecilia indulged in one more characteristic escapade by eloping to Gretna Green; an unnecessary proceeding which must have been very annoying for Mrs. Piozzi, though she makes no allusion to it in the letters. Their married life was but short, as Mostyn died in May 1807. His widow survived him just half a century, and died at Silwood House, Brighton, 1st May 1857, at eighty.

Mrs. Siddons' brother, Stephen Kemble, had taken the Theatre Royal, Edinburgh, in 1789, but from the first was involved in disputes with his intended partner and an unsuccessful competitor. He tried to escape from these by opening the New Theatre in 1793, only to

Cecilia Mostyn

find that the legitimate drama was altogether prohibited there, as infringing the rights of the Theatre Royal. He returned to the latter in the following year, but disputes and litigation still continued, so that in spite of his sister's assistance it could not have proved a very profitable situation; but he did not resign till 1800.

STREATHAM PARK, *Sat.* 13 *Jun.* 1795.
My dear Mrs. Pennington will be pleased to hear that our Cecilia is married, and happy, and gone down with her very amiable husband

to Llewesog Lodge, near Denbigh, N. Wales, the seat of *his* mother, Mrs. Wynne. A letter from you, so directed, will be a pleasure to her. We cannot get down as early as we wish, tho' things here are so high-prized, *that* circumstance alone might drive one if one's heart were not, as much of mine now is, in the country with Mrs. Mostyn. These really are sad times, are they not? A cessation of hostilities without any peace, a pause somehow more shocking than war, like the pause in a pulse lately hurried on by *fever*, now stopt by a symptom more dreadful than the fever itself.

The elements too are really very severe of late; the Park is converted into what farmers call Lay—*our* Park; it will not pay the haymaking. It is a new sight to me, and a mournful one, and the weather is like a cold October.

What becomes of our friends the Whalleys? I never hear of them, and what do they say to these terrifying moments? They will be sorry for those who are starving. My daughters tell me that the little sheds about St. George's Fields are full of Emigrée French dying of actual want; having exhausted the Charity so much—indeed so *justly* admired in our beneficent nation. Poor things! They expire quietly now, and say nothing; but stirring up Oatmeal and Cold water together, live on *that* while they can get it, and then—perish. Countesses and children of high quality in France, thus lost amidst the crowds of thieves and blackguards that infest the environs of London. How very dreadful! How very poignant the reflexion! ...

Charming Siddons is somewhere in the North, setting up the individuals of her family, like Ninepins, for Fortune to bowl at, and knock down again. *She* meantime secures glorious immortality in both worlds ...

Streatham Park, *Fryday* 26 *Jun.*
My dear Mrs. Pennirgton may assure herself I know no more of Helen Williams actual situation than I do of Colonel Barry's address. I have seen him but for five minutes since I saw *you,* and 'twas his diversion then, (in his clever way,) to make out her defence against some of the company who sported the reports you mention.

Mr. James, whom you have heard me speak of, died in a French prison, poor fellow! His widow and children are returned; they have suffered greatly, but the pressure is nearly general, and these last riots truly tremendous. If we do not catch the Corn Fleet going from America to France—the Lord have mercy upon us!

Turning towards individuals is the likeliest method to find some happiness, yet *you*, my dear Friend, complain, and poor Mr. Whalley's sufferings will be *too* great, if his wife really should *die* in consequence of his Niece's naughtiness. Oh surely I hope that will never be. Can any beside parents feel *mortal* anxiety? I hoped not.

Sweet Cecy is loaded with comforts and pleasures; the family she falls into adores her, and the peasants take off the horses and draw her about in triumph. Her sisters too are *now* contented, and express their approbation, etc., in bridal presents. May she but be sensible of her felicity! The lot she has drawn is indeed a very great one; personal beauty, birth, unblemished character, and gentle manners in one man united, is no common prize …

My Girls always say how they wish for your acquaintance. I will not yet despair of seeing you next Spring, for we *have* a project, but I must not mention it yet.

Mr. James was a portrait painter at Bath, who was elected A.R.A. in 1770. He was imprisoned during the Terror, but was apparently released after the fall of Robespierre, as he actually died at Boulogne.

Lord Howe had put out in the spring to find the French fleet, but returned on hearing that it had been damaged by a storm, and had put into Brest to refit. Though in failing health he remained in nominal command, but the English fleet was actually led by Alexander Hood, Lord Bridport, who, three days before Mrs. Piozzi wrote, gained a notable victory, with a much inferior force, over the French Fleet of twenty-two ships off L'Orient.

A letter of thanks from Cecilia for Mrs. Pennington's congratulations follows. Her condolences on Mrs. Whalley's supposed death were somewhat premature. Subsequent letters show that she made a satisfactory recovery from the effects of her niece's "naughtiness," whatever it may have been.

LLEWESOG LODGE, *July the 2d.*

MY DEAR MRS. PENNINGTON,—I am extremely obliged to you and Mr. Pennington for your kind congratulations, and should have written to thank you sooner had I been quite well. Now the correspondence has begun, may I hope it will continue, for I have now not the same means of knowing how you all go on. I am not likely to see my dear Mother for at least two months, as their house goes on very slowly here. Wasn't there a talk once of your coming into Wales? Sure it would be a good as well as an agreeable plan. How glad we should all be to see you. Do let me know if there are any hopes of such a thing; or to have a pretty little cottage—how nice it would be. Any body may live here without money almost, every thing is so cheap.

I have this moment heard of poor Mrs. Whalley's death. How grieved you must be, and poor Mr. Whalley; indeed I am very sorry. That dreadful Mrs. Mullins was, I suppose, the cause; do you know what is become of her? …

Ever yours,   CECILIA MOSTYN.

By the autumn the Piozzis were established in their own house, which Mrs. Piozzi for some time continues to write as Brinbella. Though commenced only as a "cottage," Mrs. Piozzi states in her Commonplace Book that the total cost was over £20,000.

BRINBELLA, *Wednesday* 21 *Oct.* 1795.

......

My Master is just recovered from a fit of gout, which, coming at so very untoward a moment, left me no leisure for thinking at the time of any thing else:—but *now* I am glad that 'tis over.

We were scarce warm in our house before he was laid up, and 'twas cruel to have him disturb'd at such an hour by Workmens' hammers. *To them* the less disagreeable noise of pretty ladies' prattle has at length happily succeeded; and Mr. Piozzi gallants his wife's four daughters to Holywell Assembly tomorrow. Meantime Mrs. Mostyn *is* settled at her husband's old Family Seat at Segroid, near Denbigh; his Mama lives with *her* husband, Major Wynne, at Llewesog Lodge, about four miles from them,—I, think we at Brinbella measure eight or nine. Mr. Mostyn means to build another summer, but resides in the old Mansion while that work is going on. I hear no talk of any young ones coming as yet, but we need not despair. Harriet Lee's hour of felicity will come to me, I doubt not; *she* says, you know, that no human being is truly happy but a *Grandmother.*

Marquis Trotti is married, and Annette is gone to Manchester. I think the latter a lucky incident, she will have no one to talk the other event over to, and it will fade away the sooner from her memory. Friendship has its thorns like any other rose; a person to whom you can speak freely is a perpetual reflector of your own sensations, and if they are not agreeable, serves to double the pain. The younger sister too may make conquests in a new place, where her accomplishments are likely to strike as rareties. Such companions as our lovely Nancy will not easily be found in a trading town.

My young ladies mean to spend the winter at Clifton, I understand, but all seasons begin late now, and we shall of course endeavour to detain them here as long as possible. They have been prospect-hunting ever since June, and confess these environs very beautiful notwithstanding that Mount Edgecumbe and Penfield have been taken into their tour. They have heard much of dear Mrs. Pennington, and I dare say you will like one another exceedingly; the Siddonses and they are grown quite intimate …

The public news is dismal indeed, but my Master says *'twill mend.*

The dowager Mrs. Mostyn took for her second husband Edward Watkin Wynne, of Llwyn, co. Denbigh, the representative of a younger branch of the Wynnes of Gwydir.

BRINBELLA, 24 *Nov.* 1795.

My dear Mrs. Pennington will receive this letter from an old Friend by the hand of her Daughters; they will be pleased with your acquaintance, and you will have it in your power to shew them some attentions.

Streatham Park will serve as a common theme for the beginning of conversation, tho' Heaven knows the present times afford ample scope for talk which can scarcely avoid interesting us all. Meantime Miss Thrale has seen so much beautiful scenery in the Western Counties of our Island, England and Wales, that you will delight in making her recapitulate their peculiarities of excellence. Nobody I ever knew, who loved London society with your degree of fondness, continued to possess so strong a taste of Nature and her solitary charms; but I know not whether Clifton Hill makes you any amends yet for loss of Hanover Square.

I heard that poor Mrs. Whalley was dead, but 'tis not true, I hope; if anything will make dear Siddons sit down to write a letter, it must be asking her that question ...

Brynbella, *Monday 7.*

My dear Mrs. Pennington does me wrong in thinking I forget her; but though we live an apparently retired life, being far distant both from Bath and from the Capital, I do not perceive that more time to be disposed of falls to one's share here than at Streatham Park. Our walks, being more varied, are pleasanter, and tempt us out much more. So many *improvements* too, with *Chickens to peck, and Pidgeons to flee*, as the Fool said to Mr. Whalley; I am, I think, quite tired by 10 o'clock at night always, and yet impatient for another day, that something may get forward. We have a way too of going to dinner with our neighbours here perpetually, and of sleeping at each other's houses in good familiarity, which takes up some not disagreeable moments. Of London acquaintance we cannot be supposed to see many, but Miss Thrales and Mr. Chappelow, who have been among us, will, I flatter myself, make a good report. For conversation we talk of peace, and war, and fashions, with great success; and the price provisions bear, principally corn, is a matter of serious moment, to *us.* Strange to me how 'tis endured in the Metropolis, and stranger how the evil will be cured.

You had more need write to *me*, dear Friend, than think of letters from one who, for all topics of thought or talk, depends upon distant intelligence, and I depend upon good forage in the *Bristol quarter.* There is always somewhat going forward *there* ... Send me a yard-long letter ...

The "Fool," whose sayings are several times referred to, was doubtless the "famous mechanic, Merlin," of whom Mrs. Piozzi relates in her Commonplace Book that, hearing a discussion on the possibility of stopping the expected French army of invasion, he inquired, "Could they not stop them at the Turnpikes?"

BRYNBELLA, *Fryday* 18 *Dec.* '95.

......

Well the changes and chances of this world are many and various, and sometimes happen for the better, as they do now upon the Continent. The French run very well indeed;—I *told* you that vengeance awaited them, and 'tis coming at last.

Meantime you must do me a favour. You must enquire me a Housekeeper such as you *know* will suit us; a good country housewife, who can salt Bacon, cure Hams, see also to the baking, etc., and be an active manager of and for a dozen troublesome servants: in a word, *Abbiss* without her faults. The London women of this profession hate to leave the Capital; I should hope better from a rough inhabitant of Bristol or Liverpool, where the people keep good houses, and good order in their houses, and give excellent dinners, be the times scarce or plentiful.

You see Helen Williams advertises a new Book; *her* friends are uppermost in Paris now, but if these foreign affairs run counter so, I much doubt their ability to *stand* when general enthusiasm begins to *fall.*

Adieu, my kind friend, and do look me out a servant such as I have described; the torment these people cause me here at such a distance is intolerable; fetching and carrying them is as expensive as can be, and then the others won't live with them,—and there is no end of their worrying one. Ask your good Mother if she knows one likely to do.

Helen Williams about this time published *Letters containing a Sketch of the Politics of France, 1793-4;* she had also employed herself in making a translation of *Paul et Virginie* while in prison under Robespierre.

After his fall, the party of the Gironde to which she belonged framed the new Constitution, which came into force 28th October 1795. The Convention dissolved itself to make way for the Directory, which served as a stepping-stone for Napoleon's rise to power.

Wednesday, 20 [*Apr.* 1796], Brinbella.

What a world it is, dear Mrs. Pennington! But the amiable Whalleys have found better than they expected in it. Everybody will be glad, they are people I think particularly beloved: and since Mrs. Mullins has scamper'd off so, I hope *you* will be the only favourite, and then good will come out of evil.

Cecilia and her husband are gone to London. I am sorry for it; but she felt very tired of Wales, and he felt disposed—not to *indulge* but to *obey* her. I am sorry for *that too*, a little bridle is not amiss for a young Filly Foal like her. If she had been bringing a pretty Boy, instead of driving to Town in a dangerous Curricle, I should have liked it better, but they think of themselves, not of us.

I congratulate you upon the new Tax: there will be *many dogs the fewer for it.* Do you remember saying upon Streatham Hill, one day when I thought my neighbour's favourite Spaniel in danger from old Browney, "Let him alone; if he kills it there will at worst be *one* dog less in the world"?

The dear Lees will, I hope, be all well and happy in the success which is expected to attend Almeyda. Sweet Siddons does not write as if she was encumbered with either health or happiness, but things will mend sometime, *sure.* I wish she had done with her profession, and could buy a pretty little house and farm just by us here,—*that I do*: she would like this place better than you would. Mr. Chappelow came and spent three weeks with us, and said how beautiful the country was, and the people how agreeable. But I caught him at last rejoicing in the sight of a man that *had seen Wandsworth*; and when I observed he was a knowing fellow in his way,—"Why, yes," says he, "you may perceive he has English notions; he was bred at *Wandsworth*, etc." …

You must direct your next to me at Dr. Wynn's House, Beaumaris, Anglesey. A dip in our Irish Channel will do me good, and I shall see some waves that have been at Bristol. If we can either get or save half a crown, we will visit you next year, but these sweet grounds round the new house take up all our money. They are beautiful, however, and I do not grudge it. If we live, it will repay us in pleasure certainly, perhaps in profit. Mr. Piozzi mends the estate every day. I wish you could *but* see it. Miss Thrales like Streatham better, of course ...

Nobody ever writes me word whether Marquis Trotti has perpetuated his family by marrying this pretty young Countess, and *he* has done corresponding with me now. So melt away our quondam society, my dear Mrs. Pennington, and so melt we away ourselves, none of us quite what we were I believe, but none less changed, (tho' not well neither,) than your ever equally faithful

H.L.P.

The above letter is franked, a very unusual circumstance in Mrs. Piozzi's correspondence, by "R.W. Wynne," probably her neighbour Colonel Robert William Wynne of Garthwin, who was High Sheriff for the county.

BRYNBELLA, 1 August, 1796.

Well! dear Mrs. Pennington! this next winter, if we all live so long, will we shake hands, and tell old tales of other times over a fire together. Our dear Master has had a fit of Gout in Anglesey, and he has a fancy to have the next at Bath, and will go thither—if it please God—on the 1st of Jan^Y 1797. How many things, foreign and domestic, shall we find to chat about! How many odd and new incidents have claim'd attention since we parted! And how comfortable will it be to talk all matters over in the old way! ...

Cecilia and her husband were in London this Spring with their sisters, but as they went without taking leave of us, so they returned without taking any notice. These are *some* of the odd things.

Some of the odder still are that Mr. and Mrs. Mostyn went to Streatham Park, when tired of Town, called their friends about them there, and nobody said or wrote a word to Mr. Piozzi or me about the matter, except Miss Thrale, who beg'd permission for Susan and Sophy. Since then Lord and Lady William Russell have wished us *to let it,* and Lord and Lady Clonmel have wished us *to lend it.* My Master says he'll go next Spring and live awhile in it to spite 'em. I shall be glad when we return, for dear Brynbella has full possession of her heart who is ever faithfully yours,

H.L.P.

Brynbella, 17 Aug. 1796.

My dear Friend,—This very post brought me your kind letter; see then, if I am slow in answering it, though every day makes me hate writing more than the last day did. What can one write freely? Not about one's children, unless they were good as mine are, and giving no cause of complaint. Nor about one's friends certainly, for if they did wrong, or disgraced expectation of right, *they* are the very people one would not blame. Enemies—less still; for in that blame *some* envy or some ill-nature would very likely be mingled, and *more* be suspected at all times. Of the French, and the French only, may one write freely, and blame liberally; for though all fear, I think all (even the maddest,) begin to abhor them. 'Tis too late however, and unless some decisive blow be soon struck in Italy, (of which I am not wholly without hope,) all must go, and then politics will cease to be, as now, an extraneous subject, to keep us from talking of what truly interests our heart or purse, it will be what most immediately touches our nearest and dearest concerns. May the great battle likely to take place before beautiful Verona's gates *avert,* by the success of General Wurmser,—at least *defer,* that very dreadful moment! But there are other hopes. We *may* take Leghorn ourselves. The old Empress may think ye time come when she ought to rouze from her Northern torpor, that keeps all animals asleep till late in the season by its cold, and the whole human race *may* unite against that portion of it which so seeks the utter ruin of the rest. Any of these will do; and if nothing of y^s should happen, we must revere and acknowledge the *visible* finger of God, and prepare for what's to follow. So much for public matters …

I fancy Madam D'Arblaye lives much with foreigners. She talks of *demanding* and *according* in a way English people never talk; and of *descending* to breakfast, and says one sister aided another to rise, or lye down, as English people never do. We say *ask,* and *grant,* and *help,* and *go down stairs*, you know; the other words are French. The characters however of Mrs. Arlberry and Mrs. Berlington are surely well contrasted, and both likely enough to strike a young creature of Camilla's cast. Mrs. Mittin too has much of my applause, and Bellamy frighted me with his feigned character and his false friendship, and his pouncing upon Eugenia, so like "*one Hawk with one Pidgeon*,"— do you remember?

Cecilia is very well, and looks prettier than she used to do … She has been to see us since I wrote, both with and without her Husband. They are going into Westmoreland on a shooting party, and propose visiting my oldest friend, Mrs. Strickland. Her sisters are at Tunbridge.

Helen Williams's conduct seems to astound Harriet Lee, whose own sweetness hindered her from seeing what led to it long ago, but we must yet suspend our judgments. I expect some Harlequin escape from censure will yet be performed for our delight and her benefit.

Dr. Moore battles the Ladies on their own ground, I see. Mr. Cumberland and he come forward with novels contesting the palm against very formidable antagonists. I never saw Henry, but have heard many commend it, and from Edward I really expect a good deal.

The epilogue to Almeyda pleased me more than even the prologue, some lines of which are however exquisite. The play itself half broke my heart in reading, 'twas so tender, and somehow I had expected terror more than pity would have been produced by Sophia Lee. Like yourself, I was all for *Orasmyn*. When will these dear creatures cease their combinations of calamity? There is so much in the *real living* world at present, 'tis surprising how one can find tears for *nothing* so, and for *nobody.*

Charming Siddons has been silent ever since I refused running after her from Beaumaris to Liverpool, but such an expedition was more impracticable than she dreamt on. Mr. Pott, who I met in Anglesey, said she had lost much of health and something of good looks. Oh! for those two things, if true, *I am really and sincerely sorry …*

Mrs. Piozzi's hopes of successes against the French were doomed to disappointment. The command in Italy had now been entrusted to

Bonaparte, who won the battle of Lodi and entered Milan in May. His opponent, General Wurmser, though at the head of 10,000 Austrians, and aided by the disaffection of the States newly subjugated by France, was driven out of Italy in a week; and on attempting to retrieve his fortunes by a second campaign, was shut up in Mantua, and compelled to capitulate. Nor had the English forces fared any better, having been driven out of Leghorn and Corsica in the course of the summer.

Madame D'Arblay's new novel, *Camilla*, which had just been published, proved highly successful. Besides 1100 subscribers at a guinea, 3500 copies were sold in three months. The contemporary reviewer in the *British Critic* was struck by the genius required to bring together such a number of distinctly characterised persons, and make them act consistently, and singled out, like Mrs. Piozzi, the character of Mrs. Arlberry as one of the most highly finished portraits.

The scope of Dr. Moore's work is sufficiently shown by its title— *Edward; various views of human nature, taken from life and manners, chiefly in England.* This, being devoted to the better side of human nature, was considered much less thrilling than *Zeluco*. His third venture, *Mordaunt*, published in 1803, was tamer still, being the conventional story of a workhouse foundling, recognised by his parents through the happy accident of a strawberry-mark.

Dr. Richard Cumberland, son of the Bishop of Clogher and Killaloe, and a grandson of Dr. Richard Bentley, professedly modelled his *Henry* (published 1795) on the style of Fielding. His work was fairly well received by the public, but his peculiar temper made him unpopular with his fellow authors, of whom Goldsmith drew his portrait in *Retaliation*, while Sheridan in *The Critic* caricatured him unmercifully as Sir Fretful Plagiary.

BRYNBELLA, *Shortest day,* 1796.

How, my dear Mrs. Pennington, shall I begin a letter which is sure to be so truly disagreeable to us both? How shall I tell you that we are not coming either to Bath or Bristol? Harriet has a commission from us now to un-order the lodgings we meant to take.

Eliza (Farren), Countess of Derby, 1797

Business, and that of a mortifying nature, *drags* not *draws* us to the neighbourhood of London; it is Cecy's business chiefly, but must not be neglected. There are now but thirteen short months to her coming of age, and those who are most earnest that she should be taken care of, call to us for that assistance, which, at any rate, we are anxious to give. She has never called here, or I fancy thought of such an exertion these nine or ten weeks; but if she does not know her duty, we know ours, and will endeavour to do it:—but let us talk of something,—of *anything* else.

The pleasantest subject is the new Loan: whilst the Metropolis can subscribe half a million an hour she will *fear* no invasion I suppose, although such treasures might tempt plunder from less unprincipled robbers than the French. People make comfort out of the pecuniary distresses of our enemy too; but a wolf becomes more formidable from being hungry. I am not among the warm *hopers* yet ... My Master and I are nearly as much rusticated as you consider *yourself* to be: we shall open our eyes and ears and hope to bring both back full.

The Rebellion at the Hot Wells was a vexatious circumstance, did you conquer or compromise at last? The days of obedience are over; old Nash was the last who governed, like Elizabeth, by nicely blending love and fear together, and by so exalting the force of influence that I believe *they mistook* it for power of authority, and their subjects would not undeceive them.

Have you read all these new Romances? The Knights of the Swan for example, the terrific Lenore, and a Ballad of Alonzo the Brave? I think a great change has been made in taste of popular literature,—or rather, popular *reading*,—since we parted. People were tired of Master Jacky and Miss Jenny I suppose, and flew from insipid diet of water-gruel and chicken broth to Caviare and Cayenne, and Peppermint water for drink. The other extreme was wholesomer, and 'tis better be studying stories of little Eugenia tumbling off the plank, out from old simple Sir Hugh's arms, than follow the frightful Monk to his precipice. Send me word what your Mother says when you read these horrible tales to *her*. Sure we shall see Colonel Barry again sometime; it seems to me long since I enjoyed his conversation, his criticism is always ingenious, and commonly exact, and by perpetually filling and continually emptying his mind, it acquires peculiar clearness, like a cold bath where the stream runs *through* ...

To meet the expected French invasion, the Government raised a loan of eighteen millions, which was all subscribed before the close of the second day. The price of issue was 112, which at the time was considered low.

Beau Nash had been dead for more than thirty years when Mrs. Piozzi wrote. His reign at Bath, which made the reputation of that town as a fashionable resort, lasted for over half a century; but though his prestige suffered little diminution, he fell on evil days, and towards the close of his life lived on a pension voted by the grateful Corporation, who also accorded him a public funeral in the Abbey.

The Knights of the Swan, a romance of the Courts of Charlemagne, was translated from the French of Madame de Genlis, by the Rev. Mr. Beresford in 1796. In the same year appeared some half-dozen English versions of August Bürgher's *Lenore*; those by Stanley, Pye, and Spencer are reviewed in the *British Critic*. The poem of "Alonzo the Brave" occurs in the romance of *The Monk*, by Matthew Gregory Lewis, commonly known as "Monk" Lewis, and served as a basis for the play of *Alonzo and Imogene*.

STREATHAM PARK, *Wed.* 26 *April* 1797.

I have long promised myself the pleasure of sitting down to send dear Mrs. Pennington a long letter, but long things and little people ill agree, and I never could find time till to-night ...

Of charming Siddons every Paper can inform you. I really never saw her *so* charming; but she has a mind to exhibit age, avarice, and bitter disappointment instigating the most horrible crimes, for her Benefit, when Lillo's Fatal Curiosity will be acted. Miss Farren is bride-expectant, and everybody appears to applaud Lord Derby's choice. The Greatheeds are going to Germany next Summer on their son's account; Buonaparte is there already—on his own. His Banditti have committed dreadful ravages in the Venetian State, and among the rest of their exploits, have frighted Mr. Piozzi's good old Father out of what *remained* of life at fourscore years of age. Dreadful deeds I must confess, and horrible times in every sense of the word. But as we were speaking of individuals, I must add that Helen Williams is given up here by her most steady adherents. I am sorry ...

I have been told that Cecilia Mostyn and her husband are at Bath, but since she wrote Mr. Piozzi a letter with heavy charges against me in it, we have ceased corresponding. If you meet with her, tell me how she looks, and if there are hopes of a child; it would be the likeliest means of assuring her domestick happiness. My husband is more hurt than I am at her accusations of him for setting her horse to plough, and of her mother for wearing her clothes, and charging them as accountable to herself, besides a general charge of penurious niggardliness observed in her education, which one knows not how to contradict but by a general appeal to her own accomplishments, to her own high-bred horse,—most incapable of being set to plough. Mothers and daughters remind one of poor Lady Pitches, who dropt down dead in earnest conversation with one of her young ladies' sweethearts, or the father of one of them, the other day. I did not do so with Drummond, tho' very near it I do think in Milsom Street, Bath. So you see I am better off than some of my neighbours. The Three Thrales are at Brighthelmstone, refreshing from the fatigues of a gay winter by sea-bathing. Sophia hinted that they should like a country house near Town for summer residence, and Mr. Piozzi has requested them to *accept ours*, which he could have easily have let, I trust, for £500 o' year; but generously—as I think—preferred the future possessors as present inhabitants of old Streatham Park, which will not now look melancholy because we live in Wales. And when all debts are paid we *may* perhaps return; but my own heart being fixed on my own Country, I shall never more wish to leave it, except for a short visit to Bath and Hot Wells, a happiness I still keep in sight for a motive to go forward.

As this is a letter of all fact and no sentiment, I will tell you that poor old Flo died since we came hither, and lies buried under the tree that has a seat round it. Not only a dog the fewer as you used to say, but in his tomb lie my affections buried; I feel that I shall never fondle dogs again. Belle went to live with Mrs. Mostyn long ago, old Loup is dead, and Brown Fox struck by the palsy;—Phyllis alone remains, and is no more a parlour favourite. So fade away one's pleasures and one's plagues; but Mr. Piozzi still retains his gout, and so I dare say does Mr. Pennington.

My health is much as usual, and 'tis the speech to say that I look very well. Let me hear good from *you*; from individuals we may yet hope to find some, public calamities go on increasing in velocity and strength, like a wheel downhill. A stone or hillock may stop it for a moment, but to the bottom it must go at last.

The Lord Derby here referred to was Edward, the twelfth Earl, who created considerable sensation in fashionable society by marrying, within two months of his first wife's death, the popular actress Eliza Farren.

By this time Bonaparte had accomplished his invasion of Austria from Italy, and the Emperor, seeing his capital threatened by French troops, was compelled to cede Belgium and the left bank of the Rhine. On his return to Italy an insurrection in Venice gave him a pretext for replacing the ruling oligarchy by a republican form of government, while the territory of Genoa was transformed into the Ligurian Republic. It was no doubt the confusion consequent on these changes which hastened the end of Mr. Piozzi's aged father.

STREATHAM PARK, 1 *June* 1797.

MY DEAR MRS. PENNINGTON,—I feel your good-natured expressions very sensibly, and so does our poor dear Master; he is grown a sad invalid, always having the Gout, and crying out with pain. But the sick people *live*, whilst the well people *dye*, you know; so sings the sublime Mrs. Piozzi in her Journey to Italy, and so experience teaches.

Your Brother came here one morning last week, and brought some gentlemen with him to see the pictures in our Library. He is not altered in person, perhaps not in anything. I think character never changes; the Acorn becomes an Oak, which is very little like an Acorn to be sure, but never becomes an Ash: and if Mrs. Mostyn is, as Miss Lees say, the same Cecilia, I may add that that same Cecilia never cared a pin for me nor my husband,—and cares not now. I have not done caring for her however; somebody says she is at Bristol, tell me if 'tis for health or pleasure she goes there, and how she looks, ... and whether her husband is with her or no, and how they live together. I can trust your information and your friendship ...

I have been to the Exhibition. Lawrence is the Painter of the day; and to prove that he can shine equally in describing a *rising* and a fallen Angel, he has seated *Mrs. Siddons at Lucifer's feet*. There is a little thing of somebody's, I forget who, representing Cassandra predicting the fall of Troy, which few admire as I do, but it bears the true marks of genius and of taste. The next best thing I saw was a drawing of Pellegrini's, and no inelegant or worthless portrait of the Queen for la Duchesse de Wirtemberg.

Mr. Piozzi's state of health has hindered my waiting upon Lady Derby, but we met her in a Phaeton one day, and she stopt and spoke very prettily and kindly indeed. All the world seems pleased with *her* good fortune, and Lord Deerhurst's, to whom an old, distant relation has left no less than £80,000. It came at a nice moment to comfort them, for Lady Pitches, who I perhaps never told you, dropt down dead as she was stirring the fire, about six or eight weeks ago, and the breaking up of that house was a sad thing upon all her children …

When we go hence, Miss Thrales will enliven the spot, they are to succeed us in old Streatham Park. Whenever a loose half-crown lies in our pockets, it pays a mile's Postage towards the Hot Wells, you may assure yourself. Mrs. Siddons will see you first however, for Sally says her plan is to meet her husband and children at Mr. Whalley's, when she has been at two or three places alone. The little Baby Cecilia is the most extraordinary of all living babies; many have I seen, but none of such premature intellect. It is a wonderful infant, seriously …

George William Coventry, then Lord Deerhurst, afterwards seventh Earl of Coventry, married in 1783 Peggy, daughter of Sir Abraham Pitches, Knt., a neighbour of the Piozzis at Streatham. The Lady Pitches here mentioned was therefore his mother-in-law.

Lawrence's great picture of *Satan summoning his Legions*, exhibited this year, is now the property of the Royal Academy. Contemporary opinions differed widely as to its merits. His admirers pronounced it sublime, but Pasquin described it as "a mad Sugar Baker dancing naked in a conflagration of his own treacle." Fuseli branded it as "a damned thing certainly, but not the Devil"; but Lawrence turned the laugh against him by proving, from his sketch-book, that the idea of Satan was taken from Fuseli himself, while posing on a rock near Bristol. Nearly thirty years afterwards Mrs. Pennington saw it exhibited at Bristol, but it failed to impress her. "It is only monstrous in my mind," she writes, "it gives no idea of Lucifer son of the morning."

Mrs. Piozzi's interest in the "Baby Cecilia" is, to some extent, accounted for by the fact that she was her godchild; but her portrait by Lawrence, drawn this year, certainly suggests a remarkable and precocious infant. She was the only one of Mrs. Siddons' daughters to survive her mother.

Cecilia Siddons
By R.J. Lane after Sir Thos. Lawrence

BRYNBELLA, 10 *Jan.* 1798.

Before the long threatened Blister is put upon my right arm, I will use it once more to assure my very tenderly remembered friend that she has never been a moment *forgotten.* But I wrote so exceeding long a letter to Harriet Lee a great while ago, upon the odious subject of *self* and family affairs, and she answered me so coldly and drily, that I thought *nobody* would like a correspondence of that kind; and felt unable to try at others more entertaining. Desire to see our place and our acquaintance brought us hither for three months' amusement on the 10th of Oct.ʳ,—I mean of *August* last, and the first thing we heard was that Mrs. Mostyn had [returned home]—no doubt, said I, that she may be attended by Mr. Moore, who was so comfortable and attentive when she was in the same country confined by illness seven years ago, and dear Miss Weston offered to go with us to Lisbon upon Haygarth's saying her health required Continental air. We sent, and went, and were received *civilly*, and not *un*kindly; so I thought we were upon terms, as 'tis called, and a servant was daily dispatched to know how she went on. Miss Thrale, who was with her, always returned for answer y^t all was going as well as possible. So we went out as usual to visit our neighbours, and at one Lady's house heard *suddenly,* and *accidentally*, not only of her illness, but her extream danger. Mr. Moore was in the room where we heard it; she was attended by people from Chester and Ruthyn whom neither she nor I had ever seen, but tho' so oddly thrown aside, Mr. Moore, to calm my inquietude, ran away to learn particulars, and I sate in agony at bottom of Denbigh Town, while the footman galloped forward to request my admission. It was refused. Disastrous scenes … followed; and Mr. Piozzi shed tears at the account of her severe sufferings. In due time I was admitted, and warned to make my visit *short,* and so I did. The visit was coldly, but not *un*civilly, in course of 3 months, returned,—and all passed off quietly. The Litigation for recovery of money spent on Cecilia while she remained with us went on of course; and the other day almost, the Master made Report against Mr. Piozzi, who, he said, could *compel* no payment, but y^t Mostyn must be a *strange* man (was his expression,) to endeavour so at squeezing his wife's necessary expenses out of a Father-in-law's pocket; and added—"I can tell you, gentlemen, that had you come to me as John Wilmot, not as Master in Chancery, I should have decided very differently indeed." The Counsellors on *both sides* beg'd him *even yet* to stand between us and ye Chancellor, and act as *Referee*. "If your clients please," replied he, "so I will." Mr. Piozzi wrote to express *his consent*, but when we asked Miss Thrale concerning her brother and sister's determination, she said it was a subject that had *never employed their minds even for a moment.* I requested her to remind 'em of it, and at night came a Billet with "Proper Com^s; Mr. Mostyn will take time for deliberation." And so he does, for that's a fortnight ago.

So much for the superiority with which your poor mortified and severely humbled friend has been treated; now for domestic *comforts.* On the 20th of October my Master went to bed with a raging fit of

Gout in breast, side, back, and collar bone, but soon fixing in one heel and one toe, it *tore them open* into the most frightful *ulcers* I or poor Mr. Moore ever did behold. There has the Gout gnawed and bitten for 12 entire weeks, during which time has the truly wretched patient suffered torments inexpressible, and I believe rarely endured: his letters from Italy irritating even *that* anguish by narrations of what brothers, sisters, friends, etc. endure from the rapacity of these vile French,— false as they are cruel, and insolent as they are successful. His own particular Town has been the immediate scene of distress, and all these are completely and inevitably *ruined*. Let us thank God they have not yet been *called* hither, they will do us no harm *till they are called*. 'Tis our own traytrous Vipers I am afraid of,—not the French: and of the taxes I am not afraid, except as it gives a handle for abuse to those who object to everything proposed, and propose nothing themselves.

We are in a leaky ship, we must pump or drown, and those are the greatest enemies to general safety who cry, "Oh, don't fatigue the poor men at the pumps with such hard work; see how cruel you are to urge them thus beyond their strength!" Not at all cruel; let us pump now with spirit, and the vessel *may yet* get into harbour, but 'tis no moment this for general relaxation.

When I was going over the Alps with Mr. Piozzi, the sight of a dreadful precipice made me afraid, and I said I would walk: it was very late in a fine summer evening. "Sit still," cried my Master. " I cannot sit still," replied I, "*stop, stop!*" "You disturb the drivers, you will make them overturn us, pray sit still." No, I would *not* sit still, I would *walk*. "Well, walk away then," said Mr. Piozzi, "if you *will* walk; there are troops of wolves ranging the mountains now, I was told so at the last inn; they will find their prey out in an instant." Oh you can't imagine after that how still and quiet I sate in the carriage. Britannia, in a similar situation, must act like H.L.P. She must let the driver alone, and he will avoid the precipice; she must not expose herself to this troop of wolves.

But my rheumatic arm aches with even *thus* much writing, and my heart aches for my own mental, and my husband's corporeal sufferings; my loyal soul too aches for the general pressure upon our brave King and skilful Minister; but tho' Cecilia does refuse to repay the £1400 she owes Mr. Piozzi, I will *not* grudge the taxes nor will he try to evade them. We raised two puppies I meant to drown, that *they* likewise might be entered.

Mr. Mostyn's Mother, not *much* better treated by our haughty Cecy than I have been, has sold one of her estates for £10,000, and given the money to her *daughter*. She is gone to live at Bath, I'm told ...

When Mr. Piozzi recovers our meaning is to go to Streatham Park, and wind up our affairs, and come back hither, and live snug, and save money enough to pay our just debts, and *bury* us. If we *could* live 3 years more, we should have our income clear of every incumbrance, and I should publish another *Jest Book*: but both our healths are visibly declining. Love us, and pray for us, and write again soon ...

The friendly Master in Chancery was John Wilmot of Berkswell Hall, F.R.S., M.P. for Tiverton and for Coventry, who assumed the additional surname of Eardley in 1812, and was ancestor of the present Sir John Eardley-Wilmot, Bart.

The "skilful Minister" was of course Pitt, who had been driven into the war against his convictions, and though carrying it on to the best of his ability, lost no opportunity of working for peace. This, however, now appeared to be farther off than ever by reason of the general dread and hatred inspired by the projected French invasion.

STREATHAM PARK, 27 *Feb.* 1798.

My dear Mrs. Pennington will like to see a letter dated from old Streatham Park. We got there on Fryday, after a journey made pleasant by repeated visits on the way ... Two days were delightfully disposed of with the Recluses at Llangollen Cottage, where you would, I think, leave *your* heart a willing prisoner. They conquer and keep in their enchanted Castle all travellers passing that particular road—at least all those for whom they spread their nets. Harriet Lee escaped by some poetical chance, but they like her book. We were hungry for pleasure after so long a fast, and enjoyed everything with double delight.

My nerves are however terribly shaken, and I do believe we must and shall return home to Wales through Bath and Bristol,

Joseph George Holman
By W. Angus after Dodd, 1784

and embrace our dear Mrs. Pennington … But we will not talk of declining health. Individuals are now of less consequence than ever, while the Nation, the Continent, the World itself, seems in its last convulsions. Can too many efforts be made to keep these marauders out, these pests of Society, who have shaken such a fabric to its foundations? I think no efforts great enough, though our Ministers and Soldiers and Sailors do set a sublime example, sure; and we must all follow at distance.

We have advertised Streatham Park to be let for three years: if Miss Thrales would have accepted it rent-free, only paying the taxes, they should have had if for nothing; but some Grandee, who is reducing his establishment, shall pay us £500 o' year. I thought Mr. Piozzi most paternally kind in his offer of it to the young ladies, but they refused with disdain. They are used to *refuse good offers*, as people tell *me*.

Mr. Mostyn's Lady is of age now, and in possession of £40,000, but nothing can we get from *them* except bills of tradesmen, from whom Cecy took up articles without our knowledge or consent, whilst in our house; and those bills Mostyn meanly refuses to pay, because, as minor's debts, the people cannot arrest him. So runs the world, need one wonder if God Almighty is tired of it? I am nearly tired of it myself.

The weather however is charming. You mistake in fancying Brynbella a cold spot. The Gardener brought me in two pots of the finest Carnations I ever saw in my life upon my birthday, 27 Jan., this year; and we have no hothouse. The side of our hill is particularly warm, quite a *côte-rotie* … Surrey looks marvellous dull and dreary compared to the brilliant scenery from parlours and bed-chamber windows in Wales. But the bustle here amuses me, and I like the sight of London, looking like an Ant-hill suddenly stirred with a stick, well enough.

I have not seen dear Siddons yet, but rejoice sincerely in what I hear of her happiness. Being a lucky darling of Fortune, we got her to buy us a Lottery Ticket this year, and chuse us the number. *Joy will come well in such a needful time*,[1] as Juliet says. And apropos to Juliet, Miss Hamilton seems perfectly happy with her Romeo. Nothing was ever so kind as her parents have been. They gave her away, and they strip themselves to furnish her house, and they now add to their excessive fondness for *her*, their adoration of Mr. Holman, who, I really believe, will behave most sweetly and honourably to all …

A curious account of discoveries made in the interior parts of Africa, where large Cities and Civilised Nations are now supposed to have long resided, attracts *my* attention forcibly; and much chat will we have together when we meet upon these subjects and a thousand more …

The celebrated ladies of Llangollen were Lady Eleanor Butler, sister of John, seventeenth Earl of Ormonde, who had retired from society about twenty years previously with her friend Sarah, daughter of

Chambre Brabazon Ponsonby, a cousin of the Earl of Bessborough. They took a cottage at Plasnewydd in the Vale of Llangollen, where they lived for half a century, and were visited by most of the celebrities of the time. About two years before this date Anna Seward wrote her poem of "Llangollen Vale" in their honour. Lady Eleanor died in 1829 and her friend in 1831.

Joseph George Holman, a member of Queen's College, Oxford, though he never took a degree, made his début on the stage in 1784 at Covent Garden, where he acted till 1800. His wife, so frequently referred to in the letters, was Jane, daughter of the Rev. the Hon. Frederick Hamilton, a scion of the Duke of Hamilton's family.

In 1795 Mungo Park started from Gambia to explore the course of the Niger, and subsequently visited the States on the southern edge of the Great Sahara, returning, via America, in 1797. An account of his expedition was drawn up for the African Association in 1798, which is probably what Mrs. Piozzi had seen, but his own detailed account was not finished till 1799.

STREATHAM PARK, *Tuesday,* 27 *Mar.* 1798.
My dearest Mrs. Pennington is too good a woman to wish me to make promises I cannot keep, and too kind a friend not to be sorry that I have no certainty of one day after another. *If* we let this house as we hope to do, we may possibly, and I hope we shall be able to spend next Winter or Spring at Bath, Bristol, and its environs; *perhaps* we shall be able to coax you away with us to pretty Brinbella, where our final and favourite residence seems to be fixed. But everything is so uncertain. England, Europe, the whole World seems so convulsed, and so incapable of judging its own destiny for 3 or 4 years to come, that I absolutely consider it as presumption next to madness to promise anything about coming here or going there. We must all do what suits us at the time I fancy.

Dear Mr. Whalley above all people verifies the prophecy that "a man shall seek to go into a city, and shall not be able." He himself proposed setting out for Ireland as this very day, in company of Sir Walter James; but they will neither of them go *now,* I trust, when whole families are flocking *from* thence to Wales, etc. for refuge. We dined in his and

Mrs. Whalley's company at Mrs. Siddons's last week, and went with them at night to the Eidouranion, a pretty Astronomical Show. Maria dined in the room, and looked (to me) as usual, yet everybody says she is ill, and in fact she was bled that very evening, while we were at the Lecture. Shutting a young half-consumptive girl up in *one unchanged air* for 3 or 4 months, would make any of them ill, and ill humoured too, I should think. But 'tis *the new way* to make them breathe their own infected breath over and over again now, in defiance of old books, old experience, and good old common sense. Ah, my dear friend, there are many *new ways*,—and a dreadful place do they lead to. You should read Robinson's book, and I should translate and abridge Barruel's, if I did my duty to the Public, but I really have not time. My own long, heavy work, in which I am engaged, takes every moment that can be spared from family concerns. Mr. and Mrs. Mostyn however give me *no* trouble, I have neither seen nor heard anything from them these many months …

I wonder if the pretty Misses go in *self* coloured drawers and stockings, and Brutus Heads with you as they do here. It is a horrible sight: but no one in this part of the world is considered as ridiculous, except the Bishops and Lords who commanded the Opera Dancers to put their clothes on again, or leave the Country. *My* fair Daughters have made a league with the House of Siddons, which I feel rather cooler to me than usual. Never mind! Those who know the World wonder at nothing: those who *do not*, must learn the World, or leave it. My ever kind Mrs. Pennington is of the Old School still, and remembers the precept given by old Father Homer 3 or 4000 years ago, saying that

> A gen'rous friendship no cold medium knows,
> Burns with one love, with one resentment glows;
> The same our views, our int'rests still should be,
> My friend must *hate* the man that injures *me*.

But we will talk of public calamity, if you please, it swallows, or ought to swallow up private concerns completely. I wish you to read the True Briton of March 8. There is a letter from Venice in it which *we know but too well to be genuine.* I translated and printed it myself, that none might remain ignorant of the manner in which France treats those who never offended her. What are *we* to expect from French generosity? Let us, like the Swiss, sell our lives as dear as we can. They oppose, and are cut to pieces. Italy complies, is pillaged and undone; like what Pope says of the famous Duchess of Marlborough,

> Who breaks with *her* provokes revenge from Hell,
> But he's a bolder man who dares be well.

I wish they would put their armament in motion; 'tis possible that God Almighty may permit us to destroy it, and then the Continent may be delivered from y[s] dreadful scourge. Their Italian and Dutch subjects would soon rebel, and they would be driven about finely. Distress at home would follow ill success abroad, and they would end like one of their own air-balloons, set on fire, and blazing, and burning out, and falling to ground. *This is our only chance—the only hope* of yours ever affect[ly]   H.L.P.

The exodus from Ireland was due to the apprehended rising of the United Irishmen, which was then preparing. The principal conspirators had just been arrested when Mrs. Piozzi wrote, and martial law was proclaimed shortly afterwards.

Mrs. Piozzi's apprehensions about Maria Siddons proved but too well founded. A change of treatment was tried soon afterwards, and she was sent to Clifton in June, in the hope that a change of air and a course of "the Waters" might benefit her complaint. For a time she obtained relief, and as her mother was unable to be with her, Mrs. Pennington undertook the charge. But the disease had progressed too far, and four months later she died, tended to the end by her sister Sally and Mrs. Pennington.

John Robinson, secretary to the Royal Society of Edinburgh, and Professor of Natural Philosophy in the University, was an important contributor to the third edition of the *Encyclopædia Britannica*. The work alluded to was published in 1797 under the title of "Proofs of a Conspiracy against all the Religions and Governments of Europe, carried on in the secret meetings of Freemasons, Illuminati, and Reading Societies, collected from good Authorities." The book, which contemporary critics describe as "a hasty production," was chiefly concerned with French and German societies.

The Abbé Barruel, Almoner to the Princess of Conti, had written in 1794 a history of the clergy during the French Revolution. In 1797 he published his *Mémoires pour servir à l'Histoire du Jacobinisme*, designed to show that the Revolution was the work of Voltaire and his friends, and was aimed primarily at religion, and only secondarily at the Government. An English edition, of which Mrs. Piozzi does not seem to have heard, appeared about the same time.

The brothers Montgolfier had discovered the principle of the fire balloon in 1783, and in the same year the brothers Robert (also Frenchmen) inflated a balloon with hydrogen gas. What Mrs. Piozzi no doubt had in her mind was the tragic fate of Pilâtre de Rozier (the first human being to entrust himself to the air), who in 1785 attempted to combine the two systems, with disastrous results. The balloon caught fire, and he and his companion lost their lives.

Having humbled Austria, Bonaparte had turned his attention to England. An army was raised and marched to the Channel, to await a convenient moment for crossing, when sufficient transport had been collected. But larger schemes of an Eastern campaign were now occupying his mind, and the project of invasion was not vigorously pushed forward. Indeed it may have been designed rather to draw off attention from the preparations for his Egyptian expedition.

STREATHAM PARK, *last Sunday in April* 1798.

Well, dearest Mrs. Pennington! we have been to London since I had your last kind letter. And what did we see in London? Why we saw some pictures, the spoil of Italy and Flanders, which the French sell to those who bid highest;—and we saw charming Siddons, the boast of our own Country, more admirable than ever in this new play of the Stranger. *She* is not cold to her old friends, Heaven knows, yet there *is an iciness in the house* that I cannot describe. One reason may be that as everybody takes sides now, and many go there that are not on *your side and mine*, it *must* be as it is; and I always meet Mr.

Twiss there, a fierce man who married her sister, with a brown Brutus Head,—I feel afraid of all the men that wear it.

Have you seen my Three Warnings made political use of in a new Pamphlet? It will soon be at Bristol, no doubt, as it seems a favourite with the Public.

Mr. Whalley will soon leave these busy scenes for his Cottage, and we shall soon get *home to Brynbella*, I hope. My poor Master is too lame to *march* in the King's service, but he is a good loyalist, and a better *hoper* than his wife, though I really do think things are mending. People seem *aw'd* by the *times*, without being *afraid* of the *French*: and that is exactly the spirit I would have them show. Our sailors and soldiers are true to the cause, and an armed nation (tho' small,) is irresistible. If it should please God that the descent should be made now, and fail, England would be happier, and I fear, prouder than ever; for there is no other place left for France to conquer, and Lord Bridport promises to defend us bravely.

Mr. and Mrs. Mostyn were invited to meet us for a short dinner at Miss Thrale's the day we were *all* engaged to dear Siddons's Benefit. So we curtsied, and smiled, and drank each others good health, and ran to our *separate Boxes* at the Theatre, and 'scaped all explanations; and that did nicely. Lady Derby is so altered you would not know her,—grown so immensely *fat,* and *white,* and her hair changed,—but not her sweet character and pleasing manners, which remain still superiorly lovely. Mrs. Holman is grown actually *handsome*, and seems happiest of human beings; so here are *Braave Alteraations,* as the Fool said to Mr. Whalley. Mr. Holman is a very pleasing, and very unaffectedly agreeable man … Your old acquaintance Mr. Rogers remains single yet …

Helen Williams's last Book is beautiful, but she is a wicked little Democrate, and I'm told, lives publickly with Mr. Stone, whose wife is still alive. Nobody tells me anything of Dr. Moore, but Cumberland keeps on writing plays and romances; and I'm in the middle of a *big* book, Heav'n send it may not for y^t reason be a *dull* one; but I will be a good hoper myself. Harriet Lee never sent me the Heirship of Roselva,—tell her I say so. When come out the next Canterbury Tales? People surprize me by turning their heads so to fancy compositions—I never could do it.

Adieu! We have let this place for £550 per annum for 3 years; and if we beat the French away, and things begin to *right again*, as the Seaman's phrase is, we will come to Bath and Bristol the very first months of the next New Year …

The Stranger was a spectacular drama adapted from a tragedy by Kotzebue, dealing with the Spaniards and Indians in America, which had a great vogue in England owing to its patriotic sentiments, which were interpreted as bearing on current history. No less than four English translations, one by "Monk" Lewis, appeared in the course of this year. Sheridan's adaptation was not published till 1799.

Francis Twiss, son of an English merchant in Holland, married in 1786 Frances (Fanny), second daughter of Roger Kemble, and sister of Mrs. Siddons, who then retired from the stage and, assisted by her husband, kept a girls' school at Bath. She is described after her marriage as being "big as a house"; while her husband, who took "absolute clouds of snuff," was thin, pale, and stooping, but very dogmatic. He compiled in 1805 the earliest concordance to Shakespeare.

The political version of Mrs. Piozzi's poem was entitled "Three Warnings to John Bull before he dies, by an old Acquaintance of the Public," wherein John is exhorted to show "a unanimous spirit in assisting Government, a just and manly regard for our Established Religion, and an immediate amendment of Manners." The authorship does not seem to have been disclosed.

Helen Williams' latest work was "A Tour in Switzerland, or a view of the present state of the Governments and Manners of those Cantons, with Comparative Sketches of the present state of Paris." The tour was taken in company with Stone, who had been sent thither on a mission by the French Government.

In *The Mysterious Marriage, or the Heirship of Rosalva*, Harriet Lee introduced what she claimed as an original feature, viz, a female ghost; but this does not help the plot, which the *British Critic* dismisses as "ordinary," while the characters, whether angelical or diabolical, were but commonplace, and the verses were the worst part of the performance. The *Critic* allowed, however, that *The Canterbury Tales for* 1797, published this year, showed much ingenuity and fancy, and expressed a hope for more.

Cumberland's five-act play, *False Impressions*, appeared in 1797 at Covent Garden, and had a moderate success. The *British Critic* sums it up as "only a sketch, but a sketch by a master, which might have been worked up into something much better."

Mrs. Piozzi herself had evidently now embarked on *Retrospection*, her most ambitious, and probably her least successful work, which was not completed till 1801.

SHREWSBURY, *Thursday, rejoycing day*, 1798.

MY VERY DEAR FRIEND,—Your sweet cordial letter should have had earlier thanks, tho' warmer I possess not, but I really dreaded having it to say we could not come; so many vexations and combinations happen'd which often and often did I think would hinder us. We are however so *far* on our road ... My Master's heel is very poorly, but we shall come *hopping*; and Mr. Pennington is most excessively kind in giving us so generous an invitation. You shall do whatever you please with us for one whole week, and then we will get, if possible into a nice house at Bath, where you shall return the visit *for a month*.

And now, that things may look, may *really* look as they *used* to do, Allen is returned to my Service ... We have neither of us been well settled or happy since we parted, so we are come together again. The Maid who succeeded Allen in my place was a *Lady* of good family and agreeable accomplishments; but I believe neither she liked *me* much, nor I *her*. To my much amazement and distraction, three days before we left home, a fortnight ago, the *Lady* married our *Welsh Gardener* ... This moment however I have the comfort of seeing myself once more with my old Attendant, who, after living seven years in *my* house, hated every other ... She will rejoice to see *Dear Miss Weston* again, but whose joy can be like mine? 'tis seven years now since I was in Somersetshire, and six years since we embraced our dear Sophia. May God give us a happy meeting! but my poor Master is as lame as a tree ...

I will write a very long letter to dear Mrs. Pennington this 1st of August 1798, in defiance of Miss Owen, who says she came hither for my company, and will lose none of it. She must lose some however, for I will not part with old Friends for want of pen and ink conversation. If it *should* please God that we might meet this next year, we would have much chat,—and I will not despair … I do *think* we shall meet—and talk over the false and fading hopes which we see people entertain of Europe's peaceful re-establishment after all these commotions …

Of *my* heavy work I can give a better account by word than letter; you shall see it if we come to the West. But with regard to translating Barruel, my heart has wished to do it twenty times, only that some one has always stept in before me somehow; and rendered my trouble unnecessary.

You have Robinson's book, no doubt, and the strange coincidence between that and the French one must necessarily convince the whole world of those dreadful truths which they both assert. People should stand upon their guard at such times of enormous wickedness. Have you read Mr. Godwin's life of his deceased Lady? There's a *morality* worthy the new lights of philosophical religion: *pray* read it.

Helen Williams's Book is not without its danger. She infuses *her* venom in such sweetness of style, and in such moderate quantities; I think no corruption has a better chance to spread.

The two Emilys are delightful. Ever on the verge of impossibility, Sophia's charming pen leads one to read on, and to persuade oneself for a moment, from line to line, that a woman made completely ugly should be able to inspire the tenderest passion, and have power beside to keep a man from enjoyment of all those pleasures his rank, and that of their children, entitles him to. This *may be so*, but Lothayre's story of the skeleton is nearer to my *credence*. A wonder for *ten minutes* one's heart revolts not from, be it ever so contrary to nature and experience, a wonder for *ten years*—is a wonder indeed. The denouement however is exquisitely managed, and that return to ye subject, as Musicians call it, which marks all the last pages, bringing back the first to your remembrance, appears to me a chef d'œuvre of art and skill. 'Tis a very beautiful book.

I think Miss Seward never writes now. The Recluse Ladies at Llangollen, who pick up every rarity in literature, are much her admirers. Are *you* in correspondence with her now?

Here is my paper exhausted, and not a word of politics. But what does it signify? There are but two ways. Either you must creep to the French, as other nations do, or you must spend all your money to oppose them. I should not hesitate for *myself*; I had rather be taxed till I was forced to dig Potatoes and boil them, than I would see the Abbé Sieyes in *our* King's Drawing Room: and I hope His Majesty would rather be killed fighting at the head of his true subjects against these Atheists, than receive them into his confidence who are unworthy to stand in his sight. *He* alone, except the King of Naples, refused to be an Illuminè. You shall see *they* will last longest …

The correspondence with Anna Seward had ceased in 1791 or 1792, when the "Swan" felt it her duty to write to Mrs. Pennington, as she tells Mrs. Powys, "with an ingenuousness on my part which I thought necessary to her welfare but which her spirit was too high to brook." The breach in their friendship was not healed till 1804.

William Godwin, author of *An Inquiry concerning Political Justice*, made the acquaintance of Mary Wollstonecraft, after she had been deserted by Imlay, in 1796, and in March 1797 they were married, though the ceremony was incompatible with the opinions they both professed. She died in September the same year, shortly after the birth of their only child Mary, the second wife of Percy Bysshe Shelley. *The Memoirs of the Author of The Vindication of the Rights of Woman* were published by her husband in 1798, as were also her own posthumous works. He afterwards proposed to Harriet Lee, but was rejected.

Emanuel Joseph, Comte Sieyes, Canon of Treguier, having adopted the principles of the Revolution, became Deputy for Paris, assisted to form the National Assembly, and was one of those who voted for the King's death. He declined a seat on the Directory in 1797, but accepted it two years later, and along with Bonaparte plotted the Revolution of Brumaire.

BRYNBELLA, *Fryday* 24 *Sep.* 1798.

My dear Mrs. Pennington was very kind in thinking of old friends, when so much present matter, and so important too, was filling up both mind and time. May all end for the best!

I can no more guess where Mrs. Siddons actually is than where Buonaparte is. The Papers announce her at Drury Lane, acting for Palmer's family. A letter from a friend at Brighthelmstone tells how she is playing Mrs. Beverley for the amusement of the Prince of Wales, Lady Jersey, Lady Deerhurst, and Lady Lade; and how she lives there in a house I often inhabited before I had the pleasure of knowing *her*. What you say induces me to believe her at the Hot Wells. Wherever *she* is, there is the best assemblage of beauty, talents, and discretion that ever graced a single female character. She will have much to suffer I'm afraid, but she will suffer with gentleness and submission, propriety and patience. *You*, my dear Friend, will have your consciousness of well-doing to support you thro' the trying scene: but my heart bleeds for you, and my best comfort lies in the hope that we shall meet soon after Christmas …

Meanwhile 'tis nearly miraculous that 400 sail should thus have *slipt unperceived* away from Admiral Nelson and his fleet of *observation*. The Bishop of S. Asaph says that while we are gazing after them in the Levant, tidings will arrive that they are on the coast of Ireland. He may be right for aught I know; things happen so very wide of all expectation. You remember the meeting at Tyre, where he who first saw the rising sun was to be saluted King. All stared towards the East, of course, except one man, and he, with his back to the rest, first discerned the rays shooting upward against a high tower, in the contrary and opposite direction. We will salute our Bishop wisest of conjecturers if Buonaparte attempts the Sister Kingdom; but I shall not account the Invaders wise in delaying their invasion so long. They would *now* give Lord Cornwallis a complete triumph, and give us an opportunity of showing the world that France makes no impression upon King George the 3rd's dominions.

Did you read Mr. Siddons's incomparable Ballad upon the Great Nation? 'Tis really excellent in its kind …

If you are all *tolerably* tranquil at Dowry Square, do ask what became of an agreeable Mr. Crampton, in whose company I supped last

Sophia Lee
By Ridley after Sir Thos. Lawrence, 1809

Spring in Great Marlbro' Street, who said he was going thither, and gave me the first idea how matters really stood. I concluded him a Lover of one of the young Ladies. Pray present me to them *both*, if with you, and assure them of my sincerest wishes and *prayers*, (*they* are old-fashioned things;) and do, my dear Mrs. Pennington, keep up your own spirits, if possible, for your Mother and your Husband's sake, and a little for the sake of your ever faithful

H.L. Piozzi.

It is clear that Mrs. Pennington had informed Mrs. Piozzi of the grave Condition of Maria Siddons, and had let her see something of the anxiety she was suffering; but regarding the principal cause of this anxiety, and the tragedy which was being enacted before her eyes, she evidently maintained a strict silence to her most intimate friend—or some mention must have been made in the course of the correspondence of Thomas Lawrence. That artistic but erratic genius, after having been for some time the accepted lover of Sally Siddons, suddenly transferred his affections to Maria, not long before her fatal illness, and what is most remarkable, obtained the consent of all parties concerned. But while Maria was at Clifton he began to realise that he had made a mistake—that his heart was Sally's after all, and the fear that Maria might exact a death-bed promise from Sally (as indeed actually happened) that she would never marry him, for the time being almost overturned his reason. His agitated letters, and still more agitating interviews, did much to add to Mrs. Pennington's anxieties during this trying period. The whole tragedy, as revealed in the letters of the persons most nearly concerned, has been told by the present editor in *An Artist's Love Story*.

John Palmer, a son of the doorkeeper at Drury Lane, was an actor of some repute. His sudden death in August 1797 while acting at Liverpool in *The Stranger*, aroused much sympathy for his family, and benefits were arranged for them at Liverpool, the Haymarket, and Drury Lane, at the latter of which Mrs. Siddons seems to have assisted. Sally's letters show that Maria's condition had caused her to abandon her professional engagements and hasten to her daughter's bedside.

The Lady Lade who is included among the Prince's entourage was Thrale's sister, who in the crisis of his affairs, as mentioned in the Introduction, had lent him £5000 to help him to tide over his difficulties. Fanny Burney describes her as having been "very handsome, but now I think getting quite ugly, at least she has the sort of face I like not."

The explanation of the French fleet's escape from Nelson's watchful eye is that it went to the north of Candia, while he took the more direct course to the south of the island, and so arrived first at Alexandria, which he left in pursuit of the French only two days before they arrived.

Lewis Bagot, Bishop of St. Asaph, more successful as a divine than as a prophet, was one of the two whom Cowper (in the *Tirocinium*) excepts from his scathing condemnation of the episcopal bench.

For Providence, that seems concerned t' exempt
The hallowed bench from absolute contempt,
In spite of all the wrigglers into place
Still keeps a seat or two for worth and grace;
And therefore 'tis that, though the sight be rare,
We sometimes see a Lowth or Bagot there.

BRYNBELLA, *Oct.* 4, 1798.

Your letter, dearest Mrs. Pennington, came three days before the public prints announced the fatal tydings. I can give no consolation certainly; that which I receive is from the consciousness of the charming parent's perfect resignation to his almighty *will* who disposes everything for the best; who *snatches* Palmer from the stage of life, by means which most *impress* mankind, in order y^t general compassion may be excited for his offspring, which, had he dyed in any other manner, would have been wholly forgotten by the world, although not a whit less distressed than now. That Pow'r which in a short time after *steals* by slow degrees the long-sinking life of Maria Siddons from her friends, by means best calculated to fatigue their feelings, and blunt that acute grief which is ever caused by the sufferings of a youthful patient. I am quite confident that if Admiral Nelson by his prodigious victory could purchase peace for Europe, he might in four years time die in his own house, and not be *half as much regretted* as is the lovely object of your late attention. Every letter I receive from every creature is filled with her praise, and breathes an unfeigned sorrow for her loss. Virtue well tried through many a refining fire, Learning lost to the world she illuminated, and Courage taken from the Island protected by her arms, excites not as much sorrow as Maria Siddons, represented to every imagination as sweet, and gentle, and soothing; as *young* in short, for in youth lies every charm.

When will mankind have done hoping and expecting from a generation not yet mature that excellence which cannot be found among our own contemporaries: at least not found but with drawbacks so heavy the character can hardly carry them? Never. When

Harriet Lee says no state is so enviable as that of a Grandmother, she means that life will not last long enough to disappoint expectation of happiness to the object of attention. But poor Mrs. Hamilton can tell another tale. She is grandmother to a Lady whose husband is a frolicker; rides round his own Billiard Table on his own poney, and performs a thousand feats that may delight *his own* grandmother for aught I know, (if he has one,) but frightens his wife's ancestress out of her wits.

Well! we shall meet some time I do think, and talk all matters over, merry and sad. In the mean time tell dear Mrs. Siddons how truly I love and pity her, and accept my venerating regard for that prodigious friendship *you* have evinced, thro' the scenes I can easily imagine ...

The reference to Nelson's "prodigious victory" shows that the news of the battle of the Nile, fought on 1st August, must have penetrated to Wales when Mrs. Piozzi wrote, though Nelson's despatch dated 3rd August was not published in the *London Gazette* till 3rd October.

The next letter was doubtless a reply to one giving a more detailed account of Maria's last moments, such as Mrs. Pennington sent to several of her correspondents, and in which she dwelt at some length on the courage and resignation shown by Maria in the last days of her life.

BRYNBELLA, 22 *Oct.* 1798.

I was exceedingly glad, dearest Mrs. Pennington, when I heard *you* were released. Such fatigues fall very heavy on such feelings, but the consciousness of what you condemned yourself to suffer for the sake of a friend will act as a cordial through your whole life,—a long one, I hope and pray,—and at its end, will return warm and consolatory to your own tender heart.

Meanwhile I would not wish your indulgence of a fancy which, if not erroneous, is at least liable to gross error: and my dear *Sophia* should be *wise*, and prefer dry wisdom to brilliant imagination. There is no real inference to be drawn from peoples' behaviour in their last moments to the character they would sustain in life, was their recovery permitted. No inference at all. The great Duke of Marlborough was known to show pusillanimity at the parting hour, and people are not yet weary of saying how Samuel Johnson was afraid of death. I read in the Medical Transactions one day the account of a Mr. Bellamy, Mercer in Covent Garden, his extraordinary illness, and composed resignation, which would have done honour to a Saint, a Scholar, or a Hero. Yet was dear Mr. Bellamy quite a common man, *like the next man*, and had he recovered, would undoubtedly have returned to the same undistinguished mediocrity in which he had already lived 30 years. But his complaint itself tended by some means to remove the cloud from that celestial spark which *dwells in all*; whilst those disorders of which the Warrior and the Man of Knowledge died contributed to keep that spark from being seen. Had Heaven restor'd all three to pristine vigour, *they* would once more have shone as soldiers and instructors,—men who protect and benefit their species,—*the other* would once more have stood behind a counter and sold silks by the yard. We will not rate the dignity even of *Bodies*, much less of *Souls*, by the figure they make at their departure: nothing *goes out*, as we call it, more brightly than a fire of deal-shavings.

Now let me request you my kind, generous friend, not to suppose me deficient in concern, either for lost Maria, or her surviving admirers. The Father's sensation of loss will not abate so readily as that of our transcendant and now doubly-dear Mrs. Siddons. *She* must return to the duties and cares of life, and in them, as in her own pure heart, will find a med'cine for her grief. But *his* expectations from a daughter's beauty, *his* purposed pride in those charms which 'tis now clear that she posess'd, are blasted in the most incurable manner. I am sorry for Mr. Siddons from my very soul.

Let us now take some leisure to rejoyce in the triumphs of our own Country, and the just punishment of those perfidious enemies who, having sown the seeds of misery in every Nation, will soon see all united against them, and owing their internal safety to their outward exertions for destroying them; like poyson'd Princes in a Tragedy, who just live long enough to make the Tyrant fall, and end the Drama by a proper catastrophe. The moment we have crushed these odious French, and obtained a general peace, in that moment will the venom they have disseminated begin its work, and set a Revolution going in every kingdom. But I do think that they will be destroyed first ...

I cried over your charming letter for an hour, notwithstanding I answer it so coldly, but Truth is always *cold,* from being *naked* perhaps, and what I have said is the *truest,* though not the *prettiest* thing you have heard upon the melancholy subject ...

BRYNBELLA, *Sunday 11th Nov.* 1798.

MY DEAREST MRS. PENNINGTON,—I have got your sweet letter, and do now verily and indeed hope, trust, and believe that I shall embrace the kind writer on, or very nearly about the 6th day of December next. There is our plan *told clear*, as my Master says, and bids me *scrivere una Lettera*, (don't you remember?) and tell our true friend that we are coming.

Thus 'tis. I am appointed Queen of our County Assembly, with Lord Kirkwall who is King Consort. We take it by Quarters here, and *our* Quarter expires next Thursday sennight—the full moon,— 'tis our third and last night, and I shall come home at five in the morning,—change my dress and drink my Coffee, and set out for the famous Cottage of Llangollen Vale, where dwell the fair and noble Recluses of whom you have heard so much, Lady Eleanor Butler, and Miss Ponsonby ... Well! we spend two days with them, and then away to dear Miss Owen at Shrewsbury ... On the 3rd therefore we start from her to you, from Shrewsbury to Bristol, and I suppose Wednesday or Thursday will see our meeting, hitherto deferred for six long years. We must stay a week, no more, for I really want Bath Waters ... I hope you will come to Bath, and that sweet Siddons will meet us there; her husband gives me hopes of it, and that will be *too much* felicity: to see her where I saw her *first* with admiration, and now to see her again, with beauty unimpaired, talents improved; see her in your company at Bath, and call her Friend!!! Oh, then I *should* say the tide was changed, of private as of public affairs ...

I can talk of nothing else, so will not try.
   Call up the Chaises then, make no delay,
   Accessible is none but *Bristol Way* ...

1. "And joy comes well in such a needy time."—*Romeo and Juliet*, III. v. 106.

CHAPTER V

A NEW CENTURY

THE Piozzis were at Bath on Christmas Day, when she invites Mrs. Pennington to their lodgings for the New Year. The date of the next letter indicates that their visit lasted about four months.

BRYNBELLA, *Sunday, Mar.* 10, 1799.

First of friends in every sense of the word, dear and kind Mrs. Pennington! what a charming letter have you written me! and how consoling it was to receive such a compensation—although a small one—for the converse I have so great reason to regret.

Our journey was excellent, and mended on us ev'ry Stage, till the sun lighted up our lovely Vale of Clwydd, and never seen before ascending the last hill, has smiled upon us ever since.

I shall not begin work till after Easter, we have enough to employ us now in surveying our sweet place, and recounting the *Braave alteraations,* as the Fool said to Mr. Whalley …

Are not you sorry for the poor tricked and betrayed, but ever courageous Neapolitans; of which those were happiest who left their dead bodies in the street, defending their lovely city to the last? Vesuvius seems to have half a mind to save further disgrace on that country, and will perhaps swallow it up, *from* the French, or *with* the French; who knows?

Well! I got dear Dr. Randolph's blessing, and a kind squeeze by the hand of his amiable Lady, before we left Bath: and then I resolved to mind my own business, and let the Public think of its own affairs.

They mingle so with mine however, that I cannot separate them, as Siddons does. Her little girl seemed bent upon shewing me, that day we dined at Miss Lee's, and made our Partenza, how well you were versed in the knowledge of her family character. She is sure enough no common child, no healthy child, and no good-humoured child. If she remains at Belvedere House, she will not long be a spoiled child; for those Ladies *have the way*, and will make her a charming creature. *We parents* meantime seldom think our nestlings can be improved. It is therefore *very seldom*, (never I think,) that we feel obliged to those who bring our Babies into what the world calls good order. I should think it happiness for Cecilia to remain where she is, and felicity for Miss Lees to return her safe home again in April …

Mrs. Mostyn sent the old Nurse I told you of, over here in a Post Chaise, to see Brynbella while we were away. "What a place!" exclaimed she, "and what fools the builders to plan a thing it is impossible they should live to finish. But they have an heir now, come from Italy I find." This is the only domestic news which could interest *you*; and I know Mr. Pennington is kind enough to care about whatever concerns us and our little boy …

As far back as October 1798 King Ferdinand of Naples had raised an army to act under the Austrian General Mack, for the expulsion of the French. Nelson's arrival in December encouraged him to make an expedition against Rome which was, for the moment, successful; but in a short time the French retook it, and marched on Naples, which they occupied in January, after sixty-four hours street fighting with the Lazzaroni, the regular troops being away. The King took refuge on Nelson's ship and escaped to Palermo, General Mack and the army had to surrender, and the territory became, for a short time, the Parthenopean Republic.

The Rev. Francis Randolph, D.D., Prebendary of Bristol, and afterwards Vicar of Banwell, was a preacher of some note, and for some time acted as chaplain and tutor in English to the Duchess of Kent, at the little Court of Amorbach, shortly before the birth of the Princess Victoria.

One result of the disturbances in Italy was the bringing over to England and adoption of a son of Mr. Piozzi's brother Gianbatista, merchant of Brescia, born in 1783, and christened John Salusbury. He assumed the additional surname of Salusbury in 1813, and was knighted while High Sheriff of Denbigh a few years later. On his marriage Mrs. Piozzi gave him Brynbella and her Welsh estate, a proceeding which probably completed the estrangement of her daughters, though they had been well provided for by their father's will, and Miss Thrale had declined the offer of it as a dowry for herself.

BRYNBELLA, 5 *Apr.* 1799.

My dear Mrs. Pennington's letters are always delightful, and the little gleam of sunshine given by the Archduke's victory strikes across the middle of your last so prettily So like the darling brightness that illuminates our valley just now, with gloom and gathering storm all round it ...

You see [Mrs. Jackson's] conjectures about the Play were right after all. Mrs. Radcliffe owns herself Author, as Susan Thrale writes me word, and Jane de Montfort will come out immediately. She says not a syllable of Mr. Whalley's performance. Lord bless me, my dear! His unfortunate niece, cydevant Fanny Sage, sent to me yesterday for £20; and said she was *detain'd,* (for debt I trow,) at our poor, petty town of St. Asaph, two miles off. A tall, ill-looking man on horseback brought the letter, but will not, I hope, revenge my refusal of his Lady's request, when Dumouriez shall have set all the wild Irish at full liberty. I was half afraid, sure enough, yet little disposed to give what would make 40 honest cottagers happy, to a gay lass whom I never liked in her *best days*, and who never had any claims on my *friendship,* which she now talks so loudly of.

Well! and your little favourite John Salusbury! Susanna Thrale has been to Streatham on purpose, I fancy, to gratify hers and her family's curiosity. So she saw a little boy with my *name*, and my husband's *face*; and I know not which was the greatest recommendation of the *two*—to her ...

With regard to public affairs, our domestic traytors terrify me most; but if French valour should, by this late victory, get into discredit abroad, perhaps it would not be so much the *Ton* to imitate their proceedings here at home, and we should remember Hannah More's prediction of the *Crane-neck-turn*. If they *can* be made to *run* they will find no place that will receive them I believe. All honest men, and women too, are their natural enemies: and a Grison girl said to a gentleman I know something of—"Why, dear Sir, what should we sit still for, like figures made of Papier-machée, till our houses are burned down, our parents mangled and our free will violated? Better go out with the troops, and sell our lives at least at as high a price as we can." The same gentleman wrote his sister word that the high roads were covered with *female corpses*, which he gallop'd over. These are, far as my reading goes, new notions, and new occurrences …

The victory was no doubt that won against Jourdan and the French army of the Rhine, by a vastly superior force under the Archduke Charles, at Stockach. His despatch is dated 25th March, but the full account did not reach England till April.

Miss Thrale's information about the new play was not quite accurate. *De Montfort, a Tragedy of Hate*, was one of a series of Plays on the Passions by Joanna Baillie, but it was published anonymously, and several well-known writers, including Sir Walter Scott, were suspected of its authorship. There is a note about it in Mrs. Piozzi's Commonplace Book as follows: "I remember a knot of Literary Characters met at Miss Lees' House in Bath, deciding—contrary to my own judgement—that a *learned man* must have been the author; and I, chiefly to put the Company in a good humour, maintained it was a woman. Merely, said I, because both the heroines are Dames Passées, and a man has no notion of mentioning a female after she is five and twenty. What a goose Joanna must have been to reveal her sex and name! Spite and malice have pursued her ever since … She is a Zebra devoured by African Ants—the Termites Bellicosus.

> *Wensday* 29 *May* 1799.
> *Not one Oak in Leaf.*

On the very evening of the day I receive your last kind letter, dear Friend, I write to acknowledge both. The *home* post will tell you nothing you like tho', except that our accounts of little Salusbury are all good: but *poor Uncle* is always having a bad foot, and as you say, if it were not for the comfortable news from Italy, he would be low enough.

This blowing, blighting weather ruins us all; my poor cottagers are sick, with Agues chiefly, and Dropsies; with broken hearts too, poor things, when their horses drop under even empty carts, for full ones they cannot drag. Our Hay here has been at *one Penny* o' pound, our Beef at *ten Pence*. This approaches very near to famine, but may justly be termed scarcity; and the same dreadful wind which retards the growth of all vegetation, and restrains the hand of industry in *our own Island*, has driven our protecting fleet from Cadiz harbour, and let the French and Spaniards form a junction.

Meanwhile charming Hannah More was right in her conversation, as in her book; there has been a Crane-neck-turn, as she expressed it, and things are certainly mending on the Continent. If Ireland should come to her senses, and *unite* with us in abhorrence of French principles and French seducers, who could promise them assistance and never carry it, but go on another scheme, while the rebels *there* were waiting the Fleet's arrival—it might be lucky that Lord Bridport *did* let them escape. Poor fellow! how you do hate that man! Very comically, and very unreasonably indeed; for when we saw him he was, as the phrase is, out of his element, and looked to be sure something like a *fish out of water*. But I never heard anything amiss of him in my life, and believe he will not be found, at the critical moment, to carry "Two Faces under *a Hood*."

Have you seen Dr. and Mrs. Randolph lately? What do they say about these *Riflers of Sweets* that we hear so much of? Bath has been a scene of *odd robberies* by gay Lotharios, "who scorn to ask the lordly owners' leave." It makes me only laugh, but I trust Hannah More would say, like Benvolio, "No, Coz, I rather *weep*."[1] Glorious creature! How she writes! Finding new reasons to enforce old Virtues, and adorning her sacred sentiments with brilliancy that throws *rays* round all her periods. It would be doing her too much wrong to suppose *her* capable of regarding the nonsense talked against her by Misses mad to see their Mammas reading the new book with approbation, and looking at *them* over their spectacles at every interesting passage. She

must be invulnerable to wounds from such weak hands, sure. The old
heroes in Homer,

> By Pallas guarded thro' the dreadful field,
> Saw swords beside them innocently play,
> While darts were bid to turn their points away.

All they can say and do only contributes to shew how greatly such
a book was wanted. Mr. Whalley's thinking he has contributed to
Siddons's fame is pretty enough; she thinks *her* contribution useful to
him, no doubt. The writer of Pizarro is censured for giving *her* part
to Mrs. Jordan …

The intelligence concerning Mrs. Radcliffe's having written that play
on hatred seems to have been premature. Oh, how your account of
Mrs. Jackson's domestic situation presses Hannah More's book upon
one's heart! The Italians have a proverb to say that there are only three
things worth caring about, La Salute, l'Anima, and la Borsa; one's
Soul, one's Health, and one's Purse. *We risque all three* to make our fair
daughters *accomplish'd.* Doctor Johnson said that whoever found their
mothers admired and reverenced by that circle which forms a little
silk-worm world round every individual, would add their admiration
and reverence, merely because they saw other people pay them theirs.
"I cared," says he, "nothing for *my* parents, because nobody cared for
them." Mrs. Jackson's children cannot make that *their* excuse. She has
been a woman—since I have known her—particularly *petted* by her
friends, and those friends have been people eminent for good taste
and good sense.

Are the Canterbury Tales come out yet? Nobody sent them *me*,
and I will not write again to Harriet Lee till I have read them. Sophia
is in town with her little protégée, who, if she cannot conjure down

> The pale moon from the sapphire sky,
> May draw Endymion from the moon,

perhaps; and I really wish her good luck. Tickell's *Ætherial Spirit* is
a new med'cine much in fashion, it is so finely *dephlegmated*, the

Apothecaries say. I think there is as much pure spirit, and as little *phlegm* about the tiny Bath Belle as can be imagined. Some rich man may *take* her, I hope.

Have you felt an interest in these African discoveries? They are things of prodigious *curiosity*, rate them at the lowest. I think very seriously about them for my own part, but none of my correspondents seem caring much concerning that subject, unless 'tis Miss Thrale, from whom I get about 4 or 5 letters in a year,—and she has been ill this Spring. So has everybody. I watch the weathercock all day, but the cold blight continues. The leaves which *try* to come out look like fry'd Parsley round a dish of Soles …

In April 1797, when it was expected that the Spanish and French fleets would effect a junction, Lord St. Vincent was ordered to blockade the former at Cadiz. He held his post under many difficulties, caused by the mutinous spirit which had spread from the Nore and Spithead, through 1798, but broke down under the strain, and in June 1799 resigned his command to Baron, afterwards Viscount Keith, and husband of Hester Thrale. Meanwhile the French fleet was blockaded in Brest by Lord Bridport, now Commander-in-Chief of the Channel Squadron, but in April the French slipped out and sailed for the Mediterranean, while Bridport went to look for them off the coast of Ireland.

Mr. Whalley's play was a five-act tragedy called *The Castle of Montval*, performed "with universal applause" at Drury Lane. The *British Critic* reviewer, though he had not seen the performance, thought it interesting enough to deserve a permanent place on the stage. But the measure of success it obtained was due to the acting of Mrs. Siddons as the Countess, which the author acknowledged by dedicating the second edition to her.

Elizabeth Anne Tickell, the pupil whom Sophia Lee evidently expected to make a sensation in London society, was the daughter of Richard Tickell the dramatist and Mary Linley, the sister of Mrs. Sheridan, who had died in 1787. With regard to her beauty there was little difference of opinion, but Sally Siddons, who knew her well, describes her as an "every-day character," without talent or originality, and "never heard anything so tiresome" as her singing. She was never "taken," but died unmarried in 1860.

The "Ethereal Anodyne Spirit" was a quack medicine invented by William Tickell, a surgeon, who also lived at Bath, and may have been a relation of Richard.

BRYNBELLA, *Wensday* 17 *Jul.* 1799.

Your letter, dearest Mrs. Pennington, is like yourself, full of true friendship, honest loyalty and sound criticism. Freedom from *prejudices,* as principals are called now o' days, we must not come to you for ... I do believe you were right in that *unjustifiable* conjecture of yours concerning the death of those Deputies at Rastadt ... But *Retrospect* of past ages can shew no perfidy beyond *that,* if so it should prove upon investigation. The Archduke now seems to act with his hands untied, and co-operates with Suwarrow in everything, yet I suspect something behind the curtain still. The Emperor is willing enough to see Italy freed, but does not want Louis Dixhuit on his throne again, I suppose; whereas the Russians and English are trying to accomplish y^t purpose with all their might, and no lasting peace can be obtained but by his restoration. We shall see how 'twill end.

You are droll indeed in your account of the New Canterbury Tales, I have not read them yet ... When Romances first were written they went by the name of Incredibilities; but people soon found out that Fiction looks best the more she endeavour to resemble Truth. It grows however a mighty tedious thing, after a certain age, to keep filling one's head with flitting dreams so, turning one's mind into a Magic Lanthorn for Shadows and Ombres Chinoises to pass over, if incredibilities are desirable, *we* can hear enough of Mr. and Mrs. Mostyn. As that Lady told you at some place that Mrs. *Moyston*, as she called her, made all the talk,—*and so she does, God knows.*

Well, any nonsense but *dishonourable* nonsense, *disgraceful* folly such as Honoria Gubbins has exhibited. You know I always said she looked like a Bacchante Girl, but she admired nothing except *Siddons* I remember. In good time. Dear, charming Siddons! How triumphantly must she have looked in the first and last scene of Pizarro! And what a happy contrast Sheridan has made between her artificial character, and Cora's natural one! Yet I cannot seriously approve of a *Heroic* Tragedy in *prose*. *Domestic* Tragedy, George Barnwell, or the Gamester, or the Stranger, would lose the interest they now gain in our hearts, if they spoke any but colloquial and domestic language. Poetry is made on purpose to adorn the lofty sentiments of Rolla, and Cora's song is the sweetest thing in the whole play,—only because 'tis *verse*.

Poor Cora! She is not of *your* mind, that love is of no consequence compared with a hundred other things; and that she should have completely no *other* idea present to *her* mind, makes her so natural, so interesting, and so adorable. What is stranger than love itself, and love is strange enough too,—is that one should never have done admiring that *selfish* passion when represented in works of fancy. I remember an old Alderman of London, who, when there was loud talk of invasion 20 years ago or more, said among a dozen people once at my house: "Well! I care not, for my part, if the *Island* was *devoured* to-morrow, so as my wife and child were safe, and I had enough to keep them with." This *patriotic* sentiment met with no approbation at all from an old Alderman in real life; yet this is the sentiment that Cora expresses all through five acts, and not only her auditors in the Pit and Boxes, but Rolla himself likes her the better for it. So you see Fiction may resemble Truth in some things, while if Truth resembles Fiction we hiss her out of doors.

Poor dear old Mr. Jones is very bad, and like to die, or has been like to die, and I am very sorry indeed; for though there's but little poetry or criticism about old Mr. Jones, he is a good friend and a valuable member of society, and wishes well to my Master and to me …

Mrs. Siddons goes to Edinburgh, I hear, but by what you say of Sally, I trust she cannot be of the party. Miss Thrale is in Scotland, and will have the pleasure of seeing her, as I saw her at Bath. No letter have I ever received from Marlbro' Street but one, and *that* was from the Master of the Mansion …

The little boy comes next week, next month I mean, with Davies.

Austria, having signed the Treaty of Campo Formio, and received unexpectedly favourable terms from Napoleon, agreed to hold a conference at Rastadt, and (by secret articles) to induce the German States to cede the left bank of the Rhine to France. While the conference was proceeding the Directory had occupied Switzerland, though Massena, Jourdan, and Scherer had all suffered defeats. The French envoys were ordered to leave the town, and were murdered on the road by Austrian hussars. The Emperor expressed deep abhorrence of a crime which aroused general indignation, and helped the Directory to fill up their depleted armies.

Alexander Vasilievitch Suvoroff or Suwarrow, a Russian general, had been sent to help the Austrians. He took command of the army in Italy, where he beat Moreau, Macdonald, and Joubert, but owing to jealousy he was transferred to Switzerland, and believing himself betrayed by the Austrians, he retired to Russia, and died in disgrace.

BRYNBELLA, 21 Aug. 1799.

MY DEAR FRIEND,—Your letter is like yourself, wise and kind, and I am willing to join in your wish for early meeting this year, but not for an early winter. Oh! little do you *Towns folk* know how prejudicial is this weather to Country Farmers, Labourers, etc. The Shoemaker and his apprentice at Bristol make so many more boots and clogs, and some Bath Chairmen get a few shillings extra: but *my* honest neighbours have but just barely bread, in the *strictest* sense; mere *bread*, and that made of Barley too, for their families, during such winters as this cruel summer will infallibly produce. Mr. Piozzi and I shall scarce be suffered to get thro' the Village, they will so cling and cry round us, and beg we will stay another month, another week, etc.

When the Gardener came yesterday, scratching his head, and saying there would be no wall-fruit this year, I could hardly answer him civilly; but I *did* say, "For God's sake, think about the hay and corn, and hang the fine people and their wall-fruit." The produce of whole meadows may be seen swimming down our over-flooded River to the sea this moment, and carrying with it the subsistence of hundreds of innocents.

May this fine Expedition make amends for all! It *will*, if peace and abatement of necessary exertion be its consequences. English pride will be bravely swelled, that's certain, if we can thus give law

and order and happiness to Europe. Are such blessings within hope?
People *say* they are almost within *grasp*. Meanwhile let us try to live
that we may see these good days. Mrs. Bagot, the Bishop's wife's
death has affected my spirits strangely. I got a pain in my stomach
on the *instant* Allen told me the news, and it has never wholly left
me since. She din'd here in high spirits on our Wedding day, three
weeks ago, and expired on Saturday morning. The Ton men and Ton
women bear these things without concern, and prove that fashion
can do more than philosophy towards hardening one's heart, but my
nervous fingers shake while I write about it …

To divert thought I took up the Canterbury Tales which Mr. Gillon
had just brought me. Harriet's management of the *pretty Mamma*
making the man miserable so unconsciously is very good, and in *this
age*, scarcely violates probability. The other story is too romantic, and
the ghost part too in-artificial, one sees it could be only Carey. For
love, it abounds but little with *that,* I think. Julia keeps her passion
very quiet; one is most interested about Agnes and Carey.

Real life meanwhile affords stranger occurrences than any novel
can show. Mr. Conant, the London Magistrate, told Mr. Gillon, who
told us, the following tale not a fortnight ago. Some little London
shopkeepers sent out their girl of eleven years old, with a baby 8
months old in her arms, upon some errand, I forget what, but no
further off than the short street's end. A young woman, genteely
dress'd, stop't the girl, and beg'd her to cross over and ask the price of
a gay coloured handkerchief hanging at a window, promising that she
would hold the infant till his sister returned. When she came back
however, both little boy and young woman were vanish'd; and the girl
ran back, half wild, to her parents, and told the story. They flew from
the Counter in search of the thief, and desperate with rage and terror,
exhibited to the neighbours a certainty that the shop might be easily
plundered while their distress employed every thought. Accordingly
the *man* returning home at night, found his poor dwelling robbed
of many valuable articles, while the girl, to whom all this confusion
was owing, had hid herself under the bed for fear of a beating, and
the father was persuaded she too was lost. The mother, parting
from her husband, who had wandered over six parishes, swore she

Mrs. Piozzi (About 1800)
By M. Bovi after P. Violet, 1800

would never see home again without her baby, and remained out the whole day and the whole night in search. Morning found her, much exhausted, at a chandler's shop door in Edgeware Road, and when it opened she went in to buy a bit of cheese. A little wench went in with her, and the mistress of the house, seeing her anguish, kindly asked the cause. "I've lost my child," said she, "my dear little boy." "My mammy has found one," says the wench, "and don't know what to do with it." They ran together to a Green-stall, and found Baby safe in that woman's possession, who said a young *gentlewoman* had pretended to buy Sellery of her, and while she went backwards to look for some, threw down the infant, and was seen no more. Mr.

Conant was applied to, and found a cause for all. The well dress'd lady was a Chambermaid, who had a child for whose maintenance she was paid, altho' it died during the first week; and the father had resolved, that hapless day, to see his son. Molly had nothing for it but to borrow one, and when the purpose was served, to rid her hands on't, and no Novel can bring to a reader's fancy more perfect distress than these poor parents suffered. Their girl, however, who lay concealed till mother and brother returned, told her tale so well that a subscription was raised, and all went better than before in the little shop in Silver Street, Carnaby Market.

So instead of our best com^s to Dr. and Mrs. Randolph, instead of affec^{te} regards to Mr. Pennington, or Bon Mots of our little John Salusbury, here's a page from ye Romance of Real Life, unadorned by your true friend H.L. Piozzi, and for this you will pay 8*d*.

BRYNBELLA, 17 *Oct.* 1799.

Do you know, dear Mrs. Pennington, that Mrs. Randolph and I are in correspondence? We are indeed, and 'tis all about Bath, and Laura Place, and No. I, and Christmas Holidays, and our dear Friend from Dowry Square: and not a word of the dismal, the more than dismal gloom, which these last accounts from abroad have thickened round us once again on approach of foggy November …

We are at this instant trembling from apprehension that the French will fall upon Milan, and make an example of those that called in their enemies. I'm glad my little boy is far away from them all. I think you will find him improved, unless he falls off this half-year, and begins to change his nice little teeth etc. … All the Jacobins will be *up now*, and happy I suppose; but let them remember we have taken Surinam in one Continent, and Seringapatam in another. The money is ours, and the Commodities (which their friends the French *must* buy,) are all ours; and the very warehouses in every port are too little to hold our riches. Few of them are thinkers deep enough to know that wealth, at such a moment as this, is a mere invitation to plunder; and I wish not to remind *them* of so fatal a truth, tho' I scruple not to tell it to *you*. While it can purchase Russians to find *them* in employment, the money is useful however, and well bestow'd: and I would rather hire foreign troops with it than send out our own, who will be necessary when the war *draws nearer.* And I feel sorry the Ministers did not make more bustle in London about the capture of Surinam, for it is undoubtedly fair to rejoyce when *we* reap solid advantages from a war whence no other Country, not even that of the Victors, gains any advantages *at all.* Said I well and wisely?

Mrs. Siddons's situation does not please me, for *her* sake; for my own 'tis well enough, for we are the more likely to meet at Bath. Being at Doncaster so late in the year is a dull thing indeed. I wish she had some method of getting paid at Drury Lane, because *seceders,* if they are not called back to their seats, only look silly: and when Mr. Garrick left London for his health one year, when in the fulness of public favour, I remember he was disgusted at his return, to find the receipts of the theatre had suffered nothing at all, during an absence he thought would have broken all our hearts …

The bad news from abroad doubtless related to the Dutch expedition, in which the English troops had suffered a good deal. On 10th October the Duke of York reported the conclusion of an armistice with the French, on the conditions of withdrawing the English and Russian troops, surrendering the fortress of Helder, and restoring the French prisoners.

Seringapatam had been taken in the spring by General Harris, under whom Colonel Arthur Wellesley was serving, and Tippoo Sahib was slain. The despatch giving the details, dated 7th May, appeared in the *Gazette* of 14th September.

Sheridan's habitual unpunctuality in the matter of payments had at last driven Mrs. Siddons to revolt. She writes on 18th September: "I have just received a letter, in the usual easy style, from Mr. Sheridan, who, I fancy, thinks he has only to issue his Sublime Commands, and that they will of course be obeyed. *This time* I believe, however, he will find himself mistaken, for Sid [her husband,] does *at last* seem resolutely determined not to let me play till he has sufficient satisfaction, at least for the money which is my due; and unless something is immediately done to that end, I shall go to Doncaster to play at the Races—they begin the 24th of this month." This decisive step soon brought Sheridan to reason; there was only one Siddons, and before long she was back again, practically on her own terms.

[*P.M.* BATH.] *Saturday Night* [*Dec.* 1799.]

I shall expect and prepare for my dear Mrs. Pennington, to begin what her company will make it, a happy commencement of 1800 ... I shall feel glad *this* year to see December close upon me, which for some time has carried with it a sensation more awful than pleasing. When the sand was high in the hour-glass, I well remember longing for a New Year as if it had been a new gown; and there was a *gloss* on every 1st January *then,* that seem'd as if all misfortune would *slip over* and not stain it ...

We leave our little boy with Davies because he himself (Mr. Davies,) said that staying at Streatham in holyday time, when he could attend and tutor him with personal and *undivided care*, would bring him forward, and I call that *true regard*: but everybody must be allowed to love their own babies their own way ...

With regard to the people in power, I firmly believe they do their best, neither interest nor ambition can be gratified by failure; and tho' a dapper Postilion may injure those in the chaise by driving to an *inch,* for a wager or for a frolic, I'll trust a Coachman, because he runs equal risque with myself ...

I wish this embargo on Levantine goods was over tho', for people bring none from Turkey now: true Mocha coffee sells for 12s. the pound, it was at 3s. three years ago ...

The expected meeting was for a time deferred on account of Mrs. Pennington's ill-health. Save for one or two notes of no particular interest, the correspondence ceases till the Piozzis return to Wales.

BRYNBELLA, *Sunday* 9 *Mar.* 1800.

I hasten to fulfil my promise to dear Mrs. Pennington. We came home but last night, and I write to say that we are come home well, and find our Household well too, and truly glad of our safe and early return.

The time past at Shrewsbury was full of amusement; Miss Owen feasted and fondled us, and called all the people round to feast us and fondle us, and detain us till Thursday, which had been long bespoke, and Fryday beside, by the charming Cottagers in Llangollen Vale. *They* asked me much after that Mrs. Pennington who writes such beautiful letters, and insisted on my describing your person to them, and said they knew Miss Seward esteemed you highly, though all intimacy between you was at an end. The unaccountable knowledge those Recluses have of all living books and people and things is like magic; one can mention no one of whom the private history is unknown to them …

Let me therefore talk of Mr. Pennington, and ask how he does. You may be certain how I do, and what I do. Looking out my books, setting my places to rights, ladling out the soup to 30 families round, feeding the dogs with what *they leave*, mixed up with Potatoe peelings and so forth, is mine and my Master's and Abbiss's employment; whilst Allen blows her nose in consequence of cold catch'd in a damp bed at Worcester—and thanks God the evil ends there.

The little three-legged cur jumps into my lap, licks my face, and runs to his Master to tell the good news, how the family is come home to the Hall, and everybody and every thing looks pleased to see us … I have had a civil letter from Susan Thrale, who bids me direct to Cumberland Street, and makes commonplace lamentations concerning the *times,* but *nothing further*, nothing I mean tending towards confidence or communication.

We broke our chaise between Llangollen and Ruthyn,—no wonder! Such roads! 'Tis really frightful: but neither Mr. Piozzi nor I were hurt.

Here are no Members of Parliament, no Franks of course, so I shall write very seldom; for the joke is a good one two or three times o' year, but no oftener, when 14*d.* is to pay for 44 lines about nothing: and friendship is a fine thing, but so is fourteen Pence …

There is a Lady at Shrewsbury, born the last day of 1699, and she is very well, and plays upon the Piano e forte, as you describe Mr. Whalley's mother to do; but poor Mrs. Montague's sun is setting apace I hear. She has left her fine house, and retired into a smaller, giving up the grandeur to her Nephew, and Lady Oakley said, the estate too, but

I hope she has had *more wit than that.* Lady Oakley is very agreeable ... I saw her in a robe embroider'd (as she said,) with the wings of an Indian Fly; there is no describing its beauty or lustre ...

Mrs. Montagu does not appear to have left Montagu House permanently, for she died there the following August. Lady Oakley was the wife of Charles Oakley, Governor of Madras, who was created a Baronet in 1790.

Needless to say Mrs. Piozzi's economical fit in the matter of letters did not last long, the correspondence continues much as usual; but as a matter of fact the letters from Wales to Bristol only cost the recipient 8*d.*, not 1*s.* 2*d.*

There is no date or post-mark to the next letter, but Mrs. Pennington assigns it to April 1800.

What in the world, dear Mrs Pennington, has been doing at Bath? I wrote to Dr. Randolph about a book of his which I wanted, and his letter in return has affected me very deeply. Yours gave a hint of something like a riot, but nobody seems sensible that we live out of the world here, and know nothing of what passes in it. The newspaper we take, though it swelled and raved so about Mr. King's fire, said nothing of *this*, or so little we quite disregarded it: and yet Dr. Randolph says that *our* quarter of the Town was saved by miracle from being even now a heap of cinders.

Thank God we were come home. The slight shock of earthquake that usher'd in our Fast Day *here,* and frighted many of our neighbours, not *us*, is a light matter compared with mobs and insurrections. Let us, as King David said of old, fall into the hands of God, and not into the hands of men. The noise accompanying even this trifle of a concussion was such as to alarm Mrs. Griffiths exceedingly. She said it was like a hundred carts of lime stone overturned close by her bed. Mr. Piozzi and I never waked to hear or feel it.

Miss Thrale had not then (as now,) kept our eyes wholly sleepless by a new and violent attack on our feelings and property: sending, without notice or introduction, to our Oxfordshire Tenant, a requisition to pay *her* the rent I have hitherto received for 19 years since my first husband's death, in consequence of the Marriage Settlement signed by him in 1763, confirmed again by Will in 1781, and claim'd now, A.D. 1800, with threats (to our afflicted friend Mr.Gillon,) of making me refund all I have *unjustly taken from my daughters*. It will be soon refunded. No ass, as Moses says, of theirs did I ever take, nor no present at their hands for bribe. How cruel 'tis to sit down and accuse me so! Miss Thrale says Streatham was given me to *make up* £400 o' year, but that Crowmarsh is not liable. Now it will turn out upon examination that Crowmarsh is *first* liable, and that if my due from that estate is not paid me, I have a right to make *forcible* entry, and *take* it, *without impeachment of waste*. This, being provided in the Marriage Settlement, I understand *must* be secure, so do not you nor dear Mr. Pennington be uneasy; we shall *lose* nothing but appetite and sleep. And I was *so* well after the Bath waters! and proposed being so diligent at the Book: and now nothing but law, and letters, and Chancery suits, and false accusations and every evil plague.

No news from abroad yet that we can depend upon. Will it be good when it arrives? The times, as Dr. Randolph says, are signally aweful, and I verily think that Daemons are roaming about among us, with enlarged permission both to tempt and terrify. God preserve us! even from our own bad passions, He only can. *Mine* are sometimes ready to run away with me now, for Welsh blood heats over a fire of sharp thorns thus, till it boyls again. Oh dear! how dreadful are these days! A Lady in this neighbourhood made a grand entertainment on the Fast appointed by Government, by way of spiting that Government. They must leave off appointing such solemnities: the time is over when they did any good …

I wish Miss Case would tell me what they have suffer'd at Bath, and what they have escaped, for I cannot now make it clearly out. If harm comes to Hannah More we are all undone, *her* health is a public concern …

This earthquake was not so slight a thing as I thought it; some houses at Conway and Caernarvon were much injured, and it spread a general alarm from the *unfrequency* of the thing. Yet to people who have lived much in Italy, an earthquake that did not *wake* one seems laughable enough …

Much may, and probably much *will* happen this summer, to give us a little further insight into what's coming in earnest. The best is our seasonable and salutary change of weather; had we corn to *sow*, the ground will be in fine order for putting it in. I am glad Buonaparte sends us no corn, I was afraid of contagion in the sacks; and the thought of an expedition to Egypt and Syria frights me, lest some pestilential disease should be brought home from places so constantly infected …

BRYNBELLA, 1st *May* 1800.

My dear Mrs. Pennington is *too* apt to be right. You do not, I perceive, think us safe from this new attack upon our property, and we are *not* safe …

Thus it stands. If we litigate, such is the dubious position of Mr. Thrale's words in my old Marriage Settlement, that years will roll away, and Empires be overthrown, before the affair can be decided, and in the meantime Crowmarsh rents will be retained till the decision. A circumstance very unpleasing to us for every reason; the strongest of all, because to Miss Thrale the estate *must* go at my death, so that unless my life is prolonged beyond the usual limits of humanity, Mr. Piozzi *can* hope for nothing from a law dispute, except Attorney's Bills to pay with a diminished income. Of all *this* our fair enemy cannot be ignorant, and does not profess to desire anything but profit from the contest; so we may be *sure* she will make great terms for herself. The parley of eloquence on Mr. Gillon's side, supported by Butler's Opinion concerning our Case, is held today I think. The best thing is that Mr. Thrale confirmed his Marriage Settlement by his Will, adding the bequests in that Will to what formerly was provided in the other Instrument; but nothing has been *worded* so as to preclude discussion among eager disputants, diligent to catch and cavil, and endowed with Marianne's powers and delight in wrangling. We are in a Wasps' nest, and must make haste out, and be stung as little as we can. Resistance is vain, and will be impolitic, in my mind …

That people are quiet, and the fires accidental, I would willingly perswade myself, but cannot. That your friend Paul, Emperor of all the Russias, is a true friend and firm ally, may now reasonably enough be doubted. He wants an excuse for falling upon Turkey, and takes that of quarrelling with Great Britain. It is exceedingly offensive to be forced into submission to his caprices; but I suppose George the III at close of life will not find new enemies a good thing any more than poor H.L.P. does, or will be able, any better than H.L.P., to find *supplies* for a new contest which, like her's, *can* terminate in no advantage, and will be attended with *certain* loss abroad, increase of poverty, and of course ill-humour, at home. You may see how spiteful the people are, even by their opposition to his private conveniency in making a new road to Windsor from London. No want of spite in this world, I'll warrant, either to princes or to people; my Book will have proved that new and wise remark by this time next year. If we go to London with it, I shall vote for an apartment in the Adelphi Hotel; such a place will do well enough for November, and our income *must* be reduced, and I will not suffer *my* business or pleasures to retard my husband's long projected happiness of not having a debt in the world. The very journey is expense enough. We shall be near Mr. Gillon there, and I shall not have an acquaintance in London but Mrs. Siddons and Mrs. Holman, perhaps not the first even of those, as the seasons seem to change so; everybody makes it Summer till after Christmas, and Winter to July.

There is great talk of a new book written by Hannah More, The Progress of Pilgrim Good-intent through the Land of Jacobinism; have you read it? and is it charming? ...

The Rheumatism has caught my shoulder before Gout seized my Master's toe this year. I was to have gone in the Cold Bath this morning, but the pain prevents me ...

After the battle of the Nile, England, Russia, and Turkey had entered into an alliance against France. But the Emperor Paul, annoyed at his treatment by Austria, and accusing the allies of treachery, came to terms with Bonaparte, with whom he concerted a plan for a joint invasion of India.

Sat. 16 *May*, BRYNBELLA.

My last letter was a wretch: how could you, dearest Friend, commend it so? If I remember anything about it, it was low, cold, and flat. The usage I had received sunk my nerves down, they were not irritated. Use of the cold bath, meant to strengthen them, threw me all out in *nettle-stings*. And *now,* for crowning of all, my poor Master's torment, villainous Gout, has, as you once observed of Mr. Pennington's, watched the due time, and thrown in his assistance to the fair Ladies' cause. Their cause is cold though, and notwithstanding our defenders cannot bring matters to a decision yet, they give us hopes that little will be lost, except the arrears, worth, Mr. Gillon says, £1000. He has behaved divinely to be sure, and deserves all your generous praises of him. Nobody applauds Miss Thrale's proceedings I think. Mrs. Holman and you inveigh *loudest* against her, and it *was* a cruel thing to fly so upon that estate, which her Father would never have left *her at all,* had I not so requested him, because I thought it was unfair that, from accumulation of fortune after they lost *him*, the youngest daughter would be richer than the eldest: but I meant her to have Crowmarsh after my death, and so he meant it too. Well! one has always heard some nonsense how two negatives make an affirmative, so I suppose in *Law,* when a man gives a thing twice over, it turns out *no gift at all.* Mr. Thrale tried three times to secure his Oxfordshire property for me, and if I miss it at last, no blame can attach to *him.* The flaw was in the *Settlement* you see, and the Will confirms the *Settlement*, so God knows how 'twill end at last. The Mr. Butler employed on our side has a high character in his profession as *Chamber Council*, etc. Being a Roman Catholic he cannot reach the honours of his calling, but rests contented with the profits ...

Here's much to do with *Hate* and more with *Love,*[2] as Juliet says in Shakespear. Apropos to Hatred, I am delighted that we know the author of De Montfort: she must be a fine creature, and will excite no small share of the hatred she describes. I *felt* it was a woman's writing, no man makes female characters *respectable*—no man of the present day I mean, they only make them *lovely.* We must except *Dr. Moore*: his Mrs. Barnett and his Laura Sedlitz are all that women *ought* to wish to be.

Don't you admire at my sitting here to criticize Plays and Novels, like Miss Seward, while my Husband is lame, my fortune is crippled, and my favourite dog has but *three* legs?

Farewell, dear Friend, ... 'tis five o'clock in the morning, I was up at *four*, shall call the men and maids at six, send away this scrawl at seven, jump into the bath at 8, breakfast at 9, work at the book till 1, walk till 3, have dined by 4, fret over Gillon's dispatches and Piozzi's misery all the rest of the day: a pretty biographical sketch of your literally poor H.L.P.

Charles Butler, Mrs. Piozzi's counsel, was a brother of the Rev. Alban Butler, the hagiologist. As Roman Catholics were not permitted to be called to the Bar when he began his professional career, he took up conveyancing business, and helped to edit *Coke upon Littleton*. Taking advantage of the Enabling Act, he became a Barrister in 1791, and took silk in 1832.

4 Jun. 1800.

... The Book goes on, *lamely* perhaps, now my better half has the *Gout,* but it does go. My Master mends too, and everything mends. Miss Thrale *withdraws* (somewhat disgracefully,) the claim she could not *substantiate*: a tedious suit against this never-dying Mother would have eaten up all the profits of her hoped-for estate, and nobody would have benefited *but* the Lawyers. *Her* friends were therefore persuaded by *our* friends to *give in*, as the Boxers say, and so the battle ends; and on the last of May she writes to the Oxfordshire Tenant to pay £400 to us as usual,—that very £400 which, on the first of March, she wrote the same man word—*was incontestably her own* ...

Miss Bayley, a Lady who lives with Mrs. John Hunter, and is related to her, has at length modestly owned herself Author of a Drama that every one would have been most happy to have written: but Mr. Chappelow (no bad mirror of the fashionable world,) says people think it too *solemn,—they are not amused. I* say they are like old Polonius: see Hamlet's character of *him* as a Critic.[3]

Kemble is in high favour with the Beau Monde, I am told, and his Sister declines; but she will pick up some more guineas, and then no matter. I reckon her as having only *one* daughter to portion out; Sally will never marry, I suppose, if *half* of what I have *heard* of her ill health be true. Mr. Siddons will be a long-lived man, as sick as he is always said to be; nothing runs on like a life subject to one chronic and regular complaint, Gout, or Rheumatism. Siddons will repeat over to two or three generations the lamenting strains I heard him recite in 1788, and his Daughter will think herself young when everybody else sees her grown old, because she has a father to nurse. There was a Mrs. Shelley in Sussex, her sneering neighbours called her Epistle and Gospel, who had two maiden daughters. One broke her leg, and died at about 40 years old, but the other departed not till 5 years ago. The Doctors informed her *Mama* there was no hope, and she piously resigned to the loss. "But tell me at least," cried she, "what ails my poor child, and of what *can* she possibly be dying?" "Of age, dear Madam," answered her Physician. "Miss Shelley was never strong, and 76 years have nearly worne her out." "Oh dear! Is she really? Why I am but 94 myself, and I am not dying of age!" She spoke true, and outlived her little girl, as she called her, six years.

Adieu, dear Mrs. Pennington, and tell my *old Friend* this story ...

The asthmatic complaint from which Sally Siddons had suffered, almost from childhood, proved fatal in 1803, and she died, as Mrs. Piozzi anticipated, unmarried. Though her heart was given to Lawrence, the promise made to her dying sister, and her own strong common sense and knowledge of his character, prevented her from giving her hand. The prognostication respecting her father proved very wide of the mark, as he died at Bath only two years later.

13 *June* 1800, Brynbella.

My dear Mrs. Pennington is a true friend, and has acute feelings of friendship and of Injury. All is over between me and my *beautiful* and *deserving* Daughters—*those* were Mr. Ray's epithets ... With regard to *our cause*, mark me! Mr. Gillon, dear creature as he is, did not stop its proceedings by *perswasion*; it was carried by law, though not by litigation. Mr. Cator and Mr. Richards on *Miss Thrale's* part, and

Mr. Gillon and Mr. Butler on *our* parts, talked the matter over; and they really *withdrew* the claim they could not *substantiate*, or make creditable to carry into a Court of Judicature.

Gillon tells a laughable story of Miss Thrale's standing hard for £10 which he advanced her, of his own money, to stop further absurdity. And now let's hear no more on't, and do not, Sweet Soul! make me in love with *resentment*; for except in a friend's cause like your own, 'tis an unpleasing quality, and productive of nothing but evil. We must quote our own Book of Knowledge after all, and in the Article "Forgiveness," as I *think*, you read these words. "A *wise* man will make haste to forgive, because anger is a painful sensation, and he wishes to be rid on't. A *great* man will pardon easily, because he finds few things worthy his resentment; and a *good* man will never resent at all, knowing how much he has himself to be forgiven." I wrote to the girls by yesterday's post, exactly as if no such transactions had passed among us: so long live British Synonymy!

Well! Robinson refuses my labour'd Work. He has been at Bath and Bristol, and cannot recover his health sufficiently to *enter upon new engagements*: he is going to leave off business, and cannot prevail upon himself to undertake so large a book, he says. Did *you* see or hear of him? Or did he pass any time at Belvidere House? And does he undertake any *smaller* works, I wonder? *Lesser* is a word I will not use, but it would gratify me to know. I sent him a letter to put him in better spirits, if possible, and better humour: for tho' I despair not of selling my stuff, I shall hate hawking it about London, which will at last be the case …

The incomparable Coterie you mention as loving and remembering us with kindness, will make me rich amends in their society if I can wind up my little matters, and come to Bath in Spring. But here is a degree of scarcity and dearness, both present and expected, that worries my Master and his House Book horribly … Everything costs double, besides double Taxes, double necessity of expence, and so forth. London will be much my terror indeed, but I hope our stay will be a short one.

Oh! what would have become of my wretched nerves, had I been in the Theatre that awfully impressive night? What would have become of *your* nerves? of dear Mrs. de Luc's? The tryal would have been *too* great. Susan and Sophy were there; so was Mr. Gillon. It will go hard with the Traytor, I am told, if the Jury do not find him guilty. The King's *Guardian Angel* must appear in *person* to protect him next time, because it will be such encouragement to the Jacobins to attempt his life, that nothing *less* can save him …

George Robinson, the "King of Booksellers," who had a villa at Streatham, was born in Cumberland, and coming to London in 1755, began his career in the house of Rivington. He set up for himself in Paternoster Row in 1764, and died in 1800. It is somewhat remarkable that Mrs. Piozzi's principles allowed her to patronize him, seeing that he had been fined, not many years before, for selling Tom Paine's *Rights of Man*.

The King was shot at in his box at Drury Lane on 15th May, but the assailant, James Hatfield, proved to be a lunatic, and the attempt had no political importance.

[*July* 1800]

… I am sorry Mr. and Mrs. Whalley are declining so; their pretty cottage will be a shady retreat for them this hot weather. We are roasting here on the sunny side of a high hill, but never was such hay made before; 40 acres cut and carried in 12 days is really curious, and without *one* shower. Did you observe the odd Phænomenon exhibited on Trinity Sunday in the evening? It alarmed those who *did* observe it, and our Caernarvonshire and Anglesea neighbours, who understand not how many tricks Electricity can play, were frighted to see the sun apparently go *back* when he set, no fewer than three diameters of himself.

Mr. Lloyd of Wickwar, whom you have heard me mention as an astronomer, and a man well known at Sir Joseph Banks's, etc., said it was a surprizing thing, and, for what he had observed, wholly *new*: he attributed it to the state of atmosphere. The same appearance was noticed likewise at Shrewsbury. *I saw it not*; I was not looking …

What is this story of Harry Siddons? Is he really to marry Miss Scott, the great fortune of the North? If he does, the Sun may set in the *East* if it will, without attracting our charming Friend's attention I suppose, and no wonder. Miss Lees say nothing, perhaps think the *more*. What a thing it would be!

My Book must go to the public market and take its chance in October. Buonaparte will possibly finish it for me, and destroy the Empire as he did the Papacy. Our Ministry keep feeding Francis with money, for which he will sell, not his birthright, like Esau, but all *except* his birthright, and content himself with the old Crowns of Bohemia and Hungary, resigning even the name of King of the *Romans* to those Gauls who invaded 'em 2000 years ago, and have never lost sight of a hope so late to be accomplished as poor Rome's utter destruction. The sun may well be seen to shew signs and wonders when such occurrences are coming forward.

Meanwhile what say you to Bishop Horsley's denouncing the *Schools* of impiety and sedition? Did even our dear Dr. Randolph think that London was so far advanced in wickedness? or even Hannah More? It is truly dreadful ...

Mr. Piozzi and I have been married now 16 years, and we are used to keep our anniversary, but it happened at a perverse time of ye week and month this year. And so instead of feeding the rich, we fed the poor, and every one of our 35 Haymakers had a good noggin of soup, and a lump of beef in it, and a suet dumpling; and they were like the people in The Deserter, who sing—"Joy, joy to the Duchess wherever she goes." And my Master's health was *sincerely* drank, though not very *copiously*: for bread and beer are yet considered as *luxuries* in our poor skin and bone Country; while the Lords and Ladies round the Capital are paying five guineas for a Peach, etc., and Daughters of Liverpool spend, in one entertainment, what frighted all France when requested for a frolick of poor Antoinette,—Daughter of the Cæsars.

Well! Mr. Piozzi has gone to a little—not a very little—expense, in repairing old Bachygraig for the new tenant. Our neighbours advised him to tumble the venerable ruin quite down, and build a snug farmhouse with the materials; but he would not. And so, poking about, we found some very curious bricks with stories on them, composed in 1500, and one large one with Catherine de Berayne's arms, derived from Charlemagne. 'Twas she whose husband built ye house, you know, (Sir Richard Clough—*see Pennant*;) and being descended immediately from fair Catherine of France, whom Shakespear makes us familiar with, and who married Owen Tudor after her first husband's death, heroic Harry the Vth, drew her descent by the Mother's side from Charlemagne. I have set her achievement in front now, and a stone to say the Mansion was repaired and beautified by Gabriel Piozzi Esq. in the year 1800. It will last to the World's end now, I believe.

The dear little boy whom you used to love has spent his vacation time at Streatham again. He will, I hope, be wiser in proportion as he is less happy, and less spoiled: *safer* he certainly is, and we hear a good character of his scholarship …

The report of Henry Siddons' engagement to Miss Scott seems to have been mere gossip, as he married Miss Murray in 1802.

The account of the surrender of his titles by the Emperor Francis also seems to have been somewhat premature. He proclaimed himself hereditary Emperor of Austria in 1804, and it was not till 1806, after the formation of the Confederation of the Rhine, that he formally resigned the imperial crown, and so brought to a close the Holy Roman Empire, founded by Charlemagne, and the Kingdom of Germany. Bonaparte, however, had anticipated his resignation, and had himself appointed Emperor by decree of the Senate in 1804.

Samuel Horsley, Bishop successively of St. David's, Rochester, and St. Asaph, was the great opponent of Priestly and the Unitarians, against whom several of his charges were directed.

Pennant's account of the home of Mrs. Piozzi's ancestors runs thus (*Tour in Wales*, vol. ii. p.22). "In the bottom [of the Clwyd Valley] lies, half buried in the woods, the singular house of Bachegraig. It consists of a mansion, and three sides, enclosing a square court. The first consists of a vast hall and parlour; the rest of it rises into six wonderful stories, including the cupola, and forms from the second floor the figure of a pyramid: the rooms small and inconvenient. The bricks are admirable, and appear to have been made in Holland; and the model of the house was probably brought from Flanders, where

Bachygraig House in 1776
From a drawing by J. Hooper, 1776

this species of building was not unfrequent. The country people say that it was built by the Devil in one night, and that the Architect still preserves an apartment in it; but Sir Richard Clough, an eminent merchant of Queen Elizabeth's reign, seems to have a better title to the honour. The initials of his name are in iron on the front, with the date 1567, and on the gateway that of 1569." It is stated in *Piozziana* that the vane bore the date 1537. An account of Sir Richard Clough and Catherine of Berayne has been given in the Introduction, to which the reader is referred.

BRYNBELLA, *Sat, night, 6 or 7 of Sept.* 1800.

Dear Mrs. Pennington's eyes yet serve her, I find, to write the very charmingest letters in the world, and Dr. Randolph is of the same opinion; that to the travellers was admirable, and my own, just received, most excellent. They left Wales yesterday, and have carried ugly weather home with them; but I hope and *think* that the bright sun illuminated their last glimpse of Denbighshire, from the heights round romantic Llangollen. I never saw people so well, or so happy, or so good humoured, on a journey where inconveniences must necessarily arise, such as would teize many tempers accustomed to *home life* ...

What the meaning can be of *bread rising* is past my power to divine. Wheat falls, and grass grows, and these rains have put out the fires which injured the hilly grounds. Nothing is truer than your observation on men's counteracting Providence in all they can, but of late times some permission seems to have been given them that it *should be* counteracted. Victory bestows honour on our arms, but produces no good to our nation. Plenty creates no peace, and opulence no wealth among us: I cannot fathom it. We seem upon the eve of a general pacification thro' all Europe, but I scarce expect *quiet* in *any* Country, much less our own, to be the consequence of such extensive treaties ...

Poor dear Jane Holman complains of the Greatheeds that they were *too fine* to visit her in London. She is recovering from her severe illness, and will, I hope, be happy, though the world was all *displeased* at her connection. Mrs. Siddons will have a cruel loss if her husband dies, though he was no professed wit, nor beau, nor *Damon,* and tho' I doubt me much if he was even the *very prudent* man folks take him for. Yet will he be a loss, and "*Seldom comes a better*" is no bad proverb. Her son was expected to make his fortune among the fair at one time, but I now hear no more on't.

Mrs. Wynne, Cecilia's Mother-in-law, is come home to Wales ten years younger than she left it, and infinitely handsomer of course. I do not think that will be *my* case when I leave home next; but selling my Book advantageously will, I suppose, heighten my *bloom.* We must have *things as they are*, as Baretti used to say, when he threw ill at Backgammon. My Master's capital health must keep mine up. I never saw *him* in better looks, and Mrs. Randolph will tell you how smart he has made old Bach-y-graig, the name of which they both forgot, I'm sure, before two miles were past; and Lord Mountjoy only saw Lleweny.

Whenever Lady Hesketh crosses your walks, say to her how much I respect her, and how glad I feel that the sweet little Princess is to be happy in virtuous and wise attendants on her infancy, Lady Elgin and Miss Hunt.

Never harm, nor spell, nor charm
Will come *that* Faery's pillow nigh,
While *they* sing her lullaby.

Brynbella is the *fashion*. We have people coming to take views from it, and travellers out of number,—*Tourists,* as the silly word is. Miss Thrales are among the Lakes, I believe these are modish places now for summer, as for winter modish *Streets.* Comical enough! Yet the general face of things must be confessed very gloomy, though Stocks rise, and *that* comforts many who look superficially, or never *look at all* beyond Finsbury Square and Hyde Park Corner. My fear is lest Mr. Pitt may be one of those: if such the case, *he* will be *amazed* whenever the evil moment comes, which would only give grief, not amaze, yours   H.L.P.

John, fourth Earl of Bute, son of the Minister, was made Viscount Mountjoy, Earl of Windsor, and Marquess of Bute in 1796.

The Lady Hesketh here mentioned seems to have been Harriet, daughter and coheir of Ashley Cowper, who married Thomas Hesketh of Rufford, afterwards created a Baronet. She was the cousin and favourite correspondent of Cowper the poet, and died at Clifton 1807. Lady Elgin, the other attendant of the little Princess of Wales, was the wife of Thomas the seventh Earl, best known as the collector of the Elgin Marbles.

The prospect of a general peace proved fallacious. After the battle of Marengo in June, operations were suspended by the armistice of Alessandria, but peace was not concluded, and Austria, urged on by England, recommenced hostilities at the end of the year.

STREATHAM PARK, 6 *Nov.* 1800.

Dear Mrs. Pennington will like a letter with this date, though it tells her nothing except that we are not at home here; it is however exceedingly difficult for us to find that truth out from our good Tenant's behaviour to us, or that of his servants. They are all wonderfully kind and civil, and I fancy we shall go on as we *have* done; nothing is as yet finally settled, but we have every pleasing expectation in *prospect*. *Retrospect* is already disposed of, and you will be pleased that 'tis launched from a good aristocratic House. How does Col. Barry excuse himself *to* himself, I wonder, for his so long and so wide deviation from the train of opinions he seemed as if well rooted in, when we were first acquainted? An agreeable talker is a great loss to the good cause, and I shall be happier when you tell me that he is tired of the bad one.

We have been but once in Town yet, and that for two hours only, one spent with Stockdale, and one with Siddons, who is lean and nerve-shaken, but lovely as ever, and was preparing to shine in Elvira the evening of our visit. Her husband walked in with his two sticks, and chatted chearfully; her eldest daughter appeared to *me* in high health and spirits, and Miss Lee, who was there, made a good report of the youngest …

We live among the Commercial men here, not the professed wits, yet more love and esteem for literature it would be hard to find. Perhaps familiarity, even with *that,* lessens regard. Here has Mr. Giles laid out a Thousand Pounds (no less,) in books for our Library; and Mr. Gillon grieves when a second-hand Shakespear slips from his hand at an auction for want of courage to give beyond 20 Guineas for it. Who says money is not plenty? Truth is England contains more money than meat just now, I mean in proportion, but corn is coming in, and rice, from every quarter of the world; and I hope people will forbear to fly out, and increase their own distresses. The Coachman will get them through every bog, and safely by every precipice, I think, if they will but let the *check-string* alone, and not hinder him from saving them and *himself,* who runs *more* than an equal risque with all of us, and is in haste to find the carriage clear of embarrassments as *we* are. If we believe our eyes, all will be well; if our ears, all will be dismal. Offers of peace are talked of, and no wonder. France is afraid of being driven from Egypt, whence she means to fright our East India Company, if incapable to injure it. I hate their insidious offers, resembling those magical deceptions we used to talk about, where a friendly hand appeared as if presenting a nosegay, but no sooner was it reached at than a dagger started forward in its place. Remember that all our journey has been thro' loyal places; Sir Rich. Hill's fine seat, Lord Bradford's, and the old abiding place of virtue and learning, Oxford.

Two days the first of these sweet scenes delay'd us, and Mr. Piozzi clambered thro' the Grotto. Three days were given to the hospitalities and comforts of Weston Park, and Mr. Gray was unwilling to let me leave *their* curiosities unexamined; so kept us three days more among the Museums etc. of far fam'd Rhedycina ...

Will it raise your spirits to hear that I expect release early in January? After business must come pleasure, and for that *our* eyes turn naturally to Bath. Till then a Hotel and Tavern must be dear Mr. Piozzi's residence, in order to accommodate his wife by living close to the Bookseller's, who assures us that if we will come to Jermyn Street and mind our work closely, it may be launched with the New Year, and 8 weeks of confinement finish all. Wish it success kind Friend, and make Miss Powell and Mr. Pennington—ay and good Mother too,—drink a glass to the health of the two Quarto Vols. you saw advertised this morning under the name of your   H.L.P.

Though Stockdale's publications may have had aristocratic tendencies, the publisher himself was of humble origin and rough manners. Like Robinson he was a Cumberland man, and is reputed to have been originally a blacksmith. In London he worked his way up from the position of a publisher's porter to that of the head of a successful business. It may have been a recommendation to Mrs. Piozzi that he had printed, and partly edited, Dr. Johnson's works.

Hawkestone, near Shrewsbury, was the seat of Sir Richard Hill, Bart., M.P. for Salop, who was the elder brother of the Rev. Rowland Hill, the celebrated preacher. Lord Bradford's seat was Weston Park, near Shifnall. Its then owner was Orlando (Bridgeman), Baron, and afterwards Earl of Bradford.

Mrs. Piozzi's cicerone at Oxford was, in all probability, the Rev. Robert Gray, D.D., of St. Mary Hall, Bampton Lecturer in 1796, who was afterwards Prebendary of Durham, and appointed Bishop of Bristol in 1827.

STREATHAM PARK, *Monday Morng.* Dec. (8) 1800.
(Franked "E. Russell.")

I received, my dear Friend, your melancholy letter, and am sorry to agree with you in that croaking duet which we have long kept up together, both by letter and conversation. Things do go on very shiningly, and even brilliantly, but like the ice-island you liked so in my book, there is an unseen thaw below, and we shall topple over when 'tis least expected. Be perswaded however of England's *comparative* happiness. Every other nation suffers more than we do, more than perhaps the deepest croaker amongst us gives him leave to apprehend; and so singular is the state of Europe just now, that sudden peace would accelerate the ruin of France, of Germany, of Russia, and of the Britannic Islands. The first would then be repaid her ravages over poor dear Italy, by seeing her own hungry and desperate plunderers come home clamourous for rewards they never can receive, and food which the neglected lands could not produce for them. The second would inevitably split into divisions productive of certain annihilation to the *Empire*, leaving Francis King only in Hungary, Bohemia, etc.; while Russia, left the theatre of Paul's caprices, would heat itself into rebellion soon, and throw the North of Europe into confusions much worse than those consequent on the present war. Great Britain would feel herself restrained in her commerce, cut off from power of adding to that wealth for which she is now envy'd by all mankind. Nor could cessation of hostilities benefit any of the belligerent powers, except Rome and Turkey: and they, poor things! fated to fall, and falling, expiate their predecessor's crimes and follies, continue to foment those troubles to which, whoever conquers, they are sure to be the destined victims. I think you recollect Mr. Lanzoni; his accounts of Italian distress, public and private, would half break your heart …

Dear Siddons' story is a tragical one, but the ending has been happy, she will now, I flatter myself, be no more tormented. [Having undergone a painful operation] she is now thin as a lath, and light as air, but safe, as every body thinks. Her behaviour—angelic creature—was on *this* tryal as on *all* her tryals exemplary; firm but unostentatious. Sir James said she was a *real* Heroine, and no Actress on the occasion.

Lysons called at the Hotel, and got me a sight of some manuscripts kept in the British Museum, which I wanted for my work; but he is gone to Bath now. The work is coming quick to a conclusion, and will have a print of the Authour on its first page. My heart delights not in the notion of being Bookseller so, as well as Book*maker*; but one cannot have all as one likes, and I hope people will *buy away*. Those friends who mean to serve me *in earnest* write to Stockdale even now, desiring to be "put down for an early copy." I shall *present* you with one, but do canvass your rich friends, and get them to purchase for honour, and for profit's sake, and all. The darling Randolphs have done me all possible kindness in that way, so has Mr. Chappelow; and Stockdale shows his numerous *orders* as nest-eggs or decoys …

Meanwhile Miss Thrales drove thro' London to Brighton, the seat of gayety till Town revels commence. We dined together, and parted at the lodgings of the Show Woman called a Nyctalope or Albina, with red eyes like a white Rabbet, very curious! …

The prospect of sudden peace was the result of further French successes. Moreau and Ney had beaten the Austrians at Hohenlinden on 2nd December and an armistice was signed at Steyer ceding the fortresses of the Tyrol, &c. Another was signed in Italy, as the result of further victories there, ceding the North Italian ports. And when Murat threatened Naples, a third armistice, closing the Neapolitan ports to England, practically ended the war.

STREATHAM PARK, *Sat.* 10 *Jan.* 1801.

My dear Mrs. Pennington's two charming letters waited my arrival at old Streatham Park, whence a variety of things detained us, but people are certainly never so busy as when they have nothing at all to do. My Book, once written, was not a bit more off my hands, for Stockdale and I are partners in the property, and if he is an honest man—so much the better for your H.L.P.

Of all active, and diligent, and highly successful friends, the first must be acknowledged to wear the name of John Gillon. That extraordinary man brought a list of private orders from people of his own particular acquaintance to our *business dinner* upon New Year's day, and the list took away Stockdale's breath,—much more *mine*. It consisted of 80 gentlemen, to which ten have been added since. Not content with *that*, he made a little feast for drinking success to it at the London Tavern, and set the people all wild for *Retrospection*. This is good news, is not it? And the consequence will be great, for I shall expect a letter before the first of February to say that the first edition is wholly run off. That day will probably rise on us at Bath, if my Master keeps clear of Gout, and our plans are not broken in upon by vexations unforseen …

Things are never as good as one is led to hope, but they are seldom as bad as we are impelled to fear. The bread is at its dearest, the Enemy is arrived at its utmost pitch of insolence. France is less dangerous to Britain, altho' more formidable to other countries, than she has been. Buonaparte will not long outlive the peace, let him make it how and when he pleases. No Buonaparte *can* satisfy his *troops* when they return into the bosom of their native country, pamper'd by promises, and flushed with conquest. A furious outbreak at Paris must necessarily ensue, and you may rely on my prediction being verified.

Pretty Siddons told me about Hannah More, but I never understood the merits of the cause clearly till your letter explained it; my [heart] grieves lest it should affect her health. Our charming friend in Great Marlborough Street has never been so free from complaint since I have known her; and her appearance in the character of Constance transcends all which the stage ever shew'd *me*. The dress is so *appropriate*, and so *becoming*, that its first impression is prodigious, and would be disadvantageous to one who could not keep up the interest it excites. Kemble seems much out of health this winter, and has a *slowness* upon his manner which I do not like; but the public is in high good humour with him …

Adieu, dear Friend, send me another pretty kind letter, and a *true* account of what people say to my Book …

Hannah More's trouble arose through a Sunday school which she had opened at Blagdon in 1795, at the request of Bere, the curate, who soon afterwards complained that the master she had appointed was holding a Conventicle. This was stopped, but fresh complaints in 1800 led to an inquiry by the Chancellor and Rector, and Hannah closed the school in November. The Rector, however, thinking his curate had been too officious, tried to dismiss him, and the school was reopened in January 1801. But the curate declined to resign, and the school was again closed. When a new Bishop (Beadon) was appointed to Bath and Wells, Hannah applied to him for direction, and obtained his sympathy and support: and so after she had been, as she said, "battered, hacked, scalped, and tomahawked for three years," the unedifying controversy came to an end.

Wensday Night, READING, 21 *Jan*. 1801.

We are coming, dear Mrs. Pennington, as your good husband says, but very tardily, and much like the journey of Catherine and Petruchio; so dirty are the ways, and so many our crosses, when travelling with Rat and Mole driven by a sick coachman, who makes himself a little more sick at every stage by doing more than he is able, and by crying lest we should at length be provoked to leave him on the road. He is in no danger, poor soul! Mr. Piozzi has just sent him our chicken broth, and we wait here a day for Miss Allen to go kiss her father and mother, an errand so few folks want to go upon … I think the beds will be *aired* at least, for never were so many people crowding from one city to another as now from Bath to London.

How it rejoyces my heart to hear you *really like the book!* and that Miss Jane Powell approves of the contrasted character visible in those excellent Roman Emperors. The other volume will be most read, and the 19th chapter of *that* will perhaps be most liked. I will correct the typographical errors in *your* book with my own hand, if you will bring it with you to Bath … Stockdale was hurrying to drive out a new edition before we left London, and I was forced to *hold him in*. We shall hear all *our* faults, and the printer's too, when the Reviews make their appearance … Charming Hannah More will tranquillize her mind soon, and only dislike the Established Church a *little* more than usual, for this ill-timed bustle some individuals have made against one of the most valuable members of Society. For as Dr. Johnson says of Watts,—Such she was that every Christian Communion must have been proud of her.

Do not fear the Northern combination: we can hurt *those* fellows more than they can hurt us. And as to a French invasion, it was, in my mind, never less likely, nor ever less to be feared. That Europe is running to ruin I see plain enough, and we must go *after* the rest, but it will be after a good many of them are gone, I think ...

The combination of the Northern Powers, Russia, Sweden, and Denmark, organised by the Emperor Paul against England, was the result of the irritation caused by our insisting on the right to search even neutral vessels for enemies' goods; but was soon broken up by the battle of Copenhagen and the death of Paul.

[*P.M.* Bath] 31 *Jan.* 1801.

My dear Mrs. Pennington's is indeed a dismal letter, and our Master is truly sorry, and so am I. The amusement I get at Bath, when without your conversation, is feeling myself benefited by these darling waters, and hearing the Circulating Library men say that the book sells very well. Stockdale tells me of praises bestowed on it by the Briton, Times, and Porcupine, but I have never seen any ...

Miss Jane Powell must be left, I think, to cut out her own happiness. She is very sensible, and very charming, but you may remember that Dr. Johnson says in his tale of The Fountains, "You may be lovely, but 'tis not a necessary consequence that you should therefore be beloved." We must hope she will not fling so much merit and beauty away: but if she does, let us remember she could not have been happy *without* changing her mode of life; and those who enter on family cares now, have need of strong affection on one side or the other, to support them thro' so rough a journey as what is left of life's road is likely to afford them. The people who are *indifferent* now are truly unwise to marry.

We shall look to your *coming home* for much chat on all subjects, and principally the book which has so long plagued your   H.L.P.

[*P.M.* Bath] *Tuesday,* 10 *Feb.* 1801.

... To your enquiries how things are going here, my reply is, *never so bad*. Fish, flesh, and fowl, all are double price, and tho' we live as retired as 'tis possible, the little red book you remember of marketing expences goes on worse and worse. Even Laura Chapel is raised one third, and the journey hither cost double what it used to do. These are facts. It is equally true indeed, that the waters do my health good, but 'tis a heavy charge, *this same health*, upon one's husband, though *he* may not say or even *think* so. Bachelors live at immense costs however. Mr. Roach or Roche told us yesterday that he and his son paid £200 for 5 weeks eating and sleeping at York House: his servants at board wages all the while. Tea alone stood them in six shillings o' day. Fine times! And Mrs. Mores, our next neighbours, tell me Mr. Pitt has already quitted the helm, and old Britannia is left to weather the storm how she can, without pilot, rudder, or compass; and tow a troublesome sister after her besides. God send her safe to port! He only can ...

My own book, though much diffused, and rapidly sold, has not yet brought me a *shilling*, and it was upon that I fully depended for our reimbursement of these few weeks' charges here in Bath. *Six* only of those weeks yet remain: some of them I still flatter myself we shall still pass together ...

After the union with Ireland, Pitt had become convinced that it was necessary to carry a measure of Catholic Emancipation; but as the King felt scruples about breaking, as he believed, his Coronation Oath, by giving his assent to such a Bill, Pitt resigned, much to George's distress, and was succeeded by Addington.

BRYNBELLA, 5 *April,* 1801.

My dear Mrs. Pennington will be delighted to hear that we are got home safe, in spite of my *nose*, which is restor'd to its original size, colour, and shape: having transmitted all ill humour to the shoulder, more fit for carriage of a burden so oppressive.

Some heaviness has reached my heart tho', and some weight hangs on my spirits. The first intelligence that struck us upon the very confines of our Principality, smiling as it seemed with hope of future plenty, was the death of a friend. You have, I am sure, heard me mention as an agreeable acquaintance and excellent preacher, a Mr.

John Mostyn, Curate of Denbigh. He *perished*, it seems, poor soul, in the hard weather which succeeded that day on which we dined with Dr. Randolph, walking home from his Father's house to his own:—perish'd of *cold*! and was buried in drifts of snow,—

> How sunk his soul!
> What black despair! What horrors fill'd his heart,
> When round him night resistless closing fast,
> And o'er his inmost vitals creeping cold,
> Lay'd him on the wild Heath a stiffen'd corpse,
> Far from the track and blest abode of Man.
> [Thompson]

These verses have almost haunted me ever since; so has his figure, chearful and gay, not 38 years old. But we will change the subject and the side of paper.

Tell dearest Siddons, when you see her, that *her* picture was the first thing we unpacked, and *her* handkerchief the finest thing I appeared in while at Bath: the *only* thing I shall wear here till—till what? I can't answer that question.

Poor Harriet Lee's lowness, the day we dined at Mrs. Stratton's, affected everybody present, and she ran home, unable to bear company. Can you tell whether the conversation of approving, nay *admiring* friends, has been yet able to reconcile her to past vexations, for they scarce can be accounted calamities.

We have contagion even at St. Asaph, but 'tis occasioned by want of wholesome food. When the plenty I still predict shall once arrive, there will be no distemper but *ill-humour*. Meanwhile some cause for *that* does doubtless exist, when the ports are filled with grain, and the poor perishing of hunger. Our Bishop, detained in London by illness, is much wanted, and we came home too late to save our old favourite labourer, Edward Davies, who expired eight hours before our arrival; saying that if we made haste he *yet* should live, because we should send him something *nice* from our own *plates,* as we did when he was sick once before. When *such* things present themselves to one's mind, how vain must be the hope of Reviewers and Critics to draw it on their empty abuse! I would there were no worse afflictions to lament than those created by buzzers and stingers like *them*. Nevertheless *pray* tell me how Hannah More supports *her* torrent of scurrility. She was a kind soul, and came to see us for five minutes before we got into the Chaise at Laura Place, looking very well, thank God! Apparently not worse for her long illness and confinement. Her sister is *too* right tho' concerning the general distress for *victuals* …

I carry this letter with me to S. Asaph Cathedral, Easter Sunday, and put it in the Post Office there after service. The Ladies at Llangollen enquired much for you. They have more news and more stories than one could dream of. Their *best* however is concerning their own old Maid Mary, from whose character one would think Sophia Lee had pourtray'd that of Connor in her tale of the Two Emilys. Mary, seeing her Ladies' eyes fix'd, one fine night lately, upon the stars, said to Miss Ponsonby, "Ah! Madam, you once showed me a fine sight in the heavens, the Belt of *O'Bryan*; but I suppose we shall see it no more now, since the *Union*." To this nothing, sure, can be added.

(*P.M.* Denbigh) 26 *Apr.* 1801.

What a letter! What a pleasure to have such a Correspondent! You really can scarce imagine, my dear Friend, how completely your kind Frank-full set before my eyes the scenes I was so wishing to have witness'd. Peace and plenty are coming, and dear Dr. Randolph's first sermon after the Victory at Copenhagen, must have given a foretaste of all the felicities in their train to his enraptur'd auditors, I doubt not.

The effect of national fervour and national happiness upon Sweet Siddons charmed me; and it was so nicely accompanied too by her maternal exultation. The child in your account had suffered scarce anything from ye alarming symptoms which so frighted the whole house of Belvidere …

Why, you have had a nice Holyday time indeed! And *you*, like the dear King, will recover by dint of good news. My rheumatism has mended ever since you said how Mr. Whalley liked Retrospection, and a kind letter from Mr. Gray, saying it was well thought of at

Oxford, made me throw off a little fur tippet, which, till to-day's *post*, I wore to ward off these early winds. Ods Blushes and Blooms! The poor Cherry trees have dropt their pretty flow'rs in one night. A sturdy Pear tree or two resist all Northern Combinations against *them*: but Peaches and Nectarines we shall have none of this Summer, content to see wheat falling, Stocks rising, and damaged Rice coming in by shiploads to feed *those Pigs* which my friends on the South Parade so talked of.

Meantime it was well done of the wise and good men to go out and harangue the rioters; they will go underground again now, and give their instigators *fresh* trouble to find *fresh* arguments to set them on *fresh* mischief *in due time*. Well! God save great George our King! While he lives many a Laurel bush will be used to decorate our doors … By the time this reaches your Hot Wells, good accounts may possibly arrive from Egypt. The death of Paul will sit *heavy on the soul* of Abdallah Menou, like the Ghost in Shakespeare's Richard, and *fall his edgeless sword*.[4] May he *but* hear that news before the battle, *I'll* answer for its success.

Great credit ought really to be given to that amiable creature, the Duchess of York, for being able to make every body love *her*, while they naturally and necessarily abhor her brother. And it was pretty of her husband to cry at the tragedy: they very seldom *do* cry.

When you write tell me how Sotherby's play went off; our Newspaper never names the Theatre, so Mrs. Siddons's name reaches me only through your letters. When our Bishop returns I shall get free'd covers, and write oftener, for the sake of goading your pen to an answer … With regard to Mr. Pennington, he hardly *can* come to any real harm. The complaints of gouty men are sure to end, however they may begin, in a fit of Gout; and *better* assurance of long life is granted to no living mortal. He will quarrel with the man, and vex about the maid, and they will leave him, and then he will get others;—all will lead *uneasy* lives, but no lives will be shorten'd, except *your own*, by fretting concerning what can neither be helped nor mended …

Success had attended English efforts abroad in more than one direction. The Northern Confederation having adopted an attitude of "armed neutrality," and laid an embargo on British goods, a fleet was sent to Copenhagen under Sir Hyde Parker, with Nelson as second in command. The latter grew impatient of the cautious tactics of his chief, and his daring attack on the Danish forts and fleet on April 1, resulted in the capture of the latter, and the detachment of Denmark from the League. In Russia the assassination of the Emperor Paul on March 24 (which Buonaparte in the *Moniteur* ascribed to the machinations of England) placed Alexander on the throne, who at once reversed his predecessor's policy, and so the Confederation collapsed. In Egypt General Menou had succeeded Kleber in command of the French army, which was unable to prevent the landing of Sir Ralph Abercromby's expedition on March 2: and though the English General fell at the battle of Alexandria, that city and Cairo fell into our hands, and it became evident that the French could not maintain their hold on the country.

The shock of Pitt's resignation, and the prospect of Roman Catholic emancipation, had again unhinged the King's mind. But the attack was a brief one, and by March 14 he was sufficiently recovered to accept the formal resignation of his ministers.

Frederick, Duke of York, had married in 1791 Frederica, Princess Royal of Prussia, a state whose partitions of Poland and timid attitude of neutrality to France during two reigns, were not calculated to render its rulers popular in England.

BRYNBELLA, 22 *May* 1801.

My dear and valued Friend now receives a letter of *business* from Brynbella. The trunk with all our clothes, books, papers,—*everything*,—Hodgkins saw booked ... upon the 22d of March, is never arrived yet, and this is the 22d of May. I have heard of it just now, though, and in an odd manner. A man who says he signs for some Mr. Lye, the date, Bristol, tells me it is gone by sea to Liverpool. What madness! It was meant for *Chester Waggon*, the old conveyance by which Mr. Wiltshire has regularly sent it these three years. Could you be kind enough to enquire about it? ...

And now do, dear Friend, find me out another thing. We are told Miss Thrale is at Bath for her *health*; and the idea keeps me very uneasy, the more as she never writes. *You saw* the last letter I ever received from any of them. I dare say Dr. Parry is her Physician, and you could know from *him,* without any immediate enquiry as if *I* wished to hear, which she would consider as if intrusive and inquisitive, and would *say* it was affectation ...

Let us thank God for the happy change in public affairs at least, peace and plenty are not far off.

> From Egypt old Rome in the days of Domitian
>> To make her tyrannical Emperor smile
> Fresh roses brought over, for Winter provision,
>> That bloom'd on the Tyber as once on the Nile.
>
> But bold Abercrombie, whom Britons confide in,
>> *His Flora* sent home with far different spoil;
> The invincible army of Frenchmen deriding,
>> Their standards he seiz'd on the banks of the Nile.
>
> Thus end the exploits of renown'd Buonaparte,
>> Who fell upon Egypt with force and with guile,
> Throwing dust in the eyes of each Mussulman hearty,
>> Dust pregnant with plagues on the banks of the Nile.
>
> Of warriors ill-fated if England must tell soon,
>> Her losses, though deep, she'll repair in a while;
> With Moore, Smith, and Berry, Ball, Trowbridge, and Nelson,
>> A hero we'll count for each mouth of the Nile.

Mr. Pennington will see an allusion to an Epigram of Martial[5] in the first stanza; but never mind, 'tis a good Ballad to roar at a club, and the tune, Rural Felicity, or Ellen o' Roon. But what fellows those old Romans were after all!! Fetching (as they actually did) Oysters from England and Roses from Egypt for one winter evening's entertainment ...

1. *Romeo and Juliet,* I. i. 189.

2. "Here's much to do with hate, but more with love."—*Romeo and Juliet,* I. i. 181.

3. "He's for a jig, or a tale of bawdry, or he sleeps."—*Hamlet,* II. ii.

4. *Rich. III,* V. iii, 135.

5. Martial, *Epig.* vi. 80: Ad Cæsarem de rosis hibernis.

CHAPTER VI

TRAVELS AND THOUGHTS

THE next letter is directed to "Longford Cottage, the Seat of the Rev. Thomas Sedgwick Whalley, near Bristol," where Mrs. Pennington was staying for a few weeks.

BRYNBELLA, 3 *June* 1801.

... I do assure you that between your own house and this no greater anxiety has been felt for Mr. Whalley; he is our very true friend, and we have sense enough to know it. He is so much Miss Hannah More's friend that I am convinced of his fretting at Sir Abraham Elton's officiousness. Will you have *proof* how wrong those things are? I am frequently asked after celebrated characters when we return home to so remote a neighbourhood as this is: and to the questions asked about these exemplary Ladies I made such replies as a friend is expected to make. Some of our neighbours, however, within these three months, have had a fancy to take in a Bath newspaper, and "Oh!" says one now, and "Ah, ah!" says another, "why you never told *us*, Mrs. Piozzi, concerning this *paper war* between Miss Mores and Mr. What's his name! As good as you say they are, those who live in the world see spots in the sun, we find," etc. etc. Now would it not have been better far to have left these dear creatures round Brynbella nothing to talk about but the *going off* of Lord Kirkwall's marriage with Miss Ormsby, the *coming on* of Mr. Piozzi's gout, just at Laburnum season, the hopes of famous news from Egypt, and, blessed be God, the near certainty of immense crops to feed our poor, and damaged rice from India to feed our pigs? Would it not have been better? But we will talk of something else, if you please.

The trunk is not come, but coming, and it was kind in you to let me know how I might look after it. I had no thought of its taking such a voyage. The comical preference, shown in your letter, of a trunk to a Lady, is *more* than classical. In Homer's time they preferred a tripod to the fairest: when the tripod was chas'd, though, and the damsel a slave.

I have had a civil letter from Miss Thrale now. She is retired to a friend's Country Seat, I understand … The noise and racket of London was grown painful to her, and she longed for sight and smell of green fields. I wrote her word that if chance should bring you and her together, it would be very pleasant to you both, who have many ideas, and many expressions too, in common. I would the love of H.L.P. lived in her heart as in yours, but of *that,* as Sciolto says, "*as of a gem long lost, think we no more.*"

Do you recollect that agreeable morning dear Mr. Whalley gave us at Laura Place this Spring? and how he talked of the River Euphrates, and said it would be one day *literally* dried up for the Jews' return? And do you remember what you said, after he was gone, upon the subject? and how I exclaimed "Why, you are talking just like Miss Thrale? Well! and I begin—since he open'd my own mind,—to think that it *may* be so; ay, and without contradiction of your humourous asperity against the talkers and hearers either. Beg of Mr. Whalley, when he is better, and can amuse himself with such stuff, to look in Plutarch's Life of Lucullus, 'tis an early life, first volume, I think, and if my memory fails me not, he will find something like a confirmation of his own opinion,—and of yours. Now please to observe that I have no Plutarch *here,* nor have seen one since I saw *you.* In such an act of mere reminiscence, therefore, the mind may be mistaken, but my heart tells me that Lucullus perceived some property in the River Euphrates,—some quality rather, which would (he observed) make it fordable upon a future day, altho' so deep when he was wishing to pass over.[1] All this seventy years before our Saviour's appearance in the flesh.

I am always ready you know for a bit of *old Stilton* as Dr. Johnson called profane History. "Thou dost love," said he, "my dear, to play the part of Swift's Vanessa, who

> Nam'd the ancient heroes round,
> Explain'd for what they were renown'd, etc.

and I have *as* steadily resisted that mode of conversation;—now pray, *pray* let's have no more of it." In obedience to *his commands,* as well remember'd, sure, as Plutarch's lives, I leave this, and begin saying a good word of Mr. Murphy's book, and feel delighted that you take an interest in it too. There was some danger lest it pleased *me* merely by bringing old scenes to view, but I will trust *your* criticism. The work has more merit as Garrick and he certainly never loved each other, and you may see his praises of the man he celebrates are dictated by *duty,* while those bestowed on Barry spring from *fondness.* I had rather he had been kinder to sweet Siddons. What a thing it is that her husband cannot at least count and keep together the money she gets for him. That man has, I fear, some rage for speculation; a dangerous game. The prudent people are, for aught I observe, no better calculators than we open-pursed fools, who are cheated out of 20s. perhaps, by Bett Lewis the vagrant; while they lose £200 sterling in the management of a puppet-show that *takes fire*, or sink three times as much in a Canal that *lets out water*, or some nonsense.

We have had an earthquake here, as they say, for I felt it not, tho' I am confident I was wide awake at two o'clock Monday morning. Lady Orkney's Canary Birds fell from their perch however, and some of our Denbigh friends fancy they heard a noise. I was thinking about my master's Bavanda, and he was thinking how thirsty the gouty pains made him; so Brynbella was unconscious of the shock.

Buonaparte is supposed to be all this time under the influence of poyson administered three months ago, but I believe *that* as I do the earthquake. Poor Selim's death of the Continental Apoplexy is less improbable; so is young Constantine's hope of restoring the Greek Empire. No matter! Live our own dear King, I care for none of them. Here is his 63d birthday, and the value of his life is increased 63 times since it began. But y⁰ grand climacteric passed over, I count him safe, and would rather have an annuity upon him than on the dangerous dame we fear so justly.

Oh! I forgot to tell you, Stockdale sends word we have a wicked enemy at *Bath,* who injures the sale of Retrospection by spiteful and ingenious censures. *Who is it, I wonder*! ...

Swarms of pamphlets on the "Blagdon Controversy" were making their appearance about this time. Those which Mrs. Piozzi had in view were probably "A Letter to the Rev. Thomas Bere ... occasioned by his late unwarrantable attack on Mrs. H. More," by the Rev. Sir Abraham Elton, Bart.; which was answered by "An Appeal to the Public in the Controversy between H. More, the Curate of Blagdon, and the Rev. Sir A. Elton," by the Rev. Thomas Bere.

Murphy had just published his *Life of David Garrick* in two volumes, which was not very well received by the contemporary critics, who found fault with its clumsy arrangement, and its excessive padding with prologues, epilogues, etc. Mrs. (Ann Spranger) Barry, who died this year, was a popular actress in London and the Provinces, and was considered by the critics to equal, if not to surpass Peg Woffington and Mrs. Cibber.

Sultan Selim did not die of apoplexy, but lived to be deposed in 1807. The Empress Catherine of Russia had conceived the idea of extinguishing the Turkish power in Europe, and placing one of her own family on the throne of the restored Greek Empire. For this purpose she chose the second son of her own son Paul, had him christened Constantine to fulfil the prophecy that a Constantine should again rule at Constantinople, and educated him to carry out her plan. There seemed to be some chance of its success when the Emperor Joseph gave it his support in 1788; but Turkey was saved by Pitt's triple alliance of England, Prussia, and Holland, to restore the Balance of Power. About this period Constantine had gained some distinction as commander-in-chief in Poland.

[*Dated, by Mrs. Pennington, Jul.* 1801.]

Dr. Randolph is a wise man for not caring what these foolish fellows say, and Mrs. Randolph is a sweet lady for caring. On the like principle H.L.P. is a dunce for being *angry,* and dear Pennington is a kind friend for being *enraged* at these odious Critical Reviewers. Those who say my book is merely good for nothing cannot be answer'd. The book says something like that of itself,—but its worthlessness consists in telling people what they knew before, not in telling what is *false*, for that is the charge that offends me. Much of this obloquy might have been avoided certainly, by quoting authorities, but they would add more to the work's weight than its value, were the deed done to-morrow: and I thought it a mere insult to the Public sitting gravely to *inform* them of what they may read in the 7th Period of the 3rd Chapter of the 1st Part of Mosheim's Ecclesiastical History, edited by our friend Macleane, who, in a note, *confirms* the fact of Tiberius desiring the Roman Senate to deify our Saviour. One would really wonder at a man's assurance who, like our Critical Reviewer, boldly asserts that "this is an exploded fiction." It stood on the testimony of Eusebius and Tertullian for sixteen centuries before it was disputed: and M. Iselin, with Hase the Hebraist, and numbers more since the year 1700, have proved its truth beyond all power of denial. I saw Miss Case with Macleane's Mosheim in her hand when I last visited her. *She* need not be deceived, *she* can enquire and *see* the truth of my position. When I wrote to Mr. Gillon expressing my uneasiness under a charge of ignorance ill-deserved, he said my antagonist was a man of immense abilities, and I had better *let him alone*. But Robson the Bookseller, who sent me down the Review, liked my refutation so well that he requested leave to print my angry letter to *him* on the occasion. I suppose it resembles that I wrote to you, and you will see it in the Gentleman's Magazine for July.

I am sorry about Hannah More: these things are, upon the whole, very mortifying, and injure the cause of Religion, Virtue, and sound Literature *too much*, at a moment when enemies to all three are ready and keen to take every possible advantage.

I have a cold and reproachful letter brought me just now from Harriet Lee, accusing my heart of alienation because I made no enquiry concerning her state of mind, altho' I saw, she says, that it was an uneasy one. How unreasonable the people all are! I thought myself acting delicately to make no enquiries, where nothing was avow'd as capable of being construed into more than a past vexation about the children's sickness ... Nothing would be less pleasing to me than the thought of having offended any of the house of Belvidere. Never did I say a slight word, or write a peevish one, about them. Never did I fail to express my just admiration of their talents, or even suffer myself to be provoked to more than sorrow—not anger—when I had reason for believing that Robinson was better disposed to ye purchase of my book before his visit to Bath, than he was afterwards.

I hope she will write kindly and make all up. I am ready. If she does not—we must sing Ralph's song in the Maid of the Mill, I think.

> Nothing's tough enough to bind her,
> Then agog when once you find her,
>   Let her, let her go, let her go, never mind her, etc.

Poor dear pretty Siddons! What has she been doing to her mouth? Picking it, my master says, as I do my fingers, which, he threatens me, are one day to resemble poor Mr. Pennington's toes. But in earnest and true sadness, what can be the matter with her lips? Lips that never were equalled in enunciation of tenderness or sublimity! Lips that spoke so kindly *to* me and *of* me! Dear soul! what can ail her? She dreamed once that all her teeth came out upon the stage I remember; I told her she would go on acting till age had bereft her of them; but God forbid that she should lose them *now*. Her husband will mend at Bath ... Sally's death will be no *loss* to her dear mother, altho' a very poignant affliction without doubt; and Cecilia will be her delight I dare say: but Sally and her Father both will yet last many years I am confident. Shall we have a Bath Winter all together and be comfortable? Or will they pay her, and lure her back to Drury Lane? You must get her mouth in good order, that she may look like my *little* miniature of the *greatest and only unrivalled* female this century last expired has pretended to produce. When her lips close, what good will our ears do open? Yes, yes, they will hear Randolph preach, Piozzi sing, and Pennington converse. Comfort the charming creature all you can tho', and get her into her accustomed beauty, and tell her how she is beloved at pretty Brynbella …

P.S. by Mr. Piozzi.—

… Well! I think it time to forget the Critical Review, and Mrs. P. she is persuade to do so. The writer is a poor miserable wretch wanting bread, and so *sufficit*. Belvidere people they can write, but they cannot understand *Retrospection*. Next week Little John we expect him at Brynbella …

James Robson, like Robinson and Stockdale, was a Cumberland man, and began his career in the shop of Brindley, whom he succeeded.

Bickerstaffe's opera, *The Maid of the Mill*, was based on Richardson's *Pamela*. Ralph was the son of Fairfield the Miller.

Mrs. Siddons's trouble seems to have been erysipelas, from which she suffered a good deal in later life.

[Dated, by Mrs. Pennington, Jul. 1801.]

You are a dear Friend, and a wise Lady, and—"Conscience" (says I) "you counsel *ill*": and "Pennington" (says I) "you counsel well."[2] See the learned Lancelot Gobbo. But my heart tells me that the Gentleman's Magazine will exhibit a letter of more anger than good sense at least, being written on the spur of the moment, the very day I read my antagonist's spiteful accusations. *'Tis most likely*, for it never entered my head that Robson would print what came to him in form of complaint, just as I wrote it to you. Yet when he asked leave to show it up before the public, and said several friends in his shop advised the measure, I would not shrink from it.

Harriet Lee has sent me a making up Epistle; so we make up, but it is a cold and flat paste we make on't at last, and as little George Siddons said of his brother's friends, whom he *had* been half afraid of, "*I know what they are now.*" I know what she is, too; and worded my answer accordingly. She lamented the ill nature of the Critical Review to me with due and proper pathos. I replied lightly that they were not half as ill-natured as they were ill-informed, and that if charming

Hannah More valued such abuse as little as H.L.P. did, she would live long a *champion* of religion's cause, and not dye, as they wished her to do, a martyr to't. The truth is her controversy gets very stale now, and like her torment *Beer* (*Bere*)

Though *stale*, not ripe, tho' thin, yet never *clear*.

I will hasten to expose my Gentlemen's ignorance, and then release people to think and care about matters more worth their attention.

The loss of those two fine ships was vexatious enough, but we must have a few knocks. *Hannibal* lost one eye early in life you know: so these fellows came on the *blind* side of him, *that's all.* Our cutting the Corvette from Camaret Bay was an exploit worthy to be preserved in History till Time shall be no more. But nothing ever equalled the hardihood of Naval Officers shown in course of this war. It is a tissue of heroism, and to attempt shores so guarded would seem frenzy, had one not to recollect apparent impossibilities conquered by Buonaparte: particularly his passing Mount St. Gothard in winter, never relaxed; which however *did* yield (God only knows how) to the French Artillery, suffer'd to cross that Mountain for the sake of gaining a decisive battle at Marengo. We must have more sense, if they *do* land, than fight any battle at all with such troops; our business is to harrass them and thin their numbers, not easily repair'd; and attacking them only by *night,* assure to ourselves the advantages accrueing from our own knowledge and their ignorance of the country. Mr. Pennington will tell you I am *quite right,* and it was for want of knowing as much in old times that Harold foolishly set his Island on the hazard of one grand battle, which he lost at Hastings.

Our Secret Society men who buy up the corn and fling [it] by night into the river or sea, are far more dangerous enemies; and will, if matters ripen into reality of bustle, be less afraid of acting openly. Their present intentions tow'rds irritating our lower ranks, and making them willing to rebel, are happily counteracted by the enormous quantity of corn in the field, and ports, and harbours. *They too are known,* and people see into their machinations pretty clearly.

Bath is a well-judged place for the King during times of apprehended turbulence, and the waters may do him good, as they do me ... 'Tis a nice place beside, for a man of his open character and manners to attach individuals, and delight common folks with his familiar way. I am glad he will see *Captain* Dimond play Lothario at three score years old, to our lovely friend's inimitable Callista ...

We have got a dear Member of Parl*ᵗ* now close by us in Denbigh Town; so Heaven have mercy on the correspondents of your

H.L.P.

The loss of two ships here mentioned seems to relate to the vessels which grounded at the commencement of Nelson's engagement at Copenhagen. On his return home he was set to watch the French armament collecting for the invasion of England, under the protection of the fortified camps at Boulogne, Brest, &c. There was no opportunity for any decisive action, but Camaret Bay, near Brest, was the scene of one of the numerous cutting-out engagements in which the British commanders distinguished themselves at this period.

The "gallant, gay Lothario" was a character in Rowe's *Fair Penitent*, his victim, Callista, being one of Mrs. Siddons's favourite impersonations.

Mrs. Piozzi does not seem to have made much use of her "dear Member," for this is the only letter this year which he can have franked.

BRYNBELLA, *August* 1801.

Be in better spirits, dear Friend, or at least in the best spirits that you *can*: things will draw cross sometimes, we *know* they will:

> We know that all must fortune try,
> And bear our evils, wet or dry.

My master's misfortunes are few, but *dry* ones; he has now a chalk-stone on his *ear*, but Siddons's *mouth* is a more important ailment by half ...

Hannah More
By Scriven after Slater, 1813

What is the meaning of Hannah More's marriage being thus *gravely* announced in every newspaper, and resounding here in N. Wales from every mouth, while you say not one word upon the subject? … Give me an answer to the thousand enquiries buzzing round me, and give it quickly that the talk may end …

Our little boy is blithe as a bird, almost as wild; a model of gayety and good-humour.

> With smiling cheeks, and roving eyes,
> Causeless mirth, and vain surprise,

as Hawkesworth describes childhood, such is he: may he get safety thro' the *next stage*!

I have not yet seen Harriet's tale, and without your information should never have heard about Belinda. These soft'ning books greatly encrease the dissolution of manners, tho' each, unexceptionable in itself, cannot be complained of. The youth of our present day however *read nothing else*, and how they should escape such melting relaxers, added to their own feelings in the warm season of life, I guess not. Literary arrogance and early ambition are the only antidotes which *this* world will supply.

Education is a mere word now for a theme or subject on which to display the eloquence of teachers, and the teachers themselves— Miss More perhaps excepted,—are drawing boys and girls into Love's labyrinth with one hand, while they are pointing to distant Wisdom and Virtue with the other.

The Curate and Barber who burned Don Quixote's Library of large romances[3] would have been frighted to see them thus epitomized into the power of a school boy to purchase, as India's fragrance is happily compress'd into a Guinea phial of Odour of Roses.

Our Novel-writers have a right to hate *me,* who set my face so against fiction, and who have endeavoured (tho' fruitlessly) to make truth palatable. But when they boast that *my* book is liked only by the old Heads of Houses at Oxford and Cambridge, and chained up in the *Bodleian* or *All Souls*, 'tis such a vaunt as the French make when they chain their ships ashore.

It is in the meantime very surprising that Nelson should try again after seeing that he attempts impossibilities. I think he has play'd double or quits too often, and tempts good fortune too far. Egypt is our own at last, and will bring its *plagues* with it. For how should *we* garrison such distant possessions, which the French may disturb whenever they are disposed to rid themselves of a troublesome General and 40,000 open mouths? I wish the East Indians, for whose sake we drove these fellows out, would be pleased to keep them away now they are gone.

So my Lord de Blaquiere is run away to make drawings beyond Snowdonia, and the Bishop is in Anglesey, and no Frank, for love or money, can I get … I hear Mrs. Mostyn has a son *Arthur*. He will, I hope, fill his round table with Knights, and revive the spirit of Chivalry. M[ark] L[ane] is the great Dragon which devours us all, and 'tis said there is a train laid to rid the Kingdom of a combination so strong, that relying upon its force, a Gentleman offer'd yesterday to bet a wager that Corn would be as high priz'd next November as it was last January. But this is croaking worse than Mrs. Pennington, and I believe that the Gentleman will lose …

This month Nelson had made an attempt to cut out the French flotilla at Boulogne by a boat attack, which failed owing to the fact that the French had chained their vessels together, and were able to defend them by a heavy musketry fire from the shore.

Lt.-Col. John de Blaquiere, son of an Emigré, who had been M.P. for several English and Irish constituencies, and Lord-Lieutenant of Ireland, was created a Baronet in 1704, and advanced to the Peerage in 1800.

BRYNBELLA, [6] *Sep.* 1801.
(*Franked "de Blaquiere"*)

… Our Barometer begins rising while I write, and the plantations drink their fill from the Horn of future Plenty. Ploughing and preparing ground for next year's crop will *now* be all done by Michaelmass, and the dwellers in *Mark Lane* may pray for their own *safety*: it will be in more danger than our purses and stomachs. God Almighty will send *victuals;* and the —— may take care of the *Cooks*.

I know not how you gather'd from my letter that *I* believed in Hannah More's change of condition, tho' my neighbours did. Yet never having heard that Dr. Crossman was a married or a single man, and seeing no jokes accompany the intelligence, which came in the regular list of weddings for the week, I own myself stagger'd and now the Papers are filling with epigramn nonsense which will confirm people in their credence, if no contradiction is given.

With regard to our dear charming friend, *her* tormentors *must* be private ones. The *Public* would not suffer their truly deserving favourite to be insulted; and she should run *to*, not from the *Theatre*, for protection. I guess not what *character* it was in which, you say, she will appear no more. *Tell* me, and tell me what she thinks of the enclosed. Oh! how you and I must for ever hold abhorred of our whole souls, the human creature who can thus delight in torturing a heart like hers! Have I ever *seen* him, think you? Has he made advances to her, and been refused? Or does he protect a rival Actress, rising into fame? Or *what* inspires such horrible malignity? I pretend not to trace, as Fanny Burney and as Harriet Lee can do, vile passions to their source, but such characters prove the Play of Hatred and feelings of de Montfort not out of nature ...

My packet of macaroni came down without the book in it, so I still remain ignorant of all but what you tell me ... Well! I shall read it some time, and will learn (even without its assistance) to give my esteem where confidence would be ill bestowed. I wish all the Lees very well, notwithstanding what has passed in my own mind concerning their conduct towards *me*. We must take people as they are, and *such* people are, at any rate, extremely difficult to meet with.

Our little Boy left us yesterday, and for Mr. Davies's credit and his own, left us chearfully. A sweeter temper'd creature lives not, nor one better disposed to smooth down life's asperities before him, either by well applied strength, or by a power happier still, of rolling over them, and suffering little hurt.

Miss Thrale has written to me very civilly from Lowestoffe. We have the whole island between us; for Mr. Piozzi promises me a dip in our Irish Channel next week, and we go on Thursday next to a Bathing Place called Prestatyn, about 14 miles off. Now do not exclaim "What! are you 14 miles from the sea?" because we are scarcely 4 miles; but from any conveniences we are at least fourteen. The invasion seems to keep nobody inland, and by the King's giving up Bath entirely I gather the Ministers no longer feel apprehensions. If French chicanery cannot raise a famine or a sedition among *us*, and if "even-handed Justice does indeed return the ingredients of that poyson'd chalice to themselves," and set on foot a mutiny among their own soldiers,—*peace must follow*. I told you it was coming, and plenty too; *and what I told you then my heart adheres to still* ...

Dr. Crossman, to whom the newspapers had married Hannah More, was rector of Blagdon, the parish in which her controversy with Bere, the curate, arose.

BRYNBELLA, *Fryday Oct.* 9, 1801.

Well! my dear, tardy Friend! your letter is come at last, and a nice letter it is. I have one too this post from Mr. Whalley, so kind! He has had enough to do with his Lady Writer, but he loves both Hannah More and myself, and the least we can do in return is to be *merry*, love our friends, and forgive our enemies, forget offenders and offences, and light up our windows for the Peace. The terms are certainly in no sense disgraceful, and since we have all been saying so repeatedly, "Let us heal our own wounds, limit our own expences, and care no longer for Allies who, 'tis sure, care not for *us*;" I pronounce our Ministers fully justified to *this* Country for quitting their post, and leaving every *other* Country to the fate they would none of them resist. While France, having enlarged her own territory beyond the other proudest hope of their own proudest Monarch, has prudently bought us off from fighting Europe's battles, with two eminently rich, useful and valuable Islands: well knowing that an Englishman will always be quiet while his palate is pleased and his pockets full.

The Gold, and Silver, and Rubies, and Rice from Ceylon, sweeten'd by Sugar from Trinidad, will keep Great Britain in perfect good humour, and the Commercial Treaty will keep her employ'd; and in the meantime Alexander and Buonaparte mean to divide the Globe. Such is apparently their project for 1801; how and by what means God Almighty will render it abortive remains to be seen. The internal politics of our United Kingoms here at home offer a *fair shew* certainly, for if people are not please'd with seeing their ports fill'd with foreign corn, and their stack-yards groaning under the weight of our own harvests, what will please them? Not the price of Mutton in the markets I trow; for between the inclosing commons, and *improving* the breed of sheep in Counties where such large animals will sell for 6*d. an ounce* next year, and we shall have more mouths to feed after the War is over, unless the mortality at Liverpool goes on.

Ah! dear Friend! I told you how it would be, and true did I tell you, but no matter,

> For other thoughts mild Heav'n a time ordains,
> And disapproves that care, tho' wise in show,
> That with superfluous burden loads the day;
> And when God sends a chearful hour, refrains.
> Let us light up our windows and be merry ...

Little did I dream seven yars ago of seeing peace proclaimed between Great Britain and the *Consular State* of France. Little could I *ever* have dreamed that I should see Venice annihilated, Genoa forgotten, Piedmont's Alpine barrier insufficient to keep out invasion, even in the depth of winter; and old Rome, divided against herself, dropping into her enemy's mouth almost without invitation. The world, as it appears, consenting to all this, and even happy to think things have gone no worse. We shall see more yet, but shall not see *all*. *All*! no nor *half* ...

I wote Harriet Lee word how much her tale impress'd me. 'Tis a characteristic of this age, I think, to shew what forcible impression may be made by setting only our mean passions to work, avarice, fraud and fear; instead of generosity, love, and valour. What she has done, however is very striking; and every one I lend the book to is amazed to find Conrade the murderer of Stralenheim ...

The long-expected Peace, which gave us Trinidad and Ceylon, was not finally arranged till March, but preliminaries were signed October 1.

BRYNBELLA, 30 *Nov.* 1801.

No, thank you, my dear anxious Friend; we are pretty well, and pretty happy, as health and happiness in this world go. I have had *more* than my share of both, blessed be God. My master has an addition to *his* torments, St. Anthony's fire, in and out, but much less afflicting than troublesome. It keeps him from going to neighbours' houses, and without *that,* there is no hope of Autumnal society at Brynbella: it will keep him from going to *yours*, and then he must learn to swear of dear Mr. Pennington. Lord de Blaquiere, who used to free my covers, is gone to London, and my prudence (for the first time in my life) overbalanced my tenderness, and so I made you uneasy: and so I'm glad you *were* uneasy, and there's an end.

We have written about the house to Mrs. Garrart and to Harriet Lee both. They say my Lord Kenmare is in now, and will be out on the 12th Jan. That time will do nicely, and the poor folks round here are glad he does not quit sooner, tho' Mr. Piozzi has given a dozen of them good warm winter jackets, and a petticoat each to the wife: and barley, which last year was at 32s., they may have now at 18s., and good wheat at a guinea. So I shall leave them with less regret this year than last for all those reasons; and we employ a vast many hands in planting …

Something is the matter at Belvidere House, I do *think*. Harriet says she has the Black Dog upon her back, and writes as if wishing to be courted out of the secret. Instead of doing which, I wrote her a rhodomontading letter, all mirth and no matter[4] (as Beatrice says) to turn the course of her ideas: for I wish not confidence where real kindness has ceased to reside: and if these novel-writing Ladies fancy that they, and they alone, can read the human mind,—'tis a mistake. Your imagination is bound by the Juggler who rattles and talks while he ties a knot in your pocket-handkerchief, as surely as by the sly Thief that steals it, only the intention is more honorable …

Oh do tell the Doctor that Lord Kirkwall did *not* marry Miss Ormsby, and that everybody says it was because he felt that he liked Miss Blaquiere better; certain it is the first match went off; and if this second does not come on, I shall wonder.

You were always more sanguine about the benefits of peace than I was, but tranquillity is the best consequence it *can* have; let's not therefore disturb that by putting monopoly in people's heads, or in their mouths. Such talk leads to nothing but riot. If there is no scarcity there will be no monopoly: the people *can* monopolise nothing that is not already scarce. A peace which leaves unresisted France mistress of more territory than was ever hoped for by her proudest Monarch in his proudest day; which annihilates before her grasp principalities and powers, and leaves her tributary Republics secur'd to her services by the cheap garrison, *Opinion*, cannot be viewed without horror by the mere writer of Retrospection. Tho' such were the miseries of war, and such the acquisitions by treaty to Great Britain, that peace has a right, not only to please, but to console, and even *delight* a true English subject ...

BRYNBELLA, *Tuesday Night*, 15 *Dec*. 1801.
... Well! Time passes away, and so do torments, and poor Mrs. Whalley will have no more in this world. I shall have that of telling you that there will not be any *habitable Brynbella this Summer*, that is coming. We shall be thrown on the wide world ourselves, and mean to pass the early part of it at Streatham Park, on a visit, the latter end in Caernarvonshire, where my lease of a little estate is out, and then call here for a month or two in our way back to *Winter Quarters* ... On this hope of real comfort let us live till then, and pass some chearful hours together at dear Bath, where I would I were this moment! Mr. Piozzi playing on the Piano e forte to Mrs. De Luc, you and I listening, and hoarding up chat for the half hour after he and his auditress are abed and asleep ...

I cannot yet rid myself of this Bristol quarrel, If the Mores are, and have been always Sectaries, why do they deny it? Where's the harm done? I had rather they were good High Church folks like you, and like myself, but the religion that was good enough for Isaac Watts need not be shrunk from. What are they afraid of?

Mrs. Hamilton tells me sweet Siddons is *alive,* but I fancy she is on no stage now. Poor Mrs. Whalley's death will grieve her unaffectedly. I was never intimate enough to *feel* her loss, but she was no common character, that's certain. Half a dozen Gentlemen who lived much together abroad were so sincerely vex'd when she left presiding at their public table, that they quitted the house; a surprizing testimony to the conversation talents of one so wanting in youth or beauty ...

[*P.M.* BATH]
My dear Mrs. Pennington's friends will learn to *hate* poor H.L.P.'s name, and that of her *family*, I fear, when I have told her how my

little John Salusbury and his Preceptor, Mr. Davies, are coming for ten days in the *middle of January*, to occupy our *only apartment*, and that, as you know, a bad one. The time is past when he was *Piccolino* and slept with Allen, and play'd with the men and maids; he is a great boy now, and I would not trust him out of my own sight, except with his Tutor, for all the territory of Venice.

And now let us talk of sweet Siddons, who, next to immediate home concerns, is dear to you and me. Here is her letter back, and truly sorry am I for her. Be perswaded now, and remain convinced that neither fame nor fortune can make happiness …

How people *do* study to prolong their own existence *in* this world, and their own enjoyment *of* this world, through their offspring, may be learned by the strange tale, now revived, of Hugh Capet's being told by an Astrologer that his descendants should reign over France *not quite* 800 years. "Will it," he said, "add to their time of sitting on this throne if I do not reign at all?" "Oh! yes," replies the man, "your dynasty will then continue 806 years." Hugh Capet was, for that reason, never crowned. And if you will add those 806 years to A.D. 987, when he asked the question, they will make 1793, when his last descendant was deposed and murder'd. This story now comes in peoples' heads because of the surprising Labrador stone dug up in Russia, and containing Louis XVI's profile delineated upon it by the *hand of nature*. Miss Thrale has seen it, and there is a facsimile handed about this town; yet many think it an imposition, and those who think otherwise are ashamed to say they think so. I wish to look at it in your company, which always adds to every intellectual gratification bestow'd on yours truly,   H.L.P.

Accept our Christmas Wishes, and hope of a happy New Year.

Sat. 22 *May* 1802.
GEORGE ST., MANCHESTER SQUARE, LONDON, *No.* 5.

My dear Mrs. Pennington will begin to expect *accounts*, and I think the first thing to give account of is our house; wherein was no bed, no fire, and no spit, upon our first arrival. Here, therefore, none save a negative inventory of felicities can be given; but we hire, and we croud, and we dine out, and we endure the inconveniences with the more philosophy as neither house, nor lodgings, nor room even in a Hôtel can be got nearer to Christian dwellings than Cecil Street in y* Strand, where Governor Bruce has housed himself. So much for *residence*.

The cards of visitors and inviters, however, cover our little table, and we have already pass'd three pleasant evenings enough! The first at dear Siddons's, where Lady Percival, Mrs. Barrington, Mrs. FitzHugh, and Mr. Whalley all met us; and we talked of you, and everyone talked as you would have wished to hear; but Mrs. Siddons disclaims letter writing, and says her *friends* must be contented without being her *correspondents*. Among them they perswaded us to push for places at the Theatre next night, where Hermione's *statue* was exhibited for the last time. I never did see anything so admirable, or so much like a statue of our lovely Actress, for it really did *seem stone*; and the whole was got up with such taste and splendour that I wished for Garrick to witness the magnificence of modern Drury Lane. He would have wonder'd tho' what was become of his old Florizel and Perdita—Barry and Mrs. Cibber. Kemble played Leontes better than I ever saw him do anything since the Regent. Apropos to which, here is the Author; looking as well as ever, handsome, gay, and brilliant. Mrs. Greatheed alters, and becomes very fat. Their habitation is said to be fixed at Guy's Cliffe, though they are hastening to Paris as I understand, where Helen Maria Williams and the famous Polish hero Koschiusko attract general notice. Buonaparte is consider'd as tott'ring on an unfix'd seat of pow'r; if he can once convert it into a *throne* it will perhaps stand firmer.

We dined with Miss Thrales yesterday, the party particularly agreeable, and very good *talkers* in it. We women retired to Coffee as the clock struck *nine*; the men followed in less than an hour, and when tea was taken away at 11 *o'clock*, we came home to sleep, and the rest went out to various parties for y* *evening*.

Fryday was pass'd at Streatham; little Salusbury seems much improved. I heard his whole class say their lesson, and made observations like those of Mrs. Quickly in the Merry Wives of Windsor. It was in those characters Susanna and Sophia shone, it seems, at the last Masquerade, dress'd exactly alike, for Mrs. Ford and

Mrs. Page. I wish my rich tenant Mr. Giles would get a wife, that one might with better grace accept his kind invitations to Streatham Park, which never was so fine before ...

Charles Edward Bruce, Governor of Prince Edward's Island, was third son of Charles, fifth Earl of Elgin, and brother of the seventh Earl, who collected the Elgin Marbles.

Susanna Maria Cibber, a daughter of Mr. Arne, first made her mark as a singer, Handel's contralto solos in the *Messiah* and *Samson* being written for her. She obtained even greater reputation as an actress, and played with Spranger Barry at Drury Lane in 1748, and at Covent Garden in 1750.

Tadeusz Kosciusko, after having been educated in France, had a chequered military career in America, where he fought for the Colonists, and at home. After the second partition of his country he formed a Provisional Government, but was soon after captured by his enemies. On his release he visited England and America, but finally settled in France, where, about this time, he was forming an estate near Fontainebleau.

No. 5 GEORGE ST., MANCHESTER SQUARE.
Wensday, 2 *Jun.* 1802.

My dear Mrs. Pennington's beautiful letter is the picture of her mind, a mind which only this vast Town can fill: and she starves at pretty *Bristol,* as I call it, like a large fish put in a small pond, pining for more space, and more of something to occupy that space. My taste is different. I really feel more confounded than amused at every public place, more stunned than informed by every conversation, and more generally perplex'd than pleased with the multitude of faces, voices, and caprices that surround me. Banti and Billington sang three nights ago at Viganoni's Benefit,—we heard them,—not a duet, two separate songs of the same class, Italian Airs, and both of them Bravura. When they had done,—"I am a Bantist," says one Critic. "Ah! long live Billington!" exclaims another, "Her's is the only straight road to fortune and to fame." *All* appeared quite *distracted* with the delight they had enjoyed, yet none seemed *satisfied;* for scarce a female in the room except myself went home to bed at midnight. But some at Ranelagh, some at my Lady Pomfret's, disposed of the hours *once* consecrate to sleep: while many filled the back rooms of Fancy Dress Makers, who this year keep houses open all night for *various purposes*. The ostensible one, (and that rational enough too,) is that the women may chuse Habits unobserved by each other for these innumerable Masquerades, where two or three different characters are supported every evening by Ladies of ye Haut Ton; increasing expence, and facilitating intrigue in a manner hitherto unexampled. *One* consequence of all this is our paying half a guinea for chickens,—the *couple* I mean,—and 9d. o'pound for what I should have termed *soup-meat* at Bath Market.

Another happier consequence to Country Rustics like us will be reconcilement to quieter scenes and far more tranquil pleasures. I grow very much to resemble the ill-bred fellow you and I used to laugh about, who, when Lord Mount Edgecumbe showed him the glories of our grandest sea view, from our most cultivated spot of earth in Devonshire, commanding the exits and entrances of fleets, armies, commerce, etc. from Plymouth Sound and Dock, declared that he had been exceeding happy at *The Leasowes*, for that he liked *inland* prospects, (for his part,) and *river* fish. In no unsimilar ill-humour do I vaunt the comforts of Bath society and a Sedan Chair, when the pole of some gay carriage runs into our pannel, or when, to avoid *that,* I take a run in the rain, and wet my feet upon their wide trottoirs.

Apropos to Bath conquests made, it appears I have retained but one. Genl. Smith is *faithless,* and has so completely forgotten us he never has left a card. Mr. Simmons is a fav'rite among the Great, and we humble Lodgers are not likely to be remember'd while suites of splendid apartments in every grand street and square are open to talents—of whatever kind. Edmund Charlton alone *is true*. I have a letter from him signed my very *dutyful and affectionate friend,* and saying he is less *unhappy* now than when he wrote his Mama word he was *miserable* … Our own Titmouse bids fair to possess abilities for bustle, and by ye time he comes into ye world, it will be a mad world enough.

Well! I can yet make new conquests. Lord *Stanhope* professes himself my admirer, and the admirer of *my books*. Lady Corke call'd him and about 300 people more round her last night, on the spur of a moment, because Mr. Piozzi, who had met her in Cumberland Street, had promised to sing at a *very private* party for her Ladyship's amusement: and there was H.L.P. caressed by all the *Liberty-Lovers*: sweet Lady Derby more lovely than them all, and protesting that my husband never looked younger nor sung better. There was a Mr. Moore, a new favourite with the public, who makes his own music and poetry, and pleases people very much,—a sort of English Improvisatore,—and there were the Abrahams, and there was everybody: and all our talk was the terrors and riots of a Mask'd Ball held the night before at Cumberland House, now the Union Club. Many women were hurt, and many frighted. My Susan Thrale came off with a black eye, but her fingers were well, and she played on ye harp at Lady Cork and Orrery's. Sophia went for a Comic Muse, but said the end was very nearly tragical; those who fainted from fear were trode upon. Lady Derby stood still and *cried*, and succeeded better in obtaining compassion. The men's brutality, Mr. Andrews protests, was quite unexampled in a civilised country: but Mrs. Greatheed, a jocund young Shepherdess, went thro' the whole unhurt, under the protection of such a husband and such a son as are rarely seen, and both striving which shall most *pet* and most adore *her*. They are now all of them repairing their charms for Mrs. Drummond Smith's Assembly, and Beedle's grand Ranelagh Fête to be held next Fryday. So much for flash intelligence …

Political matters do not run quite so *even*. Buonaparte tho' is likely as we hear to be made all he wishes; and if he lives to coin the money, Apollion Buonaparte *Dei Gratia Imperator Gallorum*, it will be very curious indeed …

Elizabeth Billington, considered to be the finest singer England ever produced was engaged both at Drury Lane and Covent Garden. This year she sang in Italian opera at the King's Theatre for Banti's farewell.

Lord Stanhope must have been Charles, third Earl Stanhope, the scientist, who married Lady Hester Pitt.

The English Improvisatore was, of course, Thomas Moore, who had lately come into notice by his translations of *Anacreon.* The *British Critic* described him as "a young man of elegant and lively, though not sufficiently regulated imagination"; and predicted that if he applied himself to "more important subjects, and of a more moral tendency, few poets of the present day will equal, and perhaps scarcely any excel him."

After the Peace of Amiens the Senate proposed to appoint Bonaparte First Consul for ten years. He artfully referred the question to the people, but in the form of a consulship for life, which was adopted 9th May.

No. 5 George St., Manchester Square.
Sat. 19 *June* 1802.

… Cecy Mostyn indeed is no steady intelligencer; she says but little, and that little speaks good of but few. I could not dig from her one word, good or bad, concerning *you,* tho' Mr. Piozzi and I both mentioned Mrs. Pennington's name on various occasions, while we were *all* enjoying Mr. Giles's kind hospitalities *together* at old Streatham Park.

We are returned now like Stella, to *Small Beer, a Herring, and the Dean.* Apropos to Deans, we have lost our Bishop at S. Asaph, and the learned Dr. Horsley is expected to reign in his stead. But you had rather hear about Mara and Billington. We were at the grand Concert and Benefit when they sung a *Duet* with immoderate applause, tolerably impartial too, because Mara shone there with her *low notes.* *Agitata* however went off very coldly, under visible tremors of jealous anxiety. I could have cried almost to see 60 struggling so against six and thirty, with so little hope of success in a professional contest; whilst in all those where merit is not look'd to, *the Filly loses every heat.* Our gay Prince of Wales, gayer than ever, shines the charm of society, his charmer by his side. When his fair cousin *does* appear in public, she retires thence unnoticed except for her beauty and dress, which is always singularly rich and grand. Pretty women are common, as far [as] I observe, who think so very little about them, but I see none strikingly handsome.

Sophia Streatfield is much alter'd in person, but her manner, little changed, secures to her, even yet, *some* pow'rs of fascination. At *her* request, we *visit*; odd enough! But as Callista says, "It is no matter; she can no more betray, nor I be ruin'd …"

Well! I am really haunted by *black shadows*. Men of colour in the rank of gentlemen; a black Lady, cover'd with finery, in the Pit at the Opera, and tawny children playing in the Squares,—the gardens of the Squares I mean,—with their Nurses, afford ample proofs of Hannah More and Mr. Wilberforce's success towards breaking down the *wall of separation*. Oh! how it falls on every side! and spreads its tumbling ruins on the world! leaving all ranks, all customs, all colours, all religions *jumbled together*, till like the old craters of an exhausted volcano, Time closes and covers with fallacious green each ancient breach of distinction; preparing us for the moment when we shall be made *one fold under one Shepherd*, fulfilling the voice of prophecy.

One of the things most worthy of remark here is the surprizing increase in population. You would be astonish'd to see the Town as much *fuller* (in all appearance,) as 'tis larger. On an evening when common people come forth for amusement, all these new streets leading up almost to Hampstead, are thronged like Cheapside upon a busy day: and when I enquire if Westminster and Southwark suffer from the change of fashion, as I deemed it, the reply is that rents never were so high in *both places*, and that fresh outlets are daily forming, and ground contended for on building lease …

Mr Piozzi says the Music Carts are a proof of all I say. They are so numerous now it makes one wonder. Yet he dislikes the style in which that art is carried on; and though Vinci is a pleasing singer, she is no favourite for want of striking airs to shew her voice. Mr. Braham sang "Every Valley" so as to remind me of *old Johnny Beard*—the *manner* I mean—quite *exactly*, and you will trust my remembrance of a performer I liked so much …

On the death of Bishop Bagot, as Mrs. Piozzi anticipated, Samuel Horsley, who had previously been Bishop of St. David's, was translated from Rochester to St. Asaph.

As Mara was born jn 1749 she was not really much over fifty. She is said to have made over £1000 by her farewell benefit this year, after which she retired to Russia, and lived at Moscow till it was burnt during the French invasion.

Sophia Streatfield was one of those women who are not only irresistibly attractive to the other sex when they choose to exercise their powers, but seem impelled to exercise them on every man with whom they are brought in contact. Thrale had fallen a victim to her fascinations, and the undisguised admiration he showed for her had caused his wife much heart-burning many years before, as she describes in her *Autobiography.*

John Braham, the tenor, son of a German Jew, had been singing at Drury Lane and the Festivals of the Three Choirs for about six years. His predecessor, John Beard, born about ninety years before, began as a singer in the chapel of the Duke of Chandos at Cannons. He made his reputation in *Acis and Galatea*, and appeared at Drury Lane in 1737. His first wife was Lady Henrietta Herbert, daughter of James, Earl Waldegrave, and widow of William, Marquess of Powis.

LONDON, 16 *July* 1802.

You will wonder, dear Friend, what has delayed us here so long. I will tell you now that we are delayed no longer. In the first place our letters from Wales tell us hourly of the impropriety—impossibility I might call it—of being comfortable at Brynbella. In the next place we are paying only 4 guineas o' week here for a whole house, *such as it is*, so I see not where we could be cheaper, and many Friends that leave this Town very late, have made it agreeable to us by letting us live *in* our house very few days in every week. Mr. Piozzi says we have dined from home no fewer than 30 times …

England seems quite on fire with these odious and foolish elections. The scenes exhibited, in my young days by Johnny Wilkes could alone equal the raging uproars at Brentford during this last week. Mr. Bradford dare not go through the place to Henley on his necessary business, and the Sans-Culotte Candidate at Covent Garden keeps Westminster all in a ferment. An intelligent acquaintance newly returned from France describes that Country very differently. The people's spirit is totally broken down, he says, and any government is welcome to them that will leave quiet individuals in peaceable posession of *their lives*. Not a Country Gentleman's seat is left standing, he tells me, between Calais and Paris, nor any place of worship, except what is filled with shops, raree-shows, etc. Buonaparte's declaration, that he will absolutely hear a Military Mass four times per annum, has made them clear out one church in the Capital: but force will be found necessary to oblige his subjects to marry, as they have learn'd to live without conjugal shackles, till the gross licentiousness of French behaviour is deemed positively dangerous to population. Our Streatham neighbour, a wealthy and well accomplished friend of Mr. Giles, hasten'd to bring back again his wife and daughter: tho' when they were come home he protested that no *modest* woman was left.

What else shall I tell to amuse you? Our talk is only how unfavourable the weather is for Vauxhall: I got more rational converse at our own good Tenant's table last Sunday than I have heard now for some time … Something is however always going forward at London, and Monsʳ Garnerin's Balloon called all its inhabitants into the fields here one day, when such an exhibition of umbrellas darken'd the air as I could not have conceived without seeing. Our country servants' amazement at the numbers flocking round contributed exceedingly to *my* diversion. Little Betty was half out of her wits with wonder, and even Tom takes interest in the appearance of five or six hundred soldiers on a field-day in Hyde Park. They are going back to Brynbella immediately … Mr. Piozzi has bought a nice cart here, and a horse which draws them down in it, whilst we proceed to Tenby through Oxford and Cheltenham.

The Brentford election riots were the result of the candidature of Sir F. Burdett, who had attacked the New House of Correction in Coldbath Fields as the "English Bastille," giving rise to the following squib:

> Ho! Ho!" cries the Devil, "come, bring me my boots!
> Here's a kettle of fish that my appetite suits,
>   To Brentford an airing I'll take;—'tis past bearing

> That my friends should be fettered by Justice Mainwaring.
> But young B—tt I like; and will form a connection
>   To abolish jail, gibbet, and House of Correction.

André Jacques Garnerin made the first successful descent by a parachute. He demonstrated his invention in Paris in 1797, and this year came to London, where he ascended from North Audley Street, and descended from a height of about 8000 feet, near St. Pancras.

Tenby, S.W., *Tuesday,* 3 *Aug.* 1802.

What can be the matter, dear Mrs. Pennington? When *you* do not write something must be the matter I am afraid. We were so near you at Cheltenham; I expected letters there from all the living world, but nobody's pen stir'd, and after having drank water for a whole week, without any of the usual effects from it, we drove on through South Wales to the Sea, which always looks *homeish* to a subject of Great Britain. The beauties of Brecknockshire never seem to have been praised half enough … Our little salt water cup here is the prettiest thing possible, a caricatura in miniature of the Bay of Naples, and I hope Lord Nelson will be struck with the resemblance if he comes hither with the Hamiltons next Thursday, as we expect. Four thousand people collected in a trice to give him welcome at Caermarthen, and sung the *Conquering Hero* as he past. It was the greater proof of their gratitude because a temporary frenzy had seized all the inhabitants, who were battling an Election contest with fury unexampled, till *he* arrived, who united Reds and Blues in a momentary procession, accompanying and applauding the warrior who, by his prowess, had purchased them leisure to display their folly. The disgraceful scenes exhibited at Brentford and Nottingham are however of a far different complexion …

I dined among profess'd Democrates just before we left London, but it seemed to me as if their fondness for Paris was rather diminished than increased by their last visit to that Metropolis, where they described Buonaparte as living in a Camp rather than a Court, and with a careful brow receiving, not enjoying, the homage paid him. By their talk I gather'd that Helen Williams lives in the same Hotel with Stone; but that no scandal or idea of connection subsists for that reason; that Koschieffsky, the Polish chieftain, is her hero,—much as Miss Lee venerates General Paoli;—and that her house (Helen's) is the resort of a Literary Coterie, all *malecontents*, who tell those that get into their circle what a short duration the present order of things will be granted, and what happy days await France when the next change takes place. Was not Lord Lyttleton right enough when, walking round Ranelagh, he observed that pleasure was always *in the next Box*?

Miss Hamilton is said to be writing somewhat very entertaining in a cottage near some of the Lakes. Miss Edgeworth makes everybody laugh but me, with her Essay on Irish Bulls. Hannah More is suffering from her Pamphlet Fever still. And they tell me Helen Williams thinks of nothing with real delight except London Society, and an unsullied reputation for female honour. Her mother, yet alive, curses the atheistical notions that surround her, teaches Cecilia's Babies Dr. Watts's Hymns and our Church Catechism, prays for King George the Third morning, noon, and night, and centres all her wishes in that one of seeing old England (forsooth,) once again. Why upon earth did they leave it? …

Pasquale de Paoli had been elected Generalissimo of Corsica in 1755, and held the post till the Genoese sold the island to France in 1768, when he escaped to England, and was granted a pension. He accepted the Governorship at the Revolution, but being disgusted at the proceedings of the Convention, organised a revolt, and was again elected Generalissimo. Finding himself unable to maintain the independence of his country, he agreed to hand it over to England, and when we evacuated the island, retired to London, where he died in 1807. His remains were conveyed to Corsica in 1889.

Miss Hamilton's "something amusing" would appear to be her *Letters on Education*, published 1801-2. The *Essay on Irish Bulls* was the joint work of Richard Lovell and Maria Edgeworth. The *British Critic* deemed it "a kind of peace-offering to the Irish nation for the harmless satire of *Castle Rackrent*."

TENBY, *Friday*, *August* 6, 1802.

This is indeed a dismal end to the long silence of poor dear Mrs. Pennington. Your letter kept us both awake last night, yet I have fixed on no mode of consolation to be offer'd you in the morning. Should it please God that you were to become once more a *Single Woman*, I hope *we* should always be able and willing to afford you shelter. In the mean time it is your duty to be careful of your health, your Husband, and your Mother, who, of the three, is really most to be pitied. There is always some brighter part than the *rest,* of every cloudy sky; and that part gets more luminous as one fixes one's eyes upon it …

Be perswaded to anticipate possible, though distant, good; you *will not* believe in ills till they are near *indeed.* My croaking with regard to public matters you rejected, as disturbing your rejoycing in the peace, and the plenty, and the taking away of the Income Tax: but what I said then might now be *seen,* if we were not *blind*: it will shortly be *felt,* for feeling is a sense that will remain long after the others are blunted.

If the Parliament, by finding Sir Francis Burdett's votes illegal, make the Westminster election void, who will stand forward to oppose him? Mainwaring? And if he does, will that be very advantageous, (think you,) towards the peace of the Country and our Sovereign Lord the King? Or will his *next* opponent, if Mr. Mainwaring be weary, have any better success? And will you give the Democrates a fresh triumph, because this last is not sufficient ? If he is *outed* at a stroke, and Mr. Mainwaring called in, the consequent violence will be great indeed, and the uproar deafening. It was an ill-managed business …

What *you* have lost, could not, I suppose, have been saved; what Government loses, they do not much struggle to keep. Everything is done in a new way, and we who lived in former times do not much like it. But as Baretti said, when losing at Backgammon, "These are bad dice, but we must play them as they are." …

Sea bathing is beautifully pleasant in this little place, fertile in fish beside, but seeing no fruit makes one feel as if summer was quite over … Mr. Piozzi waits here very good humourdly till Brynbella has made her toilette. What a mercy 'tis that Gout has not yet laid hold on him! …

Mrs. Piozzi (about 1808)
By J.Bate after a medallion by Henning, 1808

Mrs. Pennington's troubles were of a financial description, and seem to have been brought about, for the second time, by her scape-grace brother.

BRYNBELLA, 30 *Aug.* 1802.
(Franked "Kirkwall.")

Sick or well, sorry or glad, nobody sure does write such letters as our dear Mrs. Pennington. It is because nobody else writes from the heart, I suppose … Mr. Pennington was always an *honourable* character, and since you are to be a dependent wife, be thankful your dependence is upon a *Gentleman* who, while he deems himself such, will never desert you. Be thankful too, that you have no young family. You *cannot now* I think, be parent of two children, and live to see the one rob the other and run away. These are sins against *Nature*! My heart recoils from thought of them. Poor Mrs. Weston!! I, who am a mother, must feel for *her*!

After long wanderings and washings, like the Lady in Hannah More's Village Politics, with hot water and cold water, salt water and fresh water, here am I returned to Brynbella, and if I thought it would divert you for a moment, I would tell you how sublime and beautiful a journey we had across this Principality from South to North. Fine Alpine scenery between Machynlleth and Bala, varying at every step; and presenting now a rough, high, uncultivated rock, and now clusters of small cornfields round a tiny village, that for aught I see *need* not be so poor, because the grass and grain are really plentiful. Small lakes among volcanic fragments are perpetually occurring, and our guide showed us one which had *literally no bottom*. From Bala Pool indeed the River Dee takes its source, and winds about with very elegant bends till it reaches Chester; but Kader Idris is the chief feature of the whole Country, and tho' far smaller than Snowdon, it is much more impressive. Our weather likewise on that day was gloomy;

> The winds were high, the clouds low-hung,
> And drag'd their sweepy trains along
>   The shaggy mountain's side.

Apropos to *Verses*, you must read the British Critic for last April, and what he says of Retrospection: it has entertained me exceedingly, and will amuse Genl. Smith and Dr. Randolph. I hope those two friends will join to console you; what talents and literature can do, *they* are, above all men I know, capable of administering: but it is a grievous thing to think how very little can be done by either talents or literature. Piety and business will effect in a month what the other two could not perform in a year. Fly to *those,* dear Sophia, and be not solitary or idle for an instant. Your situation is happy in that too it forces you on Company. Nor is it wise at any time to be fastidious; you may receive from *very plain people* very good hints, and one comes away having learn'd something where 'tis least to be expected, much oftener in this life than you would think for ...

Sir Francis Burdett, a friend of Horne Tooke, had been elected for Middlesex by a large majority over Mainwaring, a magistrate who had opposed the inquiry into prison abuses. He sat for two years, when the election was declared void, but litigation went on, at an enormous expense, till 1806, when Burdett resolved not to contest another election.

The *British Critic* describes *Retrospection* as a work "perfectly singular,—a Universal History from the beginning of the Christian Era, translated into chit-chat language, alternating with passages in an elevated style"; and inclines to think that it was originally written in blank verse, but disjointed by the printer or the author, *e.g.* (p. 76):

> Chased many Vandals from their ancient seats,
> And so increased his wild and wide domain,
> Soon to be called after his name, their founder,
> That all the Northern districts of the Empire
> Felt justly fearful of these gathering storms.

"Many, like M. Jourdain, have talked prose half their lives without knowing it, but few have written half a large book in harmonious heroics, when they meant to write mere prose. If we might advise, the ingenious Author should turn the whole into blank verse, and republish it."

BRYNBELLA, Thursday 7 *Oct.* 1802.

When a Member of Parliament says to me, "Shall I give you a Frank?" "Oh yes!" I always reply, "for Mrs. Pennington." Lord Kirkwall's generosity is the cause of *this* letter, because in these hard times one likes, you see, to get a little chat gratis. The next thing to be considered is,—what shall I ask? and what shall I tell? That my Master has had a smart fit of gout in his hands, and that I expect him to have one in his feet, may be told with truth. That the Countess of Cork and Orrery drove up to our door while he was confined, may be told with some degree of vexation, because I knew not how on earth to amuse her, but she was good humoured, and gave little trouble, and after a fortnight's visit—went away. What she related of her adventures among the crags of Kader Idris, her admiration of that wild, mountain scenery, and the contrast *our* gay prospect afforded her, will, I suppose, be served up in many a London Assembly next May.

Ladies appear now to travel all Autumn upon a foraging plan of gleaning talk for their Spring parties. They who spend June and July in London can never perswade me that they are really in search of rural pleasures the remaining part of the year in *our* cold climate, or that rural pleasure is really to be found where deformity is sought. Miss Thrales have been looking for *both*, as I understand, among the *Western Islands*, described by every traveller as barren, bleak, and dangerous. Had Mr. Piozzi and I known that they were navigating the stormy Sound of Mull when we heard the wind roar so a fortnight ago, irritated by Equinoctial Gales, we should have been in pain for *them*, not for the furniture expected from Mayhew and Ince to decorate pretty Brynbella.

All is safe however. Mrs. Bagot used to say it was superfluous to wish anybody a good journey, because, said she, *everybody* has a good journey. "Ah! dear Friend!" I hear you exclaim, "many have a good journey through life too; yet is it not superfluous to wish their neighbours one likewise; for surely mine has been a very bad one." Come, courage! The next stages will be smoother, for you shall not predict of your own fortune with that unlucky acuteness you show in discerning the future lot of others …

Sweet Siddons … writes me word from Belfast that she will call here in her hurrying journey back to our Metropolis …

The next letter was written the same day, and was evidently called forth by the announcement of an unexpected visit from Mrs.

Pennington; but neither this, nor that of Mrs. Siddons, ever came off.

BRYNBELLA, *Thursday 7 Oct.* 1802.

My dear Mrs. Pennington will have the sincerest *welcome* possible, but she will have nothing else. My volunteer letter, franked by Lord Kirkwall, will shew you that we have *no* curtains, and *no* blinds up, no anything but, as Buchetti used to say of a Spanish Posada, "Four walls! no more." Those walls will however resound with joy at your arrival, and dear Siddons's. How good and charming she is! I have a letter—three lines long—from *her too* ...

The next is written while on the way to pay their winter visit to Bath.

GLOUCESTER, *Sat. night* 4 *Dec.* 1802.

And so I lose Hannah More, and so I lose Mrs. Siddons, and so I lose dear Mrs. Pennington, and so I lose my fav'rite house at Bath.

Still drops some joy from with'ring life away!

But 'tis *all for their good*, as the children say, and I resign to my fate. Let us hope at least that increase of health and fortune may make *them* happy. My Master comes better from Brynbella this year than I scarce ever saw him ...

You caution'd me, dear Friend, not to tell of your arrangements. Assure yourself I am incapable of any such breach of trust. If one lets the Maid comb one's *own* secrets out of one's *head*, (and I have none in,) those *confided* to me are in a safer place, lodged in my *heart*. I hope your new projects will answer, and that you will tell me so on New Year's Day, after dinner ...

No. 5 Henrietta Street,
Thursday 16 *Dec.* 1802.

Dear Mrs. Pennington is always right,—the letter was a mere nothing. Such will, I hope, prove the more rationally alarming report of Constantinople's sudden and unlooked for destruction. Be that as it may, our charming Dr. Randolph took occasion to draw thence a most beautiful and impressive sermon last Sunday, when he preached better than ever I heard him, to a heterogeneous congregation, which attracted my notice as much as the discourse did: Mr. Pitt, Dr. Maclean, the Duchess of York, and Bishop of West Meath …

Harriet Bowdler is a sad loss to me, and so are the Mores. Bath is scarce Bath this year somehow: were it not for Laura Chapel and Pump, I should regret leaving solitude and Brynbella; but then Laura and Pump are two good things for soul and body, and what is all the rest? …

The Mores removed this year from Bath to a new house they had built at Barley Wood, in the parish of Wrington, and which became their permanent home. It would seem that a similar move was responsible for the loss of Harriet, (properly Henrietta Maria) Bowdler, sister of the editor of the *Family Shakespeare*. She herself was a writer of poems and essays, and also of a volume of sermons, published anonymously, which were so good that Bishop Porteous is said to have offered preferment to the unknown author.

Pitt, who was now living in retirement at Walmer Castle, was much harrassed by debts, and in October visited Bath for his health. It was for his birthday dinner this year that Canning wrote the song, "The Pilot that weathered the Storm."

The Bishop of Meath, Thos. Lewis O'Beirne, had been educated for the priesthood in the Roman Church, but received English Orders and was made Bishop successively of Ossory and Meath. He appears to have been an excellent prelate, reviving the office of Rural Dean, and carefully examining his Ordination candidates.

Tuesday, 21 *Dec.* 1802.

Well, well! as Sir George Colebrooke says, if we must not meet we may write, I suppose; and I really will try to rejoice if my absent friends are happy. Dear Siddons's letter was of more real value than you seem to think. All our News Papers and News Talkers have been telling how she was hissed in Dublin, and how ill it made her … But all is well, and so that wise man Mr. Twiss, with his clear, straightforward understanding, said it would be; and February will bring her home with all her money safe I hope …

Our weather here is wondrous mild and soft, good for Brynbella planting, and very good for the *very poor* people, who cannot keep themselves and their one cow alive in hard frost …

The hostile reception of Mrs. Siddons at Dublin was the result of an unfounded report that she had refused to act for a local charity. It appears that she gave her assent when the manager suggested it, but the latter, for some reason, failed to arrange for the performance.

The remaining letters from Bath have no particular interest, but it appears that just before her departure Mrs. Piozzi had rather a sharp attack of illness, apparently influenza.

Thursday, 14 *Ap.* 1803.

… Dr. Parry and Mr. Bowen both called yesterday to *bid* me go out at noon this memorable Thursday. So I went, but found no enjoyment, except in returning without any apparent harm, or fresh access of Fever, which they had all so imbued my mind with, that I felt nothing while from home but fears of a relapse. It does not appear however that such an accident has happen'd to me as yet: and perhaps God Almighty will permit us to see Brynbella once again.

Sunday, 17 *Apr.* 1803.

… We shall set out, if it please God, to morrow sennight, and sleep at Fleece Inn, Rodborough …

My airing in the carriage did me good, and the *knocking knees* took a walk with me yesterday, up Pulteney Street and down again,—no more. Today I will go *twice* up and down and so season myself by degrees …

BRYNBELLA, 19 *Jun.* 1803.

Assure yourself, dear Mrs. Pennington, that my thoughts towards you are in no wise changed: and if I always thought you the best letter writer in our King's dominions, (before *they* were contracted by loss of Hanover,) how much more do I think so since your last arrived, full as it is of pungent and tender reproaches …

There are two Bishops and one Dean dead, you see, and their families left low in the world; yet the Democrates keep on stripping clergymen of every reason for becoming such; and tear away tythes etc. without mercy …

Sweet Siddons is at Cheltenham healing *her* honourable heart I hope, and washing away its cares. Mr. Whalley is happy, it is a cordial to hear of *somebody* being happy. You are too nervous—as the phrase is; meaning that your nerves are too irritable to be placidly content; and that is the best state to be in …

The next letter is addressed to Miss Hannah More's house, Barley Wood, but has been re-directed to Hotwells.

Brynbella, 31 *July* 1803.

Such is the present situation of everybody and everything, that even *your* lovely description of Nature and her beauties, in some place which you, dear Mrs. Pennington, call Bower Ashton—but of which I never heard in my life before—fail to detain my mind from events in prospect, and near prospect *now,* of enormous importance indeed.

Poor Jane Holman, cydevant Honourable Miss Hamilton, is running hither for refuge from murder and massacre. She has written to-day to bid us expect her every moment; and though the ground is covered with wavy corn, and the trees are loaded with apples, pears, and all useful fruitage, my heart at this instant feels more bent on their defence than on their admiration.

I defer'd writing till the time that your letter gives me leave to suppose you are under the half sacred roof of a Lady, to whom, if we direct *in Europe,* it will find the destined way. Present me with truly respectful attention where I wish so sincerely never to be forgotten; and in return I will enclose you some Impromptu verses, which I threw across the table to Mr. Piozzi last Monday. We had no company … only one friend from Denbigh, and the Parson of the Parish, who translates Miss More's admirable stories into Welsh, for benefit of his poor and ignorant parishioners. But here are the lines to Gabriel Piozzi, 25 Jul. 1803.

> Accept, my Love, this honest Lay,
> Upon your twentieth Wedding Day.
> I little hoped that life would stay
> To hail the *twentieth* Wedding Day.
> If you're grown gouty, I grown gray,
> Upon our twentieth Wedding Day,
> 'Tis no great wonder; Friends must say
> Why 'twas their twentieth Wedding Day.
> Perhaps there's few feel less decay
> Upon a twentieth Wedding Day:
> And many of those who used to pay
> Their court upon our Wedding Day,
> Have melted off, and died away
> Before the twentieth Wedding Day.
> Those places too, which, once so gay,
> Bore witness to our Wedding Day,
> Florence and Milan, blythe as May,
> Marauding French have made their prey.
> If then of gratitude one ray
> Illuminates our Wedding Day,
> Think, midst the wars and wild affray
> That rage around this Wedding Day,
> What mercy 'tis we are spared to say
> "We have seen our twentieth Wedding Day."

If Helen Williams, ever lovely, and once so beloved! is looking towards England now in preference to France, it is a great testimony to our Island's felicity and honour. For such suffrage is not mean, and Helena has had experience of *both nations*, since she published that little book in which she charged our Londoners with harshness, avarice, and want of feeling, because they suffer'd some Monsieur de Fosseè to wear straw boots. The Londoners' behaviour *now* does them vast credit in the opinion of all thinking people, and Mr. Bosanquet's speech will doubtless be handed down to posterity as giving [a] great example. Should not you be struck with the sight of a Metropolis you lived so long in, *fortified* against *hostile force?* It would to *me* bear an extremely awful appearance ...

Mrs. Mostyn is said to meditate her return to the rustics of N. Wales, who will receive her as if she came to confer on us both benefit and honour. Such is the consequence of that lofty conduct which forces people into their *places,* as the Ton Ladies call treating their humble servants with distant and scarce lukewarm civility. Well! those who take the *other* way are worse used in *this* world, and I suppose will stand no better in the *next* for directing to *Miss* White instead of plain *Sarah.* I cure every day of some prejudice or other ...

The short-lived peace had come to an end, the English Ambassador quitting Paris on 12th May, and the old scare of invasion was at once revived. Mrs. Holman was flying from Ireland, always a likely landing-place for a French expedition. After a quarrel with the management of Covent Garden, her husband had, for a time, transferred himself to the Dublin Theatre, and subsequently took up farming.

The verses, at any rate as to their form, are modelled on those written by Dr. Johnson to celebrate her own thirty-fifth birthday, and which will be found in Hayward's *Autobiography,* i. 31–2.

The reference to Helen Williams was evidently occasioned by Mrs. Pennington having communicated the contents of a letter received from her early in the month, in which Helen justifies her journey to Switzerland in company with Stone, as previously mentioned. After expressing her regret at hearing of the death of Maria Siddons, and offering condolences to the afflicted father and mother, she proceeds: "Mrs. Piozzi's heart is then changed towards me! I am afflicted to hear it, because I cannot cease to love her. If she could look into my heart she would be very sorry for her error: she would not, I am sure, be willingly unjust to any one. Yet I should have conjectured, I own, that having suffered so much from calumny herself, she would have been slow to believe ill of others!"

Saturday, 5 *Nov.* 1803.
(Franked " Kirkwall.")

Our correspondence has languished miserably of late, dear Mrs. Pennington, but though your letters may be unacknowledged, they cannot be forgotten ...

I have heard ... how much notice you attracted from the Duke of Cumberland, while he was remaining in or near Bristol, and heard it with a great deal of pleasure. Indeed *I* ever thought it a consolatory circumstance to live where a Royal Family is established, and possessing a large stake in the country one inhabits. They are the most likely people to be active in protecting it; and the present situation of affairs in England, added to the exemplary conduct of our British Princes, makes me cling closer to my old opinions.

We have had the Duke of Gloucester's son in *this* Country; he spent some time at Llewenny Hall, and Lady Orkney came here herself to insist on my dining with him there. But Mrs. Holman was just come from Ireland, and I would not leave an old friend for a young Prince, you may be sure. His behaviour was much admired wherever he appeared.

The festivities that have *since* taken place on account of Lord Kirkwall's birthday, and his Baby's christening, had *us* for sincere admirers. It was a pretty sight to see the four generations of an ancient and noble family all in one room so: the Marquis of Thomond kissing his *great grandson*, and dancing himself at the Ball.

I hope Buonaparte will not disturb our happiness in *this* Country, which never looked more beautiful ...

We have got a Clergyman to our mind besides, and Mr. Piozzi has permitted me to pick up all my poor old Ancestors' bones, and place them in a new vault under the church, which he kindly repairs, and floors, and beautifies at no small expence. So here is a fair given account of my long silence.

Ernest Augustus, fifth son of George III, afterwards King of Hanover, had been created Duke of Cumberland 1799; he was now in command of the Severn District. The Duke of Gloucester was William Henry, third son of Frederick, Prince of Wales. His son,

William Frederick, known as Prince William of Gloucester, Colonel of the 1st Regiment of Guards, was appointed Lieutenant-General in 1799.

The four generations at Llewenny Hall were: (1) Murrough (O'Bryen), Earl of Inchiquin and first Marquis of Thomond, who had married Mary, Countess of Orkney. (2) Their daughter and heir, Mary, now Countess of Orkney, who married the Hon. Thomas Fitzmaurice of Llewenny. (3) Their eldest son John, Viscount Kirkwall, who married, 1802, the Hon. Anna Maria de Blaquiere. (4) Their infant son, born 1803, Thomas John Hamilton, afterwards fifth Earl of Orkney.

BRYNBELLA, 3 *December* 1803.

When other things go pretty well, let us not, dear Mrs. Pennington, despair of the Commonwealth. If the Ministry cannot or will not take care of us, we must take care of the Ministry: and sure I am that hitherto History affords no example of a nation enslaved, whose inhabitants resolved to be free.

For the rest, I am ready enough to confess that unprecedented occurrences are, in these strange times, to be witness'd every day, and God only knows what may happen; yet I do surely hope and trust old England will never disgrace herself ... This famous Armada however, and its Xerxes, do not seem in haste to try the courage of their *only* opponents, tho' backed with the assistance of our old Allies, and gilt with the trappings torne from our Sovreign's immediate family and possessions. *He* will be right to say as Macduff does, "Within my sword's length set him,"[5] etc. ... Mrs. Holman staid with us 8 weeks exactly, no more ... Her husband is writing for the Stage ...

The Colonel's old Papa seems likely to outlive all he ever heard of in his youth, I think; the monarchy of France, the haughtiness of Spain, the papacy of Rome, the riches of Holland, the independence of Switzerland, *and the prosperity of Great Britain*. While one general pulse however keeps beating, my hopes will live, and beat too. Buonaparte's fate draws towards a dreadful Crisis, let him *but come out*, and our Admirals will give good account of him. Miss Thrales are at Broadstairs under Lord Keith's protection, who fears them not; they row out to sea for purpose of looking at the *Wolves over the Water*, and say it is an enormous preparation sure enough, but our sailors have no doubts of the event, and Mr. Gillon's letters are encouraging. *He* likes what has been doing in West India very well. Oh! how it must provoke the Tyrant of Europe to think he cannot likewise tyrannise in America.

The seizure of Alexandria too, proves the active secresy of our Government; and I remember Ministers who would have [been] much praised for such a step. Once more adieu, and do not despair of the Commonwealth.

Our plans must wait permission from above. If these Marauders come, home is the proper place to be found in besides that my Master must see some weeks over before he becomes portable, and in those weeks!!! Oh Heavens! what is there dreadful in this world that may not happen before the 1st January 1804?

God preserve *you*, dear Mrs. Pennington, and have mercy on the anxious heart of your   H.L.P.

Though the much-talked-of invasion still hung fire, the French were able to inflict some loss on England by the occupation of Hanover this year. On the other hand, many of the French and Dutch colonies in the West Indies fell into our hands, mainly through the energy of Sir Samuel Hood, who helped to capture St. Lucia and Tobago, with Demerara and other places on the mainland.

BRYNBELLA, *Thursday* 5 *Jan.* 1804.
(Franked "Kirkwall.")

Enjoy your Ball, dear Mrs. Pennington, and be assured that all is at *least* as well with your particular Friendships as with that one great public Family to which we all belong ... Mr. Piozzi has weather'd this fit, and is come downstairs once again ... My own health will do all that is wanted from it, and as to wishing myself at Bath, *I do not.* Dr. Thackeray gallop'd over from Chester, and what he did afforded more immediate and visible relief than anything I could hope, more than I ever saw done either by London or Bath Physicians. There is besides one comfort in a country Doctor one can never have from a town one. They stay and sleep at your house, and have time to observe the progress of your complaint, and the power of their own medicines over it …

Shew Dr. Grey this letter … I am all of his mind that England *can* be no better prepared for defence, or France for attack. 'Tis a grand Tournament, on the decision of which the world waits as composedly as it did 2000 years ago, when the plains of Pharsalia determined the *names* of their sovreigns. The issue of *this* contest will settle what *Nation* the others are to serve … I do really wish the crisis was come now; for after the Dinner is once ready you know, be it little or much, it gets worse for waiting. Our Volunteers will make *themselves* work, if Buonaparte finds them none of the right sort. Let *him* once appear and we know who to turn our swords upon …

No. 11 HOLLES ST., *Tuesday*, 6 *March*, 1804.

So many things have occur'd since I received your last letter, dear Mrs. Pennington, that this will of course be a long one. The King's illness and recovery, the continued talk of invasion, the widowhood of your fair friend, cydevant Honoria Gubbins, the correspondence of those French Noblemen so fêtè and so admired in Bath and Bristol, and these present conjectures concerning Sir Sydney Smith, fill every mouth, and render me still more enraged when toothach hinders my list'ning to such interesting circumstances.

Never was there a moment more favourable for rusticated folks like myself to pick up opinions, facts, etc., and *fill my little bag.* But Lord St. Vincent's ill-timed ill health is among the things I should like to fling out of it.

Dear Mrs. Siddons is in great beauty this year: her Zara was never more passionately admired. The Kembles look happy too, and so do Miss Lees; but when I was introduced to Mr. Cumberland at Lord Deerhurst's dinner yesterday, I did not know *him,* nor he *me.* The public will not however fail to recognize him, I suppose; he tries them in a new Play very soon. Poor Holman is—poor Holman!!! and everybody seems grieved at his *double* disappointment.

Miss Thrales are well and gay; Mrs. Mostyn plump and pretty,—so are her sturdy little boys … Oxford will be rendered a fine amusing place for the gay fellows by Mrs. Lee's accusation of the Gordons: it was always a good place for those who liked looking over books, conversing with scholars, etc. We staid two days there on our journey to London, for me to make my respects to the Eleusinian Ceres; but she, alas! was gone to *the other House*, as the Players say, Lord Elgin, who sent her over, being a Cambridge Man.

The weather has been very odd this year. We enjoyed Spring at Brynbella, where birds were singing, and trees coming out, every day before we came to Town *for the Winter.* It has snowed and *blow'd,* and hail'd and rained, ever since, I think; and the Thames looked all in a storm to-day from dear Lady Orkney's beautiful apartments at Chelsea …

The King had a slight return of his malady in January. On his recovery Addington, who had lost his majority, resigned, and Pitt succeeded to the Premiership in May.

Sir Sydney Smith had been appointed in 1803 to a small squadron acting under Lord Keith off the coasts of Flanders and Holland. He now seems to have been watching the French preparations for invasion. Lord St. Vincent's suffering was probably more mental than physical. His exposure of the gross corruption prevalent in the Naval Administration had drawn down upon him a storm of abuse and misrepresentation, in which even Pitt joined.

HOLLES ST., *Monday Ap.* 16, 1804.

Dear Mrs. Pennington's beautiful letters shall lie no longer unacknowledged. Mr. Parsons brought me the first … Dr. Gray came to see us since that, for the first time, but *his* appearance spoke happiness, and his *conversation* unaltered friendship to you and to ourselves. He is a good man, and he liked our little Boy, who was at home just then for Easter Holidays … As to dear Lady Orkney, she takes her lodgings on a Milestone, I believe, for there is no catching *her,* Town or Country … Lady Hesketh will be amused to hear that the people who have seen her cousin Cooper's snuff-box, or the seat his favourite Mary sate in, cry "Touch me, touch me, that you may say you have touched the person who sate in Mrs. Unwin's chair, or handled Cooper's snuff-box." This is all good, is it not? for Mr. Hayley.

Cumberland's Play keeps the stage, in spite of younger wits who wanted people to laugh at the Author instead of the Comedy; but Mrs. Abingdon and I,—veterans like himself,—are glad that he succeeds; for as she expresses it, "He has a graceful mind."

Miss Lees and we have met twice or thrice, but either the Life of a Lover, Sophia's new novel, is not out, or I have not seen it. Holcroft's Paris, and Miss Edgeworth's Popular Tales are the only books found in windows, on toilettes, etc.

No tales of wonder, and such are *not* hers, can equal the death of Le Duc D'Enghien, or the apprehensions seriously entertained at present for Mr. Drake, British Ambassador in Bavaria, and our good friend, as you remember … He married Miss Mackworth, and now we expect him to be *hanged*, as he surely will be, poor Fellow! if Buonaparte catches hold of him. These are novelties at least, though not novels; yet few romances would have ventur'd such an incident …

Mrs. Mostyn is full in feather, and high in song, as the folk say who keep Canary Birds, and her immense Aviary put me in mind of the phrase. She has three very sturdy Boys beside. De Blaquieres, Kirkwalls, all Holles Street I believe, dined with her yesterday, and among the rest my gay Master, and his and your   H.L.P.

Harriet, wife of Sir Thomas Hesketh, was a daughter of Ashley Cowper, the uncle of the poet. The latter died in 1800, and his biography by his friend William Hayley was published 1803.

In 1803 Sophia Lee gave up the school at Belvidere House, and devoted herself to writing. Her first important work, published the following year, took the shape of six volumes of letters, entitled *The Life of a Lover*.

Thomas Holcroft, shoemaker, actor, and dramatist, had been living for five years on the Continent to escape his creditors. On his return he published in 1804 his *Travels from Hamburg through Westphalia, Holland, and the Netherlands, to Paris*, in 2 vols. 4to.

It was apparently with the idea of arousing prejudice against England that Bonaparte brought an unfounded charge of plotting his assassination against Mr. Drake and Mr. Spencer Smith, our envoys at Munich and Stuttgard, and procured their expulsion by the courts of Bavaria and Würtemburg.

The treacherous seizure of the Duc d'Enghien in March in the neutral territory of Baden, his condemnation by a court-martial on no specific charges, and hurried execution, was a tragedy which shocked all Europe. It was this inexplicable incident in the career of Bonaparte which gave rise to the well-known *mot* of Fouché, "It was worse than a crime, it was a blunder."

BRYNBELLA, *Sunday Morng*, 19 *Aug.* 1804.

I am the wretchedest Quarreller on earth, dear Mrs. Pennington, and not the most ingenious Reconciler. Like mine Hostess Quickly, I am the *worse* when one *says*—quarrel:[6] nor did ever the Country Gentleman in Ben Jonson need London instructions in the art of angry reciprocation more than I do. Let us leave a subject I really understand so little, and lament that the universal Quarreller, Death, has been so busy among our common acquaintance since we parted.

How senseless, not to say offensive, must yours and my Master's mutual complaints appear in the eyes of poor Mrs. Dimond just now! Such a son!—the parents' just pride and joy—so snatched! And that unhappy Mrs. Adams who, you may remember, said she had heard the bell ring for her own execution; she has lost the daughter she alone desired to live for. Few people find the way of being happy, and those who throw little Hedgehogs in one another's paths, like the rioters, to make them stumble and roll about, have none of my approbation …

You will not be talked to (you say), of the Cat, and the Dog, and the times, and the weather; tho' really the first of these subjects is not amiss for you quarrelling disciples, and I will not, like Grumio, talk to *you* of how bad my poor Master was when your letter came to *him*, and in what a shocking situation his fingers have been placed by the last fit of gout, no nor what a loss we have sustained in poor Hodgkins, nor what a successor we picked up for him. But all these wonders, as old Shakespeare says, shall now be buried in oblivion,[7] as shall all my true expressions of admiration at your letters, which still exceed every one the last received. Farewell then, and be merry, and believe me with every possible good wish, your ancient Jigg-Maker,

H.L.P.

1. Vol. iii. p. 258 of Clough's translation.

2. "'Conscience,' says I, 'you counsel well.'"—*Mer. of Ven.*, II. ii. 21.

3. *Don Quizote*, Bk. I. chap. vi.

4. *Much Ado*, II. 1. 344.

5. *Macbeth,* IV. iii. 234.

6. "By my troth, I am the worse when one says Swagger."— 2 *Henry IV*, II. iv. 113.

7. "Things of worthy memory which now shall die in oblivion."— *Taming of the Shrew.*, IV. i. 85.

CHAPTER VII

RENEWAL OF FRIENDSHIP

THE last letter shows the appearance of the little rift in the lute of friendship, which was destined to silence its tones for so many years. Its origin remains obscure. If Mrs. Pennington received no letters between April and July, she doubtless had some reason to feel aggrieved, but the reference to the "mutual complaints" of Mr. Piozzi and Mr. Pennington suggests that they had met in the interval, and that some disagreement had arisen, which had been taken up by their respective wives, and it is probable that some letters during this period may have been destroyed. Mrs. Piozzi clearly had no desire to keep up the quarrel, whatever it was; but it may be that her attempt at reconciliation was not worded in a way which would commend itself to the sensitive mind of Mrs. Pennington, smarting from some real or fancied slight to her husband or herself. And so the correspondence was not resumed for fifteen years.

Meantime much had happened. In 1807 Sophia Thrale married Henry Merrick, third son of Sir Richard Colt Hoare, Bart., of Stourhead; and in the following year her elder sister, Hester, became the second wife of Viscount Keith. The marriages seem to have brought mother and daughters more closely together, for they paid a visit to Brynbella this year. In 1809, the gout from which he had suffered so long and so severely proved fatal to Mr. Piozzi. He had for some years conformed to the English Church, and in his last illness received the sacrament at the hands of a clergyman at Bath. He was buried 26th March, in the vault he had constructed in what Mrs.

Piozzi calls Dymerchion, now Tremeirchion Church. She began her Commonplace Book the same year.

The "little boy," John Salusbury Piozzi, had finished his education at Oxford, and having grown to man's estate, and assumed the additional surname of Salusbury, married in 1814, Harriet Maria, daughter of Edward Pemberton of Ryton Grove, Salop. In 1816 he was appointed High-Sheriff of Flint, and was knighted in the following year. To provide for the young couple, Mrs. Piozzi made over to them Brynbella and her Welsh estate, and retired to her beloved Bath, to live on the income from the English property settled on her by Thrale, and some £6000 which Piozzi's careful management had saved from their income. She had therefore—on paper—something like £2000 a year, but her generosity to her adopted son, and to her daughters in the re-fronting and fencing of Streatham Park, added to her love of entertaining, and a carelessness in money matters perhaps inherited from her father, left her in continual monetary difficulties.

Living so near Mrs. Pennington, and with so many common friends, it was hardly possible that they should not be brought together again, though there is no evidence as to how the reconciliation was effected. The correspondence was resumed in July 1819, but letters written by Mrs. Pennington somewhat later show that it was equally desired and equally genuine on both sides.

On Mrs. Pennington's side the rupture of one old friendship almost coincided with the renewal of another. On 18th October 1804, Anna Seward wrote to Mrs. Powys that she had been staying at Mendip Lodge, and that Dr. Whalley had undertaken to bring about a reconciliation with Mrs. Pennington, after twelve years of estrangement. "She received me with tears of returning love, and our reconcilement was perfect. She made me promise to stay with her a few days on my way back."

Her husband had a serious illness in 1813, as the result of which he resigned the office of M.C. at the Hot Wells, which he had held for nearly thirty years, in an address which "powerfully affected the feelings of all present." But his successor turned out to be quite unfitted for the post, and as Pennington's health had been improved by a stay at Weymouth, he was induced to take up the work again for a short time. Not long afterwards Mrs. Pennington's mother died at the age of ninety-seven. She had lost nearly all her faculties, and had been for some time unable to recognise even her daughter.

Mrs. Pennington to Maria Brown
WESTON-SUPER-MARE, 9 *Oct.* 1819.

… I shall not be sorry to return, tho' I leave dear Mrs. Piozzi behind, with whom I have passed some hours of every day, and our evenings *always* together, in the most perfect harmony. We seem entirely to have regained our former footing, and to revert to past times, persons, and anecdotes with *mutual* pleasure. She has sought no other, indeed sedulously avoided all other society since we have been here, and is happy and chearful when with us, as I ever saw her. It is not however with *me* exactly the *same* thing. I *was Prima Donna*, I now feel that many new friends and new connexions, with new interests and novel attractions, occupy the ground that *I* exclusively possessed; and I can only expect, in future, to be *one* of this larger groupe. I think the character of her mind was always rather *kindness* than *attachment*. I know not whether you admit the distinction; I *feel* it, and that I must henceforth be satisfied with such general proofs of this sentiment as opportunity may *throw* in our way.

The friend to whom this was written came to occupy much the same position with regard to Mrs. Pennington as the latter had done to Mrs. Piozzi. After Mrs. Pennington's death, the whole of her carefully treasured correspondence passed into her hands, including, besides the present series of letters, those relating to the Siddons-Lawrence tragedy, which were published in *An Artist's Love Story*, and others from Anna Seward, Helen Williams, the Randolphs, and Whalleys, and others of her correspondents.

In a letter to Miss Brown's mother, dated 28th February 1820, she pursues the same theme. "You judge," she writes, "very correctly of my feelings respecting my dear restored friend. It gives an interest to my life that nothing else could, and what is better, it seems to be felt mutually. We never are so happy as when together, and her letters, which come twice or thrice a week, are a perpetual source of amusement."

WESTON-SUPER-MARE, *July* 1819.

Sick or well, dear Mrs. Pennington is ever kind and obliging, but why empty her veins at such a rough rate? Were they bursting with heat? A Bath friend writes me word that the people *there* do feel themselves heavily oppress'd by a weight of atmospheric air, and walk about, he says, like somnambulists, with salmon-coloured faces. We have sea-breezes here that refresh our spirits, and send us out at night to stare after the Comet, which looked very pale last evening I saw it, but not, I hope, for anger.

There are other fiery fellows in the *North*, more dangerous by far, of whom I feel more afraid; but the Regent went safely, and was applauded it is said, and the Reformers will work no reformation at Smithfield under Mr. Hunt's guidance. He tried in vain to make the Basket Women at Bath hate *Sinecures*; tho' one of them said she knew he meant the *Signing Curs*, kept by Ministers to *sign* whatever they bid them,—comical enough!

If all goes on regularly and well, I shall certainly call on you, dear Madam, in my return. When that will be, however, is hard to say, for I have just hired myself a clean Cottage,—the Hotel is very noisy, and surprisingly expensive,—and since the Bathing agrees, I mean to try another tide or two by the way of making myself young, or making myself *believe* that I am younger than my neighbours of the same standing ...

People are visiting-mad here, as everywhere else. Do you remember Mr. Pennington saying he hoped there were no Evening Parties in Heaven? He will not escape them till he gets thither, nor shall, without the utmost difficulty his and your ever faithful and obliged

H.L. Piozzi.

I saw Miss Williams spreading the Bread Fruit with butter, and eating it at her tea, ten days before I left Bath,—but it was kind in you to send me some.

The comet of July 1819 was that now known by the name of Winnecke, who, in 1858, identified it with one previously observed by Encke.

Henry Hunt had for many years been associated with the leading agitators of the time. He made the acquaintance of Horne Tooke in

1800, shared imprisonment with Cobbett in 1810, and allied himself with Thistlewood and his friends in 1816. He took part in the Spa Fields meeting, presided at the Reform meeting at Smithfield which took place on July 21, and at the "Peterloo" meeting, held on August 16 that year.

WESTON-SUPER-MARE,
Saturday Night, 4 *Sep.* 1819.

Dear Mrs. Pennington's letter came late last night; our poor Postman cannot get his walk finished,—how should he?—till near 12 o'clock, which is one of the discomforts incident to our fav'rite Weston. This morning the Grinfields of Laura Chapel, Bath, left us, and you may have half their house for two guineas and a half o' week. They paid five for the whole, and had 7 or 8 Babies inhabiting it, with a proportionate number of nurses, etc. But send an immediate answer, or it will be gone … If you come quite alone, our Baker, Mr. Cooper, will accommodate you with one chamber up a ladder-like staircase, and one sitting room: but such a lodging too nearly resembles that in Coleman's Broad Grins;— one guinea and a half is, I think, *too much* for that, though 'tis struggled for!! …

Oh! what heavenly weather here is! And oh! what fools is it flung away upon! who will not gather up the harvest, but run about reforming errors in the State. They have got a wiser head now, who is better qualified to do mischief, and accordingly we read that yesterday's meeting passed off without any mad frolics on which to fix the stigma of treason or insanity:—two things so difficult to prove they oblige us to adopt Elbow's method in Measure for Measure, who says, "they must continue in their courses till we can tell what they are."[1] …

WESTON-SUPER-MARE,
Tuesday, 7 *Sept.* 1819.

Your letter came too late last night, dear Mrs. Pennington, for me to take any measures concerning the House … You will have it, as a favour, for three Pounds o' week;—cheaper than mine certainly.

The list of things wanted is just *everything*: knives, forks, spoons, plate, linnen: Weston affords only beds, tables, and chairs. Yes, yes, they do give us crockery, and there were *two* books in the town when I came, a Bible and a Paradise Lost. They were the *best* you know.

I am no better pleased with the complexion of the times than you are, but feel much more sympathy with the Mob than with their Galvanizers, who mean to give just the portion of excitement they choose, in order to deplace, *dis*place I mean, one set of Ministers, and put up another set in which they take deeper interest. In this *virtuous* cause they care not what lives, or whose peace they endanger. But let them be cautious, or the Mob will make them *their tools,* to help break down the gates which, when thrown back as those of Hell in Milton, *they* will start to see

> Before their eyes in sudden view appear
> The secrets of the hoary deep, a dark
> Illimitable Ocean without bound,
> Without dimension: where length, breadth, and height,
> And time and place are lost'[2]

Noblemen and Gentlemen are of *necessity* Aristocrates in earnest: and the numbers who now stand aloof, looking how it will end, and being—as we used to say of dear Siddons—no *-crates* at all, will even *die* with terror, and the conscious certainty that the great folk who assisted in the work at first, broke *open,* but to *shut* excelled their power. An ambitious Sovreign meanwhile, *might* while his army continues true to him, make them all *his* tools; suffering them so to destroy the House of Commons that he could reign in future without a Parliament, only just cajoling the Reformers between to-day and the year 1820. And *such* madmen are those who wish the overturn of constituted authorities …

Poor dear Mrs. Lambart can hardly *hear* these strange tales, I believe; she is at least seven years older than myself, but does not like, it seems, to tell her age; *My* Register, clearly written, as Bishop Majendie says, points out 1740.

On September 12 Mrs. Pennington writes to Miss Brown that she is going to Weston. "Dear Mrs. Piozzi is there, we shall be within two or three doors of her. She has been as active and anxious to serve us in this particular as she could have been at any former period ... If the air of that place, the fine weather we *seem* likely to have, and *her* charming society, does not restore me to something like health and spirits, I shall give up the point altogether."

The Card Table Riddle, which appears in the next letter, is taken from Mrs. Piozzi's Commonplace Book; where she remarks that "it has been plundered, and played tricks with, and published in Pocket Books, &c., but these are the genuine verses."

Sat. Oct. 17, 1819.

My dear Mrs. Pennington charged me to send her the Riddle, and Miss Camplin asking for commands, I thought it a good opportunity, therefore

> A place I here describe, how gay the scene!
> Fresh, bright, and vivid with perpetual green.
> Verdure attractive to the ravished sight,
> Perennial joys, and ever new delight,
> Charming at noon, more charming still at night,
> Fair Pools, where Fish in forms pellucid play,
> Smooth lies the lawn, swift glide the hours away.
> The Banks with shells and minerals are crown'd,
> Hope keeps her court, and Beauty smiles around.
> No mean dependance here on Summer skies,
> This spot rough Winter's roughest blast defies.
> Yet here the Government is curst with change,
> Knaves openly on either Party range;
> Assault their Monarch, and avow the deed,
> While Honour fails, and Tricks alone succeed.
> For bold Decemvirs here usurp the sway,
> Now all some single Demagogue obey,
> False Lights prefer, and curse th' intrusive day.

Oh! shun the tempting shore, the dangerous coast,
Health, Fame, and Fortune, stranded here, are lost.

This Riddle I gave Salusbury when he was a boy, "But what is it, Aunt? What can it be?" "Why, replied I, can't you perceive that

A Card-table charms men from morning till night;
Where, angling with skill for some innocent fool,
A Card-table's green is perpetual and bright,
Their thoughts are still fixed on the Fish and the Pool;
While Guineas and Counters, promiscuously heap'd,
With hope fills those pockets whence pelf has escap'd.
Thro' Winter and Summer and demi-saison,
This occupies Ladies and Lords de Bon Ton.
For Knaves are successful at Limited Loo,
At Whist the odd Trick makes all Honours look blue.
The Ten, at Casino, Decemvir we call,
And Aces, at Commerce, take tribute from all.
Wax Candles superior to Sunshine they boast,
While Time, Fame, and Fortune for ever are lost."

BATH, *29 Oct.* 1819.

I certainly do not remember a word about Siddons, and probably I did not get dear Mrs. Pennington's letter. It is no joke that my feelings grow torpid; I have had so much of the torture in my life that it is really a natural consequence, and if some odd things (kindness is one) *do* keep me awake *this* year, I shall certainly sleep out the next …

Conway's name is on the Posts as having renew'd his engagements, but he possesses many perfections, and leaves writing letters to you and me. Cecy Mostyn is a most entertaining correspondent. She is at Florence now, making good sport of her Cavaliere Servente, the Marchese Garzoni, but remembers your Mother still, and says I must mind and keep as bright as she *did* to 90 years old.

All you say of these horrid Blasphemers is said with truth and wisdom, but Dr. Gibbes and Mr. Mangin both protest to *me*, and they are no strait-laced moralists, that Carlisle and all his crew are white to Lord Byron; whose book is so seducing, so amusing, and so *cheap*, it will soon be in every hand that can hold one. Upham sent it me, thinking of course it could not hurt an old woman; but I held my crutches fast, for 'tis no fun to have them kicked from under one at fourscore—and the Scriptures *are* my crutches. If these gay fellows delight in obliterating the direction posts for Youth in the journey through life, they some of them *may* get into the road again; but as Carter said, my religion is my freehold estate, and whoever tries to shake my title to it is an enemy.

Dr. and Mrs. Whalley seem to have been giving la Comedie gratis here while the Theatres were shut up. Incidents are certainly not wanting, and the Catastrophe kept quite out of sight, as Bayes recommends, for purpose of elevating and surprizing. Those who come to hear what *I* say on the subject, go home disappointed, for I say nothing, and have indeed nothing to say ...

Helen's sinking into oblivion is no proof of the people's good taste, for she is a clever creature, though no one less approved of her Classical Elopement—Helen to Paris—than I did. Is Mr. [Stone] dead, or only his wife? He was a *Radical* before they had taken *root* ...

Lady Baynton has not improved her beauty by living in France: her son however does surprize me. A Titmouse scarce out of the egg when last we met, a Boy now of elegant carriage and behaviour; not a little *manieré*, perhaps too much so for rough England ...

In this letter occurs the first mention of William Augustus Conway, who engrossed such a large share of Mrs. Piozzi's interest, and even affection, at this period of her life; filling, it may be, to some extent, the place formerly occupied by her adopted son, now launched on an independent career. That she felt a great admiration and real affection for the handsome young actor is obvious, and she set herself to forward his interests with as much assiduity and enthusiasm as if he had been her son. It has been suggested that her feelings towards him were quite other than maternal, and certain "Love Letters," purporting to be written by her, have been adduced in support of this theory. But the way he is spoken of in this

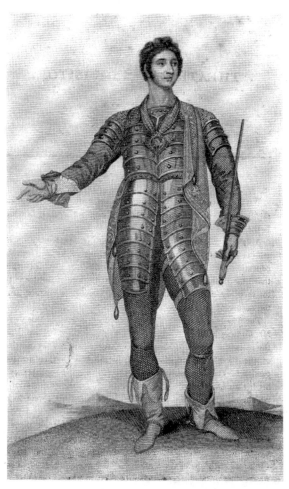

William Augustus Conway (As Henry V)
By Rivers after de Wilde, 1814

and other genuine correspondence of hers should be sufficient to disprove the suggestion. It must be admitted that her admiration led her to credit him with talents which were not obvious to other eyes. He was a man of striking appearance, of gentlemanly and attractive manners, and a tolerably good actor, but gave little indication of the genius which she discerned in him. He had acted with some success at Dublin and Covent Garden before he came to Bath in 1817, where he acted in tragedy and comedy for some three years. Only a few days before her death, according to Macready, she sent him a cheque for £100, but this he returned to the executors. The same year (1821) he left the stage, on account of an attack attributed to Theodore Hook, and sailed for America. He played again at New York in 1824, but seems to have intended to devote himself to the ministry. For some unexplained reason he threw himself overboard, while on a voyage to Charleston, in 1828, but the seven "Love Letters" above referred to were not published till 1843. They are, in the main, undoubtedly from the pen of Mrs. Piozzi, though possibly touched up in places to make them a little more sensational. But, taken by themselves, and without any reference to the circumstances under which they were written, they might easily be misunderstood—as it was perhaps intended they should be. For the editor was either unaware of, or ignored the facts which appear plainly enough in the present correspondence; that Conway was at the time engaged to a lady at Bath; that Mrs. Piozzi was deeply interested in this little romance, and promoted it to the best of her power; and that the most emotional of the letters was written to console him at the moment when the engagement had been broken off. Her attitude all through is that of an anxious mother, seeking to ensure the happiness of a dearly loved son.

Doctor, afterwards Sir George Smith Gibbes, physician to Queen Charlotte, and author of a Treatise on the Bath Waters, was one of the first explorers of the Bone Caves of the Mendips. He attended Mrs. Piozzi on her death-bed, as described by Mangin.

The Rev. Edward Mangin, who had been a naval chaplain, and Prebendary of Killaloe and St. Patrick's, was a notable dramatic critic, and at this time a recognised leader of the literary coterie of Bath. He was thus brought into close touch with Mrs. Piozzi, and the result of their intimacy was his *Piozziana*, published anonymously in 1833, now rather a scarce book, which contains many of her letters as well as his personal recollections of her later years.

Carlisle was the publisher of Tom Paine's *Age of Reason*, and other works of a like character.

Dr. Whalley's first wife had died in 1801, and two years afterwards he married a Miss Heathcote, who died in 1803. In 1813, when nearly seventy, he made a third venture by marrying the widow of General Horneck. The lady was of extravagant habits, and came to him in debt to the extent of some thousands, for which he found himself responsible. Mutual recriminations followed, and in 1814 he went to France, leaving his wife behind. A formal separation took place in 1819, after which he again went abroad, and died at La Fleche, 1828.

Of Byron she remarks in her Commonplace Book: "My own idea is that he resembles the Dead Man's skull animated by a Toad, and made to hop, in such a manner that it attracted notice from the Lord Chief Justice Willes, enabling him to detect a murder."

Sat. Night, 6 *Nov.* 1819.

Dear Mrs. Pennington will believe the torpor when I confess the Siddons' story not new to me, and it is quite in his character who once quoted Cowley's verses to me in conversation as descriptive of his wife's person.

> Merab with spacious beauty fills the sight,
> But too much awe chastis'd the bold delight:
> Like a calm sea, which to the enlarged view
> Gives pleasure, but gives fear and reverence too.

"*Too grand a thing.*" I hope some one will take your Grand Thing off your hands. We shall be wondrous rich if seven's the main. Your friend's fancies about *seven* are few in comparison with mine. Why seven is the perfect number, and the word implies and expresses perfection in Hebrew. Everything indeed goes by septenaries among us all day long. At seven years old the Baby becomes a Boy, changes his teeth, and his evidence is taken in a Court of Justice. Two sevens produce the change from Childhood to Youth, and the third emancipates the Minor. Don't ask me to go on; my conjectures would take 7 days writing, and all would not be finished this day *seven-night*. I enclose a Pound Note, and for the *seven* shillings it will be good luck to wait.

One would be frighted at your prognostics if you were a *seventh* son instead of an only daughter,—so sadly have the Rogers family justified your odd predictions … Conway, poor fellow! will sure enough come to the case you assign for him:—work, and die nobly, or starve, and pine away. Old Bartolozzi, a veteran servant of our English Public, was censured for leaving us in the last years of his life. "It is because I know them," he replied. " Whilst I can work for them, and do what no one else *can* do, they will pay me liberally, and when my eyes fail, I may retreat to an Hospital erected for the *Indigent* Blind. I will," continued he, "go to Portugal, and accept a moderate annuity from the Sovreign." So he did, and died there,—out of an Hospital:—but Waltzing is better sport; so

> The three black Graces, Law, Physic, and Divinity,
> Walk hand in hand along the Strand, and hum la Poule.
> Trade quits his Compter, Alma Mater her Latinity,
> Proud and vain with Mr. Paine to go to School.
> Should you want advice in Law, you'll little gain by asking it,
> Your Lawyer's not at Westminster, he's busy Pas-de-
> Basqu'ing it:
> D'ye want to lose a tooth, and run to Waite for drawing it?
> He cannot sure attend, he's Demi-queue-de-Chating it.
> Run, neighbours, run; all London is Quadrilling it,
> While Order and Sobriety dance Dos-a-dos.

Brackley or Brockley Combe I know by heart, and very pretty 'tis, and Cheddar Cliffs: more like good genuine mountains than most *British* imitations are. For your complaints, I do pronounce them the effect of shocks upon the nerves, and sorry am I that the sea air did you so little good. *I* certainly liked it, and found Weston very agreable, and 'tis the true Ton to say how the place agreed with Mrs. Piozzi. So it will now become the fashionable retreat for old-age and *haggardism*,—a new word of my own making.

Mr. Stone was a raging Democrate, an Enragé; so he is not wanted, we have enough such. I fear Helen deserves some *whipping*, but so we do all: as Hamlet says, "Give us our deserts, and who shall escape whipping?"[3]

What, I wonder, put me in mind of poor old long-dead Demosthenes Taylor, a Doctor in the Commons? The torpor, I suppose, for I can tell but one story of him,—who told no stories at all. Johnson said once, "That man had credit for knowledge, perhaps he possess'd it, but I have dined six times in his company, and never heard him utter but *one word,* and that word was Richard."

My story must necessarily be this. He lived a Scholar's life, you may conclude, threescore years ago at Amen Corner, near St. Paul's Churchyard; studying Greek books and collating manuscripts all morning; smoking his pipe at night, and indulging in a game at All Fours with a distant and dependant relation,—a young Surgeon in the neighbourhood. One evening they were at play together. "Doctor," exclaims old Taylor, "I have got the *Belly-ache* so bad, we won't above finish this game." "Right, Sir," was the reply, "take something very hot, and go to bed. If you are worse, call me. If not, I shan't come till Wednesday, for very good reasons." "Ay, ay, my lad; mind thy business," was the monitory answer; and they parted at 10 o'clock Monday night. On Wednesday young Stevens came, according to custom. The pipe was smoked, and the game played, and "Doctor!" exclaims our old Demosthenes, "dost remember how bad my Belly ached o' Monday night?" "Yes, sure, Sir; and I beg'd you to take something hot, and go to bed." "Why so I did, a great rummer full of hot Brandy." "Heavens!" cried the Surgeon, laughing, "I did not mean *so.*" "Well, young man, it cured me. I went to sleep, and lay very late in the morning, and have no feeling in my Belly now *at all*: none in the least." "Lord! Sir, how you alarm me! *No feeling*?" "No, on my honour." "Good God! Let me look at it directly." So he did. The mortification had spread rapidly, and good old Taylor was a corpse in four and twenty hours.

Dr. Whalley has seen me at last, and told his tale. The loss of Mrs. Lutwyche's good opinion hurts him; as to mine, it is nothing impair'd. What astonished me was his saying that he was annoyed by Creditors when we were at Mendip in the year 1813;—living like the Dukes of Bedford or Marlborough. Mr. Arnold or Almond, his fine Man, shewed Bessy and me twenty Pounds *worth*, not 20 lbs. *weight* of meat in the Larder one day, design'd, *he said,* for the stew-pan. Is it not time to beg and pray for torpor? Sensibility would drive one distracted, sure. So good night, and give my true regards to those you love best; believing me your fast-asleep Friend,

H.L.P.

Francesco Bartolozzi came to London from Florence in 1764, as engraver to the King, and was one of the Foundation Members of the Royal Academy. He left England to take charge of the National Academy at Lisbon, where he died 1815.

The Rev. John Taylor, LL.D., F.R.S., and F.A.S., was the son of a barber at Shrewsbury. He gained a Fellowship at St. John's, Cambridge, and became Chancellor of Lincoln, Archdeacon of Buckingham, and Canon of St. Paul's. His great work, from which he gained his sobriquet, was what was intended to be a complete edition of Demosthenes, published between 1748 and 1757.

The origin of Dr. Whalley's matrimonial troubles has already been explained: it was about this period that the final rupture took place. In the first of the so-called "Love Letters," written 1st September 1819 from Weston, to Conway at Birmingham, she alludes to the recent scandal of "old Mr. Whalley's wife running away from him, and settling in Freshford."

The reference to Helen Williams is no doubt connected with a letter written by her to Mrs. Pennington, dated 26th June 1819, mentioning that Stone was "now reposing in his grave," and giving an account of her life and connection with him, as previously quoted. She then proceeds to refer to the reconciliation of the long-parted friends. "How much in contrast with my sad details is your brilliant account of Mrs. Piozzi;—what a privileged mortal! But really you seem to me to love her much better than she deserves; what excuses the 16 years of separation? The fault must have been hers: she always seemed to me kind and warm-hearted, but with no deep sensibilities."

The lines on dancing are quoted from her Commonplace Book, where she assigns them, on the authority of Mrs. Hoare, to "Smith, author of *Rejected Addresses*."

4 *Dec.* 1819.

To no one else in the world would I have written, dearest Mrs. Pennington; but you are so good and so partial. Other friends can find signs enough of torpor. Miss Williams's Beau, as we call him,—Mr. Wickens,—found me fast asleep on the sopha; he is a good creature and was sorry:—said the world was now coming to an end most surely, when such symptoms attacked, in the middle of the day, your H.L.P. If it goes on, my favourites must contrive to do without me. Our old King came into the world but a short time before his dutyful subject who writes this, and who hopes to get away in his train—if possible.

I have little thought to bestow on Dramatick Exhibitions; but Mr. Mangin, who is a classical Scholar, and has leisure to amuse himself with those who provide pastime for the rich and idle, said, when Conway acted Coriolanus here, that he had never seen the Roman Toga worne so gracefully. He has not yet left London. Macready was a fine promising Actor when I saw him last, three or four years ago: a very gentlemanly man too. We dined together at dear Dr. Gibbes's.

Mr. Pennington has, I hope, taken a new lease. Gout is a pledge of long life, if long life be indeed desirable. I begin to find it very burthensome to myself and my attendants, out of whose power it is to alleviate anything I feel. Dr. Whalley will do well enough among nieces and nephews, devoted to him of course, if he has retained any thing to divide among them at the hour of dissolution.

The Dipper at Weston super Mare came here on a visit yesterday, bringing me Fish and Poultry; how good natured! But I hear of a still cheaper and more charming place along the Cornish Coast, where chickens for 6*d.* each may yet be had, and Fish for almost nothing.

Meanwhile the Great are not exempt from ill-health or cares, any more than we. A general mourning will come, consequent on the Duchess of Gloster's death as on that of the King, and both will alike ruin my wretched Fête;—a foolish promise! but I must keep it now, and it will be the *last folly.*

With regard to Politics, they go very ill no doubt. My long life can call up but one year in which the machine went so as to please everybody: and there was printed at the beginning of the new Almanacks these words, observed perhaps by no one but myself,

> In seventeen hundred and sixty—tis written,
> All strife and contention shall cease in Great Britain.

In effect there was but this dispute in Parliament, whether our Success was the cause of our Unanimity, or our Unanimity the cause of our Success. And Garrick's song ending every stanza with

> Cheer up, my Lads, with one heart let us sing
> Our Soldiers, our Sailors, our *Statesmen*, and *King*,

shews the same spirit. I believe they were never so praised *en mass*e but that one time, which nobody recollects except—Yours and Mr. Pennington's   H.L.P.

In 1760, the year of George the Third's accession, Pitt's vigorous administration had, for the moment, annihilated party feeling. Wolfe's victory at Quebec had terminated the French rule in Canada; the battle of Plassey had given us Bengal; the French power in Southern India was broken by Coote; the engagement in Quiberon Bay testified to our power at sea; and England stood forth as the first maritime and colonial power in the world.

Tuesday, 7 *Dec.* 1819.

Threatening me as you do, dear, nervous Mrs. Pennington, I will, I must write directly. But surely we are neither of us such younglings as to fancy things at 80 years old can go on as they did at 40. We might then be shown for a show. It would be silly to believe my inside possessed its pristine strength, and the want of that strength leads to various uneasinesses, ill-described in a letter. We will do as well as we can.

Meanwhile assure yourself that *one* wonder *does* wait upon your newly-restored friend. At four-score years old her *outside* is the best of her. Dr. Gibbes is too wise a man to wish to *attend* much; he knows there is nothing to be done, and what would you have him do? Mr. Cam the Baby Catcher would have suited me better to-day. The late Duke of Glo'ster kept one in the house the last six weeks of his wretched life's wretched end.

Weston did me nothing but service; gave a power to the unelastic nerves, and consoled body and mind. All is as it should be, though I do not think Conway's all-expressing countenance showed him contented with the looks of his Patroness yesterday, when he dropped in among other morning callers. I will mind Mr. Pennington's good advice and yours, and not disappoint the Boys and Girls of their Gala.

Salusbury and his wife will soon be here, I hope you will like them …

There is a pretty Book come out, very pretty indeed, against the Blasphemers; but I will not put *my* feeble hand to the Ark, assure yourself. That women should keep silence in the Church is a good injunction, and should be obeyed now more than ever …

BATH, 10 *Dec.* 1819.

Well now, dearest Mrs. Pennington, I have got a complaint I *can* talk of, or write about—a sore throat!—tho' never out of this warm room since Sunday. I fancy it is caused by relaxation,—talking about *you* to Mr. Conway, who saw your charming letter … Tho' I did say, in a prudent humour, that he should see as little as possible either of your letters or yourself …

How is your fortune going forward? Smilingly I hope; and how will my Gala get forward if I do nothing but write funny letters to Mrs. Pennington, instead of calling names over to fill up the Cards with, or sit and chat with dear Conway concerning past sorrows and future prospects. He says he is come to act Master *Slender*: and *thin* he is most certainly: but so young-looking, *never*. I hope we shall make a full house to witness his first performance in *Coriolanus* next Monday. Can't you come over anyhow without serious risque? It would be pity to miss such an exhibition, and your retentive memory has Kemble's mode of acting it well impress'd. Mine reflects back only one Scene, I think, and *he* never saw Emperor John in *his* short life.

The Salusburys come next Tuesday sennight, and where shall I get them lodgings? I am all in a *fuss*, as the Ladies say; and wish you were helping me to do the nothings I busy myself about.

The world looks white, but it is not the robe of innocence; gilt and gloom lie under, and will burst out—upon the thaw. Conway's account of Carlisle's tryal froze me with horror ...

The last appearance of John Philip Kemble was at his Benefit at Covent Garden in 1817, so there is no reason why Conway should not have seen him, though perhaps not in the part of Coriolanus.

Fryday night, 17 *Dec.* 1819.

... On Wednesday Conway acts Iachimo to Warde's Posthumus. They neither of 'em ever performed the characters, and it will be a pleasure worthy of Mrs. Pennington. How will you manage? Better make business subservient to enjoyment, and *come*. The Coriolanus electrified us all; and my amiable friend gets admirers and invitations every day. We spent our *last* evening at the Fellowes's. The Hon. Mr. Burrell *there* promised to introduce him to some Club of Gentlemen, who will all attend when Benefit time comes on, and will, I hope, compensate him in some measure for his past sufferings ...

I suppose [the Salusburys] will just come time enough for my Foolery, which plagues me to death already. "Would it were night, Hal! and all well!"[4]

John Prescott, who assumed the additional stage-name of Warde, had appeared at Bath in 1813, and till shortly before this date had been acting at the Haymarket. Mrs. Piozzi had a great admiration for his talents, and had helped to organise a Benefit for him in March.

Monday, 20 *Dec.* 1819.

Well, dearest Friend, I sent your letter to Conway, who is already in love with you, and wishes the impression he has already made *not* to be taken off by Iachimo. His wishes of being presented to you are most warm and cordial; he thinks you love his little Patroness, and *I* feel happy in the fancy that you will one day love each other, and talk confidentially concerning your poor H.L.P. when she is supposed to be far out of hearing ...

My winter is not tedious for want of engagements. I am torne to pieces with invitations, and am forced to dine at Archdeacon Thomas's on Thursday, when I wished to be in the Theatre: but our Friend says we have time before us. So *he* has, if it please God, and so have *you*; but 80 years of my life are past, and I wish this winter was past too, that spring might make our intercourse more easy.

My Ball and Supper begin to be a plague to *me*, but I somehow hope and fancy that they may be of use to *him* whose welfare is really very near the heart of yours faithfully,   H.L. Piozzi

In a note written three days afterwards Mrs. Piozzi announces that she and Conway are hoping to pay Mrs. Pennington a visit the following week, and then goes on: "Mrs. Stratton bore true witness to your impatience of our Separation; and indeed when the fine Statue we disagreed about has been pulled down a dozen years!!! 'tis fit the cobwebs should remain no longer." Can this really have been the origin of a misunderstanding between two sincerely attached friends, which lasted for fifteen years? It seems almost too ridiculous, but is the nearest approach to an explanation of the mystery afforded by the letters.

In spite of a snowstorm, the proposed visit was duly paid, and Mrs. Pennington writes to be assured that Mrs. Piozzi had taken no harm, and to express her pleasure at the meeting. "It was an hour of true, intellectual enjoyment, of *real* happiness." Conway evidently made a very good impression. "Of your Friend and *mine*, since so kindly permitted to use the, to me, always *sacred* distinction, I can only say he appears worthy of all the esteem and regard he has been so fortunate to obtain in your opinion. If that fine, ingenuous countenance, conciliating voice, and gentle, elegant demeanour deceive me, I will never trust to those tokens again. There is a certain *something* in his appearance that interests me more strongly in his happiness, than I ever felt on so short an acquaintance; and I long for an opportunity of discussing with you, dearest friend, those points that are most immediately connected with this object."

P.M. Dec. 30, 1819.

My dear Mrs. Pennington is a kind and generous friend, but her *anxiety* was superfluous. We got home without an atom of anything resembling alarm, or *cause* for it; and found the way short—I speak for myself—it was shorten'd by talking of you. Conway does certainly merit all our care, and all our admiration; may he be as happy as deserving! ...

How good Mr. Pennington was to us! and all your friends: and how far from cold it was going home with that Eider Down bag that covered us so. I wonder where such things are to be had! ...

The Salusburys will not come this fortnight, the *Ladies* God knows when ...

In a letter, dated "Friday the last of 1819," Mrs. Pennington writes: "Remember me kindly to dear Conway, towards whom I feel disposed to indulge more kindness than I ever thought to entertain again on so slight an acquaintance. I hope *personal* knowledge has not injured the impression your partial friendship sought to create on *my* part. On his, the materials, all in prime keeping, are too excellent and admirable to admit any doubt on the subject. But we are, alas! something fallen into 'the sere and yellow leaf,' and cannot cope with these summer blossoms. If however not downright *scarecrows* to the young, 'the beautiful, and brave,' we may at least be useful land-marks and monitors, if they will permit us. Pray tell him from me, that in the experience of more years than I think it necessary at this moment to enumerate, I never knew either man or woman *compleatly ruined* until they were *married.* Observe, I do not say nor *always* so then, and I heartily wish him the best luck in the world in that fearful and doubtful Lottery. But I entreat him, by the friendship you have united us in, that he will not be hasty in chusing his *Ticket,* and that he will endeavour, as coolly and dispassionately as possible, to examine the *Number* before he makes his election.

"The *Eider Down* that was so comfortable to your dear Friend, I imagine can be procured at any of the capital Furriers, at least in London, tho' I know Paris is the place to get them in perfection. A Lady of my acquaintance purchased a delightful *Pillow* there, of an immensely large size, which wrapped about her head, or feet, or served her as the warmest and lightest coverlid possible. The Custom House Officers took it from her at one of the Ports, and she was fearful of not getting it again, or at least not without a heavy premium; when, strolling about, she happened to look into the Custom House to make some enquiries. No one being there, and seeing her treasure of a Pillow lying in a corner, she clapped it under her arm, and walked off with it, fortunately unmolested, on the principle that every one had a *right* to their *own*."

In a postscript she expresses a wish that "my dear, and pretty Maria Brown ... was *rich* enough for *our* Conway, I would trust his happiness with her."

2 Jan. 1820.

No proof more perfect can be given or received, dear Mrs. Pennington, of our hearts being well united once again, than your sudden as surprising impression in favour of our common Friend's *happiness*. I have studied nothing else since I knew him: yet must confess his power of raising such *real interest* is a singular one ...

I passed yesterday at Mrs. Lutwyche's, and missed the Comus my heart was set upon, but Sir James Fellowes dropt in while I was writing this letter, and said it was *inimitable*. "Ay," replied I, "the Scholar's correctness, levigated by the Wit's elegant hiliarity." The answer was that Conway should have a patent for acting, and I should have one for praising him ...

A few days later Mrs. Pennington paid a visit to Bath, and on her return was escorted home by Conway. She gives her impressions in a letter dated January 17:

"We had as pleasant a ride as it was possible to have on a road that carried me 12 miles from *you*. So interesting was our conversation that we felt no cold, and were surprised when we reached the end of our little journey. You may easily guess our subjects; but I am sorry to say that in the discussion of certain points, I cannot find reason to think our dear and amiable Friend so near the goal as your ardent and benevolent spirit is disposed to believe. The fair lady is, I have no doubt, as amiable as he conceives her; but the timidity and diffidence which renders her more lovely in his eyes, creates obstacles and difficulties that demand a bolder spirit, and more self-confidence than she possesses, to overcome. *Love*, all powerful *love*, which sees *in the object* the ultimatum of all its wishes, and overlooks all contingent and subordinate circumstances, only can do this. We shall see whether such is hers. Such only, in my opinion, can deserve the man who gains, every hour that I see more of him, such an increasing interest in my regard, that my anxiety for his happiness is become painful. My dear Husband is highly taken with his fine manners and intelligent conversation. He says he has seen no such man since the prime days of his friend, Governor Tryon, who was reckoned the handsomest man and finest gentleman of his time.

"Oh! no Lady need fear she can lose consequence by the side of *such* a man, who will always cast a lustre about whatever profession he may follow. Perhaps it is the very circumstance of holding the power of decision wholly in her own hands, that renders her so cautious, lest *others* should suppose she has not used the responsibility wisely. Oh! love, real *love*, knows no such reasoning as this! *you* know, dearest friend, it does not.

"I am on very ill terms with myself respecting the silly speech I made about your pretty *Silver Tea Pot*. You have shown me you cannot leave it me, and I *will not* deprive you of the use of it. That would be foolish indeed; for *I* want no remembrancer of you, and *have many*: besides I do verily believe I am not likely ever to receive it on the terms I *asked* it. Sincerely and fervently do I pray and believe you have many more years before you, than I have any right, from constitution and the present state of my feelings, to reckon upon. And it would be worse than absurd to rob you of an article of daily use, to throw it into the hands of other people. All I *can* consent to therefore is, that you continue to use it, dear Friend. Long may you do so, and should the most fatal deprivation I can now ever feel (but one) befall me, desire Betsey to deposit *that* with dear Conway's watch, and I will drink my tea from it for the rest of my life, and mingle my tears with the fragrant libation."

The teapot was destined to be a source of much heart-burning, as will be seen later on.

The Lower Rooms, seen from the North Parade
By W.J. White after H.O. Neill

Tuesday, 18 *Jan.* 1820.

Well, dearest Mrs. Pennington, you sent home our favourite Friend ready to cry: he! whose business it is *to make us all cry.* But he swears you were so pathetic, and your kindness—so kind! His spirits required spurring for the evening at Mrs. Pennell's. I have not seen him since, save on the Stage ...

If the Salusburys are not snow'd up upon the road, they will be here to-night: how shall I *thaw* them? We will make them a little *no* Party for the 20th ...

Conway surpassed *himself* in Pierre last night; he has long left all *others* behind. It would grieve me should he meet mortification where he looks for happiness; though such things *do* befall the wise, the witty, and the beautiful. I wish he would stand prepared for endurance of an evil 'tis possible may be hanging over him. *I* have no guess how matters stand but as *he* tells me; and to-day his not calling, added to your letter, gives me apprehension.

Adieu! I have been to the cold Rooms arranging my supper, etc. Oh Heavens! what a foolery! It will utterly ruin your poor

H.L.P.

Something appears to have gone wrong with this letter, as Mrs. Pennington writes on January 20 in an agitated strain to enquire whether Mrs. Piozzi's silence is due to "a return of those frightful Cramps," or some other ailment. "Keep me not [in] suspense," she continues, "it is not wise to indulge so intense an interest as that I feel for you, and all that relates to you. I live on your letters, and literally think of nothing but you, and *our common Friend*. Would to God *he* was as deeply seated in the heart of his *Beloved* as he is in *ours*! But is it reasonable to expect that a mere girl should be able properly to appreciate the rich treasure of his love. No, it requires something more, rather more mature in judgement, discrimination and feeling. I was willing to be sceptical as long as I could, as to the nature of his attachment, and its extent; but I am convinced it is ardent, pure, and *deep-seated* ... She cannot know the value of *such* love by the objections she makes, and the indecision of her conduct. She thinks perhaps that the *next* Lover will love as well; but if she lets him go she will lose an unique, a noble fellow, and find too late that *such* love is seldom any woman's lot, and never more than *once*.

"I cannot think what has created such an interest in my mind;—yes, I can,—it is *you,* who have been, and are almost (I must not for shame say more) everything to me ... Give my love to the Chevalier [Conway]. Did he tell you that after all the confidence reciprocated in our pleasant ride, I sealed the bond of friendship we have sworn with a kiss (as chaste as Dian ever gave) at parting, which he was to leave on your dear hand?"

Mrs. Piozzi's letter, written on Tuesday, did not reach Clifton till Friday, January 21, when Mrs. Pennington writes complaining of the bad management of the Bath Post Office, and then touches on the subject of Mrs. Piozzi's great Birthday Fête.

"I begin to feel considerable uneasiness on the subject of your Gala. I fear indeed, dear Friend, you will be run to an enormous expence ... I have enquired, and know that the thing was done at Clifton, and *very handsomely*, at half a Guinea per head, *wine included*: for after all there is very little drank at a Supper where women are the half, or larger proportion of the company." She

Programme of Mrs. Piozzi's Concert, 1820
With Ms. Notes by Mrs. Pennington and Maria Brown

then returns to Conway's affairs. "Entre nous, I cannot persuade myself the girl has spirit or stamina to set her above, and carry her through those disadvantages which others (called the World) would see and condemn in such a connexion. If she insists on his giving up his profession, he is shorn of half his beams; more especially as her fortune will not supply that independent respectability which would be some compensation for the loss of the *eclât* he cannot fail of deriving from the exertion of his talents. If she cannot make up her mind to take him *as he is*, I verily think she does not deserve him. The objections she lays stress upon are not to be found in Love's Calendar ..."

Fryday, Jan. 21, 1820.

... Don't be alarmed. Our Chevalier will do *well*, I hope in *every* sense of the word. But happy or unhappy, he will do *right* I am sure, and *more* than well. James Harris says, you know, nothing *can* happen that shall prevent a wise man from behaving wisely, an honourable man from behaving honourably; and for *his* conduct I will stake my life.

He must be diligent to-day, for he is to act Mark Antony to-morrow, and you will not see him, which will mortify us both, but he had no notice till this morning ...

I am sick of my Foolery before it begins, *very* sick indeed, tho' people send me kind encouragement too ...

James Harris, M.P. for Christchurch, whom Johnson set down as "a prig, and a bad prig," is best known as the author of *Hermes,* of which he gave Mrs. Piozzi an interleaved copy before her first marriage.

Monday 24.

My dearest Mrs. Pennington must stay over Saturday; our Chevalier comes out in a new character, and seems to like it. His Mark Antony transcended all I ever saw of scenic perfection,—dramatic rather. The tender pathos with which he said, "Oh! pardon me, thou bleeding piece of earth,"[5] was beyond all praise, and *Lady* Salusbury liked it. Sir John seems to consider Conway as much inferior to Warde in beauty, voice, and action: and the Chevalier's bright eyes, seeing how opinion goes, drop when he enters the room. They have dined but once together indeed, but both can see into a mill stone as far as most men. We meet at Bourdois' and Burney's to-morrow, and he acts Moranges on Wednesday. He will be introduced to the Masonic Honours on Thursday; and then give you, whom he justly adores, the meeting at my Concert. If he does not dance with the proper Partner, it will vex you and me both: but he *will*—surely he will. Meanwhile here's a flood to fright one. He, and all the people at the bottom of our town are in real danger …

The weather hurts everybody, and the applications to me for cards make me, like Othello, *perplex'd in the extreme*.[6] Here comes a tempest of visitants; no gloomy sky keeps them away …

On the following day Mrs. Pennington replies:

… This weather will thin your room and lessen your expences, notwithstanding the unreasonable demands upon you for additional cards of admission. One half of the people originally invited will be laid up in their beds, as my dear Husband is at this moment with the Gout … There is not now a chance of his being able to move by Thursday … I am more than sorry, I am *grieved*! I feel *nobody* amongst numbers without my Husband. He will not however hear of my staying at home. He says I must have the satisfaction of seeing you in your glory, surrounded by all those who best love, and most admire you …

Every tribute paid to the dear Chevalier delights me … I am perfectly *up* to the preference given to Warde's talents and beauty. *I foretold it*. Our favourite is so very superior that he is much more likely to excite envy than admiration from his own sex. In this instance it is indeed Hyperion to a Satyr …

Ah! I am just informed of the sad news. The Duke of Kent is no more! What heavy afflictions fall on the House of Coburg! That poor Lady, left a stranger in the land, is much to be pitied! They were happier, as married people, than those of their rank can in general boast of being …

Her great fête to celebrate her eightieth birthday passed off most successfully. The concert, ball, and supper drew a crowd of over 600 people to the Assembly Rooms on January 27. Her health was proposed by Admiral Sir James Saumarez, and received by the company with three times three. She opened the ball with Sir John Salusbury; dancing, as Mangin remarks, "with astonishing elasticity," but in spite of her exertions the callers next day found her as well, and as mirthful and witty as usual.

Conway was present among the crowd, but in such a state of suffering, mental and physical, as prevented him from enjoying the entertainment himself, or contributing to the enjoyment of others. A letter from Mrs. Pennington dated Sunday, January 30, gives an account of a visit she had paid him the previous day, just before her return to Clifton, when she found him "like 'mobled Hecuba,'[7] hooded up in handkerchiefs and bandages," suffering from what she calls a tumour.

Sunday, 30 Jan. 1820.

My dearest Mrs. Pennington's sweet silver tongue has done our noble blooded, noble minded Friend more good than all my *written wisdom*. He promises me now explicitly, (and Conway will keep his word,) that he will in all things take your advice. "Kind, charming Lady!" is his expression, "she has bound me to her with ribs of steel." ...

What a world it is! and you, and I, and he *all* proud of our talents, if we would confess it. Fine folly!

> Is it of intellectual powers,
> Which time developes, time devours,
> Which forty years we may call ours,
>   That Man is vain?
> Of such the Infant shows no sign,
> And Childhood dreads the dazzling shine
> Of knowledge, bright with rays divine,
>   As mental pain.
> Worse still, when passions bear the sway,
> Unbridled Youth brooks no delay,
> He drives dull Reason far away,
>   With scorn avow'd.
> For forty years she reigns at most,

> Labour and study pay the cost;
> Just to be raised, is all our boast,
>> Above the crowd.
> Sickness then fills th' uneasy chair,
> Sorrow succeeds, with Pain and Care,
> While Faith just keeps us from despair,
>> Wishing to die.
> Till the Farce ends as it began,
> Reason deserts the dying man,
> And leaves,—to encounter as he can
>> Eternity.

… Bessy's increasing illness grieves me. Dr. Gibbes *tries* to save her from Consumption. We could not call him sooner. She is now cover'd with Blisters, after which come Leeches and James's Powder, with orders to eat *nothing at all* but—Milk.

The noble blood attributed to Conway evidently refers to a story, mentioned later by Mrs. Pennington, that he was a natural son of one of the Marquis of Hertford's family. He appears to have made an attempt to obtain some acknowledgment of his relationship from his putative father, but without much success; and the failure may have had something to do with his determination to leave England.

King George III died on January 29, six days after the Duke of Kent, and the new king, who was too ill to be present at his father's deathbed, nearly followed him to the grave. He had caught a severe chill, and to relieve the inflammation his medical advisers saw fit to relieve him of 130 ounces of blood, which all but killed him. Yet he was convalescent by February 6.

On February 2 Mrs. Pennington writes: "Your verses, my beloved Friend, are above all praise, for *yours* they must be, as no one else can delineate such profound thinking with the same ease and perspicuity. The late events do indeed give a grave and solemn tone to one's reflections, and these awful death-bells sounding from every quarter in one's ears, fill me with trembling apprehension for everything that is near and dear to me. I rejoice that George IV was not proclaimed on the anniversary of the Martyrdom of Charles the 1st. To my easily alarmed mind it would have seemed frightfully ominous! …

"I do not wish [Conway] to be in too much haste to renew his visits in Camden Place. I would strongly recommend him to play a *back* game, and see how absence, and some degree of solicitude, which surely his illness must excite, operates there. It is of the first consequence to *his* and to *her* future peace and happiness, that *she* should be able to appreciate, and *he* to ascertain, the degree of affection existing on her part. If she *has* mistaken the sentiment, I think she will now be able to detect the mistake; as nothing is more likely to bring out the truth, than any real or imaginary danger respecting the object. And if the same futile objections remain, depend upon it she has mistaken the feeling, whether she knows it or not, and she would do better to put an end at once to all suspense on the subject …"

                                                        3 *Feb.* 1820.

I am glad dear Mrs. Pennington approved my Verses, your taste is so good. They are like lines written in 1712, not at all of a modern sort. You have seen our Chevalier since I did; he keeps close, and Bessy, whom I sent to comfort him in his illness, brings me no good accounts. She is bad enough herself, poor girl, but pities him: I wish they were both at Clifton under your care …

Death is near us all, and after death, judgment. Poor Mr. Eckersall has had a stroke of Apoplexy or Palsy, but the family seem little aware o'nt: and I was seized with such a lethargic stupor after dinner yesterday at Dorset Fellowes's, I was forced to play Loo to keep myself awake, and lost four shillings …

This Recess, shocking as the cause may be, is fortunate for our Chevalier; and I hope he will shine out and dazzle all beholders at his Benefit. Don't you remember Siddons saying she never acted so well as once when her heart was heavy concerning the loss of a child?

I break off to say the present King is dying. God's judgments are abroad. Write to dear Conway, and with your sweet eloquence persuade him to sink all thought of his own calamities in those of the Nation he is an honour to …

On February 5 Mrs. Pennington replies. "Your letter, dearest Friend, nearly paralysed me. Poor Bessy ill!—Dear Conway no better!— Everybody sick or dying! I am absolutely ill with terror and solicitude! I was quite afraid to enquire for the Papers today but, thank God! the accounts of the King are more favourable … The first impressions I had of perfect manly grace, and princely dignity, were drawn from the fine form and gracious manners of our present Sovereign. Early impressions are always the most lasting. Never have I seen, but in our favourite, dear Conway, anything to compare with him, nor ever shall I see his equal again; and I feel that my affliction would be almost *personal* grief, should anything fatal happen to him at this time … God, of his mercy, avert this great additional calamity from us, I most heartily pray …

"Everybody was pleased with the *respectful* and affectionate attention [of Sir John Salusbury] at the Ball … I was surprised at some hints dropped at the chagrin he felt on the subject of your *increased* acquaintance; and could not help telling him, tho' in perfect good humour, that *my* claims in that line were prior to his own. I was sorry I did not recollect to observe to him, that it was a maxim of Dr. Johnson's, whose wisdom no one could question, 'that we should renew, and keep our acquaintance and our friends in *repair*, as we did our wardrobes, *because they would wear out.*'"

BATH, *Sunday 6 Feb.* 1820.

Bessy is safe; dearest Mrs. Pennington, by dint of bleeding, starving, blistering. Bessy is safe, … and our noble-minded, tender-hearted friend … is better too; I shall not outlive *all* that love me. It is a trying time, and some affliction falls on every family, the Royal Family worst.

> As if Misfortune made the Throne her seat,
> And none could be unhappy,—but the Great.

Of the present Sovereign I know nothing *personally*. From the old King I got a kiss when presented, and the late Regent made application thro' Murphy, for my acquaintance 20 years ago. But as

Mr. Thrale's *daughters* were then upon a visit to Streatham Park, and not their own Father master of the house, I declined all such honours: and therein acted wisely, which I seldom do ...

What you say of an exacting, authoritative friend is most true. One thinks immediately of Marmontel, "Je baisse les *liens* de l'amitie,—j'en redoute la *chaine*." I'm willing still to kiss the links of friendship, but from the chain I fly. Those *I* have never found *me* exacting, or (without request,) interfering. Friendship is far more delicate than love. Quarrels and fretful complaints are attractive in the last, offensive in the first. And the very things which heap fewel on the fire of ardent passion, choke and extinguish sober and true regard. On the other hand, time, which is sure to *destroy* that love of which half certainly depends upon *desire*, is as sure to increase a friendship founded on talents, warm with esteem, and ambitious of success for the object of it. Such feelings depend on the merit of the man or woman that excites them, and can be *dull'd* only by their conduct.

So here's a fine heap of *wise nothings*, as you call your own preachments,—which I hope our dear Chevalier will thank you for.

The King is safe,—as well as Bessy. Equal in the sight of Him who created and redeem'd them: very unequal in importance to those who look up to them for support and assistance.

They *live* however, and so for awhile does dear Mrs. Pennington's poor old friend   H.L.P.

Mrs. Pennington replies in a long letter dated February 9, from which it appears that Conway's love-affair had come to the conclusion she had anticipated. Miss S[tratton] could not stoop to the position of an actor's wife, and insisted on his abandoning his profession, if he was to aspire to her hand, a step which he could not bring himself to take. While full of sympathy for the suffering this decision had caused him, she is quite convinced that, as far as his career is concerned, it is all for the best, and concludes thus:

"I shall hate a *Miss* something more to the end of my life for his sake, and what is worse, notwithstanding the just and high regard he entertains for you, and his *new liking* for me, I fear he will contract a hatred for Bath, and I shall see little more of him for the rest of my life: and then what a silly thing have I done to interest myself thus deeply in his concerns! The most astonishing thing of all is the power he possesses of creating so strong and pure an interest in his favour, especially with me, who have long since ceased to feel the influence of that sort of enthusiasm, and am become fastidious from disappointment. In very few instances have I *ever* experienced the attachment I feel to him! It seems as if that Girl alone was exempt from the power of the magic he bears about him. Well, let her go!— sit down at ease with a Country Squire, 'suckle fools, and chronicle small Beer.' ... But as you say, while we do right, and honourably, and wisely, (and when he has recovered the proper use of his reason—I am sure he will do,) all will ultimately go well, and *better* than if it had gone *our* way, depend upon it."

The two "Love Letters," so called, written to Conway on February 2 and 3, when read in connection with those to Mrs. Pennington, show not Mrs. Piozzi's doting fondness for the handsome actor (as the Editor evidently desired to insinuate), but her deep concern for his welfare, and her anxiety lest he should damage his professional prospects by giving way to despondency or despair as the result of his rejection. In the first she subscribes herself "your more than Mother, as you kindly call your H.L.P." In the second she mentions having received a call from the Strattons, and that she could not bring herself to touch the hand of Mrs. S., whom she evidently held responsible for the rupture. She refers to them in her Commonplace Book, in a passage evidently written about this date. "Strattons, a family here, pretended passionate love [for Conway,] and I thought them in earnest, ... dined with me yesterday, and said *all was over*, because the girl's friends would not agree to the connection." The words in brackets have been carefully obliterated, but there is little doubt about them, as Conway's name has been similarly treated in several other places. The last of the "Love Letters "is dated February 28.

Thursday Evening, 10 Feb. 1820.

My dear Mrs. Pennington's prognostics are always wise, lucky, and fulfilled; and I doubt not but we shall lose our accomplished

Chevalier,—after this Season,—for ever. Let us get him a good Benefit first, and send him down the wind, with fav'ring gales. I will leave, in the vulgar phrase, no stone unturned to serve him. Meanwhile he is in London, escaping our wise letters of good advice; of which, if now *weary*, he will on a future day be *proud*. The world is full of incident, and some good ones may illuminate *his* Drama.

Yesterday's post brought word that Lady Salusbury's Father was most alarmingly ill. To-day's post said he was *dying*. Yesterday at dinner Salusbury broke one of his fine teeth. To-day it was drawn, and they are gone to Shropshire. So runs the world away. Jealous of Aunt's favour, and glad to carry little Wifey far from that widely spreading influence which, as you say, throws an attractive halo round us all: which *she* feels among the rest, for who can 'scape? Sir John's chagrin won't kill him: and he says he will perhaps come again—*by himself*—but he will find enough to do at home.

Our Benefit will probably take place towards the end of this month. Conway comes back to open the Theatre with a swarthy face on the 18th, in a new Play written by Mr. Dimond;—St. Clara's Eve. That young man's brother, Charles Dimond, who I used to say resembled a Thames Smelt, and who has long been settled in London, marries a girl with £10,000, and pretty besides, a Miss Wood. Leoni Lee too has found a maid with the *love-beaming eye*; he took her to St. James's Church yesterday.

The King's calling to his bedside the Duke of Sussex is a pretty and a tender anecdote. "My Father and my Brother are lying dead now," said he, "your life, my dear Augustus, is very precarious, my own saved almost by a miracle. Let us not quarrel more with each other, while Death is at hand so to quarrel with us all." Everybody says that Prince's amiable son will marry a daughter of the Duke of Montrose.

I hope you will begin the next month with *me*, under St. Taffy's influence: and if you invite me early in the Spring, when our tall Beau is gone, or going, I will come to Clifton, and escape visitors. My door never rests here, and when once out of town, they may knock in vain. But till the Theatre is shut, or the great Light of it extinguished, the halo hangs round me, and I shall neither be willing nor *able* to stir. The less indeed, because persuaded that his return hither, (unless either the Gentleman or Lady is married,) is very unlikely, and would perhaps be imprudent. I mean his professional return, as now, in the character of principal performer.

Adieu, dear Mrs. Pennington, continue to him your regard; do not willingly lose sight of him; your value is by him duly appreciated, and I depend on living long in *both your memories.* You will often talk together of yours and his true friend and faithful servant

H.L.P.

The "amiable son" of the Duke of Sussex, Augustus Frederick, born 1794, who took the name of d'Este, died unmarried.

On February 15 Mrs. Pennington replies in two closely-written sheets, full of indignation at the girl who, she is convinced, could never have felt any real love for Conway, or she could not have dismissed him without "one word of sympathy, one token of pity, or sentence of consolation." ... "It was most silly and illiberal to tell him 'she could not support the idea of being sunk in her rank of life, and looked down on,' etc." ... "I trust, as Dr. Johnson would have said, he will never think of hunting down a *Kitten* again."

She goes on to refer to the story of his being the son of William Conway, an old college friend of Sir Walter James, who had remarked on the likeness between them. His reputed father must therefore have been Lord William Seymour Conway, sixth son of Francis, first Marquess of Hertford.

Sir Walter "said of his acting, that he was the best Pierre he ever saw, though he had a perfect recollection of Holland, who was thought *perfection* in the character. That he would advise him by all means to keep clear of the London Theatres for two or three years, and then burst upon them, a *finished* actor. He said it was remarkable they never received an Actor as *such*, whatever his merits, so young, or so young-looking, as Conway, until more matured by experience and knowledge of the business; and instanced Mrs. Siddons's failure in early life, Mr. Young's, etc. It was some years before Kemble made his way to the popularity he at last attained ... Sir Walter says your verses are the best he has seen of modern verses, and like those sterling things of 50 years back ...

"I wonder what the generality of people would think if they were to pick up our letters?"

16 *Feb.* 1820.

Thank you kindly, dear Mrs. Pennington, for your kind letters. Our Chevalier longed to see them whilst in London, and I disappointed him by not sending them forward. It was the first pain I ever put him to, and it shall be the last. Our business is to soothe and solace, not to chide him, or add a particle to what he suffers. If female friendship is worth anything, let us benefit and please him all we can. Your part must be to advise, mine to console; and both of us will try to get him a blazing night, when once the time is appointed ... Sir Walter James is very unwell, and I am sorry for it. He always instinctively loved our friend Conway; and the last time we changed a word about him, his expression to me was, "I think that young fellow is all that a man ought to be." ...

Sir Walter James Head, of Langley Hall, Berks, who assumed the name of James, and was created a Baronet 1791, was the great-grandfather of the present Lord Northbourne.

On February 18 Mrs. Pennington writes: "I begin now to get very anxious on the subject of *our Benefit*. I know, by experience, that only *general* and simultaneous impulse will *fill* a Theatre or a Ball Room. The Pit and Galleries are prime objects, a showy-play is the best attraction there. The boxes there can be no doubt about, and Bessy must exert all her influence with your tradespeople, not only to *take* Tickets for the other parts of the House, but to *dispose* of as many as they can. Not a word however about these sordid matters to our high-minded Friend, whose feelings *I* would not hurt in any way, intentionally, for the world ...

"The King was saved to a minute! Dr. Tierney had the courage to do what others durst not hazard;—but his worst sufferings, I fear, are yet to come with that *bad* woman,—and what mischief have not *such* women effected? The Duke of Berri's assassination has congealed us all with horror! It is plain that unfortunate family is to have no successor."

Another letter follows, dated February 22, written in much the same strain, and giving an account of a visit from Conway, who acted as the bearer of Mrs. Piozzi's last.

On the 24th Mrs. Piozzi writes a note to say that the Benefit is fixed for March 11, and to arrange for Mrs. Pennington's visit on the 1st. She concludes: "I hate such short letters, but *my* goose-quill,—poor old Goosey!—is *moulting* as it appears. The Pens and Paper are worse than ever I remember: Yours at Bristol are better perhaps, I'm sure it *seems* so."

Mrs. Pennington replies the next day: "What will the S—ns do on *the* Night? If they absent themselves, known and marked as they [have] been, as dear Conway's staunch and particular Friends, surely it will excite remark? And yet how *can* they be there? At any rate, if they are, I trust it will be in a situation not to meet *his* eyes;—I should dread the consequences, at least I know I shall feel it for him in every Nerve. You talk, (with little reason,) of Bath stationery! I cannot get a sheet of paper that is not greasy and full of hairs, nor a pen that will pass over them without blotting, and when I look at your beautiful writing, I think my own letters only fit to bolster up candles, or for the Pastry Cook's use."

As Mrs. Pennington was staying at Bath, there are no letters to give an account of the Benefit, but there is not much doubt that Mrs. Piozzi made it a success. She evidently returned with Mrs. Pennington to Clifton, and the next letter is written immediately after her return home.

Begun Thursday Night, 24 *Mar.* 1820.

Dearest Mrs. Pennington will be glad to hear that four horses, and three able-bodied men, brought my little person safe home … at 9 o'clock last night. Had I died, like Mrs. Luxmore, of cough and strangulation, I should not have seen our tall Beau for 5 minutes after breakfast:—*a morning call.* He looked in high health and good spirits, said your eloquent praises had produced others, which Miss Williams sends me this moment, and I really think them very good indeed; he does deserve *all* praise in every situation,—in all situations of life,—and his adoring mother says he was from infancy the best boy upon [earth]. We had no time to talk of plans, present or future, [he] will go to London next week, whether to return again I know not …

Captain Marshall has got what he wished and wanted. How long will he be happy in the Prize he has so contended for? Mr. Mangin said to me once, that if he were to go to Heaven, (unlikely enough, added he,) it would be disagreeable to him for a week at least,—the *first* week,—but he should grow reconciled to it. Would not *that* speech make a good note to some of the observations in Johnson's *Prince of Abyssinia*? It would at least do well for Sophia Lee, whose misanthropism I reverence, while others ridicule it. Why should she let the people in to *visit* her, as it is called? She knows they come for curiosity, not from affection; and I suppose her means of doing good have been curtailed by accident, her powers of pleasing by infirmity and age. Why should she then exhibit the *Skeleton* of Wit?—or Beauty, if she ever possessed it? Is there no time when one may be permitted to die in a corner [after] arranging our little matters for the Journey? Lord! I [shall have] to expire in a Curtsey and a Compliment, and request the Spectators [to] honour me with *their commands*—to the next World …

Mrs. Pennington writes on March 26: "I was indeed glad to get your letter, dearest Friend, for tho' I entertained no fears for your personal safety, I was anxious lest the evening air should increase the *choaking,* and in great dread of dear Bessy's everlasting displeasure for suffering you to depart at *half past 5 o'clock,* without anything to sustain you on the way. There was more danger of your dying from inanition than suffocation. Poor Mrs. Luxmore was, I believe, a full liver. You and I shall not hasten the end of life *that* way. However we certainly carried the starving system to excess the day you honoured Dowry Square with your presence; for if we had had the common sense to have sat down to Dinner an hour sooner, you would have been tempted, from mere good humoured compliance with our wishes, to have taken *something* and a glass of wine to have supported you. But I was sick at heart, and could feel only regret at parting from you, and the rest of the party lost all their useful recollections in the pleasure of listening to you, and looking at you. They declared they would have gone without dinner for a week to have prolonged the gratification.

"Maria [Brown] is a paintress, and a really *good* amateur artist;— she says she cannot take her attention from your *forehead and eyes*,— the unfurrowed smoothness of the one, and the lucid, sweet, and bright lustre of those blue orbs, giving a youthful expression that might pass for 20! It is *this* that Jagher has hit off so happily, and that Roche could not touch. I *must* have a copy of that picture some day or other, if I sell my silver spoons, for my Tea Pot I will never part with; but mind, I am not begging, nor whining. I will never have it from *your* purse." …

At the close of a long letter she returns to the subject of Conway. "Dare you hint to him before you part our *only* fear? and venture to tell him that your, and his *saucy Friend* says that if he goes to that odious Ireland, and pours as much wine down his throat as his strong head will bear, in a few years he will look like a moving steeple, with a blazing Beacon at the top? Oh! if he ever Carbuncles that beautiful nose, or heightens the natural colouring of that charming face, I will never give him another kiss. A tremendous threat, to be sure, considering the time I am looking forward to, especially as I am getting fast to poor Miss Wren's *ashey* tint: but I intend to be beautiful again one of these days. *Ninon* was charming at a much more advanced age, and wore spectacles as *we* do.

"I have been told I have a cast of her in my character, with a *total exception*, I beg leave to be understood, as to her physical and constitutional propensities, (as also to her erudition,)—but that she was fair and gentle, with my stature and carriage;—often serious;— generally rather tender, interesting, and amusing, than brilliant, tho' sometimes gay and sprightly,—

From grave to gay,—from lively to severe.

I wonder how all this nonsense came into my head? … If our dear Chevalier mars what God has made so exquisitely well, and stamped so clearly an impress of the Divinity upon, it will be a *great sin*."

28 *March*, 1820.

My dear Mrs. Pennington's *gratuitous* letter gives me the best certainty of her returning health and spirits. This answer to it will cost no more.

My health has little to do, at 81 years old, with cramming or starving, and if I am to be *blest*, as you seem to think it, with "second childishness and mere oblivion;"[8] to sit, like old Elspet in her wicker-chair, turned over by *kind* inquirers, like a last year's Almanack:—why, be it so! This is a week of mortification and resignation, and I will endeavour to endure the degrading idea.

The loss of *his* company and talents will be a great privation to me, but on *his* account my heart feels no fears. Conway's virtues are not, I trust, what Johnson would call ambulatory, meaning dependant upon climate and company. He will come home to *you* I hope, in seven years time, two or three little children at his side, his own incomparable soul unsullied, his merits unmolested, his beauty unimpair'd …

Mr. Hunt's being elected into Parliament is another tub for the whale; so if old Britannia like her daughters, must live to be sick and superannuated, why, Henry Hunt and Horace Twiss may hold the smelling bottle to her nose.

I have at last seen a man who profess'd himself *happy*. It was Captain Marshall. But as he left me, and dress'd for the Member's Dinner, to which he went in a Sedan, a wagon overset his little vehicle, ran over his Chairman, breaking both his thighs, and brought *him* to the Hall—too late for Dinner.

Those who converse with the Great expect our King to be crowned on his birthday, the 12th of August. My dividends will be come in by then, and Salusbury may have his promised £100, to see the Coronation. I hate being worse than my word. Our friend Fellie may not perhaps find *her Grandees* so scrupulous. But she has had many assurances of the Herb-woman's place, in the Procession, which I have heard was £400 or £500 o' year for life. She is a sweet Lady, but ladies *are* charming creatures, of course; *yours* most particularly so *surely*, when they think it fit to fling so much flattery away upon your poor affection[e] Friend

H.L.P.

Miss Fellowes as Herb-strewer at the Coronotion of Geo. IV
By M. Gauci After Mrs. Baker.

Hunt was tried for his share in the Peterloo meeting this year, and sentenced to two years imprisonment. He was, however, actually returned to Parliament for Preston in 1830, in which capacity he presented the first petition in favour of Women's Rights.

The actual date of the coronation was 19th July 1821, when "Fellie," otherwise Miss Anne Fellowes, the sister of Mrs. Piozzi's friend and executor, Sir James Fellowes, did officiate as Herb-Woman.

Monday, 10 *Apr.* 1820.

My dear Mrs. Pennington is but too kind in excusing my peevishness, but this sharp weather freezes all my faculties: it is as cold as January *ought* to be. You will have a sad loss in Maria Browne, and I have a sad loss in dear Conway; and his steady resolution never to write is such a bad trick. Siddons has the same you know: and Dr. Johnson used to complain, I remember, of David Garrick. "One would believe," said he, "that the little Dog loved one, if it was only by conversation one knew him: but 'out of sight, out of mind,' is an old proverb, and they have all of them so much to do."

If my coming to Clifton depended on my being weary of Bath, you would see me soon indeed; but till July dividends I have no money for *move-about.* Lord bless me! I wonder how other people's Bank Notes hold out. Mine melt away like butter in the sun. 'Tis a great mercy that the Stocks hold firm with a well organised rebellion in the Island. In *my* time, had such a state of things existed, people would have laid down knife and fork, and fallen to praying: those I mean who did not *fight* either on the one side or the other. We do not now lay down even our Cards. My friend Dr. Gray however, whom you do, or you do *not* remember at Streatham Park, has taken serious fright, and fled to London with his family, from Durham; wishing to change his valuable living for one, even half as profitable, in the South. Altho' Miss Normans told me on Saturday, at Mrs. Pierrepoint's or Mrs. Courtenay's Assembly, that the Bishops were insulted going to Dinner with some of our Ministers of State, last week; and the circumstance created some alarm.

Mr. Eckersall says the Comte d'Artois' life has been attempted, and *that* it was gave the King of France gout in his stomach. Our gracious Queen's arrival may possibly produce a like effect in the stomach of Louis Dixhuit's personal friend.

… Miss Wroughton, in her zeal for Mr. and Mrs. Ashe, asked half a dozen amateur Gentlemen to mount the Balcony, and sing for their Benefit, because the Theatre supported by Mr. Young took all their best musicians away; just as her friends the Ashes, took away Mr. Windsor, etc.—if you recollect—from my Fête on the 27th of January. And so some laugh, and some are angry, but Miss Wroughton, tho' she cross'd *me* at every turn this Winter, begs *me* to take Tickets now for Mr. Ashe!!! I really wonder how she can think of such a thing.

Clifton must be a charming place, sure, where there is no such gossiping nonsense; and all the Devonshire coast too is so quiet, and Penzance in Cornwall will soon be fashionable;—it is so cheap, they say, and so warm ...

You do not care much, I think, about these ridiculous reports concerning Queen Caroline; how she is coming—so she is—to do wonders unheard of till now: and Buonaparte!—how he's to be let out, a Bag Fox, for all Europe to hunt again. People find torpor worse than torture 'tis plain. They long for War, a property-tax and a battle in every Newspaper: rebellion and assassination are not hot enough. As Mr. Leo was constrained at last to warm his brandy with Cayenne Pepper before his stomach could feel any effect.

BATH, *April* 22, 1820.

Dear Mrs. Pennington will be glad to see the spring coming forward so sweetly. She will be glad, too, to hear that her true friends are well; the Little Old Woman, and the Tall Young Beau. She will be glad that the Parties grow hot and disagreeable, and that I feel longing for Clifton and the 10th of June. Whether we are to be glad of the recovery of the Great Lady I know not, for tho' her life does much good, her death—poor Dear!—would have done no harm. Do you remember an impudent Comic Actor on our Bath Stage? A Mr. Edwin, and we said he resembled Dr. Randolph in the face: and how when he was addressing the audience in an epilogue upon his own Night, he suddenly turned to her Stage Box, singing

And the Duchess, who now sits so smiling here
Shall come to our Benefits every year.
Tol ol derol, Lol, etc.

I never saw any fair Female so confounded in my life. You were with me.

How the ground and the trees do sigh and pine for rain! And what a haze this odious North East wind sheds over all my prospect! The people are right enough that go abroad. I would go myself, but that I have an appointment to keep with dear Piozzi, who I brought out of his own sweet Country, to lie in the vault he made for me and my Ancestors at Dymerchion; where I am most willing to keep him company, when I have performed *more* than *all* the promises I ever, in any humour, made his Nephew; and when I have, after paying every debt, saved a silver sixpence or two for those who soften and amuse the closing scenes of a life long drawn out,—perhaps for that very purpose. Meanwhile we have a church building here, for my *particular friends*, the Blackguards and tatter'd Belles of Avon Street, and my Subscription will be soon expected.

Ay, Ay, I see where I shall pass the Winter months escaping frosts, and keeping clear of expences, in a climate better than Paris, the Latitude very little higher. But if you open your lips—Adieu! …

Dear —— says *his* health was never so perfect, and he uses horse exercise, and sends love to his Friends,—and is a good Boy. I used to bid my children when at distance, only write three words,—safe, well, and happy: his letter is just like theirs.

You are tired, are you not, of the silly talk concerning the Queen and the Radicals. They are like the Statues in the *Arabian Nights*, who clatter their armour to fright those who go up the hill: but if you walk steadily forward it ends in nothing.

We have an Italian Rope Dancer coming, *Diavol* Antonio, as they call him. Our shows have been like those in a Magic Lanthorn; so the *Devil* comes at last to end the whole ado.

Fryday May 5th, 1820.

… We will see a great deal of each other when Clifton becomes my place of residence for six pretty weeks. After them—old Ocean. Can aught else compleatly wash away all recollection of Bath *Parties*? That fair assemblage of glaring lights, empty heads, aking hearts, and false faces?

Who is it says the conversation of a true friend brightens the eyes? I have enjoy'd two chearful hours *talk* with our best *speaker,* best actor, best companion,—Conway. You seem to express yourself as if half sorry you loved him so much. I am only sorry that I can't love him ten times more …

Here is lovely weather for frisking up and down, and my empty pockets will not *overload* the carriage; altho' the whole *family* of *emigrants* will be packed *in, and on, and upon*, my Post chaise and four ...

Salusbury sent me a whimpering letter, and has already got his £100, which Heaven knows I owed, and much more, to the estate of Messrs. Callan and Booth, Lodging House keepers. But if I can get five Guineas o' week for No. 8, during absence, I shall bring matters round in due time: because, as Clarissa says in the *Rambler*, 'tis well known to all the Beau-Monde *that nobody ever dies.*

In her next letter Mrs. Piozzi makes arrangements for the accommodation of herself and her household, consisting of her man James, her attendant Bessy, and two other maids at Clifton.

Tuesday, 16 *May* 1820.

... I can't stir till 10th of June ... I like to be under Mrs. Rudd's roof, and mean to sleep under it next Saturday three weeks, the Pretender's birthday, when old Tories in Wales wore white Roses, the 10th day of June. Sunday's dinner I hope to eat with Mr. and Mrs. Pennington, at their hospitable board, and we will talk of anything and everything but la Partenza, which cannot be before the same day of July, as till then I have ne'er a groat. If life is lent me I will be rich that time twelve-month; and if it is *not* lent me, I shall want no money.

Meanwhile I expect no letters from our favourite Friend. I have written to him tho', and told him that you and I were his Hephestion and Parmenio; and if he does not laugh at his Blue Ladies, we are surely well off.

Do you remember Charles Shephard, I wonder? and how we petted him? and Piozzi trusted him with all his affairs, and bid me do so; and *so I did.* The envious and jealous people however, after my husband's death, (people of our mutual acquaintance,) blew coals up between him and me, and parted us with *acrimony* on his side, *mental* resentment, very strong, on mine. I express'd none however; only said, "God forgive and prosper you, farewell." Many reports would have been made afterwards concerning his *distresses,* which I regularly turned a deaf ear to; and for these last 10 years never heard his name, and scarcely ever pronounced it. Last Fryday brought me a beautiful letter from him, dated West India, congratulating me on the gay supper given last January, assuring me of his continued regard, and bidding me direct back to the Hon. C.S. etc. because he is a Privy Councillor, Chief Justice, and Lord knows what besides.

That he retains his confidence in me plainly appears from the tender enquiries he makes after his favourite Lady; of whose attachment to him, and his to her, no one ever knew but myself. So I have lived long enough to have old friends restored, and to have made *one* new one. I hope dear Conway and he will be acquainted when he comes home *rich* and—no, *not* happy, but able to spite the spiters. If I am removed before then, you will remain and introduce them to each other. It will be a mutual pleasure, and you will talk of H.L.P., and Sir John will have my letters to make money of, and give him some compensation for my extravagance in the year 1820.

Callan and Booth, the people I take my house from, have heavy claims on me *now;* so I have let it to Mr. Iveson for a twelvemonth, and mean to be smooth as Oyl'd Silk by July 1821 …

There is much for you to do as my Sentimental Executrix, so we will hear of no departure but mine for Marasion, just by Penzance …

George Hammersley has just left me and taken my Banker's Book to Pallmall to be regulated; and gives me great credit for my care and exactness in my Money Matters: bidding me make no scruple with regard to *their House*, etc., very good-naturedly indeed. But as I told him I never yet overdrew my Banker, and will not (unless something serious happens,) begin to do so in the year 1820. *One* twelve month's short-biting will set all smooth, and you shall see a merry face once more on the shoulders of yours and dear Mr. Pennington's affectionate, H.L.P.

A few days afterwards Mrs. Piozzi was much agitated, on Conway's account, by the news of the collapse of the stage of the Birmingham theatre, where it appears he was going to act; but it turned out that it was not during a performance, and the only injury done was to one of the workmen.

BATH, *Tuesday* 23 *May* 1820.

... I shall sleep at your Crescent House, Mrs. Rudd's, as we agreed long ago on Saturday night, 10 June, if it pleases God, and go to your Bristol Cathedral on Sunday morning: dine in Dowry Square, chat with you all the evening, and pass a comfortable night,—altho' the Queen is coming near enough to put every one in a heat; if perhaps she may forbear to light up a *fire* in our Nation for purpose of roasting her own chicken to her own mind.

Public and private villainies on the increase, as Dr. Randolph used to tell us long ago. He did recommend Charles Shephard's father for the education of young Salusbury, and the son recommended *himself* by his useful talents to dear Piozzi; by his brilliant ones to me. I am happy to find he will be *rich* and *prosperous*; happy he scarcely *can* be from the nature of his attachment; but 'tis happy to feel attachment at all, for when that's over, all's over ...

... At a wedding breakfast we were invited to yesterday Dr. Wilkinson harangued in praise of Marazion, and our friend Mr. Gifford said that when he was a young Officer, he treated his brothers of the Corps with a dinner; two dishes of fish, one ham, three chickens, a pigeon pye, and a plum pudding;—the cost, 14 shillings ...

Meanwhile Sir Wm. Hotham says the Levee was a Bear Garden. Miss Knight's letter to Mrs. Lutwyche says it was full of Grocers, Silk Dyers, and Upholsterers. And *I* say it was a *Levy-en-Masse.*

The Bath people must get substitutes for H.L.P. and W.A.C. as they can. I fancy young Roscius will be the man, the woman is yet to be looked for.

Admiral Sir William Hotham, one of Nelson's officers, was made a K.C.B. in 1815, and became one of the Gentlemen in Waiting to the King.

The young Roscius (William Henry West Betty), whose acting at the age of twelve created such a furore, and whose popularity for a time eclipsed that of Mrs. Siddons, had already appeared at Bath in 1812. He retired from the stage in 1824 and died in 1874.

BATH, *Tuesday Night*,
6 *June,* 1820.

… Mr. Ward has taken leave, and all the Ladies wept. Such was the croud, I am told, that James my man could not get in to any place he could stand upon.

The Londoners will have as good food for starers as Mr. Ward can give the Bath folks. Queen Caroline is said to be arrived, and is to inhabit Wanstead House. The rumours and reports are indeed innumerable …

Meanwhile my heart is heavy with affliction at losing an old, tried, and true friend, Archdeacon Thomas. Poor man! and poor Mrs. Thomas! for whom my heart bleeds. He was buried in the Abbey, where he was walking with Dr. Harington, his father-in-law, some few years ago. "Let us look," said they, " for a place where *we* may lie." "Ay, Thomas, so we will, for

> These ancient walls, with many a mouldering bust,
> But shew how well Bath Waters *lay the dust.*"

repeated the ever-ready Doctor.

How long, dear Mrs. Pennington, *am* I to live? How many valuable companions *am* I to lose? These gentlemen were among the very pleasing ones I have known … Thank God Salusbury and Conway—dear Lads—are young, and likely to last me out. But when they do not write my foolish heart is fluttering for their safety,—naughty children as they are in neglecting to send me a letter. I have heard but once from Brynbella since my £100 went there.

Mrs. Dimond told [Miss Williams] that Bath would have a sad loss of Mrs. Piozzi; but the Queen will put everything but herself out of everybody's head. The weather is wonderfully dull; so is my letter …

Henry Harington, M.D., Physician to the Duke of York, was a talented musician, and founder of the Bath Philharmonic Society. A letter quoted by Hayward describes him in 1815 as "listening with delight to his own charming compositions. The last Catch and

Glee are said to be the best he ever wrote." The incident mentioned above took place the same year. There is a curious little note about him in Mrs. Piozzi's Commonplace Book. "Dr. Harrington, who was then 88 years old, never took any air or exercise that he could possibly avoid, going constantly to his patients in a Sedan; and held a handkerchief before his face to keep the air away."

Another note, dated June 7, 1820, runs as follows: "Am I, H.L.P., sorry to leave Bath? No, but I should be *half* sorry to think I never should return, which it is most probable I never shall; my age so far advanced. Well, God's will, not mine, be done."

PENZANCE, Tuesday 25 Jul. 1821.
[clearly a slip for 1820.]

My dearest Mrs. Pennington will be pleased to hear that we arrived safely at Penzance last night … All we are told about the place seems true … We shall get a good house, with a sea view … upon the Regent's Terrace, paying £16 o' month, thro' the whole ten, from 1st of August next to 1st of June 1821 …

Our dear Conway's name at length appears in the *Morning Post*, summoning his troops to meet in the Green Room of the new Theatre, Birmingham. If Mrs. Rudd does not know it, do her the honour to call with the information.

I wish the ship was come with our Cook, and our books, and our luggage. A Mr. Paul shew'd me 4 fine Red Mullets he had just paid a penny each for, this very morning: yet the *Inn* gave us a stale Soal yesterday, and will charge a shilling at least for it. But Honesty is a shrub harder to raise than Myrtle, which grows here in open air sure enough, and the people are so fond of it that they plant the beautiful Bay out of their sight as much as possible, preferring green trees to blue waves completely.

St. Michael's Mount is a disappointing object, at least to me; and as to the country we came thro', nothing ever looked so poverty-stricken, except the very roughest part of North Wales in *rough* days, before they had begun enclosing. Goats browsing wild about the rocks, as in some districts of Snowdonia, serve the peasants as good substitutes for cattle, who could not pick a living so as to enable them to give milk for the innumerable children that crowd the cottages. Yet Mrs. Hill complains that they grow saucy, and refuse Barley Bread *now*, which used to be their regular sustenance. I have not, however, seen a beggar, and the shops are splendid, while the streets are *odious*,—too filthy, too mean to be endured. Bangor and Beaumaris would be ashamed of them. I might have had a good house for two Guineas o' week, but could not away with the situation, coming from Clifton Hill. Peat stacks at every turn shew what fires they use here in the winter, but till last January snow had not been seen for many years, and it lasted but *one* day. The tide here is like that in the Mediterranean, just *visible* the Ebb and Flow; tho' full moon to-day, no rise appears to *my* eyes that are unused to a land-locked bay, and which, (foolishly enough), expected an open Ocean, such as the Sussex coast exhibits. But old Neptune here puts on a quiet aspect, resembling that he wears at Weymouth or at Tenby. No mud however *offends* the Bathers, and no Machine *assists* them.

I saw the Holmes, and pretty Mendip Lodge, as we came along, and fancied I could discern Weston super Mare, whose Sea View Place is just such a row of houses as Regent's Terrace; only we have here such magnificent gardens, and one good house in the middle of the row, looking down with true contempt on the mouse-holes each side it:—and *that* Mansion I am in chase of, only suspecting that, before we knew it was to be had, I entangled myself in a mouse-hole.

The women here are beautiful. The Lady of Mousetrap Hall, with whom I have entangled myself, has eyes like Garrick's, teeth like Salusbury's, complexion like your own, but cruel as lovely. I fear she will not let me off; and in her house I should regret the *ample* space of your house, or mine at Weston super Mare.

I have half a mind not to let this go till I have finally settled this *great affair*. Great indeed just now, for as Goldsmith said

> These *little* things are great to *little* men.[9]

> And on this 26th—I shall sit, fret, and dine
> In a chair-lumber'd closet, just eight feet by nine.

For I feel myself after all condemned to the Mousehole for three months certain; £2, 15s. 0d. per week, with a view of the sea, and *then* (if we live to see November), Mr. Paul's comfortable Mansion at next door.

PENZANCE, *Wed.* 3 *August,* 1820.

Charming Mrs. Pennington's beautiful letter was indeed most welcome, tho' it does put me a little more out of humour with my runaway frolic than I was before it arrived ...

Now for Penzance and its Parties. Mrs. Hill made a splendid one, for *me* I rather think, and my black satten gown (for no other is yet arrived,) was my best garment. Bessy lent me a cap of hers, and my youthful looks were duly appreciated—my whist-playing *applauded.* We had two tables, one for shillings, one for sixpences; a profusion of exquisite refreshments, and music in another room. Oh! if I escape all temptations to sensuality, I shall live to see dear Mr. and Mrs. Pennington again, and the Hot Wells, and Clifton Terrace, where I shall surely jump for very joy. But these Red Mullets and Dorees for two pence o' piece will certainly destroy *some* of us. Poor Bessy has been *seriously,* I might say dangerously ill, from indulging in a Crab; it made James sick too; all the family half-killed,—for the small price of a groat the fish, and a Pound to the Dr. ... a real Physician, thank God, and not a country 'Pothecary ...

The people know not how to be civil enough, and if my stomach will reconcile itself to the clouted cream, I shall come home as fat as the pigs of the country, and such pork did I never see. Our own garden affords potatoes for us all, and onions etc., besides the flower plot, perfuming the very air around with carnations of every hue, Myrtles of every form, and exotic shrubs with Linnean names innumerable. The appearance of our Mansion, *pleasure* ground, and kitchen garden, reminds me of Kingsmead Terrace, Bath; but James says the houses here are by no means so *spacious* as that where your compassion carried you when our incomparable Conway was so ill. I hope he has proved himself *irresistible,* and what must the heart be over which he cannot, if he pleases—triumph? ... Oh! if I possessed an unappropriated £100 in the world, I would go see him act once again, that I would … I am glad Mrs. Rudd's heart seems lighter than when we left her; the Rogue has never written to *me,* no, not a scrap; but she had an *earlier* pretension to his regard, I think it is scarce a truer.

Meanwhile Sophia Hoare has written me a more good humour'd letter than usual, and I am *so* delighted! Maternal love is the only good thing mankind cannot throw away. It springs fresh with the least drop of water flung upon it. She wishes her illustrious Neighbour out of Town I see, and says wisely that her present residence being so near the Barracks is unfortunate, because the soldiers' wives and children are among her every night's applauders. The Hoares are used to be violent opposers of the Ministry, but Democrates like to have their property held sacred, as well as you or I; and firing houses will make no sport to the Bankers, I trow.

So now *pray* accept these *not elaborate* verses: they will amuse Mr. Pennington's gout.

> Around their *Queen*
>> Here are seen,
>>> Sharp'ning every *sting,*
> Bees,—alarming
>> By their swarming
>>> People, Peers, and King.
>
> But in their tricks,
>> Should they fix
>>> On our property;
> They must learn
>> To discern
>>> That when they *sting,* they *die.*

Surely such Cakes, Jellies, etc., as they use here for refreshments, all new and warm, were never *seen* at Bath or London, so various, so profuse. I never touch them, certainly, but never was so tempted. No Confectioner's shop visible in the place, *all made at home.*

With regard to rain, we live in a cloud of soft mist, rain, if you please to call it so; certainly a perpetual damp, warm moisture. Lady Jane James said, you know, that she never put on a dry chemise at St. Michael's Mount, and truly did she speak; but nobody ever told me that the sea here is as tame as the country is wild. Wild without sublimity, coarse externally, like other Misers; its riches all concealed underground. I saw Hay carried last night, two months after the environs of Clifton. But I have wrong'd old Neptune; he *can* roar, I hear him now, thank Heaven. Oh! how much more delightful is the music he now makes than that of the pretty Ladies of the parties, to the rude ears of dearest Mrs. Pennington's everlastingly obliged and faithful   H.L.P.

Aug 3. Fateful month! but no clothes, no books, no Cook, no Conway's portrait yet for poor   H.L.P.

Cook, books, and clothes were still in the Port of Bristol, as Mrs. Pennington writes on the 29th, waiting, as it appeared, for the captain to make up his freight; and might then be expected to take from four days to a fortnight—according to the wind—to make Penzance.

The renewed enthusiasm for Queen Caroline was aroused by the anticipation of the Bill of Pains and Penalties, intended to dissolve the marriage, which was brought in on August 14, but proved so unpopular, both in and out of Parliament, that it had to be dropped.

On August 10 Mrs. Pennington is able to announce that the *Happy Return* had actually sailed, with Mrs. Piozzi's belongings, five days before. Conway had been to see his mother, and had called on herself, rather, she thinks, from civility than from choice. "There was a polite distance assumed, evidently for the purpose of repressing enquiry … I am persuaded we trouble ourselves much more about his concerns than he either wishes or likes." She gathered, however, that he had secured some sort of recognition from his father. She alludes to the letter of "lovely Mrs. Hoare," whom "I always liked … because I thought her more personally like you than any of the Ladies."

PENZANCE, *Sunday August* 13, 1820.

Come! oh come! dear Mrs. Pennington, I see you half long to be here, and what a relief, what a comfort, would your society afford to your starving H.L.P.? Here is *no* heat, *no* dust, *no* cold: I daresay it is a very *negative* place, but I must not have you tell tales out of School. Miss Trevenan may justly disapprove my censure on the *no* picturesque of her native county: and if you read her my letters so, I must grow cautious, à la Conway. I *have* heard from him, thank God! The rogue told me nothing tho', except how charming you and I were, what admirable letters we wrote, etc. "Yea, and all *that* did I know before,"[10] as Juliet says. Quere, whether he has anything to tell; unless it be that he has at length calmed his own noble and too-feeling mind, by conduct which himself approves.

But at the same moment with your kind letter comes our long-expected ship. Cook says they have been to *Wales*; Swansea in Glamorganshire!

The day you receive this one whole month will have elapsed since I left the full moon *shining in her brightness* on Clifton Terrace. Never have my eyes seen her since. No, nor a starry night. Yet here is sun enough, and the sea so beautifully blue and clear, you would be delighted with it, as one is with a tame Lyon. Will you come? …

Much, meantime, and of much more importance, is crazing all the brain-pans of poor Europe. The revolt at Rome strikes me as very surprising. The same people who defended their Sovereign as long as they could, poor creatures! against French aggression, now fly in the face of his not only *Innocent*, but *innocuous* successor: no mortal can guess why. Ay, ay, you used to laugh when I mounted my turnep cart and preached the end of the world. But you don't like witnessing the convulsions that precede it, and which increase in violence visibly every day. Poor Ithaca! Whence Ulysses was detained, you know, by the gardens of Alcinous, has been shattered completely to pieces by an earthquake, under the name of St. Mauro; and Inspruck, where I spent a few days, has seen the destruction of her *Golden House.*

Our Queen Bee, of whom the Radicals have laid hold, will be the instrument of concussion in *our* Country; and we drones shall suffer, while the stingers go on torturing each other into madness.

The Naturalists, Pennant, Linnæus, etc., have long observed that all the *Hymenoptera* have stings. Yet I suppose that will not deter the *hopers* from *marriage* ...

Mr. Mangin's Intercepted Letter was a little Pamphlet, censuring some Authors, Actors, etc., commending others; and I got two kind lines, before we were at all acquainted,—so *that* brought on Library conversation, and he offered his services about the *Name-Book*;— took it to London for me, where it was rejected, not through any neglect on his part: and I felt myself much obliged by his attentions, and rejoiced in his good fortune when he married ...

No particulars are forthcoming respecting the "Name Book," but it was evidently a work on Etymology, written some years before, which was to have been called *Lyford Redivivus*, for which she was unable to find a publisher. A letter in Mr. Broadley's collection indicates that it was finished about 1816, when she writes to Sir James Fellowes, "I wish Mr. Jenkins had taken the Name Book."

PENZANCE, *Saturday Night*,
26 *Aug.* 1820.

Dear, kind Mrs. Pennington, I love you for wishing that you *could* come, and you ought to love me for agreeing in the notion that to come would be very foolish. One can hardly save the expences of such a journey by cheap fish, when the water 'tis boyl'd in must, every drop, be paid for. And what an idiot was James not to pay the carriage of the Turbot! When I miss'd it in the weekly account I could have cuff'd him.

The heats are equable, not strong or *starvy*; but little can be said in praise of the weather. Rain, almost incessant, keeps one at home, and to get at this lovely sea, such stinks must be encounter'd as I never knew but at Rome or Naples. Poor, dear Italy! I *did* love it however, and hear with unaffected sorrow of the pangs that are tearing it to pieces. In France *fire*-brands seem the instruments of punishment from on high. In England *one female* suffices. If nothing can be done without *more help*, my Paper says that Buonaparte is to be let loose, and that Prince Esterhazy's business here was to solicit his liberation.

Hissing the Duke of Wellington is a prelude, a pretty overture to such an Opera. Opera means *piece of work*, you know. It makes me more willing to quit the world certainly, when I see it rolling down hill so. But the whole of it must be discover'd before it is destroy'd, and the little ship *William,* a trading vessel from Blythe in Northumberland, has in effect found at last the great Southern Continent, so long supposed to exist, so completely forgotten of late years ...

Did you ever read my verses, which this discovery made by the *William* confirms? "*No*," is the answer, Well then, here they are, making part of a long poem composed 35 years ago.

> Where slowly turns the Southern Pole,
> And distant Constellations roll,
> A sea-girt Continent lies hurl'd,
> And keeps the balance of the World.
> But felter'd fogs, and hoary frost
> Defend th' inhospitable coast,
> Which, veil'd from sight, eludes the Pilot's care,
> And leaves him fix'd in ice, a statue of despair.

I hear no more of Salusbury. I never could get *him* to care about these matters: and after all, does not he act as *all* parents wish their children to act, soberly and quietly, keeping a steady eye to his *interest* in this world; not, I hope and trust, forgetful of the next. One must love the creatures for their valuable, or delight in them for their shining qualities, no matter whether they love me or no, and *in their way* they do love me. Sir James Fellowes has written kindly and good-humouredly, and my heart has entirely made all up with his. Nothing, as you say, ail'd him but jealousy; and I hold that to be what foolish Merlin, the mechanic, called a *desagreable compliment* ...

Miss Willoughby has written from St. Anne's Hill. She says Lord Erskine wishes the illustrious Lady, who causes so much talk, was *in* the Liturgy and *out* of the Country. After what past at Ephesus, I see not why one should wish any such thing; but the aggregate of understanding she is tried by will decide rightly, I doubt not ...

Well, God mend all; and give us a merry meeting on our *Happy Return* ...

The populace had been exasperated with Wellington over the Peterloo incident, and he was just now sharing the unpopularity of the Ministry, of which he was a member, on account of the Bill of Pains and Penalties designed to effect the Queen's divorce. The exclusion of her name from the Church Services had been one of the first objects of the King on his accession.

Miss Willoughby, who soon afterwards followed Mrs. Piozzi to Penzance, appears to have been a daughter of Charles James Fox.

15 *Sep.* 1820.

I hope my dear Mrs. Pennington is beginning again to look for an empty letter. Empty it *must* be of all but good will, badly express'd, for we are still-life people here, who see and hear very little, and reflect less upon what is seen and heard. I think every day more and more with our old Master Shakespear, that "there is a tide in the affairs of men, which, taken at the flood, leads on to fortune."[11] Caroline of Brunswick has surely miss'd her tide. A commotion might have been raised the first week: I now begin to doubt its possibility on *her* account. Rebellion however is *in*, as boys say of Cricket and Kite-flying, and any excuse serves in any country. When what is called a Spirit of Liberty seizes the swarthy inhabitants of Morocco, how should their old enemies, the Portuguese, escape? "When Afric *recovers*, Mundus will *end*," says an old proverb. And as dear Mrs. Pennington says, "no matter how soon, it *should* be either ended or mended." The eclipse however did nothing towards its destruction. I saw it here beautifully, but there was little apparent obscuration, tho' the Thermometer sunk two degrees. We shall have an elegant Eclipse of the Moon on our Equinoctial day, the 22d of September: and our tides become even now a little stronger in their flux and reflux. Like other quiet temper'd people, their anger, I understand is dreadful ...

Doctor Randolph's state of health grieves me, and the loss of Mr. Bayntom; on whom so many, (and those wise people too,) depended with a very firm reliance. I always wonder at *such* partiality. It has been my lot to love three or four Medical Men very sincerely, and like them in earnest for companions and friends, but would not give much of preference to any. And 'tis well that such is my humour, in a place where we send to the *Tallow chandler's* if we want drugs: no Apothecary or Chymist residing near happy Penzance. Fowls we buy in the feathers—and James says every shop in the Town sells Barley to feed them with. There are no more Poulterers than Milliners yet everybody is genteelly drest, and I warrant our Michælmas goose will be good, and cost us scarce half a crown, giblets and plumage. I should like to write you a letter with my own *quill* …

Well! now I will go work at your Fly; but even that is nonsense, for I cannot frame it, nor line it, nor put it in a box. There are no frames, no boxes, no linings, at Penzance. I cannot make it worth your acceptance; and who dreams of my living till the spring, and bringing it with me to Clifton, when I shall be going on to 82 years old? I must finish, and leave it in charge with Bessy, to save from the hands of my Executors; as I will do by Conway's portrait …

The Harvest here is beautiful and plenteous:—

> Far as the circling eye can range around
> Unbounded, tossing in a flood of corn,

as Thomson says. Industry is a rough power surely, but a kind one; working that you and I may sit idle, ploughing that H.L.P. may have leisure to work Butterflies, and weaving that pretty Mrs. Balhechet may look lovely in her various dresses.

Charles Shephard has written to me again. He likes the correspondence I suppose, for we are 4000 miles asunder. By dint of industry however, he will come home *rich*; and seeing 50 people richer than himself, will find he has exchanged honour and distinction for Coffee-house chat and Drawing-room small talk,—the food his fancy *now* is longing for, but which will grow insipid in six months; and reflection will *then* inform him that to talk of *Rum* and *Sugar* has more *spirit* and *sweetness* than to talk of *nothing*. He begs me to write, not newspaper occurrences, he says, but *stuff out of my own head*, as they say at Eton School;—the head of an old Haggard, 81 years old!!! But he is consorting with those who never heard tell about the gardens of *Alcinous*. Some one sung a Ballad in which Lethe was mentioned, not a soul in the company guess'd what was meant, till some very clever fellow found it was a river, running between Leith and Edinburgh ...

In Morocco, under Soliman, the Christian slaves were being liberated, and piracy suppressed. In Portugal, after the flight of John VI to Brazil, the government had been in the hands of a Regency, which included Marshal Beresford, who organised the army, but used its power despotically. During a visit he paid to Rio in 1820, insurrections took place at Lisbon and Oporto, the English Officers were expelled, and a Constituent Assembly formed.

The Eclipse of Sep. 7, 1820, was an annular one, well seen over the N. of Europe. Mangin relates how a similar one occurred in Mrs. Piozzi's girlhood, and an astronomical friend told her she might live to see another at 80.

On Sep. 21 Mrs. Pennington writes, much disgusted at the revelations of the Queen's trial, and apprehensive of their effect on public morals. "Not a Boarding School Miss, nor a Parish Girl, that can make out the words, but we see studying these detestable pages, and devouring their contents as they would a new Novel ... The worst part of the business is the little respect, and less approbation, felt even by well disposed and moderate persons for a certain Great Individual. The vices of debauchery offend and disgust more (with many who are not altogether disinclined to the practice,) than the downright wickedness arising from the ambition and tyranny of the worst Monarchs that ever reigned; and prove that the moral virtues are of more value than anything. Our late K—g lost 13 Provinces, and supported a war which was unpopular with a great part of his subjects, and which has ruined the Nation; yet he was loved for his moral excellence, and his memory is revered."

She deprecates precipitancy in the matter of the Butterfly, and suggests that any Carpenter, with 4 strips of wood, might make a rough, but efficient, substitute for the Tambour Frame which she thought Mrs. Piozzi could not procure.

PENZANCE, *Tuesday, Sep.* 26, 1820.

In life's last scenes, what prodigies surprise!
Fears of the brave, and follies of the wise!
SAM. JOHNSON

Poor dear Dr. Randolph! Ay, and poor dear Mr. Chappelow too! The post which brought your letter—charming friend!—brought one from his nephew, son to Soame Jenyns, saying his uncle was dead, and had left my letters carefully tied up, which he would send to Bath immediately. I wrote and beg'd him send the packet to *you*, where I shall find it safe if I live till May-day; and if *not*, you will give it to Sir John or Sir James, my Executors. He had lost his head long before he lost his life, I find. Awful reflection! For a pleasant head it was, and a world of pleasant stories were hatched in it. Would not Mr. Pennington be sorry for such a loss to his true servant H.L.P.? I am very *sure* he would; and vexations at 81 years old cannot contribute much towards holding it in its place ...

Of the discovery made by the "William," I think very seriously. It is the last place that has lain concealed, and when the Gospel has been *preached* there,—Christ does not say *obeyed,*—"then shall the end come." Distress of nations with perplexity was never, no *never* so apparent: tho' Dorset Fellowes writes me word that they say not a syllable of their own conspiracy at Paris ... You are right about the tryal ending in smoke. I daresay it will: but the people, falsely called people in *power*, are afraid of its ending in *fire*, like myself, and will therefore be glad to compound. It was never a thing of *their* seeking, and the French are all for la belle Caroline, of course; and threaten their English visitants with the speedy appearance of Monsieur le Baron Bergami. Meanwhile the fashionable joke is to say a noble Marquis, much talked of in London, is like a *comb*, all back and teeth. Yes, says another wag,—a *Horn* comb.

My fret about your Fly was for a frame, a picture frame, to hang it up in your boudoir. The only merit in my work is that it is all done upon the *hand*; I do not know how to use a Tambour. The drawing it is ill executed from represented the *Blue-eyed Paris* from Chandernagore;

a Butterfly of much dignity, according to Linnæus, but you must accept it cover'd with faults. Lady Williams of Bodylwyddan had the *Ulysses* worked reasonably well,—a dozen years ago,—and Mrs. Rudd has a Moth …

I never heard Miss Stephens sing, and what is much stranger, never heard the famous Mrs. Sheridan. But I have heard old Dr. Burney say *she* sung "Return, O God of Hosts" better than anybody except Mrs. Cibber the Actress, whose manner of delivering that air was absolute perfection. Miss Sharpe says the Kembles are well and happy at Lausanne … I hear the Twisses are returned to Bath, meaning Mr. and Mrs. Twiss; the Girls are out, like good girls, getting their living … Horace has got into Parliament safe and snug.

Poor Mrs. Rudd! I hope she will keep her houses full, and find me a lodging in some of them next Spring, before the 10th of June, that I may bustle and be busy; and get my *little things,* (as Ladies call everything,) from No. 8 Gay Street to No. 36 Royal Terrace, Clifton. But how hopeless and silly all this is at 81 years old, and dear Chappelow dead of superannuation, six years younger than myself, in whom *hope* of living six months would be *proof* of superannuated folly. We must do as well as we can, and wish we could do better. He was as temperate as I am … But when sickness comes in consequence of drinking some stuff that *pretended* to be smuggled wine, and *was* a mess made with sea water in an Alehouse; why then I *do* despair of ever again seeing any place or people that are dear to your poor   H.L.P.

Mr. Ray has long left Streatham and its neighbourhood. His mother died of cold in a rough winter some years ago. She would go and sort her apples in a loft; where being seized with a shivering fit, she was brought down,—only to expire,—at 92 years old.

Soame Jenyns, who, according to the Dictionary of National Biography, left no issue by either of his wives, was the author of the epitaph on Johnson containing the lines—

> Boswell and Thrale, retailers of his wit,
> Will tell you how he wrote, and talk'd, and cough'd, and spit.

The French conspiracy here alluded to was the plot hatched for the murder of the Duc de Bern, son of the Comte d'Artois.

Bartolomeo Bergami, who just now loomed large through the cloud of scandal which surrounded the Queen's trial, was originally engaged by her as a courier, when she retired to the Continent in 1813. His handsome person so commended him to his royal mistress that she speedily promoted him to be her equerry and chamberlain, and treated him as an intimate friend. Through her influence he was made a Baron of Sicily, a Knight of Malta, and several other orders, including one of her own devising, under the patronage of "Saint Caroline": while a number of his relatives were provided with posts in her train.

Catherine Stephens was at this date the leading soprano at Covent Garden, and afterwards sang at Drury Lane, and in the chief concerts and festivals. In 1838 she married the fifth Earl of Essex, then over eighty years of age, and died in 1882. Though she had not a finished style, she sang airs like "Angels ever bright and fair" with much pathos and devotional feeling.

The Mrs. Sheridan here spoken of was the dramatist's first wife, Eliza Ann Linley, who died 1792. Though she was the finest singer of her day, her dislike to appearing in public had much to do with her run-away match with Sheridan.

Of Dr. Burney she writes in her Commonplace Book that he "died at last, I am told, at 89 years old, and in full possession of his faculties. They were extremely good ones. He *thought* himself my friend once, I believe, whilst he thought the world was so. When the stream turned against the poor straw, he helped its progress with his *stick* and made his daughter do it with her *fingers*. The stream however grew too strong, and forced the little straw forward in spite of them."

Mrs. Pennington sends a closely-written foolscap sheet dated October 1, largely taken up with the Queen's trial, a propos of which she says: "We received a comical anecdote in a letter from Town. They say it was a common trick for the little rascally boys, if they could get hold of a stranger in the mob, to offer to *shew them the Queen for sixpence!* On receiving it they would *shout out*; on which Her Majesty would immediately appear, and smile and curtesy graciously: and the boy would then add, "*I'll have her out again presently!*"

PENZANCE, *Sunday Oct.* 15, 1820.

A propos to Kingly residence the best joke is that since Her Majesty has possessed herself of all the John *Bulls,* her husband ran to *Cowes* by way of retaliation. It would seem by the Papers now, I think, that the Tryal draws near to a conclusion. If any poor Italian should be put in the Pillory, as menaced, he never, no never, would come out alive. When Mr. Thrale and I lived in Southwark, I pass'd a poor creature in that situation, upon St. Margaret's Hill, and could eat no dinner for thinking of his sufferings and danger. "Madam," exclaimed Dr. Johnson, "give yourself no concern about him. My life for it, he is drunk by now." The hapless Lombards have no such resource, and the man I saw died before night. But Miss Willoughby tells of another joke. One says the Queen must be fatigued to death sitting in this room so, without refreshment. "No Sir," is the reply, "the Queen's not *nice*; she can take a *chop* at the King's Head";—an Alehouse in the neighbourhood.

What you observe concerning public and private virtues may be true now in 1820; in 1760 I remember, when Wilkes's moral character was objected to by the Loyalists, the Liberty Boys cried, "What care we whether he be vicious, or the man he insults be virtuous? We look to *public*, not to *private* character." In consequence of these opinions the Town was deluged with verses, of which I can call to mind one stanza in praise of the then popular Hero.

> 'Tis thus that we are told,
>   The Ægyptians of old
>   Ador'd their still *fouler* Ichneumon,
> Who alone durst engage
>   The fell Crocodile's rage,
>   With courage exceeding the human.

I forget whether the crocodile stood for King George III, or my Lord Mansfield. They equally resembled him, I believe; but 'tis plain men thought little of Jack Wilkes's vartue.

Your Butterfly, which was finished yesterday, is not less fixed in his flights than popular opinion. When Cardinal de Retz was followed up and down by an admiring mob, "Is not this fine?" said a flatterer, "to see your Eminence possess'd of so many friends and followers." "Let anybody ring a dinner-bell," said he, "and see how many would be left me *then*."

Meanwhile the storm continues very grand indeed, but something very like very dreadful. This bay looks so calm too! But sweetest wines make the sourest vinegar, and no anger is so fierce or fatal as that of gentle natures irritated to frenzy. I begin to wish it was over; as I did travelling among the Alps, which at first enraptur'd, but the third day *wearied* my very heart. Effect of the true sublime ...

[*P.M. Nov.* 2, 1820.]

This will be a dull letter, dear Mrs. Pennington; I have been very ill, ill in good earnest, the pulse 92. There is a fever in the Town, and Sophy, my stout-looking housemaid, lies cover'd with blisters now ...

Let us talk of the storm, it is more entertaining, and tho' death seems, by the *describers,* to be most dreadful under the form of white breakers, it comes cleanlier, and less to my personal disliking, so, than accompanied with gallipots and all the tribe of sick-bed sorrows; for which, and the talk concerning them, my aversion was ever great ...

I continue to do what I came hither to perform, eat cheap fish, and pay old debts. Mr. Pennington will laugh, so will Dr. Randolph, if you tell them Tully's *Offices* are come to the last *chapter,* and that I shall write FINIS to *that* book, if I live the *next* month through.

Am I, d'ye think, to see the end of 1820? If I am, those who say people of letters are never people of figures, shall find themselves mistaken in H.L.P. Had I dreamed of losing £6000 at a stroke so, I would have been more prudent.

Conway was a good boy to send Partridge and pretty words to dear Clifton: he sends me no such nice things, knowing that my regard is not a ceremonious one. Marcella's speech to her lovers in Don Quixote, when they tax her with ingratitude, has the best common sense I ever read. "You love me," said she, "because I am young and beautiful and attractive by talents and graces. When you are so too

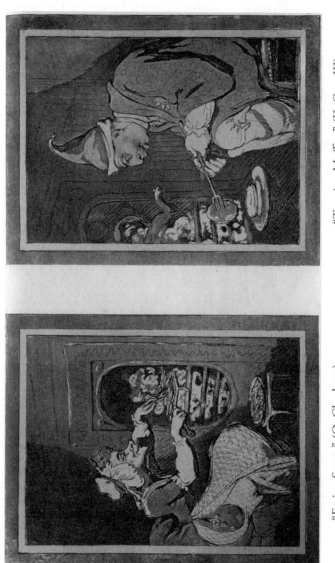

"Frying Sprats" (Q. Charlotte)   "Toasting Muffins" (K. Geo. III)

From a caricature by Gillray, 1791.

I will requite your love, but no gratitude is due for that attention which you all confess to be involuntary. Get you gone, and plague me no more. Should I want your assistance when grown old and ugly, would you give me any? No, I warrant. Then I have nothing to thank you for."[12]

Dorset (Fellowes) has been *surprisingly* kind, to me ... for after all, "Age is dark and unlovely, it is like the glimmering light of the Morn, when she shines thro' broken clouds: the blast of the North is on the plain, and the Traveller shrinks on his journey." Well! the people at Penzance do endure the dregs of the Piozzi very good naturedly; and Miss Willoughby grows much a favourite with them all.

What is to be seen at Penzance however, is a *storm.* The billows most majestic, and the sea spray tossing, foaming, as if to remind me of Brighthelmstone. For *there* alone does the salt water throw its particles into the air, so as to be carried 9 miles over the Downs to Lewes; where I have been warned to strip the Peaches of their downy coat, because they would taste of the last tempest. The shipwrecks here are shocking, and very frequent. This is no land of felicity to any but starvelings. Bessy buys five such fine Soles as I have partaken of at your table for one shilling, and they feed the family. We had a Turbot larger than that I sent to you for half a crown, a while ago. Miss Willoughby and I dined on the *fins.* But I scarce believe all fish is wholesome food, the town is full of Typhus now ...

My heart tells me that H.L.P. has made her last journey; but 'tis no matter, and will be no loss.

A new book called Nicholle's Reflexions, or Recollections, will amuse you. His opinions of the late King run parallel with yours. But I, who remember caricatures of Charlotte toasting the muffin, and George the third reaching the Teakettle, can never be made believe that modern Reformers sigh for *moral* Princes. How did Louis 16ze please the people with *his* morality? Calling his present Majesty *Nero*, is to me *comical.* Carleton House may indeed be termed Nerot's Hôtel, because the Master of it is kept, like the people of a bagnio, in *hot water*. And it seems that's the true London joke. Adieu ...

The £6000, as appears from subsequent letters, had been given to Sir John Salusbury.

The joke about "Tully's Offices" evidently relates to her paying off the expenses of her birthday fête. The supper was provided by a celebrated Bath pastrycook named Tully, and the jest originated with Mrs. Piozzi, who, addressing her guests, bade them do justice to "Tully's Offices," the name by which Cicero De Officiis was commonly known in the eighteenth century.

On November 17 Mrs. Pennington, who has herself been ill, writes in great agitation about the Typhus, entreating Mrs. Piozzi, if she will not return to Clifton, to fly to Torquay. The Randolphs report it to be a terrestrial Paradise;—the scenery exquisitely beautiful, the air pure, mild, and dry, the town clean and neat, the living cheap, (the best possible meat 6d. per lb.,) and no lack of good society. Mrs. Randolph considered that Mrs. Piozzi might keep a carriage and live there *elegantly* within £1000 per annum.

Of the caricatures she remarks that "they were no proofs of the people not *loving* George the 3rd as a good man, a good husband, and good father, but merely the result of that spirit of *persiflage* to which the people of this country are said to be so much addicted. The simultaneous expressions of joy which you and I witnessed in the Streets and Theatres of the Metropolis on his recovery, could only have been the effects of genuine love and affection. It is in the failure of these virtues that the present K—g has lost the warm hearts of so many worthy subjects."

PENZANCE, *Sunday, 12 Nov.* 1820.

I am very sorry, dear Mrs. Pennington, that I said anything about this odious Fever; it will perhaps hurt the place, and in no wise benefit me … We are surely in the hands of the same God at Penzance as at Torquay; and when *he* calls, go we must.

I cannot leave my habitation, which I have taken for a term, and must abide in till the term is over, nor will I go back without having done what I came hither to do. My friends are but too, *too* solicitous. They have all heard of this nonsensical story, and every day brings me letters full of pathetic, and I believe, *sincere* admonitions

... I wish you would all be more moderate in your kindnesses. My establishment is not a little Cloke-bag to put on my shoulder, and carry away from one place to another ... Be *quiet,* dear Friend, so I say to Miss Williams and Conway, who are half wild, God bless them!—and their loss would be nothing to what they fancy it. Yet 'tis all I can do to keep them from my door.

The world is all unhappy. This vexatious affair of the Queen has been a *Tryal* to everybody. I wish to know how the Bishops of Salisbury, Bangor, and St. Asaph give their votes. Lord Liverpool's observations are the best. If there was nothing *wrong* between the Lady and the Courier, what *was* there? Conversation was difficult, and talents there were none.

No letter has come from Brynbella this long time, but I know from Miss Williams there is nothing wrong there; meaning as to health and happiness. As to pelf I will be more prudent in future; indeed the danger is over when the money is all gone ...

Bessy and I are engaged far differently from trimming hats for parties. Housework, and nursing, and crying, and clinging about Dr. Forbes and Mr. Moyle, an intelligent Surgeon, is all we have been doing a long time ... I do believe there is always Fever of this sort in these low situations, and when we *do* move, if it be not to Dymerchion's burying ground, it shall be to the lofty Crescent at Clifton. Torquay may do for some of those future years dear Mrs. Pennington talks of ...

If you like to tell Mrs. Rudd I still hope to come early in spring, do tell her so. Her son is a good child, and will ever be an honour and a comfort to her and to your *really* obliged and troublesome

H.L. Piozzi.

Her anxiety had not been all on account of Sophy the housemaid. Her attendant Bessy was the mother of a small boy named Angelo, a great pet of Mrs. Piozzi's, who accompanied them, and whom the Fever had brought to death's door, but who was now beginning to mend. She herself had only had a feverish cold.

The Bill of Pains and Penalties, reluctantly introduced by Lord Liverpool, then Prime Minister, though it passed the third reading, was abandoned by the Government on November 10, and the next letter gives a lively picture of the demonstrations which ensued.

PENZANCE, *Nov.* 15, 1820.

I feel terribly afraid, dear Mrs. Pennington, that my state of anxiety when I wrote last, betrayed my pen into some impatience of expression; ... and the interest Dr. and Mrs. Randolph were obliging enough to take in my concerns, deserved more thanks and compliments than I had, at that moment, leisure to pay ... The weather is changed, and the Fever quenched, ... and H.L. Piozzi become less a nuisance to her active Friends ...

This town may defy any place of its size, or twice its size, for a burst of real feeling displayed in honour of the late event. All the ships in the harbour have flags flying during day time, lamps blazing thro' most of the long night. "Queen Caroline for ever" round every head in ribbons, while Laurel, Myrtle, every blooming shrub, decorates the houses that would not wish to be pulled down. And no bustle you and I witnessed in 1788, could in any degree equal the spread of influence shown on this occasion by Britons in love with morality, from Scarborough to Penzance. Popularity may be outlived indeed, as her uncle learned I trust, when shot at twice in *one* day, and nearly torne to pieces on another; when Cecil Forester, passing by accident, called up the Guards, and saved George the third's life, in his own Park, from the fury of a Mob, joined in deliberate design to murder him. I was in Wales, but could not doubt a fact so well attested. The State Coach, in which he *had* ridden that morning, was demolished, and he nearly dragged from his own private carriage. My wonder is he escaped so often, and died in his bed at last.

Our Horse's Mother, (Mr. Pennington remembers the story,) sent to me to bid me not to be frighted into illuminating my house. The Peuple Souverain say "Light your windows, or we will break them." My answer is the same to both. "We will do as our neighbours do."

16th. Wish'd morning's come. The windows unbroken. The gay fellows from Newlyn and Mousehole, (who increased our mob,) all gone home to bed, after drinking "The Queen and Count Bergami for ever," till they could scarcely reel to their wretched habitations.

But St. Michael's Mount was the beautiful sight to see. Lamps in a pyramidal form to the top, where Tar Barrels were placed, and gave a glowing light to the whole scene, resembling the Bay of Naples.

Well! the wife of George the second was just dead when my poor eyes and ears opened on talk and show. She was a writing and reading woman, who respected *herself*, and half ador'd her husband. She died detested of the people, and derided by the wits. Our next was Charlotte of Mecklenburg. "Poor ugly Pug!" cried the populace, who crowded about *her* Chair, as she went to the Theatres on her first arrival. Poor Pug indeed! when the mob met her suddenly a few years after, at St. James's Gate, with a bier and mourning apparatus; "Young Allen's body" written on it. "Young Allen, murder'd by your husband's soldiers." The Queen fainted, miscarried, and lived thirty years, when she died. The people swung a Cat about the Palace, and sung "Old Tabby's departed." *This* Lady is a *favourite*; but sure the others were not hated on account of their immorality. I never heard a fault but avarice laid to *their* charge, and *that* has been disproved …

Oh! these are pretty times in which to be caring for a *lengthen'd stay*: but I have not *that* folly to answer for. May you, dearest Mrs. Pennington, be *as* willing to lay down the burden of life, when the Angel of release comes to cut the last thread it hangs by, as is your truly sincere and faithful   H.L.P.

November 16, 1820, is the last date in her Commonplace Book which she notes was begun at Brynbella 1809, thrown aside for some years, begun again at Streatham 1814, and continued at Bath 1815.

In 1794, a year of great scarcity, as the King went to open Parliament on October 29, his carriage was surrounded by a mob crying "Bread," and "Down with George!" and stones were thrown through the window. A somewhat similar attack was made on the Queen's carriage in 1796, when she herself was hit by a stone.

In a letter dated November 17, Mrs. Pennington replies. "In an early stage of our acquaintance, speaking of you to Mr. Greatheed, I recollect his exclaiming, 'Oh if you like her so much *now*, what will you do when you see her *miserable*? She is so *comical* then, that she is quite *too* charming.' And *comical* you are, sure enough, my dearest Mrs. Piozzi! You scare one with ugly words, and then are half-angry that one is frightened. At above 200 miles distance, was it possible to hear of 'Fever and Typhus' in the town, and even in *your house,* and not be alarmed?" ...

"*All* the Bishops voted for the Bill, (with the exception of the Archbishop of York and the Bishop of Tuam,) tho' they divided on the divorce clause ... And all (with the above exceptions,) declared their perfect conviction that her Majesty was guilty, to the full extent of the charges." ...

"You remember, I daresay, Mr. Dennam's concluding sentence, in his address to the Lords, conjuring them to imitate the beneficent spirit of the Saviour, and to say to her, 'Go, and sin no more.' A blunder certainly, if he had taken the proper inference into account, worthy of *Paddy* himself, from a man advocating her *innocence.* The following lines are, I think, neat enough on the subject.

> Go, Caroline, we thee implore,
> And sin, (if it be possible,) no more.
> But if that effort be too great,
> For God's sake, go—at any rate.

PENZANCE, *Fryday* 24 *Nov.* 1820.

......

The oldest friend I have in N. Wales, poor dear Mr. Lloyd of Pontriffeth, is dying; and my earliest playfellow and cousin, Tom Cotton, is dead. We never met, of course, since my second marriage, and he was saucy. But I am sorry, for he will be saucy no more. So if *my* death prevents me from returning to No. 36, you must not wonder, tho' I will not say you must not cry ... Conway writes the kindest of letters: but Newton is tardy in his payments, and I am as low-spirited as a cat.

It would however have made me laugh to see Miss Hudson illuminating her windows, and it does *not* make me weep to observe that the Brynbella people never write. Tom Cotton's death is a bad thing for Salusbury, *his* life is in all our leases. Mr. Thrale had a proper notion of that man's longævity. He lived 77 years. Lady Keith and I are the other two. Dearest Piozzi enjoyed the estate and improved it, and never had a life to renew,—never cost him a penny. Those who do right get a little reward for it, even *here;* and now that my heart feels itself on the brink of eternity, how daily and nightly do I thank God and my parents that in my gayest hours I never did forget it …

Lieutenant Parry's voyage might supply much food for thought and chat. He has surrounded the Pole, and found the seas more open than was expected. I do not understand that we are brought nearer to America, but we are near enough to *them* for the love they bear us. 'Tis pity he lost sight of the red snow, and the savages who took our ships for animated creatures, fancying, like the Mexicans in Dryden's "Indian Emperor," that

> They turned their sides, and to each other spoke,
> We saw their words break forth in fire and smoke, etc.

It was so pretty to see his fine ideas realised.

Miss Willoughby and your most humble servant have been at a Penzance Ball, the first, (as we were told,) illuminated by Wax Candles; and the Ladies led our admiration to the lustres. They had better have led it to their own beauty, for we *had* seen lighter rooms *often, seldom* such pretty women; and all like one another …

I will live, if I can, but every day counts now, aye, and every pulse too, and 'twere a folly not to feel it. Were a soldier to sleep sound in a besieged town, Mr. Pennington would count him lethargic. But he that sleeps during the *attack*, can only be compared to that man or woman who does not prepare for death at 81 years old, but just tries to keep him *out of sight* …

It is not because I think *better* of Mortal Man than you do, dear friend; worse probably of men and morals, having seen *more*. But then I am contented with *less,* and ever thankful when things and people are no worse, surrounded with temptations as the poor creatures are, and filled with *snares, holes, gins, rotten planks*, etc., as.we all find the bridge that carries us from this world to the other. Fools flapping their umbrellas in our faces all the way, hiding the *light* from us at every step, and triumphing in slips made by their neighbours, whilst tottering along themselves, scarce able to stand or go. Do not be sorry that I have arrived at more than three-quarters over, but pity those that have many arches to pass, with broken battlements on either side, enough to giddy their brains. Salusbury's path seems clearest of difficulties, but he is in danger of drowsiness; Conway's walk is above all men's dangerous. And neither of them, poor dears! have, in their early stages, experienced the advantage of an *authorised* hand to lead or guide them. Yet you will see them both—good fellows in their way—whether they love *me* enough or not, I'm *sure* you will. Conway *certainly*, I believe *both*, do think better than she deserves of theirs and your   H.L.P.

… I am sitting without a fire, it is so warm and damp, and soft an atmosphere, we are all relaxed to rags. No sunshine.

Thomas Cotton was the fourth of the six sons of Mrs. Piozzi's maternal uncle, Sir Lynch Salusbury Cotton, Bart., and almost the only one of that large family to whom she ever alludes.

Lieutenant Parry had commanded the Brig *Alexander* in the expedition of Captain Ross to the Polar regions in 1818. In 1819 he sailed in command of the *Hecla* to discover the N.W. passage, and reached Melville Island. He returned in the autumn of this year, landing at Peterhead on October 30, and posted to town. His despatches reached the Admiralty on November 4, and he was shortly afterwards promoted to the rank of Commander.

The latter part of the letter is of course based on Steele's "Vision of Mirza," published in the *Spectator*, No. 159.

Penzance, *Thursday*, 30 *Nov*. 1820.

… This morning, all agree, is to exhibit a new procession through the streets of the Metropolis, which, with its consequences, may justly fill thinking people with alarm. How much benefit can result from invective meanwhile, I see not. Insult is harder to forgive than injury, and for the best reason, it does the insulter *no good*. A man may fill his purse by robbing me, while he who flings dirt sometimes forgets that there's a pebble lodg'd within, which cuts so sharp as to excite lasting hatred; and all for what? Reformation never yet was effected by scurrility. And if the Fourth Estate of the Nation, as some Member of Parliament called the newspapers, were less violent on both sides, it would be better. Irritating an already much offended and dangerous *enemy* is, surely, not prudent. Better get rid of such a one without submission, but without harsh language.

> If *then* we fail, the world will only find
> Rage has no bounds in slighted womankind.
>   DRYDEN.

When the Orientals go out Tyger hunting, they try to *finish,* not to *wound* the creature. But I am wearied with conjecture, and must wait the result as I can …

No new book has reached us but *the Abbot,* an odd novel enough, but to me a dull one. The Edgeworths have always *humour,* and often some good information.

Jeffrey Crayon's *Sketch Book* is pretty enough. How oddly the things come round! There was just such an out-of-the-way writer entertained the Town about 66 or 67 years ago. He called his book *Sketches,* and assumed the name himself of Lancelot Temple. But 'tis strange how names are left behind, when the books are forgotten that first used them. John Bull is in every mouth, and every Pamphlet, yet people do not seem to know who first called Old England by that very appropriate appellation. Mr. Pennington, I dare say, well recollects that it was Dean Swift: when, to reconcile the Nation to Harley's Peace of Utrecht, and the loss of their Bonfires for Marlboro's victories, he and Arbuthnot planned a little work called *Law is a bottomless Pit*; in which he represents Great Britain as engaged in a litigious quarrel with Lewis Baboon, by which name he designates Louis Quatorze, and shows how we were cheated by our Allies, Nic: Frog for Holland, my Lord Strut, for the Emperor of Germany, and so on. Of all this rubbish, composed of wit and malice and mummery, little now sticks in any but such memories as mine; remembering *old* stuff better than new …

The invention of the phrase "Fourth Estate" is attributed to Burke, who, referring to the Reporters' Gallery, said, "Yonder sits the Fourth Estate, more powerful than them all."

Mrs. Piozzi was not much interested by Scott's earlier productions. Mangin notes that she thought *Rob Roy* a dull book; but adds that "no one could be more ready than she to applaud the unknown author as a man of Genius." Her admiration was excited mainly by his poetry, on which the Commonplace Book contains some verses which end as follows:

> So may posterity bestow the praises which to thee we owe,
> And never be the Lay forgot of our Last Minstrel, Walter
> Scott

Geoffrey Crayon was the pseudonym used by Washington Irving, when he published his *Sketch Book* in 1820. Lancelot Temple was the *nom de plume* of John Armstrong, whose *Sketches or Essays on Various Subjects* appeared in 1758. Wilkes is said to have assisted in their production.

The procession to St. Paul's on November 30 to celebrate the Queen's acquittal, passed off without any serious disturbance. No escort of troops was permitted, but she was received as usual by the city authorities, who accompanied her to the cathedral.

[*Dec.* 14, 1820.]

My dear Mrs. Pennington says her letters are mere commentaries upon mine. What text shall I find *next* to excite her eloquent flattery? Lord Kirkwall's death is what most readily presents itself to a woman just twice his age, who little dreamed of living to lament him. Poor dear K! My heart is very heavy at the thought. And when recollection, or retrospection places him before my mind's eye, it is with a pint of curious Constantia wine under his coat, or shooting dress, to please dear Piozzi in his last illness. So kind! Well! sure the people will have done dying some day! Never was sight so wearied as my own is by reading Newspaper lists.

Mrs. Mostyn writes chearfully. Living abroad loosens all old attachments, and gives no opportunity of forming new ones. 'Tis the true mode of keeping the mind free; but then I mean roving from place to place, not being shut in an angle of the world, of which, as a Turk once said, the only merit is that Suspicion herself could not throw any light into *corners.*

Tell me sometimes about the weather—in the world. Here it is mild, soft, and just now silent; stormy enough at times, but never clear. 'Tis the anger of a puzzle-headed fellow, which elicits no spark of brilliant fire; and the inhabitants of Penzance speak of lightning as a most unusual phenomenon.

I have the comfort to hear my fair daughters praised, even in *this* odd place. They patronized some poor families, when such philanthropy was less common than now, and are remember'd with grateful tenderness. Such recollections are among the Hot-house plants which bloom in the open air of Penzance. Rough winds *break,* and heavy snows *chill* the remembrance of what is merely ornamental, producing like Oak and Ash, no lasting utility …

I can really bear a good fire with difficulty, but the smoke is scarcely lessen'd by endurance of the cold. The houses here are so constructed that, except in one particular wind, we live smother'd. Coals are however not cheaper than elsewhere; meat and fish bear no price, but we pay for every drop of water—salt or fresh—because it must be *carried.* The place is replete with objects of curiosity nevertheless, and Lady Keith gained immortal fame here, by descending 35 ladders, of 35 steps each, into a tin mine. Not the most extraordinary of all the tin mines, for there is one under the sea: a submarine residence of many wretched mortals, who seldom see light, (save such as their patron Sir Humphry Davy supplies them with,) but often hear old Ocean roaring over their heads. A wonderful situation surely! and clear of *worldly* contamination. They are innocent of all that we are saying and doing.

Meanwhile I am glad you have been amused by Matthews. Even I, who naturally hate buffoonery, was much diverted by his story of the Yellow Soap, which dear Sir George Gibbes never wearied himself with repeating. My heart tells me that Matthews has a brother, who wrote a Pamphlet called the *Nutcracker,* meant as a sort of mathematical puzzle; that he planned the new fine Bedlam Hospital,

The Burning of the Kingston Rooms from a Ball Ticket, 1821,
And Ticket for Mrs. Piozzi's Fête

just off Westminster Bridge, and requested a particular apartment for *himself*, conscious of his own infirmity; that he actually resides there, much respected and visited by the great Mechanics, who do nothing without consulting him. The Comic Actor calls him cousin, but the relationship is nearer ...

Sir Humphry Davy, who was born at Penzance, invented his safety lamp in 1815, and was created a Baronet in 1818. He had just been elected President of the Royal Society.

Charles Matthews the actor was now giving his "At Homes." The Sketch Mrs. Pennington saw was probably that entitled *Country Cousins*, produced in 1820.

John, Viscount Kirkwall, born 1778, was the only son of the Countess of Orkney, who was still living.

On December 23 Mrs. Pennington writes: "As you say, the Abbot is indeed a very dull book. I begin to question whether a *well-known* point in History *can* be a good foundation for a Novel. There can be little interest where the event is more than anticipated, and if extraneous characters and circumstances are too freely introduced, we quarrel with them, as interfering with the truth.

"There is some pretty writing in the first volume of the *Sketches*, but the second falls off lamentably, and is downright stuff ...

"You will be shocked on seeing, in the Bath papers, the entire destruction of the Kingston Rooms by fire!!! No one seems to know by what means. Those very rooms in which, near to the same time last year, you made above six hundred people so happy! Everybody, I believe, but me and Conway, who you certainly desired should have been most so: but he was wretched, and infected me with his misery, so perversely does everything go in this world."

PENZANCE, 27 *Dec.* 1820.

......

Well! at 82 years old, and my 81st Birthday is hard at hand, one is easily convinced of money's importance to felicity. No suicide, or comparatively none, is committed but for *lack of pelf*. Yet money, if people are *stuffed* with it, like a Fillet of Veal, does not keep them alive. Do you remember a comely Mrs. Taylor, who had married an old man, and possessed herself of his riches to an *immense* amount? She sent dear Conway £5 for a Benefit Ticket, tho' being just left a widow she could not go to the Play. *She is dead*: a woman about 40 years old, I suppose, apparently strong and healthy.

This is *stranger*, though not so dreadful, as the fire, of which your kind letter gave me the first account. I suppose it was occasion'd by some of these new devices to snuff candles by conjuration, or fill your teapots by steam. They cook their dinners by stratagem, and assassinate those whose talents lighten the cares of life, best illuminated by *genius*, like that of unfortunate Naldi, charming creature as he was!!—and to die *such* a death! My heart bleeds for his handsome wife and pretty daughter,—highly accomplished *both;* and left to *starve* on the remembrance of his unrivalled powers.

Cruel reflexion! But all reflexion is cruel, and so we run to get rid of it. My own conscience however congratulates *me* that I had discharged Upham's long Bill; so if he had suffer'd it would not have been by *my* fault or folly. I have not lived on fish in a foggy atmosphere and smoky house for nothing, when comforts like those come smiling to my heart …

Miss Willoughby is in the highest favour here. She plays Country Dances, Waltzes, etc. for the boys and girls to dance, after winning their money—or that of their parents—at sixpenny whist; and she makes riddles and charades to amuse us all, and is very entertaining.

Adieu! Here is no room to tell of a shipwreck and a *Parrot*, with two other *two*-legged creatures, saved out of thirty eight, coming from Surinam. Wretched Sailors! now begging their way to London, with only what they sold the bird for in their pockets …

Guiseppe Naldi, who had distinguished himself in Italy and London as an Actor, Singer, and Musician, had lately met his death in Paris, by the explosion of a newly invented Cooking Kettle, which he had been invited to inspect at the house of a friend.

On January 8, 1821, Mrs. Pennington writes to report an unexpected visit from Conway, on his way to take up another engagement at Bath, in spite of the ill-treatment he considered he had received from the Management of the Theatre before he left. But he had not fared much better, pecuniarily, at Birmingham, where he had been a leading Actor and Stage Manager for four months, but was only given £106 as his share of his own Benefit. "Detestable Mechanics! I hope he will waste no more such powers on them." This short interview, however, served to reinstate him in Mrs. Pennington's favour, and she writes of him with all her old enthusiasm. "Anything so noble! so manly! so graceful! so *handsome* as his figure at this time I really never saw."

PENZANCE, CORNWALL *Saturday*, 13 *Jan*. 1821.

......

'Tis a cordial to hear about Conway. My heart entertains no fears for his reception among old acquaintance, and I can't cry because his Benefit brought only £106. The people in London get very little. Mrs. Hoare says she saw excellent acting to completely empty benches: I forget at which Theatre. Indeed my mind has been so taken up by a new attack upon my property, that I have thought on nothing else. A Mr. Kenrick, of whose name or situation in life I am totally ignorant, writes to ask me very *peremptorily* what I did with the stock of some Mr. Giffard, who died he tells me, before Mr. Thrale did!! Lord! what should I do with the man's money? His name is new to me now, but he says it stands joined with that of my first husband, to whom I am executrix. No sum is specified, but 'tis probably a large one; and I am a bad Lawyer, and easily alarmed. I was *so* bad a self-carer, that when the death of my four Coadjutors left me alone to manage the Trust Money as I pleased, I begged of my Lord and Lady Keith to name those that should be substituted in their places; and I *think*, but have forgotten, whether Mr. Hoare, Sophia's husband, is one. Surely *they* should bear me out harmless, but God knows whether they will or no; and *you* know I have parted with my patrimony and my savings to Sir John Salusbury, who always complains for want of money, and I daresay justly enough. Mr. Thrale's estate is doubtless chargeable with any mistakes of this sort; but I should hope the Widow's jointure is guarded from such attacks. Nevertheless my spirits are flutter'd and affected, and I am as hoarse with nervousness as if I had caught twenty colds ...

Miss Willoughby dined with me yesterday. She says Coriolanus is an unfavourable character for Actors to appear in just now, when insulting language to our Peuple Souverain will perhaps be treated as it was in Rome. I shall be happier when I see the Newspaper, and learn how our Friend has been received; but do not fright Mrs. Rudd about it, perhaps she may get good intelligence before the common Prints of the Day come out. If the Play should be disapproved, every kind, good-natured acquaintance will inform her ...

How is poor dear Mr. Pennington? Better, I'm sure, and always kind to *me*. I used the word Joynture improperly; tell him so: £800 pr. ann. was appointed me by Marriage Settlement, in return for Ten Thousand Pounds I brought with me to Southwark. The rest was hard worked for, and left me by Will, in consideration of my Welsh estate, enjoyed by Mr. Thrale for 9 years, and offer'd him *for ever* had he wanted it. *That* money may be liable for ought I know, but I hope not ...

Thursday, 1 *Feb*. 1821.

I like the Tailpiece best, dear Mrs. Pennington, and feel deeper interest in Macready's Acting than in Lord Castlereagh's. For as Dr. Randolph said to our sweet Siddons once, coming out of Laura Chapel, "*All are Actors*": and I am most contented to hear the Oppositionists are likely to be hissed.

But I want you to tell me a *truth* before we leave Penzance, a truth of a very different *taste*. Will it be worth our while (says Bessy,) to send half a doz: hams by the "Happy Return," for which we *must* give seven pence halfpenny a Pound *here*? ... The *Fish* would be worth carrying to begin Lent with at the Pope's Court; but fish won't carry. Our oysters are better than those Vitellius sent to Sandwich for; and such Cod, Mullet, and Flat fish of all denominations no tongue can enumerate. Our Crocuses, Primroses, and Honeysuckle leaves, all bursting now every day, are lovely likewise;—but what wretched pens to describe them with!

You are a comical Lady in your fears lest Miss Willoughby should make me a Radical. Salusbury seems, by his letters, to have fears lest she should be hovering over my *death-bed,* to his disadvantage. I hope to hold fast both life and loyalty one little while longer, and cannot believe she will help hurry *either* of them away. Poor Miss Willoughby! were it not for *her* I should not have known Milton from Shakespear by this time: for to no other creature here are those names familiar.

God forgive me! but talking on the subject reminds me of the days when H.L.P. was young, perhaps agreeable, and supposed to have interest among the grave and gay. When I was solicited on behalf of a decayed Gentlewoman, such as H.L.P. may one day become, for aught I know, whose friends wish'd to get her into a *then* famous refuge for distressed females, Lady Dacre's Workhouse, or rather Almshouse, I tried, and succeeded; but beginning to harangue my Protégée upon the neatness of her new establishment, the decent society she would be introduced to, etc., "Ah! Madam," said she, "but will there be any one there who ever frequented the Opera? For I love musick so, I can *talk* of nothing but Mingotti." Such a companion in my retirement has been to me Miss Willoughby.

I think the attack upon my property, made with *no gentle strokes,* will at length be parried, so as to fall on *none* of us. The dividends remained unclaimed for 25 years, and were often advertised before Mr. Thrale's daughters ever enquired about them. Mrs. Hoare, your namesake, kind Sophia, has written to me very good-naturedly; says it is impossible I should have to *refund* money I never *received*; that my name alone was lent for *them* to receive it; and that my letter to the Claimant was the comicallest thing in the world. But my Correspondent saw *no joke* in it, and sent it for their perusal to Mr. Merrik Hoare.

Well! sure if I do write funny letters from Penzance, I must borrow the salt from the Sea Tang that they manure their Strawberry Beds with, in this place. Apropos, how do those agreeable Brownes do, that I met once in Dowry Square? I loved Maria for her non-affectation about reading before Conway or Piozzi. She took her book up and began *so* prettily, and *so* sensibly, where another Miss would have mimp'd. I *valued* her.

No Bath news but what the Papers tell. London is in expectation of a *new* Miss O'Neill of consummate beauty, to draw the world off from The Wilson; whose style of singing—Sophy H says—is like that of Billington. Dear Siddons holds her own I hear. Welcome intelligence! when every day takes some old acquaintance off the Stage of Life, leaving sad, and solitary, and desolate your poor

H.L.P.

Mary Anne Lane made a brilliant début at Drury Lane in 1821, as Mandane in *Artaxerxes*, but going to Italy for further study, she overtaxed her voice, which never entirely recovered its tone. Regina Mingotti, *née* Valentini, sang with great success in Italy, Germany, France, Spain, and England. She came to London in 1755.

PENZANCE, February 10, 1821.

Thanks, dearest Mrs. Pennington, for your kind letter, speaking the words of truth and soberness. We will send Hams and Bacon by the Happy Return, most certainly. The Butter here is *poyson*, whether in pot or pan.

All you can say of poor dear Miss Willoughby is true to a tittle. Sir John is very ill-natured in detesting everybody who contributes to my comfort, and I hope not *quite correct* in supposing that neither you, nor she, nor Conway would endure my company an hour but for interest. Sophia Hoare's civilities will make him very angry indeed when he hears me say I *delight* in them: but he deserves such sort of vexation.

So you see Horace Twiss is the man at last, who, when Public Virtue finds herself sick and squeamish, holds the successful smelling bottle to her nose. And are they not all Actors on both sides? Surely they are. That Titmouse began his literary career by criticising and ridiculing H.L.P. in Magazines, Reviews, etc.; and afterwards begged my pardon at a party Mrs. Siddons gave one night at Westbourne. We shook hands and drank each other's health, and I wished him the success his audacity deserved.

This world is made for the bold, daring man,
Who strikes at all, and catches what he can.
Virtue is nice to take what's not her own,
And while she long debates, the glittering prize is gone.

So sung Johnny Dryden, whose *family* had every claim to match even with a Howard. Addison was Secretary of State, and if his wife was insolent, he *needed* not to have cared. Would Mr. Canning care? But times have changed.

But there is a passage in the Bath Paper that interests, and ought to interest me much more than Marriages or Merriment. A woman dying in the act of supplication to Almighty God; past 80 years old, found dead at her prayers! I used to say that no death ever pleased me, but here is one at last with which my heart would be content indeed. Why did she not take me with her? If however the next month carries me to Clifton, and treats me with a sight of *true friends,* I shall think leaving me behind was merciful, and feel replete with gratitude. Conway has written to me very kindly ...

If I should live to see a Jeweller's Shop once again, I would evince my gratitude to Sophy Hoare. What she wants is out of my power,—children to enjoy hers and her husband's fortune. Salusbury has got a new Baby—William Edward—I like the name, but have made no offer of Gossiping. Dear Mrs. Pennington is *too* sharp a discoverer in the Terra Incognita of human hearts. Mahomet says there is a black Bean in that of every one; and that the Angel of Death *plucks* it in our last agonies. I am trying to loosen mine before the dreadful day arrives, that it may hurt me less at final parting. Poor dear old Cookey! whom I have so much reason to love! Cannot, Doctors Dixon or Carrick *warm her up again?* It is not wholly for *interest* however that I wish her well. She is going *my road*, and my heart hopes she will feel it not very rough ...

PENZANCE, *Sunday 25 Feb.* 1821.

My last letter to dear Mrs. Pennington should be a pretty one, but it will only be dull; replete with Kitchen-griefs, and thanks to Heaven that they are my worst afflictions. Mr. Kenrick's insults have brought me civil letters from Lord and Lady Keith, kind ones from Mr. and Mrs. Hoare, and all will end—in nothing, as they hope, and as I firmly believe. Pray do not suffer your good husband, (so much younger than myself,) to grow old. He and I mean to keep on this many a day, and we will not *shew teeth* when *biting* is over with us.

Now for the Kitchen-griefs. James has behaved monstrously ill, "beaten the Maids a row,"[13] like the fierce fellow in Shakespear, and forced reproofs even from *my acquaintance* by his *out-door* conduct. This has been going on a long while, but I forbore to speak to you about it, till it suited me to say—do, dear Mrs. Pennington, get me a Footman. Not a fellow to wear *his own clothes*; I must have a *Livery Servant*, who will walk before the Chair, and ride behind the Coach, and be an old-fashioned, tho' not ill-looking servant. My little Plate, so small in quantity, is easily clean'd, but *clean* it must be. For I will not live in a state of disgust when I have a decent mansion over my head, and James was too dirty and slovenly, even for a wretched smoky closet like that I inhabit at Penzance: he is a sad fellow …

& now

Let me tell you the sights that we have *seen*. I always like them better than the tales that we have *heard*; and to-day the tales are truly melancholy. Lord Combermere has lost his only child, a son; so his honours and titles are gone, and the estate will fall, I suppose, to Willoughby Cotton, son of the Admiral, my Uncle's *second* boy. He had nine. *This* young fellow was a Colonel in what Regiment I know not, and married Lady Augusta Coventry, who brings Babies every year:—but these are *not* the sights I meant to tell you of.

On last Wednesday then, a memorable day, Mr. George Daubuz John undertook to show us the Land's End, and we did stand upon the last English stone, jutting out from the Cliffs, 300 feet high, into the Atlantick Ocean, which lay in wild expanse before us, tempting our eyes towards the land Columbus first explor'd, Hispaniola. Dinner at a mean house, affording only Eggs and Bacon, gave us spirits to go, not forward, for we could go no further, but sideways to a tin and copper mine under the sea. Aye! 112 fathom from the strange spot of earth we stood on, in a direct line downwards, where no fewer than three score human beings toil for my Lord Falmouth in a submarine dungeon, listening at leisure moments, if they *have* any, to the still more justly to be pitied Mariner, who is so liable to be wrecked among those horrid rocks, proverbial over all the kingdom,—Cornish rocks! ruinous to approach, as difficult to avoid. The men go up and down in buckets, with two lighted candles each, into a close path, long and intricate. And should their lights go out before their arrival in the open space where their companions work, there they must remain till the hour of relieving one wretched set by another comes to set them free. Billows meanwhile roaring over their heads, upon a stormy day most dreadful, threatening to burst the not very thick partition of solidity that divides them from the light of heaven, bestowed on all but Miners. This place is called Botalloch, whence we drove home our half-broken carriage but not even half-broken bones; having refreshed at the house on which is written "First Inn in England," on one side the Board, and "Last Inn in England" on the other. By "us" and "we" I mean Miss Willoughby and H.L.P., but we took our two Maids, Bell and Hickford, on the Dicky, and James rode. Four horses were not too many for such an exploit, tho' one of them was a Waterloo warrior …

We will go to Conway's Benefit certainly, if I get home time enough: Miss Willoughby will wish herself of the party most truly. But for *her* I should have pass'd many a dreary hour …

With regard to Lord Combermere's son, Mrs. Piozzi's information was evidently mistaken. Field-Marshal Sir Stapleton Cotton, Bart., G.C.B., Commander-in-Chief in India, grandson of her uncle, Sir Lynch Cotton, Bart., was created Viscount Combermere in 1814. He married thrice, and by his second wife had two daughters and a son, Wellington Henry, born 1818. The latter did not die in 1821, but succeeded to the title, and was grandfather of the present Viscount. His cousin, General Sir Willoughby Cotton, G.C.B., was Colonel of the 32nd Regiment of Foot.

Sunday, 4 *March* 1821.

I swear I think my dear Mrs. Pennington is one of the very best subjects the King has in his dominions, which contain very strange and contradictory people and things. Battling now about the tenets of Romanism, when Rome is itself in danger of almost immediate destruction from those who know no other tenets but hers. Well! you know I was always mounting a Turnep Cart to predict the end of the world, (not, I hope, forgetting my own all the time). It will vex me, in the last stage of life, to see the death and downfall of the Bourbons, but so it *must* be, without doubt, if they can live till I get safe to Clifton. Dubious enough, poor Souls! for the plot thickens apace, and Sovereigns have hourly more reason to fear the loss of all that's dear to them. Authority melted from their grasp long ago, and influence is sliding down the hill, of course.

Mr. Pennington must try keep up his spirits. So must we all, but mine often prove *false* ones, as when I took Geneva for Brandy; but the people here are *such* knaves! …

The day of our arrival how can I *certify*? My hope is to see you sometime on Tuesday 13; but Lord! I was so ill on Fryday night I hardly felt anything *like* certainty of ever seeing myself out of Penzance *alive*. Never mind that tho'; and say nothing about it; for the people make such an *ado* I dare not confess that anything ails me, like other old women. It is really troublesome to excess.

We have got Kenilworth among us, everybody admiring and even extolling it. *Your* strange book has a rival, Mr. Pascoe says, in Anastatius, but I have seen neither. Clifton will be nearer both to books and men. Dr. Randolph must be careful of his highly valued life. No one respects his abilities, or would regret the loss of them more sincerely than H.L. Piozzi, whose comfort it is, that she is likely soon to escape the truly uneasy sensation of outliving friends and enemies, and standing alone upon the Stage of Life, till hiss'd off for being able to furnish no further amusement. After having been at home on the Boards, like Matthews the Buffoon, so many silly years. Bear me however witness, that [I am] all but weary, and only kept from confessing myself so because I think it wrong. What however must this world be that even a *Frenchman* should leap into Vesuvius to get rid on't; and he did *not* get rid on't as he expected; the very Mountain vomited him back, and reproached his unrepented suicide … Everybody seems to approve my sitting down at Clifton, as neither in the blaze of Society nor the obscurity of Solitude. We will make out the close of the Game as chearfully as we can; and if you ask me to dinner on Wednesday the 14th, a refusal need not be apprehended from your poor   H.L.P.

The allusion to the danger of Rome appears to relate to the insurrection in Piedmont, where the King was driven to abdicate on March 13. Later on other revolts broke out in Naples and Palermo. In France plots were being hatched against the life of the Duc de Bordeaux (afterwards Comte de Chambord), posthumous son of the Duc de Berry, and grandson of Charles X.

The *Memoirs of Anastatius*, an autobiography of a Greek renegade, was a novel by Thomas Hope, and was considered his masterpiece. It appeared in 1819.

PENZANCE, 5 *Mar.* 1821. *Monday.*

... This is a short letter, but I am on the eve of a long journey, and the kind friends here require many visits, and notes, and thanks, and so forth: and some of them have lent me Kenilworth, so *that* must be galloped through. Forgive me therefore, and accept my positive answer by securing me this good lad, who I like the better for his name, Sam. I had once a Footman so called, who could not, and would not be spoiled. He is dead, and poor Hodgkins too, that said he was going to *take places* for me, with his last breath. *He* was *Sam* at the first. I shall be glad to see them both, and remain meanwhile dear Mrs. Pennington's and her good husband's ever obliged and faithful
                                                        H.L.P.

Mrs. Piozzi evidently left Penzance in the course of the week. On Saturday she was at Exeter, and after sitting up writing letters till the small hours of the morning, retired to rest, using a light chair to climb up into the bed, which was a high one. But the chair slipped, and gave her a violent blow on the leg, causing a severe bruise and a slight wound. However, she attended the cathedral service next day, though she could hardly kneel, and in due course reached Clifton; taking up her quarters at 10 Sion Row till Mrs. Rudd should be ready to receive her at the Crescent. The accident caused some alarm to her friends, but according to Mrs. Pennington's account, the wound healed rapidly and no evil consequences ensued. But internal troubles followed which neither physicians nor surgeons could overcome. The few short notes which follow, mostly undated, were written during her illness, of which no one for some time anticipated a fatal termination.

SION ROW, *No.* 10,
Tuesday, 10 *Apr.* 1821.

Addressed—

Mrs. Pennington, Dowry Square
With 1000 Comˢ —Sickly ones—from a Taker of Castor Oyl.
(She encloses a letter from Conway).
I got a letter from Mr. Roberts, the Curate of Dymerchion, begging me to make the Parish the present of a Bier, to carry the dead Poor. So I finished my Epistle to Salusbury, which *you* saw, with letting *him* know the request; and "tell Roberts," said I, "the favour is immediately granted"; for *this* is a debt I cannot, surely, be blamed for; and if I am, dear Salusbury must at last be contented to consider me as his *unaccountable*, no less than his Affecᵗᵉ Aunt,   H.L.P.

SION ROW, *No.* 10,
Thursday, 11 *Apr.* 1821.

'Tis I shall be made happy, dear Mrs. Pennington. Our kind and skilful Dickson is just gone. He only waited till things were in the state they *should* be, I perceive; and to-day he brought the tall man again, who performed the *operation,* and praised my courageous endurance. This for your own kind heart's private information. *Mine* is completely satisfied of their skill and management.

A thousand respectful compliments await Mr. Davenport, love to Mr. Pennington, threats of *ruin* at Cards to Mrs. Bellhatchet, and humble service to Miss Wren.

All that was done yesterday and to-day, (rough usage on the whole,) has *raised*, not *lowered* the spirits of your ever obliged and faithful

H.L.P.

Undated, on a Visiting Card.

I have been to the Crescent by the Surgeon's permission, and now comes the Doctor to insist upon my eating. I *must* obey you all, or I should deserve to be neglected by every living creature; and so far as I can, I *will* obey you.

Poor dear Dr. Dickson! he is as low spirited as myself, he has been among the Lunatics.

On miniature notepaper.
Dated Tuesday.

Very little better, dearest Friend, but certainly not worse, and though unmoved by all the *new things swallow'd*,—dying for a *Paper*. Can you direct James where to find one? Shame and Bessy have struggled all night, and the first gets the better. She *cannot* go to dear Mrs. Pennington without *me* to *help* her,—to words, I suppose.

Mrs. Pennington to Mrs. Brown

3 Jun. 1821

… I knew you would feel for my loss, an irreparable one to me, for if twenty years ago I could find nothing to replace it, I am not likely, in the winter of life, and more particularly after two years of almost daily intercourse, which, by the endearing restoration of *more* than former kindness and confidence, doubled its value …

At present I can think of nothing, talk of nothing, nor dream of anything but my lost friend …

My best comfort is that I attended my beloved friend to the last moment. For three days and nights I never quitted her bedside, where, at *my summons*, I had the satisfaction to see her attended by her three charming daughters, and *more* charming women I know not. Oh! what a sum of happiness did she throw from her, through the *misapprehensions,* etc., which separated her from them! But in this respect Retrospection is both useless and painful. She was absolutely lost from inanition! She either *could* not eat enough to support nature, or had brought herself to it from a mistaken system; till, on a slight disorder, a sudden prostration of strength took place, and nothing *could* be done! She had her wish, however, which was never to live to support the mere *dregs* of life; and would have made, I think, rather an impatient invalid, under the suppression, or deprivation, of those uncommon powers which rendered her the delight of every one that came near her, to the last. I hope you saw my character of her in the Papers. I should not have had the temerity to have attempted it, but at the earnest request of her daughters, who feared it might be attempted by some one who did not know her as well, and might not have written so much to their satisfaction. It has answered the purpose by silencing all other scribblers on the subject, and met with much more general praise and approbation than it deserves ...

Mrs. Pennington to Maria Brown

23 *Jun.* 1821.

... It is a new thing to me, dearest Maria, to feel reluctance in addressing you. But such is the effect of a late melancholy event, that I shrink from all exertion. It has impressed a languor on my spirits more fatal than grief, and more distressing than positive pain. It was a blow for which I could not be prepared, if indeed we are ever prepared for the loss of those we love; as only ten days before, she had dined with us in a party of ten or twelve persons, and was, as usual, the delight and soul of the company. And the sudden reverse appears to me, even now, at times, more like a frightful dream than a fact! I actually detect myself expecting to *see* or *hear* from her, until the sad reality forces itself upon me, and convinces me that time does not lessen those regrets, that time only more clearly and strongly discovers to us the value of what we have lost ...

If twenty years ago I could find no substitute, I am less likely when two years of almost daily association, with, as it should seem, *increased* affection and renewed confidence, gave additional interest to our connexion. While the apparent, but deceptive vigour of her corporal powers, held out a promise of many years of future enjoyment. I firmly believe she fell a victim to the *extreme* abstemiousness of her habits; actually sunk under inanition! Attacked by a slight disease, there was no reaction in the system. She suffered little and died easy. So far she had her wish, which was always to escape the tedium and imbecility of invalidism, and to preserve her faculties *unimpaired* while life remained. I had the mournful satisfaction of ministering to her last hours, and of seeing her close those brilliant eyes in the presence of her children; their tears I trust embalmed, and their affectionate attention soothed her last moments. But from better acquaintance with these ladies a new source of regret has opened upon me: that through some strange misconstruction of circumstances, and *perversion* of mind, my beloved friend should have lost such a sum of happiness, as, but for some most mistaken conclusions, these daughters (the most charming women I have almost ever met with,) could not fail to have imparted. But Retrospection is useless as painful, and it is best to draw an indulgent veil over the imperfections of poor human nature on *all* sides. They remained at Clifton a week, during which time I was almost constantly with them. It was only from me, they said, that they could gain any accurate idea of their departed Mother's habits and connexions. They were never weary of the interesting subject, and unbounded in their acknowledgments to me for affording them, by timely information, an opportunity of performing their last duty to their parent. I have had the kindest and most flattering letters from them since their return to Town, with an elegant remembrance, from each sister, of my dear deceased friend. It was at their earnest request I had the temerity to give to the Public the last tribute I could pay, which probably you have seen, as it was copied into all the London Papers, and has had much more praise than it deserved. That it answered the end proposed, by silencing certain writers, who, these Ladies were apprehensive, might have given "*the Celebrated Mrs. Piozzi's* Character" in a manner less agreeable to their feelings, is indeed highly satisfactory to me; and their warm approbation the best recompense and sweetest incense I could receive …

The Obituary Notice, by Mrs. Pennington, mentioned above, ran as follows:

DEATH OF MRS. PIOZZI.—Died at Clifton on Wednesday, night, the 2d of May, in the 82d year of her age, after a few days' illness, HESTER LYNCH PIOZZI, the once celebrated MRS. THRALE, descended both on the paternal and maternal side from the ancient and respectable families of the Salisburys and Cottons, baronets in North Wales, but still more distinguished as the intimate friend and associate of Doctor Johnson, Burke, Sir Joshua Reynolds, Garrick, Goldsmith, Murphy, and most of those literary constellations who formed the Augustan galaxy of the last century. The world has long known in what estimation her society was held in that circle where these illustrious men, with Mrs. Montague, Mrs. Carter, Vesey, Boscawen, and many others, formed a coterie never surpassed in talent and acquirement, in this or any other country. The vivacity of this lamented lady's mind was a never-failing source of pleasure to all who had the good fortune to enjoy her society, while the brilliancy of her wit, tempered by invariable good-humour and general benevolence, delighted all who approached her, and offended none. Her manners were highly polished and graceful—her erudition, the result of a regularly classical education, under the learned Dr. Collyer, was much more profound than those who only conversed with her superficially were likely to discover; for, wisely considering the line usually prescribed in such pursuits to her sex, she made no display of scholarship, yet was always ready to give her testimony when properly called out; indeed, on those occasions, it was impossible altogether to conceal the rich and rare acquirements in various sciences which she possessed. Her writings are many of them before the public, and if some incline to condemn a colloquial style, which perhaps she was too fond of indulging, all must admire the power of genius and splendour of talent she displayed. She was particularly happy in *jeux d'esprits*, numbers of which lie scattered amongst her friends, and we hope will be collected. Her *Three Warnings* have long been enshrined, and held in universal admiration as a specimen of the precocity of her talents; on graver subjects, those who knew her best will say she most excelled. Her religion was pure, free from all wild speculative notions—her faith was built on the Scriptures—that rock of our salvation, the continual perusal of which was her delight. She knew "in whom she trusted," and in the fullest conviction of those sacred truths, she closed a various life, declaring to a friend, who watched over her last moments, that she quitted the world in the fear and trust of God, the love of her Saviour, and in peace and charity with her neighbours and with all mankind. Her fine mental faculties remained wholly unimpaired; her memory was uncommonly retentive on all subjects;—enriched by apt quotations, in which she was most happy, and her letters and conversation to the last had the same racy spirit that made her the animating principle and ornament of the distinguished society she moved in, at a more early period of her life. Those who have to regret the loss of such a friend and companion, though continued to them beyond the usual date of human existence, will feel persuaded that as this admirable Lady was *unique* in the acquirements and combinations that formed her character, so are they sure that they shall never "look upon her like again."

Mrs. Pennington reverts to the same topic in a letter written to Miss Brown on December 3, 1821, in which she regrets that time, and care, and various other circumstances have dulled her powers to render her correspondence interesting and amusing.

"My dear, lost Friend possessed that talent in a wonderful degree. Her letters, however frequent, never ran into commonplace, but were always novel, and had the peculiar tact of always supplying matter for a reply. Never was there a mind of such varied resource as hers! The more I think of it, the more I am astonished that it was not even *more* appreciated and valued. Because I am persuaded, as Dr. Carrick said, when she lay, an inanimate corpse, before our eyes, that 'the world had nothing to compare with her. *She had left no equal.*' And that having *again* found her, she is lost to me for ever, is a subject of regret that no time, during the short remainder of my pilgrimage, will ever lessen. Her advanced age was no preparation to me, because wholly exempt from all those infirmities which usually attend that stage of our existence, and prepare others, if not ourselves, to look to the end. Appearing to have as much the advantage of me in vigour of constitution as in intellect, I looked forward to a few years of cordial and rational enjoyment, and really expected we should have run our race on nearly equal terms, happy to think it would be *together*. The change was so sudden, that at times I can scarcely persuade myself it is not a dream! and the disappointment so severe it seems to have annihilated all capacity for enjoyment or pleasure in *anything* …"

Among the friends to whom Mrs. Pennington wrote an account of Mrs. Piozzi's death, was Helen Williams, who replied in a letter dated October 28, 1822: "I read with warm interest all you wrote of the last scene of Mrs. Piozzi, and above all, your article, which is admirable; full of judgment as well as feeling, neither saying too little nor too much, in short, worthy of your pen: but I think you are too indulgent in respect of her daughters. I never could be satisfied with people who testify their tenderness to their friends only when they are at the last gasp. Above all, in the sacred relation which exists between a parent and a child, I think reconciliation and pardon should precede the act of dying: and Mrs. Piozzi being eighty years of age, her daughters must have known there was no time to lose, even before you summoned them to receive her last breath. They had reason to be offended at her second marriage, but life is too short for eternal resentments. Why do you not become her biographer? I am sure no one would write her memoirs half so well as yourself. I shall always love her memory, tho' she never forgave me for coming to France, and severed me from her affections because we differed in politics. If she could have known all I have suffered amid the convulsions of States, her good-natured heart would have been more disposed to pity than condemn."

Soon after the loss of her friend, Mrs. Pennington came into collision with her executors, Sir John Salusbury and Sir James Fellowes. By her will, dated March 29, 1816, she had left everything to Sir John, except legacies of £100 each to her maid Bessy, her old steward Leak, and his son, and one of £200 to Sir James. But outside the formal bequests of her will, she had intended that certain articles should be given as memorials to Conway and Mrs. Pennington. The former was to have her watch, and an annotated copy of Malone's Shakespeare, and the latter the silver teapot and stand which she habitually used, and which is referred to in Mrs. Pennington's letter of 17th January 1820, quoted above. What became of the watch does not appear, but letters in Mr. Broadley's collection show that Conway got his Shakespeare from Sir John, who may have been the more inclined to regard his claim with favour if, as is stated, Conway had just returned the £100 which Mrs. Piozzi had given him just before her death. Mrs. Pennington could offer no such inducement to favourable consideration, and perhaps her remark at the Bath Fête, that her claims to Mrs. Piozzi's friendship were of longer standing than his own, had not been forgotten or forgiven. It appears from Mr. Broadley's letters that she had applied in the first instance to Sir James Fellowes, urging her right to the teapot in somewhat strong terms, on the ground that her friend had actually given it to her, though it had not been handed over; and that she could produce witnesses to that effect, whose testimony would be accepted in any Court. Sir James no doubt referred her to his co-executor, to whom she next applied, though in a more humble strain, asking for it not as a right, but as a favour; reminding him that she had a larger collection of dear Mrs. Piozzi's letters than any other correspondent, and was in fuller possession of her opinions on all subjects, private, public, and literary, possibly than any other person in the Kingdom, which she should carefully preserve. This, she hints, would be practically indispensable to any intending biographer. But Sir John was not to be tempted or cajoled, and returned only three curt lines, declining to discuss the matter at all; while he told Sir James that he should hand over any future letter on the subject to be dealt with by his lawyer. So neither her long friendship nor her loving care for his aunt were deemed worthy of even this not very extravagant recognition.

Her relations with the daughters were far more cordial. In the summer of 1824 she paid a visit to London, where, she tells Miss Brown, "I experienced much kindness, and more attention than I had any right to expect; chiefly indeed from my late dear lamented Friend's three charming daughters, who seemed as if they never could do enough to prove the sense they entertained of my *true* friendship to their mother. In Town they assisted me to see everything that time and circumstances would permit; and I spent ten delightful days at Miss Thrale's beautiful Villa in Kent, surrounded by Nobleman's Seats, which we visited in our daily morning drives. Knowle Park, the residence of the Duchess of Dorset, is the finest specimen, I believe, of *Baronial* grandeur in the Kingdom; and the Park (fourteen miles in extent) they say has the noblest Timber of any in England. She kindly carried me to Tunbridge, where we spent two days very agreeably, and we parted with (I am persuaded) mutually increased esteem, and sensible regret."

Thomas Sedgwick Whalley, D.D.
By J. Brown after Sir Joshua Reynolds

The following winter Mr. Whalley (as appears from his published Letters) spent in her house. Writing to him in October with regard to his proposed visit, she tells him that she has for some time given up public and private parties. Pennington is tolerably well, "but we are both fallen into the sere and yellow leaf. I do not find my mind get older in proportion to my body. I have as keen a relish for intellectual enjoyments as ever I had. My spirits are rising in anticipation" of the visit and conversations to which she was looking forward with great pleasure. Her subsequent letters to Maria Brown are full of laments for the loss of such intellectual enjoyments, owing to the continual growth of Bristol, and the gradual decay of the Hot Wells as a health resort. The last of them was written in April 1827, when she had just had a severe illness, and on 1st August she died, aged seventy-five years, as stated on her mourning ring.

It is somewhat remarkable that neither her children, who showed so much attention to their mother's oldest friend, nor her heir, who handsomely acknowledged on paper his obligations to his aunt, cared to perpetuate Mrs. Piozzi's memory by any kind of monument. Perhaps they thought it needed no such artificial aid. It was reserved for the present century, and for a descendant of her other executor, to erect a simple white marble slab in Tremeirchion (formerly Dymerchion) Church, with the following inscription:

NEAR THIS PLACE ARE INTERRED THE REMAINS OF
HESTER LYNCH PIOZZI,
"DOCTOR JOHNSON'S MRS. THRALE."
BORN 1741. DIED 1821.

WITTY, VIVACIOUS AND CHARMING, IN AN AGE OF GENIUS
SHE EVER HELD A FOREMOST PLACE.
THIS TABLET IS ERECTED BY ORLANDO BUTLER FELLOWES,
GRANDSON OF SIR JAMES FELLOWES, THE INTIMATE FRIEND
OF MRS. PIOZZI, AND HER EXECUTOR,
ASSISTED BY SUBSCRIPTIONS,
28TH APRIL, 1909.

1. "Let him continue in his courses till thou knowest what they are."—*Measure for Measure*, III. i. 196.
2. *Paradise Lost*, ii. 890.
3. "Use every man after his desert, and who should 'scape whipping?"—Hamlet, III. ii. 556.
4. "I would 'twere bed-time, Hal, and all well."—I *Henry IV.*, V. i. 125.

5. *Julius Cæsar*, III. i. 254.

6. *Othello*, V.ii. 346.

7. *Hamlet*, II. ii.

8. *As You Like It*, II. vi. 165.

9. *The Traveller.*

10. *Rom. and Jul.*, II. v. 47.

11. *Timon of Ath.*, IV. iii. 218.

12. *Don Quixote*, Bk. II., Chap. xiv.

13. *Comedy of Errors*, V. i. 170.

INDEX

C